THE DEVELOPMENT OF SENSORY, MOTOR AND COGNITIVE CAPACITIES IN EARLY INFANCY: FROM PERCEPTION TO COGNITION

The Development of Sensory, Motor and Cognitive Capacities in Early Infancy: From Perception to Cognition

Edited by

Francesca Simion
University of Padova, Italy

George Butterworth
University of Sussex, England

Psychology Press
a member of the Taylor & Francis group

Psychology Press Ltd
27 Church Road
Hove
East Sussex, BN3 2FA
UK

British Library Cataloguing in Publication Data

A catalogue record for this book is available from the British Library

Library of Congress Cataloging-in-Publication Data are available

ISBN 0-86377-512-8 (Hbk)

Typeset in Times, by Facing Pages, Southwick, West Sussex
Printed and bound in the United Kingdom by Biddles Ltd, Guildford and King's Lynn

Contents

Contributors

Janette Atkinson, Visual Development Unit, London and Cambridge. Department of Psychology, University College London, Gower Street, London WC1E 6BT, UK.

Josiane Bertoncini, Laboratoire de Sciences Cognitives et Psycholinguistique, CNRS–EHESS, 54 Boulevard Raspail, 75270 Paris Cedex 06, France.

Henriette Bloch, Laboratoire de Psycho-Biologie du Developpement, EPHE – CNRS, 41 Rue Gay-Lussac, 75005 Paris, France.

Marc H. Bornstein, Child and Family Research, National Institute of Child Health and Human Development, 9000 Rockville Pike, Building 31, Room B2B15, Bethesda, MD 20892–2030, USA.

J. Gavin Bremner, Department of Psychology, Lancaster University, Lancaster LA1 4YF, UK.

Ian W.R. Bushnell, Department of Psychology, University of Glasgow, 56 Hillhead Street, Glasgow G12 8QB, UK.

George Butterworth, School of Cognitive and Computing Sciences, Arts D Building, University of Sussex, Falmer, Brighton BN1 9QU, UK.

Leslie B. Cohen, Department of Psychology, University of Texas, Austin, Mezes Hall 330, Austin, TX 78712, USA.

Scania de Schonen, Center for Research in Cognitive Neuroscience, Unit of Developmental Neurocognition CNRS, 31 Ch. Joseph Aiguier, F-13402 Marseille Cedex 20, France.

Rick O. Gilmore, Department of Psychology, Carnegie Mellon University, Pittsburgh, PA 15213–3890, USA.

Brian Hopkins, Department of Psychology, Lancaster University, Lancaster LA1 4YF, UK.

Mark H. Johnson, Medical Research Council, Cognitive Development Unit, 4 Taviton Street, London WC1H 0BT, UK.

Scott P. Johnson, Texas A&M University, College of Liberal Arts, Department of Psychology, College Station, TX 77843-4235, USA.

Frederique Liegeois, Center for Research in Cognitive Neuroscience, Unit of Developmental Neurocognition, CNRS, 31 Ch. Joseph Aiguier, F-13402, Marseille, France.

J. Mancini, Service de Neuropédiatrie, CHu La Timone, F-13005 Marseille, France.

Olga Maratos, Department of Preschool Education, University of Athens, 33 Hippocrates Street, 10680 Athens, Greece.

Louise Rönnqvist, Department of Psychology, Umeå University, 90187 Umeå, Sweden.

Kerstin Rosander, Department of Psychology, Umeå University, 90187 Umeå, Sweden.

Alan Slater, Department of Psychology, Washington Singer Laboratories, University of Exeter, Exeter EX4 4QG, UK.

Francesca Simion, Dipartimento di Psicologia dello Sviluppo e della Socializzazione, Università di Padova, Via Venezia 8, 35131 Padova, Italy.

Carlo Umiltà, Dipartimento di Psicologia Generale, Università di Padova, Via Venezia 8, 35131 Padova, Italy.

Eloisa Valenza, Dipartimento di Psicologia dello Sviluppo e della Socializzazione, Università di Padova, Via Venezia 8, 35131 Padova, Italy.

Claes von Hofsten, Department of Psychology, Umeå University, 90187 Umeå, Sweden.

Some New Possibilities in Explaining the Relationship Between Perception and Cognitive Development

Research on the development of perceptual, motor and cognitive capabilities in early infancy has undergone dramatic changes in recent years. With improvements in experimental procedures numerous studies have demonstrated that human infants are biologically capable of processing constrained classes of perceptual input. Nevertheless, this innate endowment only becomes realised through interaction with the environment. The newborn is now considered to be predisposed to make sense of specific sources of information, whether in vision, audition or touch, and experiments now focus on how different perceptual systems interact with environmentally derived information. This leads to new opportunities for understanding the relation between the initial state of psychological organisation and its subsequent development.

This book addresses several possibilities in explaining the relation between infant perception, action and cognitive development. These include a reconceptualisation of perception as being at the origins of development, a tentative reconciliation of psychophysical and ecological approaches to infant perception and building bridges between biological and psychological aspects of early development, especially in terms of species-typical brain structure and function. This preface will serve to make a case for the fundamental importance of perception in early human development which will be elaborated in the various chapters that follow.

This book originates in the European Research Conference Series, "The Development of Sensory, Motor and Cognitive Abilities in Early Infancy" which was funded by the European Science Foundation. Two meetings were held which were specially organised to make-up-to-date work of established scientists accessible to young European researchers. Discussions were focussed on recent discoveries in very early human development and on the utility of a positive characterisation of the abilities of young babies. We found that a close analysis of early human development can be a powerful tool to achieve a better understanding of the structure of the nervous system in relation to perception, action and cognition. The chapters gathered in this volume are just a selection of some of the topics that were discussed.

A basic concern of all the chapters here is how to characterise the origins of development. Psychologists no longer conceive of the newborn infant as an empty organism, capable only of reflex action. Nor do we stress the "half empty" view in which limited abilities are rather grudgingly acknowledged but given little subsequent role in development. The emphasis is now more optimistically placed on the adaptive nature of the initial state of organisation. We no longer stress what the newborn infant cannot see because, for example, there is poor visual acuity, or because the newborn baby's eyes operate at a fixed focal length, but ask what is the adaptive function of this initial state?

The first part of the book is concerned with the basic exploratory processes of early visual perception, especially the control of eye movements. The chapters review the developmental evidence on early vision in relation to the theory of two visual systems, one specialised for the perception of form and the other for orienting in space. How these systems may influence the organisation and control of eye movements for the uptake of information in early development is discussed and some implications for understanding the perceptual world of the neonate are reviewed. (Chapters by Atkinson; Gilmore and Johnson; von Hofsten and Rosander.)

The chapters grouped in the second part of the book are specifically concerned with the infant's perception of faces. Restrictions in the visual acuity of the newborn may confine attention to significant objects in near space, such as the mother's face, which set in train species-typical outcomes in person recognition. In this area of research tighter theoretical distinctions are now being drawn between psychophysical (i.e. energy based) and categorical explanations for the well-established newborn preference to look at face-like patterns. Such a preference for faces may be based simply on energy characteristics of the face (e.g. because faces correspond with a preferred contrast sensitivity or luminance function). Alternatively, there may be a predisposition to attend to the typical form of the human face. In the extreme version of the psychophysical account, there is no need to postulate a particular, innate structure which has specifically evolved for face recognition, since the immature perceptual system is constrained more generally in transducing the energy in patterned light. On the pattern selective account, however, it is necessary to postulate a preference for the actual form of the face, notwithstanding the infant's apparent psychophysical limitations. Contemporary research is concerned not only with behavioural evidence on face perception but also with the precise ways in which the brain is involved in perceiving faces. The chapters consider recent evidence on newborn face perception and the different ways in which such perceptual abilities might be interpreted (Bushnell; Simion, Valenza and Umiltà; de Schonen and Mancini; Slater and Johnson).

The third section of the book groups chapters on perception and action with discussions of species-typical aspects of human communication, both in newborns and older babies. The papers are concerned with imitation, perception of the phonetic structure of speech, manual pointing and the origins of handedness in human development. Imitation in newborn babies has been a controversial issue in early human development and although it is now a well-established phenomenon, many questions about its mechanisms and functions remain. The case is made here that neonatal imitation is substantially different from imitation among older babies. It serves a fundamental communication function in early development, especially in relation to the perception of emotion. Elsewhere in Part 3, innate components of speech perception are discussed. Cross-linguistic studies of speech perception in newborn babies show a universal ability to process speech sounds, both in syllabic and associated prosodic properties. It is suggested that the perceptual system is innately "set" to perceive syllables and this allows the infant to carry out first-level segmentation of the auditory stream typical of the native language.

Later appearing behaviours, such as manual pointing, may nevertheless have innate, species-typical foundations. This thesis is discussed in relation to the transition from communication by means of gesture to speech. The pointing gesture is a specialised orienting response, closely linked with processes of joint visual attention between adults and infants, with vocalisation in the baby and with the transition to language. The final chapter in this section reviews evidence on the origins and development of handedness in babies. Right-handedness, typical at the population level, is a characteristic of humans often closely linked to speech and language. It is argued here that handedness is actually more ancient in evolution than speech. If so, the cerebral asymmetries underlying handedness may have originated prior to cerebral specialisation for language. Handedness fluctuates, it is not at all easy to define and it is not an invariant, fixed attribute in the early months of life. (Chapters by Maratos; Bertoncini; Butterworth; Hopkins and Rönnqvist.)

The final section of the book contains theoretical contributions on the relation between early perceptual abilities and later cognitive development. The Gibsonian and Piagetian views on perception and cognition are reviewed. The basic issues here concern the relation between perceiving and knowing, and how best to characterise them, whether as implicit versus explicit knowledge, or as a distinction between sensori-motor and operational knowledge. The two concluding chapters are examples of early development where continuity between perception and cognition may be postulated. The information-processing approach to object categorisation, as revealed by habituation studies, supposes that categorisation in babies, at the outset of their cognitive development, is fundamentally similar to categorisation at more advanced levels of cognition. The last chapter reviews evidence from habituation studies as a predictor of IQ. This also suggests there is a degree of stability in mental development from infancy to early childhood. Since selective attention measures predict later intellectual abilities, perception may be one of the foundational, component processes of intelligence. (Chapters by Bremner; Bloch; Cohen; Bornstein.)

In conclusion, the focus of this book is on perception, action and cognition from very early infancy. The psychology of infancy has made much progress since scientific enquiry began into the origins and development of babies. From a time when perception was relegated to a position of secondary importance in theories attempting to characterise the relation between the infant and environment, it has moved into the foreground as one of the primary mechanisms of infant adaptation. Perception is nowadays more adequately considered as a fundamental building block for the rapid intellectual changes observed in infancy. The theoretical distance between perception, action, language and cognition has been drastically reduced as we have come to understand better the biological and psychological foundations for the early development of babies.

Francesca Simion and George Butterworth March 1997

ACKNOWLEDGEMENTS

We are very grateful to the European Science Foundation for financial support to hold two conferences[1] on early human development, "The Development of Sensory, Motor and Cognitive Abilities in Early Infancy". We are particularly grateful to the office for European Research Conferences and to Dr. Josip Hendekovic and his colleagues who ensured that both meetings ran smoothly and efficiently for more than two hundred participants from all over Europe and the United States.

---

1   The first meeting in the series, "The Development of Sensory, Motor and Cognitive Abilities in Early Infancy: From sensation to cognition", was held in Maratea, Italy in 1994, and the second meeting was held in San Feliu de Guixols, Spain in 1996 on "Antecedents of language and the symbolic function". The meetings were coorganised by Francesca Simion, George Butterworth and Scania de Schonen. This book contains material drawn mainly from the first conference but Chapter 8 is based on material presented at the second conference.

PART I

The Visual System
in Early Development

CHAPTER ONE

The 'Where and What' or 'Who and How' of Visual Development

Janette Atkinson
University College, London, UK

A number of neurobiological models of visual development have been put forward over the past twenty years. One popular idea is that of two visual systems: a primitive, evolutionarily older subcortical system controls orienting responses which define crudely 'where' an object is located and triggers foveation, while newer cortical mechanisms define 'what' is actually in the foveated area. Using this idea, Bronson (1974) suggested that newborn vision is totally subcortically controlled with the cortex starting to mature at around 2 months postnatally. Atkinson (1984) put forward a modified model in which the newborn visual system is largely subcortically controlled, with executive control of vision being taken over by a number of cortical modules postnatally. These cortical modules can be thought of as a number of cortical streams, each specifically processing particular types of visual information and each becoming operational at different ages.

These hypotheses have been updated in the light of both recent infant data and ideas arising out of models of adult vision. The first model of the adult visual system is based largely on primate studies, which have dissociated a 'where' and a 'what' system *within* the cortical pathways. Zeki and his co-workers first defined an area selective for motion information (V5 or MT) and a colour specific area, V4 (Zeki 1974,1978,1983). Ungerleider and Mishkin (1982) suggested that the two streams are associated with different visual capacities – a largely parietal module is involved in localizing objects within a spatial array and is intimately linked to eye movement mechanisms of selective attention, while the temporal lobe contains mechanisms tuned to 'what' aspects such as form, colour and face recognition. Clinical observations of patients with specific focal lesions have shown a dissociation between loss of position or movement perception and deficits of object recognition (e.g. Damasio & Benton, 1979; Milner & Goodale, 1995; Zihl et al., 1983).

The second model of the adult system is based on the idea of parvocellular and magnocellular streams. The two streams are distinct at ganglion cell and LGN levels, project to different parts of primary visual cortex, V1, and continue within independent cortical streams to V4 and V5 (Livingstone & Hubel, 1988; Maunsell & Newsome, 1987; Van Essen & Maunsell, 1983). The parvocellular-based system is proposed to subserve detailed form vision and colour, while the magnocellular system subserves movement perception and some aspects of stereoscopic vision. Comparisons have been made between psychophysical data on adults and the functioning of the parvo-based and magno-based pathways. Similar comparisons are made from looking at the time course of development of specific cortical modules in infant development. It appears that there is some evidence to suggest that parvocellular-based systems may become operational slightly earlier than magnocellular-based systems (Atkinson, 1992).

Goodale and Milner (1992) suggest that the distinction between the 'where' and 'what' cortical streams is not one for separating different properties, such as colour and movement, but rather two broad categories of visual coding. One stream is useful for perception and one for action. As the ventral pathways contain specialized areas for face perception and the dorsal stream contains systems for controlling eye movements, reaching and grasping, we can rename these systems the 'who?' and the 'how?' mechanisms. Rather than two distinct streams, Goodale and Milner suggest multiple streams, loosely connected into two broad modules, with each operating in an internal coordinated fashion. The relatively fast 'action' module has a very short memory and is for automatic 'unconscious' immediate responses whereas the ventral stream controls 'conscious' awareness and interactions with more long-lasting elaborate memory stores. When this model is applied to human development we can see that it is not only possible to have differential timing of functional development between the two major streams, but it is also possible to have differential development, internally, within each stream. A very obvious example is the differential development in babies of 'action' modules for reaching and grasping as opposed to walking. Both these action programmes must involve some spatial analysis of the visual layout, but there may be quite different scales used, one involving nearby space relative to the infant's body and one involving peripheral vision and spatial layout some distance from the child. So although some initial perceptual analysis will be common to both reaching and walking, the integration of this information from the ventral stream with the appropriate motor programmes and spatial maps in the dorsal stream may be different and have different functional onsets.

This means that our theory of visual development involves a first stage with development of functioning in specific cortical channels, followed by a second stage where information is integrated across channels within a single stream so that complete objects and people can have an internal representation, and this is followed by a third stage for directing actions to this object or person. We can think of the first and second stages taking part largely in the ventral stream, with dynamic online information added to this from the dorsal stream at stage three. Of course integration between information regarding colour, shape and texture and information about movement, must take place at a relatively early stage to enable separation of one object from another and each object to be separated from its background (figure–ground separation). These two processes of integration and segregation take place continuously and simultaneously, to provide smooth uninterrupted perception of a dynamically changing visual world. We do not as yet have a complete neurobiological model of these processes in adult or infant perception, but recent results on 'structure from depth' and 'structure from motion' do start to address these issues (e.g. Braddick, 1993).

In this chapter I will attempt to briefly summarize some of our current understanding of visual development from the neurobiological modelling perspective. For the sake of clarity I will divide visual development into three processes, although in the developing brain these processes are unlikely to be completely distinct. Our model will be considered to consist of three overlapping stages or processes:

1. Development of specific cortical modules. Here selectively tuned pools of cortical neurones become operational for processing distinct visual attributes such as relative size, shape, colour and movement.
2. Development of integration ('binding') and segmentation processes within and between ventral and dorsal streams. Here integration and segregation between and within subcortical and cortical modules become operational. These processes allow infants to recognise objects as a whole and to understand the dynamic spatial layout of the visual world. In any adult visuomotor act information must also be smoothly integrated from the ventral (perceptual) system and the dorsal (action) system. In this chapter I will discuss two new paradigms we have been using which show that even beyond infancy in early childhood this integration does not always happen. The child does not always seem to be able to integrate.
3. Development of selective attentional modules. Here attentional modules become operational, allowing the infant to shift visual attention from one object to another and shift between different levels of processing within a single object, e.g. local versus global processing in attending to a particular feature rather than the whole object.

As many of these areas have been discussed at length elsewhere, only a brief summary will be given in this chapter. Throughout this discussion I will use the term *'module'* to describe a collection of brain areas thought to be interconnected regarding their functional significance in behaviour. The use of the term *'stream'* implies some serial order between modules or within a module.

DEVELOPMENT OF SPECIFIC CORTICAL MODULES

Rationale ('designer stimuli'): From primate electrophysiology we know that the adult visual cortex contains populations of neurons specifically sensitive ('tuned') to specific visual attributes. For example, a population of cortical neurons will give their maximum response to lines which are vertically oriented. We also know that neurons within the subcortical system are indifferent to many visual attributes. For example, neurons in subcortical visual areas are indifferent to the orientation or slant of a grating pattern. A general strategy to separate cortical functioning from subcortical functioning is to use 'designer stimuli', chosen to be appropriate stimuli for particular types of cortical neurons, which are within particular cortical streams.

Below, I describe briefly how we have used this approach to gauge the development of the infant's sensitivity to a number of visual attributes. The examples considered are of course by no means exhaustive. In each case, we have designed our test so that, if the infant shows a discriminative response between two stimuli, which differ in only one dimension of one visual attribute, we can argue that the infant must have working neurons operating to enable discriminative responses. For example, if the infant shows a discriminative response between two grating patterns which differ only in the slant of the lines in the pattern, then we argue that the infant must have working cortical modules which are sensitive to differences along this particular dimension. The examples are given for changes of orientation, direction of motion and disparity.

Example 1: Development of the orientation module

Infants of a few days of age have been shown to discriminate between differently oriented static grating patterns (Atkinson et al., 1988; Slater et al., 1988). However, if dynamic stimuli are used, as is necessary in recording visual evoked potentials (VEPs), the age at which the first reliable VEP is recorded varies with the temporal parameters of the stimulus. In general if the stimulus changes in slant or orientation at relatively low rates (three times per second), a significant VEP is seen at a median age of three weeks postnatally. The discriminative response is found at an older age (around two to three months) if the stimulus changes orientation more rapidly (Braddick et al. 1989; Braddick et al.,1986a; Wattam-Bell, 1985). If the infant is shown a phase-reversing (PR) grating, where the grating is in a constant orientation, but the black and white stripes are periodically interchanged at 3rps or 8rps, a significant PR-VEP can be recorded for infants from birth. These results support the idea of very rapid development (or sensitivity at birth) of cortical modules for processing changes of orientation. But the response depends on the temporal properties of the stimulus as well as the spatial, and it seems that both spatial and temporal sensitivity improve with age. Different ranges of temporal and spatial sensitivity have been found in the cell properties of the magnocellular and parvocellular pathways (Derrington & Lennie, 1984). One plausible interpretation is that the magnocellular pathways are involved in fast temporal analysis, while the parvocellular pathways carry only slow temporal information. By analogy, we can argue from our results with infants that the orientation discrimination we see in the first few weeks of life is more likely to be related to parvocellular-based activity than to magnocellular-based modules.

Example 2: Development of the motion module

The results from infant studies on sensitivity to motion are quite puzzling. Motion provides a very direct source of information concerning the contents and layout of the environment and it would seem reasonable to imagine that modules for sensitivity to motion might be the first to become functional in development. It is of course true that young infants prefer moving to static visual stimuli. However the ability to distinguish between moving and stationary stimuli may reflect sensitivity to temporal modulation rather than motion as such and it is well known that infants show a preference for full field flicker (Regal et al., 1983), i.e. temporal modulation which lacks coherent motion. In general, true motion detectors are in evidence if a differential response to different directions of motion can be demonstrated

Indeed the newborn does have a crude directional system already operating as is evidenced by the optokinetic system, a stabilizing mechanism which is present in some form in the visual system of virtually every species. If newborn infants view with both eyes open a large or full field of random dots, moving horizontally at a relatively low velocity, optokinetic eye movements (OKN), with the smooth component of the eye movement following the direction of movement, can be elicited to both the left and right. In newborn infants viewing with one eye alone, monocular optokinetic nystagmus (mOKN) can only be driven by a stimulus pattern moving nasalward (i.e. towards the nose): mOKN is not elicited by movement in the opposite direction (Atkinson, 1979; Atkinson & Braddick, 1981). Neurophysiological studies suggest that OKN is mediated by a subcortical nucleus, the nucleus of the optic tract (NOT). At birth each NOT is driven only by direct crossed input from the contralateral eye, and responses of neurons in each NOT show the same asymmetry of OKN as newborn infants. This means that the newborn binocular response can be generated by stimulation of one NOT from the right eye for rightward movement and stimulation of the other NOT and eye for leftward movement. It is proposed that at a later age an indirect pathway from visual cortex to NOT becomes functional, allowing symmetrical OKN responses with monocular viewing.

To measure cortical directional mechanisms in infants, we have used designer stimuli consisting of two-dimensional random dot displays, which can have a particular direction of motion without the confounding presence of any dominant orientation component. In a similar way to the OR-VEP technique, we can generate a VEP to a change in the direction of motion of a set of random dots (Wattam-Bell, 1988, 1991). The first significant motion VEP for a velocity of 5 deg/sec appears at around 6-8 weeks of age, with onset for higher velocities occurring later (Wattam-Bell, 1991). Parallel behavioural studies show once again that the velocity is a critical determinant in obtaining discrimination of relative motion at different ages (Wattam-Bell, 1990) but true cortical directional detectors have not as yet been demonstrated prior to 6–8 weeks of age with many variants on both behavioural and electrophysiological methods (Wattam-Bell, 1996).

From neurophysiological studies, the magnocellular-based stream running from ganglion cells to V1, V2, V3 and V5 seems to be specifically selective for information about direction. In particular in adults, recent studies using fMRI indicate that V5 and V3A are critical areas for human motion perception (e.g. Tootell et al., 1995; Zeki, 1974, 1978, 1983). From the results on infant discrimination of direction, discussed above, we have argued that cortical directional systems, subserved by this magnocellular-based system, are necessary for both symmetrical mOKN responses and sensitivity to relative directional motion and that these modules become functional at around two to three months postnatally. Before this age, subcortical systems operate on their own. As such it would seem that the magnocellular-based modules may become operational a little later than parvocellular-based modules for orientation and shape discriminations and that both cortical modules take over executive control of visual behaviour from neonatal subcortical modules.

However, two recent results on asymmetries of motion responses may require us to elaborate on this simple 'cortical takeover' model. The first result is that we found that two infants who had undergone hemispherectomy surgery in the first nine months of life, to relieve intractable epilepsy caused by congenital unilateral megalencephaly, showed marked asymmetry of OKN for both binocular and monocular viewing (Braddick et al., 1992) OKN was elicited for stimulus movement in the direction towards the decorticate half-field (i.e. contralateralwards with respect to the damage) but not for the opposite direction of pattern movement. If a subcortical system alone was adequate to sustain OKN in children of this age, then with binocular stimulation OKN should be elicited in both directions because the subcortical systems of these children are intact on both sides. There are several possible explanations for the asymmetrical OKN in these children. One possibility is that we are wrong about OKN generation being possible with only subcortical systems operating. Instead, there may be two cortical systems involved in generating OKN, with the crossed system operating from birth and the uncrossed system becoming operational later. A second possibility is that the subcortical response is programmed to drop out once the cortical system is supposed to become operational in normal development, i.e. at 2–3 months postnatally (even in infants where one cortex is completely non-functional). The third possibility is that in these children the remaining good cortex suppresses the subcortical NOT responses on the other side, thus giving rise to the persistent asymmetry. This seems the most plausible explanation, although the other two explanations cannot be ruled out at present.

The second finding which casts doubt on the model of the cortical motion module becoming operational at around two months postnatally is that an asymmetry in a particular type of motion VEP has been found in infants before two months of age. Now it seems likely that VEPs are dominated by activity in cortical rather than subcortical visual areas (probably V1 and V2) .The left/right directionally asymmetrical VEP, found in young infants' responses to an oscillatory displacement of a vertical grating appears to be a very similar type of asymmetry to that shown in mOKN (Braddick, 1996b; Norcia et al. 1991). The result might give support for the idea that asymmetries of mOKN are not due solely to an absence of cortical functioning, but rather that there are directional asymmetries in cortical as well as subcortical motion processing.

In all of the motion studies described, the motion within the stimulus has been along a single dimension, with motion being reflected by a change in luminance. More recently we have examined infants' preferential looking responses to stimuli which require more elaborate processing to detect the motion. In 'second-order' or 'drift-balanced' motion displays (Cavanagh & Mather, 1990; Chubb & Sperling, 1988; Koenderink & Lelkins, 1984) movement information is carried by some property of the pattern without any directional energy in the spatio-temporal pattern of luminance. Our work uses random dot patterns in which bands of dynamic noise are successively displaced with interleaved bands of stationary dots. This can be compared with a 'first-order' motion display, in which the dynamic noise bands and the interleaved bands have stationary boundaries, but the dots within the interleaved bands move coherently. Second-order stimuli require an extra non-linear processing stage before directional processing. It has been suggested that this stage occurs in the pathway from V1 to MT via V2 (Yo & Wilson, 1992). In both two-month-old and four-month-old groups, we find significant preferences for second-order as well as first-order motion stimuli over equivalent stimuli without directional motion; performance on both improves with age, and at both ages is better for first- than for second-order stimuli, but there is no evidence of differential age of onset for the processing requiring the non-linear stages.

Interestingly, several perceptual discriminations dependent on relative motion detection can be demonstrated in relatively young infants. For example, four-month-olds can distinguish between three-dimensional forms which differ only in terms of 'structure from motion' cues in random dot displays (Arterberry & Yonas, 1988). Many of the experiments on infants' abilities to make avoidance responses to looming objects (e.g. Yonas, 1981) and to reach for nearby objects demonstrate how the infant integrates spatial and temporal information into a unified percept of an object in a given location. However, many of these abilities may depend on applying crude heuristic rules (e.g. getting bigger means nearer) rather than using specifically tuned orientation and relative direction detectors to calculate the precise shape and direction in which the object is moving.

At present there seems to be a conflict between the results of detailed experiments on discrimination of orientation and direction and the apparently sophisticated discriminations demonstrated in the newborn's capacity to make facial imitations. In particular, some theorists (e.g. Bower), have claimed that newborns use the higher order variable of 'pure movement' to imitate facial movements. Bower (1989) has suggested that newborns not only imitate real faces but will also correctly imitate the facial expression represented only as a series of strategically placed light bulbs (on the lips and corner of the mouth). This type of capacity seems to involve at the very least relatively finely tuned spatial and temporal detectors, which have not so far been in evidence in many of the psychophysical studies on older infants cited previously.

Example 3: Development of the disparity module

The input information from the two eyes remains segregated in subcortical structures with the first level of interaction being within the cortex. This means that any response dependent on detection of binocular correlation or disparity must be dependent on the operation of cortical rather than subcortical mechanisms. An example of such a response was first demonstrated using a sucking habituation paradigm (Atkinson & Braddick, 1976). Such responses are first seen on average around 3 to 4 months (Braddick & Atkinson, 1983; Braddick et al., 1980; Braddick et al., 1983; Fox et al., 1980; Held et al., 1980; Petrig et al., 1981). Binocular correlation and disparity detection appear to have the same onset time in individual infants, with significant VEP responses usually being recorded one to two weeks before significant behavioural preferential looking responses (Smith et al., 1988). These studies indicate that the onset of functioning of cortical binocular mechanisms is clearly postnatal and such mechanisms cannot be used in any depth or distance judgements involved in spatial localization made prior to 3 months of age. As the thick cytochrome oxidase staining stripes in V2, which receive input largely from the magnocellular system, are thought to be the predominant location of disparity selective neurons, it seems likely that development of functioning in this pathway takes place a few months postnatally in the case of human development.

It seems plausible to argue that once stereoscopic vision is established information from this would be used to guide the actions of reaching and grasping. We have measured the course of visually guided reaches in infants who have just started reaching (6–9 month-olds), comparing their ability with both eyes viewing to a situation where one eye is covered. If stereoscopic information is used to control reaching, then covering one eye should reduce the accuracy or efficiency of the reach. We have used the ELITE motion analysing system which uses video tracking of lightweight reflectors on the skin to register and analyse the kinetics (three-dimensional trajectory, velocity and timing) of a limb movement. In 6–9 month-olds reaching consists of a number of segments, each segment defined by an acceleration followed by a deceleration. The most extreme case of this is where the hand comes almost to rest in an incorrect position, and this misreach is then followed by one or more corrective movements. Thus an increased number of segments indicates greater inaccuracy and uncertainty in the initial ballistic action. We have found an increased number of segments and peak velocity to occur in monocular viewing conditions (Atkinson et al., 1994a). This result suggests that stereoscopic information is one form of information which allows the infants to make accurate rapid reaches. We intend to study development of reaching in infants who do not have stereoscopic vision because of early onset convergent strabismus (cross eyes). There are of course two possibilities here. One is that strabismic infants will show more imprecise slower reaching behaviour than normal infants. The other possibility is that strabismic infants will have developed strategies to use more fully monocular cues to depth and distance than their normal peers.

From these findings it seems that initial onset of functioning in cortical modules for orientation discrimination, directional motion and stereopsis is largely postnatal. We have some support for the idea that orientation selectivity may develop before selectivity to motion and disparity. This may suggest that parvocellularly based modules become functional before magnocellularly-based modules. Although it is not discussed here, infants in the first few weeks after birth show relatively sophisticated ability to detect differences based on colour alone, using isoluminant displays. This might be taken as further evidence for a dissociation between colour/form information and motion/depth information in early infancy.

DEVELOPMENT OF INTEGRATION AND SEGMENTATION

Integration within specific cortical streams We have already really considered these processes above for motion and disparity detection. In fact, it is precisely because of these integration processes between neurons showing similar sensitivities to a particular visual attribute, that we are able to demonstrate motion and disparity discrimination.

Example 1: Integration and segmentation in the orientation module

Another example of integration and segmentation can be given in the domain of orientation. Here we test the ability of the infant to recognize an area containing identical single features, such as an area composed of similarly oriented short-line segments. This segmentation process would take place after primary visual mechanisms have registered the simple stimulus properties of orientation, and would be used to define distinct surfaces or objects. In adults, the presence of orientation differences between line or edge segments making up two areas is very effective in determining visual segmentation (Beck, 1966; Nothdurft, 1990; Olson & Attneave, 1970). Several models of cortical mechanisms responsible for these processes have been proposed (e.g. Nothdurft, 1985; Sagi & Julesz, 1985). Their principal component is local differencing operations, acting on the output of neurons which are visual filters for specific properties. The differencing function may depend on connections within the cortex providing mutual inhibition between pools of neurons specifying differing orientations.

We have measured the infant's ability to orient towards a rectangular area in the visual field, whose boundary is defined by a change in orientation of the line segments making up the display. The rectangle is presented to either the left or right of a central fixation point. Using the forced choice preferential looking technique (FPL), we measure the infant's ability to detect the change of orientation within the rectangular patch compared to the background. What we have found is that this appears to be an impossible task for infants up to four months of age, and even at this age the response appears relatively weak (Atkinson & Braddick, 1992; Braddick & Atkinson, 1991; Sireteanu & Rieth, 1992). This relatively late onset of ability to segment on the basis of orientation suggests that other mechanisms for segmenting and localizing objects in the visual world, such as contrast cues and differential motion, may be more robust and useful in the first few months of life. Of course it may be that even in adult vision, the primary segmenting mechanisms use crude intensity differences to parse the visual scene and that these decisions are then confirmed by additional information provided by more elaborate texture comparators. It may also be that the orienting mechanism, necessary for rapid detection of objects in the peripheral field rather than central part of the visual field, does not use information processed in the cortex very effectively, but relies instead on crude information provided by the superior colliculus. To test this we will need to carry out further studies, presenting the segmented area of uniform orientation in the centre of the infant's visual field, rather than in the periphery.

Example 2: Integration and segmentation for perceiving texture

Julesz (1981) has proposed a theory of preattentive processing, defining classes of local features called 'textons' (such as edge segments and edge terminators) which enable us to rapidly segregate one texture from another which is useful for separating one object from another and one depth plane from another. Textons are thought to encode local phase relationships (i.e. the relative phase of the spatial frequency components making up the pattern elements), with certain phase relationships considered as 'special' because they correspond to physical features of the outside world. For example, the peaks-subtract phase relationship specifies a square-wave edge and allows analysis of the edges of objects to separate one object from its background or another object. Many models of relative phase discrimination propose perception of configuration to be dependent on comparator detectors across spatial frequency channels. Such phase selectivity might, for example, be embodied in channels having even- and odd-symmetric receptive fields, and such mechanisms exist only in the cortex and not in subcortical modules.

Applying these models of adult vision, we can use tests of relative phase and texton discrimination to infer cortical functioning in young infants. What we have found is that newborns are insensitive to changes in relative phase, when viewing complex gratings made up of several superimposed spatial frequencies (Braddick et al., 1986b). Nor do they discriminate between texture patterns, differing in the type of texton detectors proposed for adults (Braddick et al., 1986a). Three-month-olds have no difficulty with both these discriminations (relative phase and textons) which suggests that these integrative mechanisms get underway in the first few months of life.

Two examples of integration within each of the ventral and dorsal stream without full integration across streams

Example 1: Orientation matching and posting. A task (called the 'letter posting' task) has been developed which appears to dissociate performance in the dorsal and ventral stream in some neurological patients (Goodale et al., 1994, Stelmach et al., 1994). The task involves orienting a rectangular card (the 'letter') to be aligned with a postal slot, which can be varied in orientation. There are two tasks, a perceptual matching task and a posting task: in one the subject has to match the orientation of the letter with the slot, and in the other the subject has to post the letter. The posting task is thought to involve largely dorsal processing, while orientation matching involves the perceptual ventral module. We have measured the accuracy of orientation matching in the matching and posting task using both video and the ELITE motion tracking system (BTS Milan) (Atkinson et al., 1996). The system involves small infrared markers whose position on the corners of the card are tracked during the matching and posting tasks. The average orientation error (difference between the orientation of the slot and the letter at the point in the reach when the letter is 2 cm from the slot) is plotted in Fig. 1.1 for both a normal 4- and 7-year-old and a 9-year-old Williams Syndrome (WS) child. As can be seen, the 7-year-old shows similar size of error on both the matching task and the posting task (around 2–3 degrees). Both the WS child and the 4-year-old show more accurate matching than posting. Although they are able to perceive and correctly match the orientation they are not able to use this information fully to accurately control the reach and posting. This would seem to suggest that normal children up to at least 4 years of age show some lack of integration for information gained in the two streams. WS children seem to show a similar dissociation on this task, with a possible deficit in dorsal stream processing. This is in line with a number of other findings we now have for WS children on a variety of spatial and visuo-motor tasks.

Example 2: A dissociation between discriminating and copying spatial constructions. From a number of studies we have found that there is an improvement between 18 months and 5 years of age in the ability of young children to construct reasonable copies of different brick constructions. Two-year-olds are

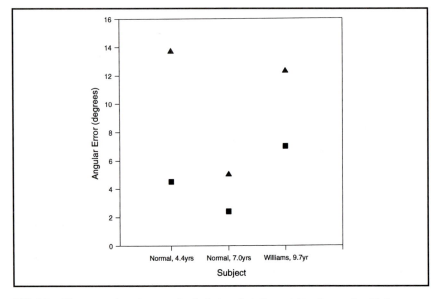

FIG. 1.1:   The mean orientation error for the letter orientation matching (squares) and letter posting (triangles) tasks for two normal children and a 9-year-old Williams Syndrome child. The orientation matching task involves orienting a rectangular card (the 'letter') to be aligned with a postal slot, which can be varied in orientation. In the letter posting task the subject has to successfully post the letter.

usually able to understand and copy a stack or tower of small bricks whereas five-year-olds are able to make quite elaborate copies in two dimensions involving angles, corners and conjunctions, with a continuum between the two ages correlated with constructional complexity (e.g. Atkinson et al., 1994b; Stiles-Davis, Sugarman & Nass, 1985). In one study we tested two age groups of children (19–24 months, 31–36 month olds) on both a discriminative task and a constructional copying task. In the discrimination task we first asked the child to make a copy of one of the constructions, D and H, in Fig. 1.2. We then showed the child two identical copies of the construction, putting the second copy by the side of their attempted copy. We then placed a small teddy bear on the experimenter's original model, saying it was the teddy's house. We then gave the child a second teddy and asked them to put their teddy on another house which was the same as the experimenter's teddy's house. Only 2 out of the 16 children in the younger age group made a similar construction to D consisting of a stack and a row (of any number); nearly all the other children in the group made either a single stack or a single row. However when asked to place their teddy on the 'house' (construction) which 'looked' the same as the experimenter's, 9 out of 12 children correctly discriminated between the two constructions, placing the teddy on the identical construction to the experimenter's. The same dissociation was found using construction H for the older

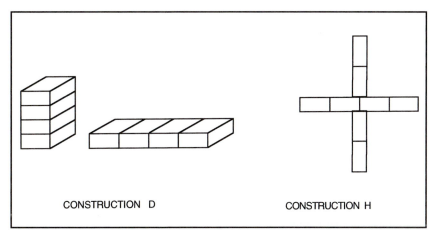

CONSTRUCTION D   CONSTRUCTION H

FIG. 1.2:   Constructions used in the block copying task. There are two tasks: in one task the child has to copy either construction D or construction H; in the second task the child has to discriminate between their copy of the construction and a perfect copy of the construction.

age group. Although only 3 of this group made similar cross construction to the original, 16 out of 19 were able to place the teddy on the identical cross construction.

For both these age groups perceptual matching and discrimination of the overall shape of the construction is possible, but this information cannot yet be integrated with the appropriate series of motor actions to construct a similar copy. It is not a question of the child not understanding what making a copy which is 'the same' is, because when they are asked which one is the same in the teddy task most of them have no difficulty. Again it looks like a failure of integration across cortical streams, with the dorsal stream lagging behind the perceptual mechanisms in normal development.

DEVELOPMENT OF SUBCORTICAL AND CORTICAL ATTENTIONAL SYSTEMS CONTROLLING HEAD AND EYE MOVEMENTS

If a conspicuous large moving object is made to appear suddenly in the peripheral visual field, infants will often move their eyes to foveate the object centrally. This has been called *overt orienting* and is usually taken as an indicator of an attentional shift. Many previous studies indicate that this response is present but unreliable in newborns, but becomes a robust response by three months of age (e.g. Atkinson & Braddick, 1985). We can question what factors control this improvement. It could be the relative visibility of the target above threshold contrast or acuity limitations.

In a calibration study (Atkinson et al., 1992; Braddick & Atkinson, 1988) we showed that the orienting response is indeed modulated by the contrast of the peripheral stimulus. We were able to equate overt orienting in 1- and 3-month-olds (in terms of number of refixations and/latency of response) to a peripherally placed stimulus, whose appearance was synchronized with the disappearance of an identical central target, by using a higher contrast for the younger age group than the older infants. The large conspicuous target consisted of one cycle of a grating pattern which alternated in phase, the target being matched in mean luminance to its background. In a second *competition condition* the central target remained visible throughout the time that the peripheral target appeared, so the two targets were competing with each other for the child's attention. Even when the peripheral targets are equated for visibility above contrast threshold, one-month-olds tend to be a little slower in refixating, and often fail to refixate at all under *competition* conditions. The one-month-olds seemed to have a problem 'disengaging' from the central target if it was still visible. By analogy from results of primate lesion studies and neurological patients with parietal lobe damage, we suggested that this additional factor in attentional control between 1 and 3 months was likely to be related to the onset at around 3 months of age of functioning in additional cortical attentional systems, involving superior colliculus, striate and extrastriate connections in the parietal lobes, with the 1-month-old's behaviour being largely under subcortical control in the colliculus (Atkinson & Braddick, 1985; Atkinson et al., 1992; Braddick & Atkinson, 1988). For example, the inability of 1-month-olds to shift fixation to a peripheral target if a central target is already fixated, called 'sticky fixation', has been found in a neurological condition called 'Balint's syndrome'. The problem is not one of 'neglect' or optic apraxia but rather concerns the coordination of mechanisms controlling saccadic eye movements and selective attention to provide accurate spatial localizing. Balint's syndrome involves bilateral lesions in parieto-occipital areas but may also involve the circuitry between the superior colliculus and parietal lobes for controlling shifts of attention (review by de Renzi, 1988). Very similar behaviour to Balint's patients has been seen in primates with bilateral parietal damage (Mountcastle, 1978) although Schiller (1985) has also reported similar deficits with damage to the superior colliculus and frontal eye fields. Again, the evidence for development of cortical streams lends support to the idea that crude localizing of single targets can be carried out by subcortical collicular mechanisms, while more elaborate selective processes, to shift attention from one object to another, require executive control from the striate and extrastriate cortex. These latter networks are likely to involve the functioning of the pulvinar for linking subcortical and cortical areas (reviewed by Robinson & Petersen, 1992) A similar idea concerning the sequencing of development in attentional systems from birth to 6 months, has been put forward by Johnson and Morton (Johnson, 1990; Johnson & Morton, 1991; Johnson, 1992; Johnson, 1996). Johnson suggests a slightly later age for 'ready disengagement' from a central target than that from our earlier studies (4 months rather than 3 months). An additional inhibitory mechanism has also been suggested by Johnson which operates in 1-month-olds and was not operational in newborns. There is, as yet, very little direct empirical evidence for this change over the first month of life, but a number of studies in addition to those mentioned above show marked changes between 1 and 4 months. Perhaps a study gathering longitudinal data to compare the same infants from birth for the first 4 months postnatally, on a variety of these attentional paradigms, will allow us to pinpoint these changes more exactly and to understand the relationship between different measures. The course of development of an additional attentional mechanism called 'inhibition of return' has also been investigated (Hood & Atkinson, 1991; Hood, 1993; Johnson, 1994). Here a covert cue in one location, which does not elicit orienting, can nevertheless reduce the speed of response to the same location for the target which is oriented. Both 'facilitation' and 'inhibition' of orienting by a covert cue can be demonstrated in infants; the effect of cueing depending on the timing of the sequence of events, as is the case in adult studies of attention. Heart rate changes as well as latency measures have been used to monitor attention in infants during orienting (e.g. Richards, 1991). Both exogenous and endogenous cues can be found to affect sustained attention as monitored by heart rate changes. The increase in response time when heart rate deceleration indicated sustained attention is presumed to be due to cortically mediated pathways in the frontal lobes which inhibit the colliculus. Whether this mechanism is entirely separate from the aforementioned disengage mechanism remains an open question.

Further support for the idea of a cortical mechanism becoming operational to allow rapid disengagement from a foveated target comes from our study of the two infants who had undergone complete hemispherectomy in the first year of life (Braddick et al., 1992). Appearance of single conspicuous targets, with the central target simultaneously extinguished (non-competition), in the periphery of the half-field contralateral to the removed hemisphere could elicit fixations, implying detection and orienting by a subcortical system similar to that reported for some blindsight patients (reviewed in Weiskrantz, 1986; Cowey & Stoerig, 1991). However when the central and peripheral targets appear together and compete for attention, the infants fail to refixate, and show sticky fixation only when the peripheral target is on the side contralateral to the removed hemisphere. Although this can be taken as evidence for cortical involvement in disengaging and shifting attention between competing targets, we do not know from these studies which particular cortical areas are required.

There are many paradigms, which can reveal development of attentional mechanisms besides that of fixation shifts. One example which we have interpreted as a deficit in selective attention is that of the 'externality effect', initially identified by Milewski (1976) defined as the inability of very young infants and primates with V1 lesions to discriminate a change in shape in an internal contour, if the outer contour remains constant. This can also be demonstrated in young infants' difficulty in recognizing faces if the outer hair lines of both faces are made identical using swimming caps (Bushnell, 1982). The reverse effect can be seen where infants fail to process the outer contour if their attention is captured by dynamic inner contours (Bushnell 1982). This reversal supports the idea that the attentional salience of a stimulus is markedly changed by its dynamic properties, so that the hierarchy of salience can be reversed or adjusted by changing the relative dynamics of the display.

Of course, in these studies we are not gauging overt attention directly from eye movement analysis, rather we are assuming a correlation between longer looking times and increased sustained attention. In other studies we have taken a change in accommodative focusing mechanisms in the eye, for targets at different distances, as a measure of attentional shifts. Yet another measure for gauging attention over distance is to measure the distance at which the infant loses eye contact and looks away (Macpherson et al., 1994). Here we are interested in the ease of distractibility of the child's attentional system. These later measures, have been used to look at the extent of failure of sustained attention in children with focal and global brain damage (Mercuri & Atkinson, 1996). Different types and degree of attentional deficits are among the commonest problems in clinical paediatric populations, but we are only just starting to correlate different types of attentional deficit with damage in different underlying brain areas.

DO WE ALWAYS FIND A CLEAR ASSOCIATION BETWEEN BRAIN STRUCTURE AND BEHAVIOUR IN DEVELOPMENT?

In clinical populations we already see some clear correlations between a physiological change in development and abnormal development of some aspect of vision. One of the most straightforward examples is the correlation that we see between adults who have been strabismic (cross-eyed/ misaligned eyes) from an early age and a lack of disparity detection as adults on standard clinical stereo tests. However, even this relationship is not completely watertight. We find that some strabismic children who obviously lack good stereoacuity nevertheless give a significant VEP to a relatively large change in disparity, when tested with red/green correlograms or stereograms (Smith et al., 1988).

Another way to study the relationship between changing behaviour and brain development is to look at children with identifiable brain lesions around birth and find out how visual development is affected. Over the last few years we have been looking at children with brain lesions (some focal, some more global) and correlating this with visual development, looking at a number of different aspects of vision. Here we find quite large variations in the range of visual delays or defects associated with similar degrees of perinatal damage, as imaged on serial MRI records (Atkinson & Hood, 1994; Mercuri et al., 1996). A somewhat intriguing recent finding is that perinatal basal ganglian damage alone is quite often associated with delays in development of attentional mechanisms and delays in the onset times for orientation-reversal cortical VEPs. Indeed, in a number of children, the visual delays are more pronounced in children with perinatal basal ganglian damage than in children with quite extensive cortical damage to both temporal and parietal lobes. Exactly which circuits are involved in this reduced plasticity for recovery in the basal ganglia is a current question. Three distinct areas of cortex have been identified as important for shifts of attention in both adults and infants. These are the frontal eye fields, posterior parietal cortex and prefrontal cortex. Each circuit is likely to have both a distinct role to play in attentional control (for example, the prefrontal role is likely to involve endogenous attention with time delays before a shift of attention is allowed), but they are also unlikely to ever be in operation completely independently. All three circuits involve pathways to and from the basal ganglia (Alexander, DeLong & Strick, 1986, review). It seems quite possible that disruption to this integrating basal ganglia circuitry from birth will mean delays and possibly defects in developing attentional systems involving eye movements. However, the delays in cortical VEP onset would seem to be harder to explain. The answer is likely to be related to the temporal frequency tuning of the cortex, as the likelihood of a significant cortical VEP is related to the temporal parameters of the stimulus (slow reversal rates give bigger VEPs and are significant earlier than do stimuli rapidly reversing). A much more fundamental deficit in inhibitory circuitry of the basal ganglia may mean that synchrony of cortical circuits is lost, preventing a coherent time-locked potential to build up and generate a fast averaging signal.

SUMMARY

In summary it appears that infants are born with operating discriminatory mechanisms linked to appropriate orienting responses, which enable them to set out a crude spatial map of the world around them. These mechanisms are initially largely under subcortical control, although some fragmentary cortical functioning may already be demonstrated in newborns. In the first few weeks postnatally many of the specialized detectors in the cortex start to operate, to enable discriminations of various visual attributes such as orientation, colour and size. Integration of information within channels and across channels, subserving different attributes, extends throughout infancy and even beyond into childhood. There are some obvious but curious omissions of integration even in school-age children. Simple structure-function relationships in single areas have not generally been found in looking at developing vision. Rather we must think in terms of interacting modules and streams, with the gradual slow integration across streams taking several years to develop. Many aspects of this integration are still to be investigated if we are to have a complete understanding of human visual development.

ACKNOWLEDGEMENTS

I thank Oliver Braddick and all the other members of the Visual Development Unit who have been involved in the research reported in this chapter. I thank the Medical Research Council, UK, the University of Cambridge and University College London for supporting the research of the Visual Development Unit.

REFERENCES

Alexander, G.E., DeLong, M.R., & Strick, P.L. (1986). Parallel organization of functionally segregated circuits linking basal ganglia and cortex. *Annual Review of Neuroscience 9:* 357–382.

Arterberry, M.E., & Yonas, A. (1988). Infants' sensitivity to kinetic information for three-dimensional object shape. *Perception and Psychophysics 44:* 1–6.

Atkinson, J. (1979). Development of optokinetic nystagmus in the human infant and monkey infant: an analogue to development in kittens. In R.D. Freeman (Ed), *NATO Advanced Study Institute Series*. New York: Plenum Press.

Atkinson, J. (1984). Human visual development over the first six months of life: a review and a hypothesis. *Human Neurobiology 3:* 61–74.

Atkinson, J. (1992). Early visual development: differential functioning of parvocellular and magnocellular pathways. *Eye 6:* 129–135

Atkinson, J., & Braddick, O.J. (1976). Stereoscopic discrimination in infants. *Perception 5:* 29-38.

Atkinson, J., & Braddick, O.J. (1981). Development of optokinetic nystagmus in infants: an indicator of cortical binocularity? In D.F. Fisher, R.A. Monty & J. W. Senders (Eds), *Eye Movements: Cognition and Visual Perception.* Hillsdale, NJ: Lawrence Erlbaum Associates Inc.

Atkinson, J., & Braddick, O.J. (1985). Early development of the control of visual attention. *Perception 14:* A33.

Atkinson, J., & Braddick, O.J. (1992). Visual segmentation of oriented textures by infants. *Behavioural Brain Research 49:* 123–131.

Atkinson, J., Braddick, O.J., Anker, S., King, J., Mercuri, E., Nokes, L., & Hartley, T., (1996). *Perceptual, cognitive and motor aspects of vision in young Williams Syndrome children.* Paper and poster presented at the Williams Syndrome Association Seventh International Convention, Philadelphia.

Atkinson, J., Braddick, O.J., & Hood, B.M. (1994a). Kinetics of infants' reaching with monocular and binocular vision. *Infant Behaviour and Development 17:* 504.

Atkinson, J., Gardner, N., Tricklebank, J., & Anker, S. (1989). Atkinson Battery of Child Development for examining functional vision (ABCDEFV). *Ophthalmic and Physiological Optics 9 (4):* 470.

Atkinson, J., & Hood, B. (1994). Deficits of selective visual attention in children with focal lesions. *Infant Behaviour & Development, 17:* 423.

Atkinson, J., Hood, B., Wattam-Bell, J., Anker, S., & Tricklebank, J. (1988). Development of orientation discrimination in infancy. *Perception 17:* 587–595.

Atkinson, J., Hood, B., Wattam-Bell, J., & Braddick, O.J. (1992). Changes in infants' ability to switch visual attention in the first three months of life. *Perception 21:* 643–653

Atkinson, J., Macpherson, F., Rae, S., & Hughes, C. (1994b). Block constructions in young children: development of spatial grouping ability. *Strabismus 2 (1):* 41

Atkinson, J., & Mercuri, E. (1995). Visual development in infants with neonatal focal brain lesions. *Strabismus 3 (4):* 178.

Atkinson, J., Wattam-Bell, J., & Braddick, O.J. (1986a). Infants' development of sensitivity to pattern 'textons'. *Investigative Ophthalmology and Visual Science 27*: (Suppl.) 265.

Beck, J. (1966). Effect of orientation and shape similarity on perceptual grouping. *Perception and Psychophysics 1*: 300–302.

Bower, T.G. (1989). The perceptual world of the new-born child. In A. Slater & G. Bremner, *Infant Development*. Hove: Lawrence Erlbaum Associates Ltd.

Braddick, O. (1993). Segmentation versus integration in visual motion processing. *Trends in Neurosciences 16*: 263–268.

Braddick, O. (1996a). Binocularity in infancy. *Eye, 10*: 182–188.

Braddick, O. (1996b). Motion processing: where is the naso-temporal asymmetry? *Current Biology, 6*: 250–253.

Braddick, O., & Atkinson, J. (1983). Some recent findings on the development of human binocularity: a review. *Behavioural Brain Research, 10*: 141–150.

Braddick, O.J. & Atkinson, J. (1988). Sensory selectivity attentional control, and cross-channel integration in early visual development. In A Yonas (Ed), *20th Minnesota Symposium on Child Psychology*. Hillsdale, NJ: Lawrence Erlbaum Associates Inc.

Braddick, O.J., & Atkinson, J. (1991). Infants' and adults' segmentation of oriented textures. *Investigative Ophthalmology and Visual Science 32 (4)* (Suppl.): 1045.

Braddick, O.J., Atkinson, J., Hood, B., Harkness, W., Jackson, G., & Vargha-Khadem, F. (1992). Possible blindsight in infants lacking one cerebral hemisphere. *Nature*, 360: No. 6403, pp.461–463.

Braddick, O.J., Atkinson, J., Julesz, B., Kropfl, W., Bodis-Wollner, I., & Raab, E. (1980). Cortical binocularity in infants. *Nature 288*: 363–365.

Braddick, O.J., Atkinson, J., Smith, J.C., & Hood, B. (1989). Behavioural and VEP measures of developing contrast sensitivity and binocularity: do they reveal different mechanisms? *Ophthalmic and Physiological Optics 9*: 471.

Braddick, O.J., Atkinson, J., & Wattam-Bell, J. (1986b). Development of the discrimination of spatial phase in infancy. *Vision Research 26 (8)*: 1223-1239.

Braddick, O., Atkinson, J., & Wattam-Bell, J. (1993). Infant's sensitivity to second order motion. *Strabismus, 1 (4)*: 212.

Braddick, O.J., Wattam-Bell, J., Day, J., & Atkinson, J. (1983). The onset of binocular function in human infants. *Human Neurobiology 2*: 65–69.

Braddick, O.J., Wattam-Bell, J., Marshall, G., & Atkinson, J. (1986a). The orientation specific VEP shows marked horizontal vertical anisotropy. *Perception 15*: A22.

Bronson, G.W. (1974). The postnatal growth of visual capacity. *Child Development 45*: 873–890.

Bushnell, I.W.R. (1982). Discrimination of faces by young infants. *Journal of Experimental Psychology 33*: 298–30.

Bushnell, I.W.R., Sai, F., & Mullin, J.T. (1989). Neonatal recognition of the mother's face. *British Journal of Developmental Psychology. 7*: 3–16

Cavanagh, P., & Mather, G. (1990). Motion: the long and short of it. *Spatial Vision 4 (2/3)*: 103–129.

Chubb, C., & Sperling, G. (1988). Drift-balanced random stimuli: a general basis for studying non-Fourier motion perception. *J.Opt.Soc.Am. A5*: 1986–2007.

Cowey, A., & Stoerig, P. (1991). The neurobiology of blindsight. *Trends in Neurosciences 14(4):* 140–145.

Damasio, A.R., & Benton, A.L. (1979). Impairments of hand movements under visual guidance. *Neurology 29*: 170–178.

de Renzi, E. (1988). Oculomotor disturbances in hemispheric disease. In C. W. Johnston & F. J. Pirozzolo (Eds), *Neuropsychology of Eye Movements*. Hillsdale, NJ: Lawrence Erlbaum Associates Inc.

Derrington, A.M., & Lennie, P. (1984). Spatial and temporal contrast sensitivities of neurons in lateral geniculate nucleus of macaque. *Journal of Physiology 357*: 219–240.

Fox, R., Aslin, R.N., Shea, S.L., & Dumais, S.T. (1980). Stereopsis in human infants. *Science 207*: 232–324.

Goodale, M.A., Jacobson, L.S., Milner, A.D., & Perrett, D.I. (1994). The nature and limits of orientation and pattern processing supporting visuomotor control in a visual form agnosi. *Journal of Cognitive Neuroscience 6 (1)*: 46–56.

Goodale, M.A., & Milner, A.D. (1992). Separate visual pathways for perception and action. *Trends in Neurosciences 15 (1)*: 20–25

Held, R., Birch, E.E., & Gwiazda, J. (1980). Stereoacuity of human infants. *Proc.Natl.Acad.Sci. USA 77*: 5572–5574.

Hood, B.M. (1993). 'Inhibition of return produced by covert shifts of visual attention in 6-month old infants. *Infant Behaviour and Development 16*: 245-254.

Hood, B., & Atkinson, J. (1991). Shifting covert attention in infants. *Abstracts of the Society for Research in Child Development.*

Hood, B., & Atkinson, J. (1991). Shifting covert attention in infants. *Investigative Ophthalmology and Visual Science 32 (4)* (Suppl.): 965.

Johnson, M.H. (1990). Cortical maturation and the development of visual attention in early infancy. *Journal of Cognitive Neuroscience 2*: 81–95.

Johnson, M.H., & Morton, J. (1991). *Biology and Cognitive Development: The case of face recognition.* Oxford: Blackwell.

Johnson, M.H. (1992). Cognition and development: four contentions about the role of visual attention. In D.J. Stein & J.E. Young (Eds), *Cognitive Science and Clinical Disorders,* pp.43–60. San Diego: Academic Press.

Johnson, M.H. (1994). Visual attention and the control of eye movements in early infancy. In C. Umiltà and M. Moscovitch (Eds), *Attention and Performance XV: Conscious and Nonconscious Processing,* pp.291–310. Cambridge, Mass: MIT Press.

Johnson, M.H. (1996). The development of visual attention: a cognitive neuroscience perspective. In M. Gazzaniga (Ed), *The Cognitive Neurosciences*, pp.735–747. Cambridge, MA: MIT Press.

Julesz, B. (1981). Textons, the elements of texture perception, and their interactions. *Nature 290*: 92–97.

King, J.A., Atkinson, J., Braddick, O.J., Nokes, L., & Braddick, F. (1996). Target preference and movement kinematics reflect development of visuomotor modules in the reaching of human infants. *Investigative Ophthalmology and Visual Science 37*:S526.

Koenderink, J.J., & Lelkins, A.M.M. (1984). Illusory motion in visual displays. *Vision Research 24*: 1083–1090.

Livingstone, M.S., & Hubel, D.H. (1988). Segregation of form, color, movement, and depth: anatomy, physiology, and perception. *Science 240*: 740–749.

Macpherson, F., Rae, S., Hughes, C., Atkinson, J., & Anker, S. (1994). Atkinson battery of child development for examining functional vision (ABCDEFV). *Strabismus 2(1)*: 49.

Mason, J., Grey, N., & Atkinson, J. (1992), *A preliminary study of the development of spatial grouping ability in young children.* Unpublished Part II project, Emmanuel College, Cambridge.

Maunsell, J.H.R., & Newsome, W.T. (1987). Visual processing in monkey extrastriate cortex. *Annual Review of Neuroscience. 10*: 3416–3468.

Mercuri, E., Atkinson, J. (1996). Visual function and perinatal focal cerebral infarction. *Fetal and Neonatal 75(2)*: 76–81.

Mercuri, E., Atkinson, J., Braddick, O., Anker, S.E., Nokes, L., Cowan, F., Rutherford, M., Pennock, J., & Dubowitz, L. (1995). Visual maturation in children with focal brain lesions on neonatal imaging. *Neuropediatrics 26*: 348.

Mercuri, E., Atkinson, J., Braddick, O.J., Anker, S., Nokes, L., Cowan, F., Rutherford, M., Pennock, J., & Dubowitz, L. (1996). Visual function and perinatal focal cerebral infarction. *Archives of Disease in Childhood 75*: F76–F81.

Mercuri, E., Atkinson, J., Rutherford, M., Cowan, F., Braddick, O., Anker, S., Nokes, L., Pennock, J., & Dubowitz, L. (1996). *Maturation of visual function in infants with HIE*. Transactions of the British Paediatric Neurology Association XXII Annual Meeting, Southampton.

Milewski, A.E. (1976). Infants' discrimination of internal and external pattern elements. *Journal of Experimental Child Psychology 22*: 229–246.

Milner, D.A., & Goodale, M.A. (1995). *The Visual Brain in Action*. Oxford: Oxford University Press.

Mountcastle, V.B. (1978). Brain mechanisms for directed attention. *Journal of the Royal Society of Medicine 71*: 14–28.

Norcia, A.M., Garcia, H., Humphry, R., Holmes, A., Hamer, R.D., & Orel-Bixler, D. (1991). Anomalous motion VEPs in infants and in infantile esotropia. *Investigative Ophthalmology and Visual Science 32*: 346–439.

Nothdurft, H.C. (1985). Sensitivity for structure gradient in texture discrimination. *Vision Research 25*: 1957–1968.

Nothdurft, H.C. (1990). Texton segregation by associated differences in global and local luminance distribution. *Proceedings of the Royal Society of London B 239*: 295–320.

Olson, R., & Attneave, F. (1970). What variables produce similarity grouping? *American Journal of Psychology 83*: 1–21.

Petrig, B., Julesz, B., Kropfl, W., Baumagartner, G., & Anliker, M. (1981). Development of steropsis and cortical binocularity in human infants: electrophysiological evidence. *Science 213*: 1402–1405.

Regal, D.M., Ashmead, D.H., & Salapatek, P. (1983). The coordination of eye and head movements during early infancy: a selective review. *Behavioural Brain Research 10*: 125–132.

Richards, J.E. (1991). Infant eye movements during peripheral visual stimulus localization as a function of central stimulus attention status. *Psychophysiology 28*: S4.

Robinson, D.L., & Petersen, S.E. (1992). The pulvinar and visual salience. *Trends Neurosciences 15*: 127–132.

Sagi, D., & Julesz, B. (1985). 'Where' and 'what' in vision. *Science 228*: 1217–1219.

Schiller, P.H. (1985). A model for the generation of visually guided saccadic eye movements. In D. Rose and V.G. Robson, *Models of the Visual Cortex*, pp. 62–70. Chichester: John Wiley.

Schiller, P.H. (1985). The superior colliculus and visual function. In I. Darian-Smith (Ed), *Handbook of Physiology: The Nervous System III. Sensory Processes, Part I*. Bethesda MD: American Physiological Society.

Sireteanu, R., & Rieth, C. (1992). Texture segregation in infants and children. *Behavioural Brain Research 49*: 133–139.

Slater, A., Morison, V., & Somers, M. (1988). Orientation discrimination and cortical function in the human newborn. *Perception 17*: 597–602.

Smith, J., Atkinson, J., Braddick, O.J., & Wattam-Bell, J. (1988). Development of sensitivity to binocular correlation and disparity in infancy. *Perception 17*: 365.

Stelmach, G.E., Castiello, U., & Jeannerod, M. (1994). Orienting the finger opposition space during prehension movements. *Journal of Motor Behavior 26 (2):* 178–186.

Stiles-Davis, J., Sugarman, S., & Nass, R. (1985). The development of spatial and class relation in four young children with right cerebral hemisphere damage: evidence for an early spatial-constructive deficit. *Brain and Cognition 4*: 388–412.

Tootell, R.B.H., Reppas J.B., Dale A.M., & Look R.B. (1995). Visual motion after-effect in human cortical area MT revealed by functional magnetic resonance imaging, *Nature 375(6527)*: 139–141

Ungerleider, L.G., & Mishkin, M. (1982). Two cortical visual systems. In D.G. Ingle, M.A. Goodale and R.J.Q. Mansfield (Eds), *Analysis of Visual Behavior*, pp.549–586. Cambridge MA: MIT Press.

Van Essen, D.C., & Maunsell, J.H.R. (1983). Hierarchical organization and functional streams in the visual cortex. *Trends in Neurosciences 6*: 370–375.

von Hofsten, C., & Rosander, K. (1996). The development of gaze control and predictive tracking in young infants. *Vision Research 36*: 81–96.

Wattam-Bell, J. (1985). Analysis of infant visual evoked potentials (VEPs) by a phase-sensitive statistic. *Perception 14*: A33.

Wattam-Bell, J. (1988). The development of motion-specific cortical responses in infants. *Investigative Ophthalmology and Visual Science 29* (Suppl.): 24.

Wattam-Bell, J. (1990). The development of maximum velocity limits for direction discrimination in infancy. *Perception 19 (3)*: 369.

Wattam-Bell, J. (1991). Displacement limits for the discrimination of motion direction in infancy. *Investigative Ophthalmology and Visual Science 32 (4)* (Suppl.): 964.

Wattam-Bell, J. (1996). The development of visual motion processing. In F. Vital-Durand, O. Braddick, & J. Atkinson (Eds), *Infant Vision*, pp.79–94. Oxford: Oxford University Press.

Weiskrantz, L. (1986). *Blindsight: A case study and implications*. Oxford: Clarendon Press.

Yo, C. & Wilson H.R. (1992). Moving 2-dimensional patterns can capture the perceived directions of lower or higher spatial frequency gratings. *Vision Research 32(7)*: 1263–1269.

Yonas, A. (1981). Infants' responses to optical information for collision. In R.N. Aslin, J.R. Alberts & M. R. Petersen (Eds), *The Development of Perception: Psychobiological Perspectives*. New York: Academic Press.

Zeki, S.M. (1974). Functional organization of the visual area in the posterior bank of the superior temporal sulcus of the rhesus monkey. *Journal of Physiology 236*: 549–573.

Zeki, S.M. (1978). Uniformity and diversity of structure and function in rhesus monkey prestriate visual cortex. *Journal of Physiology 277*: 273–290.

Zeki, S. (1983). Colour coding in the cerebral cortex: the responses of wavelength-selective and colour-coded cells in monkey visual cortex to changes in wavelength composition. *Neuroscience 9*: 767–781.

Zihl, J., von Cramon, D., & Mai, N. (1983). Selective disturbance of movement vision after bilateral brain damage. *Brain 106*: 313–340.

CHAPTER TWO

Learning What is Where: Oculomotor Contributions to the Development of Spatial Cognition

Rick O. Gilmore
Carnegie Mellon University, Pittsburgh, USA

Mark H. Johnson
University College, London, UK

INTRODUCTION

Perceiving where things are in the environment poses a fundamental problem for mobile animals. The perception of external space demands the capacity to detect, represent and transform information in multiple sensory frames of reference since the body's sensors have different intrinsic geometries and move relative to one another. Similarly, even the simplest forms of action involve the identification of a goal in one frame of reference, such as the limb's desired position in space, and the transformation of those spatial coordinates into motor commands in another frame of reference that move the limb into the appropriate position. Between visual perception and visually guided action lies a rich repertoire of spatial cognitive abilities that participate in transformations between signals derived in different sensory modalities and integration among them.

Several lines of research have been brought to bear on these general questions. Recordings from neurons in behaving animals have provided information about the retinal-, head-, body-, and even arm-based codes used by the nervous system to support spatial perception and action (Andersen, Snyder, Li & Stricane, 1993; Graziano, Yap & Gross, 1994; Stein, 1992). Behavioral studies of brain-injured adults have suggested how the normal and injured brain processes spatial information (Farah, Brunn, Wong, Wallace & Carpenter, 1990; Moscovitch & Behrmann, 1994). Computational models which parallel sensorimotor transformations have suggested how spatial processing might occur in the brain (Goodman & Andersen, 1989; Guenther, Bullock, Greve & Grossberg, 1994;

Olson & Hanson, 1990; Zipser & Andersen, 1988). Developmental evidence has suggested that different sources of information influence object search and orienting behavior at different ages and that spatial processing matures gradually in the first year (Acredolo, 1990; Bremner, 1978; Piaget, 1954; Piaget & Inhelder, 1948). Nevertheless, few have attempted to incorporate neurobiological, computational, and developmental aspects of spatial perception and action simultaneously, despite the fact that spatial behavior and its brain substrates undergo rapid and dramatic maturation early in life.

The neurodevelopmental perspective we have adopted attempts such a synthesis by exploring the development of spatial perception and action in terms of the neural systems and computational processes which support it. Development in infants' neural structures, their brain's computational capacities, and behavior proceeds in a rapid, interdependent, and mutually reinforcing fashion. Consequently, patterns of change in the brain and its information-processing capabilities may provide fundamental constraints on infants' spatial behavior. We will explore the nature of these constraints on infants' developing spatial capacities by examining the neural structures, computational mechanisms, and development of one of the simplest sensorimotor behaviors that permits exploration of the environment, eye movements. Specifically, we will address the following questions: What spatial information is used for directing eye movements? How do infants' eye movements change in development? How do the neural substrates of eye movements develop? What do patterns of change in infants' eye movements and their neural substrates imply about the development of spatial information processing?

In answering these questions, we will argue that perceptual and motor limitations over the first several months of life severely constrain the range and accuracy of spatial information available to young infants from vision and visuomotor behavior. This specifically limits the ability of the immature visual system to represent space in multiple head-, trunk-, hand-, or environment-centered coordinate frames crucial for controlling complex and flexible forms of spatial behavior such as reaching and locomotion. However, improvements in the ability to detect accurately and integrate systematically spatial information from visual and non-visual sources permit spatial representations coded in higher-level frames of reference to emerge and influence behavior several months after birth. We will argue that the maturation of functional brain circuitry involved in spatial perception and eye movement control plays a central role in the development of infants' spatial processing and orienting behavior.

In the first section, we review the sources of spatial information which influence eye movements. Next, we describe the neural pathways that control eye movements in adult primates and developmental evidence which suggests that these pathways develop gradually in the months following birth. Then, we will describe recent behavioral research in our laboratory which explores what spatial information and which brain systems guide saccade planning at different points in early infancy. This evidence suggests that visual spatial processing progresses from retinal- to head- or body-based representations in the first six months of life, in accord with the development of mechanisms in the cerebral cortex which integrate multimodal spatial information. We will conclude with some remarks about the implications of these findings and the neurodevelopmental approach for spatial cognition in general.

SPATIAL INFORMATION PROCESSING IN OCULOMOTOR BEHAVIOR

One general view of sensorimotor processing postulates that it involves converting spatial goals from perception into spatial targets for action which move the body into some desired position and configuration. The transformation of spatial information from perceptual to motor coordinates may involve representations in frames of reference (see Fig. 2.1) defined relative to multiple points on the body or features of the environment (Andersen et al., 1993; Feldman, 1985; Marr, 1982) depending on the desired behavioral goal; for example, looking at a face versus touching it. Unlike limb control which has at least as many frames as there are joints, three frames appear immediately relevant for eye movements: a *retinocentric* frame which defines the position of an object relative to the center of the retina or

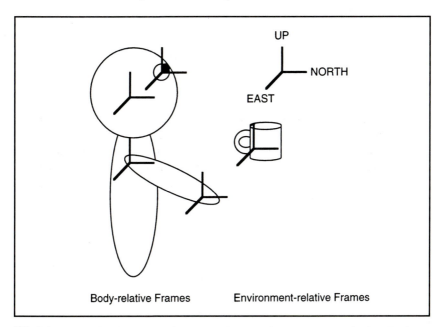

Body-relative Frames   Environment-relative Frames

FIG. 2.1:   Illustration of two types of coordinate frames useful in perception and action planning: body-relative frames anchored to different sense organs or effectors, and environment-relative frames anchored to objects or physical features of the landscape.

fovea; a *craniocentric* frame which defines locations relative to the head; and an *egocentric* frame which defines locations relative to the center of the trunk. These frames follow a logical hierarchy. Craniocentric coordinates combine retinocentric location and eye position relative to the head; egocentric coordinates combine retinocentric location, eye position relative to the head, and head position relative to the trunk. Specifying a target location in coordinates relative to any body part other than the retina requires the systematic integration of visual information, its position or velocity relative to the retina, and somatosensory information, eye, head, or body positions and velocities. A brief consideration of what spatial information influences eye movements illustrates how signals coded in these frames might have different effects on behavior.

Spatial signals in eye movement control

Saccades shift the center of gaze from one point to another with extremely rapid and essentially unmodifiable trajectories. This implies that online feedback has limited influence and that in some circumstances saccades involve prospective control—predictions made in advance about where in space a target is located. That spatial goal might be coded in any one of the three frames just mentioned. The simplest scheme proposed to account for saccade control transforms a target's distance from the fovea into motor commands which center the target on the retina (Young & Stark, 1963). As we will discuss later on, critical saccade-related brain structures appear to transform retinal position into corresponding saccade commands (Robinson, 1973) making this retinocentric scheme an initially appealing model. Unfortunately, it has several weaknesses in accounting for adult visual behavior. Information about the eyes' position and movement influences the perception of the relative directions of visual targets flashed during saccades and the production of saccades to them (Becker & Jürgens, 1979; Hallet & Lightstone, 1976a; Hallet & Lightstone, 1976b; Matin & Pearce, 1965). If eye position information influences saccade planning, then craniocentric or possibly egocentric coordinates may control mature saccade processing. The fact that adults make accurate saccades to auditory and visual targets suggests that a craniocentric representation might underlie a unified saccade planning scheme since the ears are fixed with respect to the head. On the other hand, egocentric coordinates could guide gaze shifts which combine eye and head movements.

Retinal-, head- and body-centered frames of reference influence other forms of eye movements as well. Smooth pursuit involves detecting a target's velocity and issuing an eye velocity command. In principle, target velocity could be coded relative to the retina, head, or trunk depending upon whether coordinated eye and head movements are involved in tracking the target and whether retinal-relative velocity is combined with eye or head position information in generating a pursuit command. The vergence system provides another example. It takes as input two retinocentric representations of the field of view from the left and right eyes. By determining their lateral disparity and the eyes' angular positions relative to the head, the vergence system presumably computes a signal specifying distance relative to the head and from it new positions of the eyes. Even fixation involves spatial signals in multiple frames of reference. Retinal information specifies whether the target remains on the high acuity foveal region, while eye and head position information is needed to stabilize the position of the eyes relative to the head and the head relative to the body. In adults the visual localization of objects in the dark and spatially coincident lights and sounds does in fact rely on accurate eye position signals (Matin, Stevens & Picoult, 1991) supporting the argument that craniocentric or egocentric information influences mature spatial perception.

Oculomotor development and its implications

The head- and body-based frames which control mature visual exploratory behavior rely upon precise integration of visual and somatosensory information; however, changes in oculomotor behavior in the first six months suggest that the developing system does not employ the same highly tuned mechanisms. Milestones in the development of the infant visuomotor system have been reviewed elsewhere (see Aslin, 1987; Johnson, 1990). Here we highlight two principal limitations on spatial representation in multiple frames of reference implied by the patterns of infant oculomotor development:

1. *Poor visual acuity*: At one month of age, visual acuity and contrast sensitivity are an order of magnitude worse than adult levels but improve steadily thereafter (Banks & Dannemiller, 1987). Poor acuity also affects infants' perception of optical motion. Young infants show sensitivity to some patterns of visual motion such as those specifying impending collision (Nanez, 1987). However, 2- month-olds' abilities to detect (Wattam-Bell, 1990; Wattam-Bell, 1991) and respond to a range of velocities (Atkinson, 1979; Naegele & Held, 1980; Naegele & Held, 1982) are an order of magnitude lower than adults. Diminished acuity has widespread impact. It limits the spatial resolution of retinocentric information about position and velocity and consequently the precision of perception and action systems that depend on this information.

2. *Poor eye and head control*: Changes in the precision of visual information no doubt make significant contributions to infants' increasingly precise control over the eyes and head in the first six months, but accurate motor control also involves comparisons between actual and predicted or desired movements. Consequently, improvements in infants' abilities to sense where the eyes and head are positioned must also occur. We know little about the development of somatosensory information that specifies positions of the eyes and head or other parts of the body. But, infants' vergence, pursuit, saccade, and tracking responses suggest these signals provide initially inaccurate information about the position and velocity of the eyes and head.

Patterns of infant saccade development provide evidence for initially poor eye position control. Newborns saccade in the general direction (left/right, up/down) of salient peripheral stimuli, but they make large errors in amplitude compared to adults (Aslin & Salapatek, 1975; Harris & MacFarlane, 1974; Lewis, Maurer & Kay, 1978), and their saccades may be less sensitive to visual feedback than adults' (Salapatek, Aslin, Simonson & Pulos, 1980). Aslin (1993) has suggested that postnatal calibration between visual and motor commands might contribute to improved saccade accuracy. If visual and motor commands require postnatal calibration, then eye position signals do not provide reliable information until the tuning process terminates. Visual pursuit also shows initially poor, but gradually improving control over eye velocity. Intermittent smooth pursuit of moving visual targets appears between 6 and 8 weeks (Aslin & Salapatek, 1975; Hainline, 1985; McGinnis, 1930), but there is an upper limit on target velocity that elicits pursuit, eye position lags target movement and corrective saccades are common (Aslin, 1981). By 12 weeks, however, many infants anticipate the future location of a moving stimulus by making tracking responses which exceed the velocity of the moving object (Aslin, 1981). Finally, changes in the magnitude and direction of vergence suggest that eye position information regarding relative angular deviation of the eyes is unreliable until 3 to 5 months of age (Aslin, 1987), a time period in which stereopsis commonly emerges (Birch, Gwiazda & Held, 1982; Gwiazda, Bauer & Held, 1989).

Similarly, information about static head position may not be especially reliable until infants gain skill in holding their head erect and stable without support. Information about head rotation, however, drives compensatory vestibulo-ocular responses (VOR) by 1 month of age (Regal, Ashmead & Salapatek, 1983) and this behavior comes to closely approximate adult magnitudes by approximately 4 months (Reisman & Anderson, 1989). Infants as young as 2 months show compensatory cervico-ocular reflexes (CORs) when the head is held fixed and the body rotates relative to it (Reisman & Anderson, 1989). Similarly in head free conditions, infants tested from 11 to 28 weeks of age showed steady improvements in matching the velocity of their head to the motions of a visual target, but much slower improvement in matching eye velocity to target velocity (Daniel & Lee, 1990). So, infants 2 to 4 months of age appear to have access to increasingly accurate vestibular and proprioceptive information about head rotation which drives compensatory eye movements or pursuit. Whether and how this head velocity signal is integrated for more general purposes, such as determining head position, is unknown.

There are no doubt many interacting factors that contribute to the development of eye and head movement control and their integration. The combined effect of these limitations, however, is to make eye and head position signals less reliable sources of spatial information for computing head- or body-centered representations.

Implications

This discussion supports several generalizations about the spatial information which controls visual exploratory behavior:

1. Neonates' limited visual acuity diminishes the resolution and accuracy of spatial information derived from vision.
2. Changes in the accuracy of eye and head control suggest that young infants do not have initially precise information about eye and head position.
3. Adult visual perception and oculomotor behavior involves the systematic integration of visual and somatosensory sources of spatial information which permit craniocentric, egocentric, or other body-based frames of reference to guide behavior.
4. Consequently, the period from birth to 6 months, in which oculomotor capacities develop rapidly, may involve changes in the frames of reference which govern visual perception and action.

Since large-scale development in the brain's visual and spatial processing circuitry occurs in the same time period (Johnson, 1990), understanding these patterns of brain growth may provide constraints upon what spatial information characterizes early visual behavior, in which frame or frames of reference it is coded, and how changes in neural circuitry contribute to the development in infants' spatial processing.

NEURAL BASES OF VISUOSPATIAL INFORMATION

The neural mechanisms for skilled spatial behavior must integrate visual and somatosensory spatial information in a systematic, precise, and flexible way. Reviews of physiological and anatomical evidence concur that the parietal lobe of the cerebral cortex plays a central role in these processes (Andersen et al., 1993; Stein, 1992). However, in several accounts of the relation between infant visual behavior and brain development (Atkinson, 1984; Bronson, 1974; Johnson, 1990) it has been argued that cortical circuitry is largely immature at birth and that infant visual perception and eye movement planning involves a gradual shift from subcortical to cortical control in the first several postnatal months. This implies that two possibilities may account for early infant behavior. The early maturing subcortical systems may systematically combine visual and somatosensory information providing an immature, but functional representation of visual space in head- or body-centered terms. Subsequent cortical development provides increasingly accurate and flexible information in multiple frames of reference which supersedes subcortical control. Alternatively, these representations do not emerge until the appropriate cortical circuitry becomes functional some months after birth; in the meantime, simpler, presumably retinocentric information dominates visual perception and visually guided eye movements. We explore these possibilities by reviewing the neural circuitry for eye movement control and the kinds of spatial information instantiated within these systems.

Oculomotor pathways and spatial processing

Several brain systems, each with distinctive functional properties, operate along parallel pathways to control eye movements. Our account of the principal functional pathways that control shifts of gaze in primates is modified from one originally described by Schiller (1985) (See Fig. 2.2). The pathways are as follows:

1. A subcortical pathway from the retina to the upper layers of the superior colliculus (SC).
2. A cortical pathway from the retina to the primary visual cortex (V1) via the lateral geniculate nucleus (LGN). From primary visual cortex, this pathway splits. One component projects directly to the intermediate layers and deep layers of the superior colliculus. The other projects to the middle temporal area (MT or V5) and from this and parietal regions (e.g. Brodmann's area 7a and the lateral intraparietal area, LIP) back to the intermediate and deep layers of the superior colliculus.
3. A cortical pathway projecting to the frontal eye fields (FEF) from several higher order visual areas including V4, MT, and posterior parietal cortex (areas 7a, LIP).
4. A mainly inhibitory projection from the substantia nigra in the basal ganglia to the intermediate and deep layers of the superior colliculus.

Johnson (1990) suggested that each of these parallel systems develops gradually with a different timecourse, and that infant orienting behavior at a given age reflects the patterns of relative maturity among the systems. For brevity the discussion is restricted to the subcortical pathway (1.) and the cortical pathways (2. & 3.).

Spatial information processing in the subcortical pathway

Retinal input to the subcortical pathway terminates densely in the upper layers of the superior colliculus in a pattern which maintains the topography of the retinal map (Schiller, Malpeli & Schein, 1979). Upper cells in the colliculus respond both to static targets and to the motion of visual targets relative to a static surround, and their receptive fields are retinotopic: each cell responds to stimulation in a fixed portion of the retina and there is a point to point mapping from the retina to the colliculus. When stimulated electrically, many cells elicit saccades which bring the eyes to fixate on the center location of the cell's receptive field, suggesting that these neurons code the retinotopic goal of an eye movement (Robinson, 1973; Schlag-Rey, Schlag & Shook, 1989). Many cells in the intermediate and deep layers of the colliculus, which project directly to the brainstem oculomotor nuclei, also fire when subjects make saccades of a certain direction and amplitude (Schiller & Stryker,

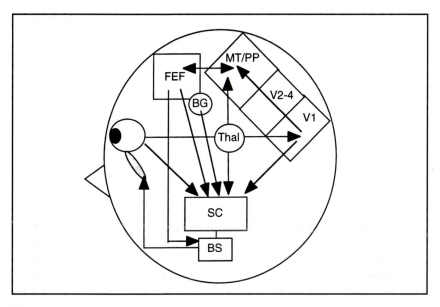

FIG. 2.2:   Schematic of primate oculomotor pathways adapted from Schiller (1985). Thal:
thalamus; V1-4: *Primary and extrastriate visual processing areas*; MT: *middle temporal area*; PP:
posterior parietal cortex; FEF: *frontal eye fields*; BG: *basal ganglia*; SC: *superior colliculus*; BS:
brain stem oculomotor nuclei.

1972; Sparks, Holland & Guthrie, 1975), and the saccade responses are topograph-
ically organized (Robinson, 1972; Sparks et al., 1975), so that cells near one another
respond to movements of a similar direction and amplitude. Electrostimulation of
the deep layers of the structure results in saccades of fixed amplitude and direction
independent of eye position (Robinson, 1972), leading to the proposal that this
nucleus transforms retinocentric position into eye movement commands directly.
More recent evidence suggests that this pathway incorporates information about the
location of a target stimulus in craniocentric or egocentric coordinates (Mays &
Sparks, 1980b), but the eye or head position signals originate from sources external
to the SC (Schlag, Schlag-Rey & Dassonville, 1991).

Despite retinal immaturities which contribute to poor newborn acuity (Abramov
et al., 1982; Banks & Shannon, 1993; Mann, 1964), the retinocollicular pathway
appears to support functional oculomotor connections prior to actual visual
experience (Stein, Clamann & Goldberg, 1980). The frame of reference for saccade
signals in young animals has not been investigated systematically. However,
evidence from the development of orienting to both visual and auditory targets
suggests that a period of postnatal tuning of visual — retinocentric — and auditory —
craniocentric — information occurs in owl hatchlings. The calibration is mediated
by changes in the receptive field properties of the optic tectum, a homologue
of the mammalian superior colliculus (Knudsen & Brainard, 1991; Knudsen

& Knudsen, 1990). So, if eye or head position was either unavailable, due to immaturity in the regions where these signals originate, or inaccurate, due to the need to calibrate retinal positions and eye movement commands, then retinocentric, but not cranio- or egocentric information would govern spatial processing in the subcortical pathway of neonatal animals.

Spatial information processing in the cortical pathway

In contrast to the limited spatial processing in the subcortical pathway, neurons in the cortical pathways combine visual and somatosensory information in increasingly complex ways.

Visual cortex

Most cells in primary visual cortex have retinotopic receptive fields (Felleman & Van Essen, 1991) and many modulate their firing patterns depending on eye convergence (Trotter, Celibrini, Stricanne, Thorpe & Imbert, 1992; Weyrand & Malpeli, 1989). Stimulating cells in the cat visual cortex results in saccades that vary depending on the position of the stimulus in the cortex, but are otherwise fixed in size and consistent with eye movements that would fixate a stimulus at a given retinal position (McIlwain, 1988). These response patterns suggest that eye position signals project to this part of the cortex (Ashton, Boddy & Donaldson, 1984; Buissaret & Maffei, 1977), but that the primary representation of visual space in this region is retinocentric (Pouget, Fisher & Sejnowski, 1993).

How do these adult response patterns relate to those in early infancy? Johnson (1990) proposed that while some cortical visual processing can be carried out at birth, immaturities in primary visual cortex create a bottleneck which limits the quality and availability of cortically processed visual information to subcortical and cortical targets downstream from primary visual cortex. Specifically, the tendency of deeper layers of the cortex to mature earlier than upper layers (Conel, 1939–1967; Purpura, 1975; Rabinowicz, 1979) suggests that pathways which originate in deeper layers and project to subcortical structures will mature before pathways which originate in upper layers and project to other visual areas in the cortex concerned with higher levels of processing (Johnson, 1990). Beyond the limitations of primary visual cortex on downstream processing, the developmental course of some oculomotor behaviors almost certainly reflects changes in the underlying substrate within this region. For example, Held (1985) has argued that the initial lack of segregation of inputs from the two eyes in the primary visual cortex is a crucial limiting factor which prevents aspects of binocular function—e.g. accurate eye convergence and stereopsis—from emerging earlier than the fourth postnatal month. Related factors might be immaturities in the middle layers of visual cortex where cells sensitive to binocular disparity are found (Johnson, 1990), failures to derive accurate eye convergence information, or inadequate integration of retinal and eye position information.

In short, the neural evidence concerning the spatial processing of primary visual cortex suggests that this region sustains largely retinotopic representation of visual space, but plays a central role in computing relative distance from the viewer in craniocentric or egocentric coordinates using vergence and stereopsis. Since, maturational limits within visual cortex at birth appear to constrain both spatial processing within the region and the extent to which downstream subcortical or extrastriate regions receive functional input (Johnson, 1990) from it, this region is unlikely to provide a source of head-, trunk- or other body-centered spatial information in early infancy.

Areas MT, MST and parietal cortex

Cells in the middle temporal (MT) and medial superior temporal (MST) areas receive broad-band input both from the dorsal "where" stream (Ungerleider & Mishkin, 1982) of visual processing originating in primary visual cortex, and from the upper layers of the superior colliculus via the thalamus. These regions respond selectively to visual motion, disparity, and optic flow (see Stein, 1992, for review), appear to influence directly perceptual judgments about the direction of visual motion (Newsome, Britten & Movshon, 1989), and play a role in smooth pursuit by means of projections to the colliculus (Schiller, 1985).

The middle and medial superior temporal areas also project to the parietal cortex which receives information from and projects to visual, somaesthetic, proprioceptive, auditory, vestibular, oculomotor, limb control, and limbic centers (see Stein, 1992 and Andersen et al., 1993, for reviews). Damage to parietal cortex causes a variety of spatial orienting and cognitive deficits in humans which appear to reflect the influence of multiple, body-centered and even object-based frames of reference (Behrmann & Tipper, 1994; Farah et al., 1990; Moscovitch & Behrmann, 1994). The majority of cells in two critical eye movement areas, 7a and LIP, are visually sensitive with large retinocentric receptive fields. Some 30% of cells have response properties that vary systematically with changes in the position of the eyes in the orbit (Andersen, Essick & Siegel, 1985), and others when both eye and head position is varied (Brotchie, Andersen, Snyder & Goodman, 1995). This supports the argument that parietal neurons embody a distributed representation of space in multiple coordinate frames (Andersen et al., 1993). Further evidence comes from neural network models of visual spatial processing which have shown that by systematically combining retinal and eye position signals, units whose receptive fields approximate those of parietal neurons emerge (Goodman & Andersen, 1989; Pouget et al., 1993; Zipser & Andersen, 1988). Moreover, the networks generated simulated saccadic output in head-centered coordinates following the activation of these parietal-like units (Goodman & Andersen, 1989).

Although the direct anatomical and physiological data are limited, the posterior temporal and parietal regions of the brain appear to mature later and more slowly than primary visual cortex. The association of the middle temporal area with smooth pursuit led Johnson (1990) to argue that the onset of smooth tracking at approximately 2 months may mark the delayed functional maturational of this region. Similarly, in parietal cortex, only minimal changes in metabolic activity measured by positron emission tomography (PET) were observed by 2 months of age compared with marked changes at 3 to 6 months (Chugani, Phelps & Mazziotta, 1987). Part of the limitation on early parietal activity may be due to incoherent or insufficiently strong inputs from primary visual cortex to extrastriate visual regions (Johnson, 1990). In general, the neural evidence supports the argument that the perception of spatial representations in retinal-, head-, trunk-, or other body-centered coordinate schemes involve computations by circuitry in several higher order visual regions of the posterior parietal and temporal cortex. Nevertheless, the gradual postnatal development of these regions probably limits the availability of craniocentric, egocentric, or other higher order spatial information until several months after birth.

Frontal eye fields (FEF)

Neurons in the frontal eye fields fire in association with the execution of purposeful saccades to visual, auditory or remembered targets; and to saccades with specific directions and amplitudes (Bizzi & Schiller, 1970; Bruce & Goldberg, 1985; Bruce, Goldberg, Stanton & Bushnell, 1985; Mohler, Goldberg & Wurtz, 1973). Saccade-related neurons in this region project to the deep SC (Seagraves & Goldberg, 1987) in a topographic pattern. Electrostimulation of FEF cells can evoke saccades of a particular direction and amplitude (Dassonville, Schlag & Schlag-Rey, 1992b; Goldberg & Bruce, 1990), which are largely independent of initial eye position. However, studies of saccades elicited by stimulation during another visually guided saccade have led to the hypothesis that the frontal eye fields code the retinal error of a stimulus with respect to an eye position that preceded the actual stimulation (Dassonville, Schlag & Schlag-Rey, 1992a). Consequently, neurons in this region do appear to have sensitivity to both retinal and eye position signals in some form. However, there is no evidence that cells in the frontal eye fields respond to changes in eye and head position in the systematic way that posterior parietal cells do, despite extensive patterns of interconnection between these areas.

There is limited anatomical or physiological evidence about the development of frontal cortex, but several behavioral indicators suggest a delayed developmental time course. Johnson (1990) argued that the increasing control over both the initiation and inhibition of eye movements beginning at 3 to 4 months of age marks the emergence of frontal influence over gaze. For example, 4-month-olds show more anticipatory saccades to stimuli that have been associated with spatial locations in a training task (Johnson, Posner & Rothbart, 1991), and can learn to reduce the number of eye movements they make toward a stimulus appearing on one side of a display and redirect their eye movement toward the appearance of another stimulus which appears slightly later on the opposite side (Johnson, 1995).

By 6 months, infants show memories over several seconds for cued target locations when performing a memory guided saccade task associated with activity in the prefrontal cortex (Gilmore & Johnson, 1995). Other authors have shown that infants between the ages of 3 and 6 months can learn to direct their gaze to specific locations based on predictive visual patterns (Haith, Hazan & Goodman, 1988). However, the available neural evidence is consistent with this region having a slower, and longer developmental time course than the behavioral evidence might suggest (Huttenlocher, 1990): Glucose metabolism in frontal cortex begins to increase by 6 months of age and continues to do so over the next several months, but significant increases in activity are not observed until 8 months of age (Chugani et al., 1987). In summary, the delayed developmental time course of these regions most likely limits their functional contributions over gaze shifts until several months after birth.

Summary of neural circuitry

The available neural evidence supports the hypothesis that newborns have rudimentary representations of visual space dominated by retinocentric sources of information derived from the subcortical pathway. The maturation of the primary visual cortex and other cortical pathways during the following postnatal months permits the parietal and other parts of the cortex to begin influencing gaze shifts. These regions instantiate retinal, head-, trunk-, and other body-centered representations in adult animals. The increasing influence of parietal circuitry over infants' visual behavior leads to a gradual shift in dominance from retinocentric to cranio- or egocentric information. In the next section, we will summarize several recent experiments which provide behavioral support for such a shift.

FRAMES OF REFERENCE FOR INFANTS' SACCADES

If the subcortical retinocentric information dominates orienting responses of younger infants until cortical systems mature, then retinocentric information should influence younger infants' eye movements more strongly than older ones. We tested this hypothesis with three separate experiments.

A retino- to egocentric shift

The double step saccade paradigm (Becker & Jürgens, 1979; Hallett & Lightstone, 1976a; Hallett & Lightstone, 1976b) was specifically designed to determine whether retinal position alone or some combination of retinal and eye or head position signals was used in controlling saccades. In adult versions of the task, observers were instructed or trained to make saccades to sequences of two visual cues flashed extremely briefly in a dark visual field; the second stimulus appeared and disappeared shortly before or during the first saccade. Retinal information alone did not permit observers to plan a saccade to the second target accurately since the saccade to the first target shifted the center of gaze and with it the second target's position relative to the retina. Accordingly, to make accurate saccades to the location of both stimuli viewers would have had to plan the direction and magnitude of their saccades-based targets positions defined relative to the head or body which remain stationary or relative to the predicted position of the eyes at the end of the first saccade (Dassonville, Schlag & Schlag-Rey, 1993). In fact, adults made accurate saccades directly toward the second target without delay or significant error in most circumstances (Becker & Jürgens, 1979; Hallett & Lightstone, 1976a; Hallett & Lightstone, 1976b). This suggested that adults typically code saccade targets in cranio- or egocentric coordinates.

We adapted the double saccade paradigm (Gilmore & Johnson, 1997) in order to distinguish the influence of retinal, and eye or head position signals on eye movements—and by extension, the development of head- and trunk-centered representations of visual targets—in infants 4 to 6 months of age. In one experiment, infants viewed a display that attracted their attention to a central computer monitor and was followed by a sequence of two brief (200 ms) visual cues flashed 30 degrees to the left or right of the center of fixation one after the other in a randomly selected left–right or right–left pattern (see Fig. 2.3A, first column). In a second experiment we flashed the targets for 250 and 150 ms respectively and tested separate groups of 4 to 5-month-old and 6-month-old babies. In both experiments, the targets elicited sequences of eye movements that were recorded on videotape and subsequently coded for direction and latency. Sequences were classified as *retinocentric* if the subsequent second saccade ended at the midpoint of the center screen, or *egocentric* (since the head was fixed, not free) if the sequence ended at the midpoint of the screen where the second target had appeared (see Fig. 2.3A, third column). Single-target control trials (Fig. 2.3B) were presented as a control for the possibility that 4- and 6-month-olds could differ in their capacity to make long eye movements independent of the specific form of spatial representation.

The results from both experiments are summarized in Fig. 2.4. It shows that 4-month-olds made significantly fewer egocentric responses than did their 6-month-old counterparts. There was a marginally significant difference in the proportion of long looks observed in the control trials in the first study, but this was not replicated in the second study. The smaller proportion of egocentric saccades to the target location in the 4-month-old group suggested that younger infants less reliably integrated retinal and somatosensory sources of spatial information and therefore relied upon a retinocentric coding of visual target position in planning saccade sequences. The fact that the mean proportion of successful long saccades in the control trials did not differ significantly argues against an alternative explanation in terms of differences in the ability to make long saccades.

Decline in vector summation

Recall that stimulation of many cells in the superior colliculus elicits saccades equivalent to the retinal error between the current fixation point and the center of

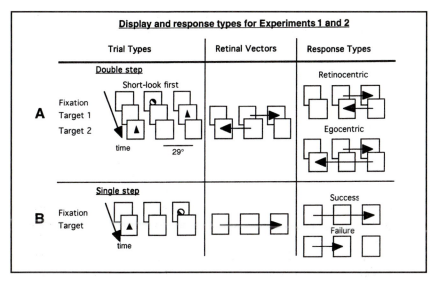

FIG. 2.3:   Description of infant double step saccade experiments. Stimulus sequences are in the first column, retinal position vectors in the second column, and response types in the third column. (Gilmore & Johnson, 1997). Fig. 1, p.225. Copyright © 1997 Cambridge University Press. Reprinted with the permission of Cambridge University Press.

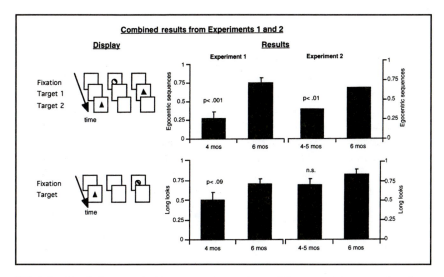

FIG. 2.4:   Results from two double step saccade experiments. The mean relative proportion of egocentric relative to retinocentric saccades is plotted for the experimental trials in the first experiment while the proportion of total egocentric to retinocentric sequences is plotted for the second experiment. The mean relative proportion of successful long looks to failures is plotted for the control trials. (Gilmore & Johnson, 1997). Fig. 2, p.227. Copyright © 1997 Cambridge University Press. Reprinted with the permission of Cambridge University Press.

the cell's receptive field (Mays & Sparks, 1980b; Robinson, 1972; Schlag-Rey et al., 1989). The stimulation of two or more such cells results in a saccade which is the sum of each stimulated cell's retinal error or movement vector (Robinson, 1972), suggesting that normal saccade commands involve vector summation (Mays & Sparks, 1980a; Van Gisbergen, Van Opstal & Tax, 1987) or weighted averaging (Ottes, Van Gisbergen & Eggermont, 1984) of responses associated with the active population of cells.

We reasoned that since the summation of retinal position vectors is a hallmark of the superior colliculus, the prevalence of vector summation in infants' saccades may serve as a marker for the extent of influence of the subcortical retinocollicular pathway. Accordingly, we recorded the saccades of 12 infants in each of three age groups (2, 4, and 6 months) who viewed pairs of brief (200 ms) visual targets presented simultaneously in a two-dimensional array (see Fig. 2.5). We predicted that the extent of spontaneous saccade errors to the retinal vector sum location would decline in older groups of infants. As Fig. 2.6 shows, the proportion of vector sum responses did decline between 2 and 6 months as predicted. A follow up analysis ruled out the possibility that younger infants were simply less accurate in their eye movements. The decline in retinal vector summation with increasing age provides further evidence for maturation and increasing influence of cortical centers which influence saccades via craniocentric (Zipser & Andersen, 1988), or egocentric (Brotchie et al., 1995) coordinates (Andersen et al., 1993).

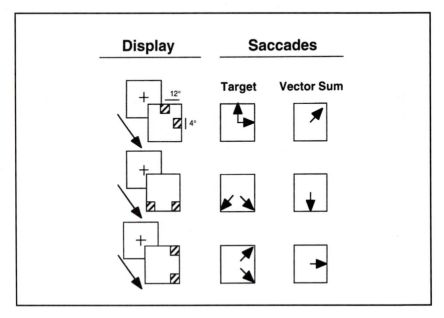

FIG. 2.5:   Description of vector sum experiment. Stimulus sequences, retinal vectors and response types are indicated in columns 1–2 respectively.

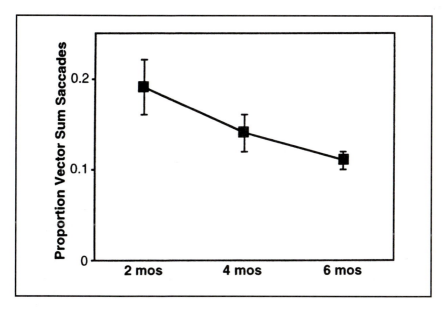

FIG. 2.6:   Results from vector sum experiment showing decline in the mean proportion of saccades to vector sum locations as the age of infants tested increases.

OCULOMOTOR CONSTRAINTS ON THE DEVELOPMENT OF SPATIAL COGNITION

We have argued that a neurodevelopmental account of human infants' oculomotor capacities provides a framework for exploring how infants' perceptual and cognitive systems come to integrate multiple sources of spatial information into a coherent framework for guiding visually controlled action. In asking what spatial information drives adult oculomotor behavior, we suggested that retinal-, eye- and head-position sources contribute to the representation of visual space in eye-, head-, and body-based frames of reference. However, infants' visual exploratory abilities suggest that simpler, less highly tuned spatial processing systems dominate the earliest visual behavior, and that rapid postnatal development in these skills occurs between birth and 6 months of age (von Hofsten & Rosander, this volume). Evidence concerning spatial information processing in the adult brain and the patterns of development in these systems during early infancy led to the hypothesis that retinocentric information characteristic of the early maturing subcortical pathway dominates spatial processing in neonates and young infants. Subsequent maturation of cortical systems, especially in the parietal cortex leads to the gradual emergence and increasing influence of head- and body-centered representations of visual space. Results from three experiments with infants from 2 to 6 months of age provided behavioral evidence for this proposed shift in visual representations.

This account has highlighted the development of spatial information for saccades, but the eye movement system has many components which interact extensively in the context of mature spatial perception (Owen & Lee, 1986) and whose development is not yet well understood. However, other evidence supports the development of increasingly elaborate and flexible representations of space in infancy. For example, infants between 2 and 6 months show increasing sensitivity to self versus object patterns of motion (Kellman & von Hofsten, 1995), accuracy in orienting toward the location of sounds (Muir & Field, 1979), and precision in reaching with visual feedback (von Hofsten, 1984) or without it (Clifton, Muir, Ashmead & Clarkson, 1993). From 6 to 12 months, spatial processing continues to develop, with infants showing increasing sensitivity to landmarks or environment-centered spatial information in searching for hidden objects or predicting interesting events (Acredolo, 1990; Bremner, 1982). Detailed computational analyses of these multimodal spatial behaviors, their neural underpinnings, the relationships between different perception and action systems, and the processes of their development remain challenging problems for future research.

From a broader perspective, we believe that the development of perception and action systems offers the neonate a challenge and an opportunity. The challenge stems from the behavioral demand to develop precise patterns of movement in space derived from initially imprecise sensory information and immature effector systems. The challenge is complicated by the relative immaturity of neural systems which sustain spatial representation and processing. The opportunity stems from the fact that a simple mapping from sensory to motor coordinates provides the infant with a limited ability to interact with the visual environment, to orient toward or away from sources of stimulation, and ultimately, to detect regularities between the position and motion of objects in the world and movements of the body. In this way the spatial representations based on simple sensorimotor systems may provide the infant with opportunities to gather information from experience that is necessary to construct more elaborate body-centered mappings of space, encoded perhaps in the newly maturing, powerfully flexible cerebral cortex. These representations in turn provide new opportunities for action and learning. With this in mind, we believe that the neurodevelopmental analysis of visuospatial behavior illustrates the promise of an interdisciplinary effort that incorporates computational, biological, and behavioral constraints in order to illustrate both the nature of infants' changing spatial representations and the processes that transform them.

ACKNOWLEDGEMENTS

Rick Gilmore acknowledges graduate fellowship support from NIMH grant MH19102-04, the NSF Neural Processes in Cognition Program, and a Grant-in-aid of Research from the National Academy of Sciences, through Sigma Xi, The Scientific Research Society. Mark Johnson acknowledges financial support from the National Science Foundation, the UK

Medical Research Council, and the Human Frontiers Scientific Foundation. We thank Karen Adolph, Marlene Behrmann, and Jay McClelland for productive discussions and suggestions.

REFERENCES

Abramov, I., Gordon, J., Hendrickson, A., Hainline, L., Dobson, V., & Laboussier, E. (1982). The retina of the newborn human infant. *Science, 217*, 265–267.

Acredolo, L. (1990). Behavioral approaches to spatial orientation in infancy. *Annals of the New York Academy of Sciences, 608*, 596–612.

Andersen, R.A., Essick, G.K., & Siegel, R.M. (1985). Encoding of spatial location by posterior parietal neurons. *Science, 230*, 456–458.

Andersen, R.A., Snyder, L.H., Li, C.S., & Stricanne, B. (1993). Coordinate transformations in the representation of spatial information. *Current Opinion in Neurobiology, 3*, 171–176.

Ashton, J.A., Boddy, A., & Donaldson, I.M.L. (1984). Directional selectivity in the responses of units in the cat primary visual cortex to passive eye movement. *Neuroscience, 13*(3), 653–662.

Aslin, R.N. (1981). Development of smooth pursuit in human infants. In D.F. Fisher, R.A. Monty, & J.W. Senders (Eds.), *Eye movements: Cognition and visual perception* (pp. 31–51). Hillsdale, NJ: Lawrence Erlbaum Associates Inc.

Aslin, R.N. (1987). Motor aspects of visual development in infancy. In P. Salapatek & L. Cohen (Eds.), *Handbook of infant perception: From sensation to perception* (pp. 43–113). New York: Academic Press.

Aslin, R.N. (1993). Perception of visual direction in human infants. In C.E. Granrud (Ed.), *Visual perception and cognition in infancy*. Hillsdale, NJ: Lawrence Erlbaum Associates Inc.

Aslin, R.N., & Salapatek, P. (1975). Saccadic localization of visual targets by very young infants. *Perception and Psychophysics, 17*, 293–302.

Atkinson, J. (1979). Development of optokinetic nystagmus in the human infant and monkey infant: An analogue to development in kittens. In R.D. Freeman (Ed.), *Developmental neurobiology of vision* (pp. 277–287). New York: Plenum Press.

Atkinson, J. (1984). Human visual development over the first six months of life: A review and a hypothesis. *Human Neurobiology, 3*, 61–74.

Banks, M.S., & Dannemiller, J.L. (1987). Infant visual psychophysics. In P. Salapatek & L.B. Cohen (Eds.), *Handbook of infant perception: From sensation to perception* (pp. 115–184). New York: Academic Press.

Banks, M.S., & Shannon, E. (1993). Spatial and chromatic visual efficiency in human neonates. In C.E. Granrud (Ed.), *Visual perception and cognition in infancy*, (pp. 1–46). Hillsdale, NJ: Lawrence Erlbaum Associates Inc.

Becker, W., & Jürgens, R. (1979). An analysis of the saccadic system by means of double step stimuli. *Vision Research, 19*, 967–983.

Behrmann, M., & Tipper, S.P. (1994). Object–based attentional mechanisms: Evidence from patients with unilateral neglect. In C. Umiltà & M. Moscovitch (Eds.), *Attention and Performance XV: Conscious and Nonconscious Information Processing* (pp. 351–375). Cambridge, MA: MIT Press.

Birch, E.E., Gwiazda, J., & Held, R. (1982). Stereoacuity development for crossed and uncrossed disparities in human infants. *Vision Research, 22*, 507–513.

Bizzi, E., & Schiller, P.H. (1970). Single unit activity in the frontal eye fields of unanaesthetized monkeys during head and eye movement. *Experimental Brain Research, 10*, 151–158.

Bremner, J.G. (1978). Egocentric versus allocentric spatial coding in nine-month-old infants: Factors influencing the choice of code. *Developmental Psychology 14*, 346–355.

Bremner, J.G. (1982). Object localization in infancy. In M. Potegal (Ed.), *Spatial abilities: Development and physiological foundations*. New York: Academic Press.

Bronson, G.W. (1974). The postnatal growth of visual capacity. *Child Development, 45*, 873–890.

Brotchie, P.R., Andersen, R.A., Snyder, L.H., & Goodman, S.J. (1995). Head position signals used by parietal neurons to encode locations of visual stimuli. *Nature, 375*, 232–235.

Bruce, C.J., & Goldberg, M.E. (1985). Primate frontal eye fields: I. Single neurons discharging before saccades. *Journal of Neurophysiology, 53*, 603–635.

Bruce, C.J., Goldberg, M.E., Stanton, G.B., & Bushnell, M.C. (1985). Primate frontal eye fields: II. Physiological and anatomical correlates of electrically evoked eye movements. *Journal of Neurophysiology, 54*, 714–734.

Buissaret, P., & Maffei, L. (1977). Extraocular proprioceptive projections to primary visual cortex. *Experimental Brain Research, 28*, 421–425.

Chugani, H.T., Phelps, M.E., & Mazziotta, J.C. (1987). Positron emission tomography study of human brain functional development. *Annals of Neurology, 22*, 487–497.

Clifton, R.K., Muir, D.W., Ashmead, D.H., & Clarkson, M.G. (1993). Is visually guided reaching in early infancy a myth? *Child Development, 61*(1), 1098–1110.

Conel, J.L. (1939–1967). *The Postnatal Development of the Human Cerebral Cortex* (Vols. I–VIII). Cambridge, Mass.: Harvard University Press.

Daniel, B.M., & Lee, D.N. (1990). Development of looking with head and eyes. *Journal of Experimental Child Psychology, 50*(2), 200–216.

Dassonville, P., Schlag, J., & Schlag-Rey, M. (1992a). The frontal eye field provides the goal of saccadic eye movement. *Experimental Brain Research, 89*, 300–310.

Dassonville, P., Schlag, J., & Schlag-Rey, M. (1992b). Oculomotor localization relies on damped representation of saccadic eye displacement in human and nonhuman primates. *Visual Neuroscience, 9*, 261–269.

Dassonville, P., Schlag, J., & Schlag-Rey, M. (1993). Direction constancy in the oculomotor system. *Current Directions in Psychological Science, 2*(5), 143–147.

Farah, M.J., Brunn, J.L., Wong, A.B., Wallace, M.A., & Carpenter, P.A. (1990). Frames of reference for allocating attention to space: Evidence from the neglect syndrome. *Neuropsychologia, 28*(4), 335–347.

Feldman, J.A. (1985). Four frames suffice: A provisional model of vision and space. *Behaviour and Brain Sciences, 8*, 265–289.

Felleman, D.J., & Van Essen, D.C. (1991). Distributed hierarchical processing in the primate cerebral cortex. *Cerebral Cortex, 1*, 1–47.

Gilmore, R.O., & Johnson, M.H. (1997). Egocentric action in early infancy: Spatial frames of reference saccades. *Psychological Science, 8*(3); 224–230.

Gilmore, R.O., & Johnson, M.H. (1995). Working memory in infancy: Six-month–olds' performance on two versions of the oculomotor delayed response task. *Journal of Experimental Child Psychology, 59*, 397–418.

Goldberg, M.E., & Bruce, C.J. (1990). Primate frontal eye fields: III. Maintenance of a spatially accurate signal. *Journal of Neurophysiology, 64*, 489–508.

Goodman, S.J., & Andersen, R.A. (1989). Microstimulation of a neural network model for visually guided saccades. *Journal of Cognitive Neuroscience, 1* 317–326.

Graziano, M.S.A., Yap, G.S., & Gross, C.G. (1994). Coding of visual space by premotor neurons. *Science, 266*, 1054–1057.

Guenther, F.H., Bullock, D., Greve, D., & Grossberg, S. (1994). Neural representations for sensorimotor control: III. Learning a body-centered representation of a three-dimensional target position. *Journal of Cognitive Neuroscience, 6*(4), 341–358.

Gwiazda, J., Bauer, J., & Held, R. (1989). From visual acuity to hyperacuity: A 10-year update. *Canadian Journal of Psychology, 43*, 109–120.

Hainline, L. (1985). Oculomotor control in human infants. In R. Groner, G. W. McConkie, & C. Menz (Eds.), *Eye movements and human information processing*. Amsterdam: Elsevier.

Haith, M.M., Hazan, C., & Goodman, G.S. (1988). Expectation and anticipation of dynamic visual events by 3.5-month-old babies. *Child Development, 59*, 467–479.

Hallett, P.E., & Lightstone, A.D. (1976a). Saccadic eye movements to flashed targets. *Vision Research, 16*, 107–114.

Hallett, P.E., & Lightstone, A.D. (1976b). Saccadic eye movements towards stimuli triggered by prior saccades. *Vision Research, 16*, 99–106.

Harris, P., & MacFarlane, A. (1974). The growth of the effective visual field from birth to seven weeks. *Journal of Experimental Child Psychology, 18*, 340–348.

Held, R. (1985). Binocular vision: Behavioral and neuronal development. In J. Mehler & R. Fox (Eds.), *Neonate cognition: Beyond the blooming, buzzing confusion*. Hillsdale, NJ: Lawrence Erlbaum Associates Inc.

Huttenlocher, P.R. (1990). Morphometric study of human cerebral cortex development. *Neuropsychologia, 28*, 517–527.

Johnson, M.H. (1990). Cortical maturation and the development of visual attention in early infancy. *Journal of Cognitive Neuroscience, 2*(2), 81–95.

Johnson, M.H. (1995). The inhibition of automatic saccades in early infancy. *Developmental Psychobiology, 28*, 281–291.

Johnson, M.H., Posner, M.I., & Rothbart, M. (1991). The development of visual attention in infancy: Contingency learning, anticipations and disengaging. *Journal of Cognitive Neuroscience, 3*, 335–344.

Kellman, P.J., & von Hofsten, C. (1995). The world of the moving infant: Perception of motion, stability, and space. In C. Rovee-Collier & L.P. Lipsitt (Eds.), *Advances in Infancy Research* (Vol. 7, pp. 147–185). Norwood, NJ: Ablex.

Knudsen, E.I., & Brainard, M.S. (1991). Visual instruction of the neural map of auditory space in the developing tectum. *Science, 253*, 85–87.

Knudsen, E.I., & Knudsen, P.F. (1990). Sensitive and critical periods for visual calibration of sound localization by barn owls. *Journal of Neuroscience, 10*(1), 222–232.

Lewis, T.L., Maurer, D., & Kay, D. (1978). Newborns' central vision: Whole or hole? *Journal of Experimental Child Psychology, 26*, 193–203.

Mann, I. (1964). *The development of the human eye*. London: British Medical Association.

Marr, D. (1982). *Vision*. San Francisco: W. Freeman.

Matin, L., & Pearce, D.G. (1965). Visual perception of direction for stimuli flashed during voluntary saccadic eye movements. *Science, 148*, 1485–1488.

Matin, L., Stevens, J.K., & Picoult, E. (1991). Perceptual consequences of experimental extraocular muscle paralysis. In J. Paillard (Ed.), *Brain and space*. Oxford: Oxford University Press.

Mays, L.E. & Sparks, D.L. (1980a). Saccades are spatially, not retinocentrically coded. *Science, 208*, 1163–1165.

Mays, L.E., & Sparks, D.L. (1980b). Dissociation of visual and saccade related responses in superior colliculus neurons. *Journal of Neurophysiology, 43*, 207–232.

McGinnis, J.M. (1930). Eye movements and optic nystagmus in early infancy. *Genetic Psychology Monographs, 8*, 321–430.

McIlwain, J.T. (1988). Saccadic eye movements evoked by electrical stimulation of the cat visual cortex. *Visual Neuroscience, 1*, 135–143.

Mohler, C.W., Goldberg, M.E., & Wurtz, R.H. (1973). Visual receptive fields of frontal eye field neurons. *Brain Research, 61*, 385–389.

Moscovitch, M., & Behrmann, M. (1994). Coding of spatial information in the somatosensory system: Evidence from patients with neglect following parietal lobe damage. *Journal of Cognitive Neuroscience, 6*(2), 151–155.

Muir, D.W., & Field, J. (1979). Newborn infants' orient to sounds. *Child Development, 50,* 431–436.

Naegele, J.R., & Held, R. (1980). Optokinetic nystagmus shows asymmetry in human infants. *Investigative Opthalmology and Visual Science, 19* (Suppl.), 210.

Naegele, J.R., & Held, R. (1982). The postnatal development of monocular optokinetic nystagmus in infants. *Vision Research, 22,* 341–346.

Nanez, J. (1987). Perception of impending collision in 3- to 6-week-old infants. *Infant Behavior and Development, 11,* 447–463.

Newsome, W.T., Britten, K.H., & Movshon, J.A. (1989). Neuronal correlates of a perceptual decision. *Nature, 341,* 52–54.

Olson, C.R., & Hanson, S.J. (1990). Spatial representation of the body. In S. J. Hanson & C. R. Olson (Eds.), *Connectionist modeling and brain function: The developing interface* (pp. 193–254). Cambridge, MA: MIT Press.

Ottes, F.P., Van Gisbergen, J.A., & Eggermont, J.J. (1984). Metrics of saccade responses to visual double stimuli: Two different modes. *Vision Research, 24*(10), 1169–1179.

Owen, B.M., & Lee, D.N. (1986). Establishing a frame of reference for action. In M.G. Wade & H.T.A. Whiting (Eds.), *Motor development: Aspects of coordination and control.* Dordrecht: Martinus Nijhoff.

Piaget, J. (1954). *The construction of reality in the child* (M. Cook, Trans.). New York: Basic Books.

Piaget, J., & Inhelder, B. (1948). *The child's conception of space* (F.J. Langdon, & J.L. Lunzer, Trans.). London: Routledge & Kegan Paul.

Pouget, A., Fisher, S.A., & Sejnowski, T.J. (1993). Egocentric spatial representation in early vision. *Journal of Cognitive Neuroscience, 5*(2), 150–161.

Purpura, D.P. (1975). Normal and aberrant neuronal development in the cerebral cortex of human fetus and young infant. In N.A. Buchwald & M.A.B. Brazier (Eds.), *Brain mechanisms of mental retardation.* New York: Academic Press.

Rabinowicz, T. (1979). The differential maturation of the human cerebral cortex. In F. Falkner & J.M. Tanner (Eds.), *Human Growth: Vol. 3. Neurobiology and nutrition.* New York: Plenum Press.

Regal, D.M., Ashmead, D.H., & Salapatek, P. (1983). The coordination of eye and head movements during early infancy: A selective review. *Behavioral and Brain Research, 10,* 125–132.

Reisman, J.E., & Anderson, J.H. (1989). Compensatory eye movements during head and body rotation in infants. *Brain Research, 484*(1–2), 119–129.

Robinson, D.A. (1972). Eye movements evoked by collicular stimulation in the alert monkey. *Vision Research, 12,* 1795–1808.

Robinson, D.A. (1973). Models of the saccadic eye movement control system. *Kybernetik, 14,* 71–83.

Salapatek, P., Aslin, R.N., Simonson, J., & Pulos, E. (1980). Infant saccadic eye movements to visible and previously visible targets. *Child Development, 51,* 1090–1094.

Schiller, P.H. (1985). A model for the generation of visually guided saccadic eye movements. In D. Rose & V. G. Dobson (Eds.), *Models of the visual cortex* (pp. 62–70). Chichester: Wiley.

Schiller, P.H., Malpeli, J.G., & Schein, S.J. (1979). Composition of geniculo-striate input to superior colliculus of the rhesus monkey. *Journal of Neurophysiology, 42,* 1124–1133.

Schiller, P.H., & Stryker, M. (1972). Single-unit recording and stimulation in superior colliculus of the alert rhesus monkey. *Journal of Neurophysiology, 35,* 915–924.

Schlag, J., Schlag-Rey, M., & Dassonville, P. (1991). Spatial programming of eye movements. In J. Paillard (Ed.), *Brain and space* (pp. 69–78). Oxford: Oxford University Press.

Schlag-Rey, M., Schlag, J., & Shook, B. (1989). Interactions between natural and electrically evoked saccades. I. Differences between sites carrying retinal error and motor command signals in monkey superior colliculus. *Experimental Brain Research, 76*, 537–547.

Seagraves, M.A., & Goldberg, M.E. (1987). Functional properties of corticotectal neurons in the monkey's frontal eye field. *Journal of Neurophysiology, 58*, 1387–1419.

Sparks, D.L., Holland, R., & Guthrie, B.L. (1975). Size and distribution of movement fields in the monkey superior colliculus. *Brain Research, 113*, 21–34.

Stein, B.E., Clamann, H.P., & Goldberg, S.J. (1980). Superior colliculus: Control of eye movements in neonatal kittens. *Science, 210*, 78–80.

Stein, J.F. (1992). The representation of egocentric space in the posterior parietal cortex. *Behavioral and Brain Sciences, 15*, 691–700.

Trotter, Y., Celibrini, S., Stricanne, B., Thorpe, S., & Imbert, M. (1992). Modulation of neural stereoscopic processing in primate area V1 by the viewing distance. *Science, 257*, 1279–1281.

Ungerleider, L.G., & Mishkin, M. (1982). Two cortical visual systems: Separation of appearance and location of objects. In D.L. Ingle, M.A. Goodale, & R.J.W. Mansfield (Eds.), *Analysis of visual behavior* (pp. 549–586). Cambridge, MA: MIT Press.

Van Gisbergen, J.A., Van Opstal, A.J., & Tax, A.A. (1987). Collicular ensemble coding of saccades based on vector summation. *Neuroscience, 21*(2), 541–555.

von Hofsten, C. (1984). Developmental changes in the organisation of prereaching movements. *Developmental Psychology, 20*, 378–388.

von Hofsten, C., & Rosander K. (1998). The establishment of gaze control in early infancy. In F. Simion & G. Butterworth (Eds.), The development of sensory, motor, and cognitive capacities in early infancy: From perception to cognition. Hove: Psychology Press.

Wattam-Bell, J. (1990). The development of maximum velocity limits for direction discrimination in infancy. *Perception, 19*, 369.

Wattam-Bell, J. (1991). Development of motion-specific cortical responses in infants. *Vision Research, 31*, 287–297.

Weyrand, T.G., & Malpeli, J.G. (1989). Responses of neurons in primary visual cortex are influenced by eye position. *Abstracts of the Society for Neuroscience, 15*, 1016.

Young, L.R., & Stark, L. (1963). Variable feedback experiments testing a sampled data model for tracking eye movements. *IEEE Transactions, Human Factors, 4*, 38–51.

Zipser, D., & Andersen, R.A. (1988). A back-propagation programmed network that simulates response properties of a subset of posterior parietal neurons. *Nature, 331*, 679–684.

CHAPTER THREE

The Establishment of Gaze Control in Early Infancy

Claes von Hofsten and Kerstin Rosander
Umeå University, Sweden

Achieving gaze control is an important development during the first half-year of life. It is of crucial importance for the extraction of visual information about the world, for directing attention, and for the establishment of social communication. Controlling gaze may involve both head and eye movements and is guided by at least three types of information: visual, vestibular, and proprioceptive. The present chapter deals with how young infants gain access to these different kinds of information, how they come to use them prospectively to control gaze, and how they come to coordinate head and eyes to accomplish gaze control.

The real challenge for the gaze-controlling system is not so much switching fixation from one target to another but rather to stabilize gaze on the target once it arrives there. Stabilizing gaze is of such crucial importance for vision that it has even been suggested that the most important reason for evolving movable eyes was for the purpose of stabilizing gaze rather than scanning the surroundings (Walls,1962). There are, at least, three reasons for this. First, if detailed information is needed about an external object, it is of crucial importance to keep it within the foveal region of the visual field. Secondly, during the inspection of an object, it is of crucial importance to minimize slippage of its retinal projection: even the slightest retinal motion will cause gross deteriorations in acuity. Finally, while linear visual flow is informative of the spatial layout of the environment (motion parallax), rotational flow is not, and will, in fact, mask the information conveyed by the linear flow (Warren & Hannon, 1990). Therefore, especially rotational flow needs to be minimized.

Stabilizing gaze on a target is a dynamic problem. Even when the target is stationary, the observer moves continuously relative to it, and these movements

49

must to be compensated for. If, in addition, the target itself moves, gaze must move with it. Because of the information processing lags of the nervous system and the mechanical lags of the effectors, these adjustments must be predictive to avoid the gaze to lag the target. Secondly, if the tracking involves both head and eyes, these two movement components must be timed and scaled to each other. This is possible only if the neural system that controls the eye movements "knows" what the head is going to do ahead of time. Thirdly, if gaze is to stay on the target, eye movements also have to compensate for head movements unrelated to the tracking of the target. Such head movements may arise as a result of more gross body movements like locomotion, from external perturbations of the head, or from the internal modulations of voluntary head movements. The eye movements must predict the modulations in head movements to be able to compensate for them. It is important to note that head movements are something that the subject has to compensate for as well as being actively involved in the tracking of the target.

METHODS FOR STUDYING GAZE CONTROL IN INFANTS

Two methods have been used for studying infant eye movements, cornea reflexion and electrooculogram (EOG). The former system uses infrared reference lights (outside the visible part of the spectrum) which reflect on the surface of the eye and by comparing the positions of these reflections relative to the pupil, the direction of the eye can be calculated. In order to do this, the eye is filmed. If the reference lights are fixed relative to the head, eye direction is obtained, and if they are fixed relative to the surrounding, gaze direction is obtained. The advantage of this method is that it doesn't drift. Absolute eye and gaze direction can then be obtained. The disadvantage is that its time resolution is equal to the frame rate of the film or video used, which is generally rather low.

EOG utilizes the fact that there is a voltage difference between the front and the back of the eye. If an electrode is placed at the outer canthi, it will register the potential level of that part of the eye lobe which is closest to it. When the eye moves, the potential level will change in a way which is approximately linearly related to the change in their horizontal position, within a range of $\pm 30°$.

There are essentially two main problems when measuring eye movements through EOG. First, the absolute potential level is subject to slow drifts which makes it possible to measure only relative eye direction. Eye velocity, however, may be very precisely evaluated. Secondly, as the signal is usually amplified at some distance from the electrodes, there are impedance problems. In other words, the potential level is disturbed by movements of the wires relative to the body and wire movements may be interpreted as eye movements. Von Hofsten and Rosander (1996) have solved this problem successfully by feeding the signal through very short wires into a preamplifier attached to the head of the infant. This arrangement gave a very stable and reliable signal with high resolution.

Knowledge of where the head is turning is of crucial importance for establishing the relationship between eye movements and gaze movements. In infant studies using the cornea reflexion technique, the reference lights are most often fixed to the surrounding (see Haith, Hazan, & Goodman, 1988; Salapatek, Aslin, Simonson, & Pulos, 1980), which implies that gaze movements are recorded. If the head moves, eye movements can only be obtained by subtracting the head movements from the gaze record. If the reference lights are attached to the head and the head moves, gaze movements can only be obtained if eye and head movements are added together. This is also valid for the EOG method, which records eye movements. To get gaze movements, head movements must be accounted for.

The problem of head movements can be solved either by trying to prevent them or by recording them. Restraining the head is problematic in at least two respects. First, infants have strong inclinations to use their head in pursuing a target and they will not always accept head restraints. Secondly, because of this strong inclination to use the head in visual pursuit, it is almost impossible to hold the head of an infant completely still. Small head movements correspond to large changes in the direction of gaze. A 1cm movement at the forehead equals approximately 10° of gaze change. Thus any procedure of restraining movements of the head runs a serious risk of underestimating the gain of the pursuit. Finally, if head movements are an important part of stabilizing gaze in young infants, restraining them might distort the coordination.

Von Hofsten and Rosander (1996), recorded head movements by an opto-electronic device (SELSPOT) using infrared light emitting diodes as markers. Both the spatial and the temporal resolution of this device is very high. It was also used to record the movements of the target.

TRACKING EYE MOVEMENTS

Several studies on eye movements indicate that newborn infants have some ability to track a moving target smoothly. Dayton and Jones (1964) found that neonates pursued a wide angle visual display with smooth eye movements. They became rather jerky for a "small" target. These results were supported by several other studies. Bloch and Carchon (1992) used a red transplant ball covering 4° of visual angle and found no smooth tracking in neonates. Kremenitzer, Vaughan, Kurtzberg, and Dowling (1979) used either a vertically striped pattern covering 180° of visual angle in the horizontal dimension or a single 12° black circle and found that neonates would smoothly track both of these stimuli, however with low gain and only approximately 15% of the time. Finally, Roucoux, Culee and Roucoux (1983) using a big black circle covering 10° of visual angle found evidence of smooth pursuit in one-month-old infants, but only at low velocities and with low gain. Dayton and Jones (1964) found that those jerky eye movements underwent rapid development towards smooth following during the first months of life. The same findings were obtained by Aslin (1981) who used a black bar 2° wide and 8° high moving sinusoidally in a horizontal path. He found only saccadic following of the target up to 6 weeks of age after which smooth pursuit started to be observed.

Von Hofsten and Rosander (1996; 1997) recorded eye and head movements in unrestrained 1- to 5-month-old infants as they tracked a happy face moving sinusoidally[1] back and forth in front of them. In von Hofsten and Rosander (1996) the target measured 7° and was surrounded by a striped pattern, 0.14 cycles/ degree, which extended over the whole visual field (a drum) and moved with the target. The target speeds were also somewhat different in the two studies. In von Hofsten and Rosander (1996) the target moved over a 36° arc at 0.1, 0.2, or 0.3 Hz while in von Hofsten and Rosander (1997) the target moved over either a 25° or 50° arc at either 0.2 and 0.4 Hz. Finally, somewhat different age groups were used in the two studies. In von Hofsten and Rosander (1996) 1-, 2-, and 3-month-old infants participated while von Hofsten and Rosander (1997) followed one group of infants from 2 to 5 months of age.

The moving stripe background in von Hofsten and Rosander (1996) was introduced to facilitate tracking. It had, however, the opposite effect. While gaze gain (i.e. the relative amplitudes of the added eye and head movements relative to target movements) was around 0.7 with the striped background it was close to 1.0 without it. These figures were only marginally dependent on age and target speed.

Saccades were defined as periods of eye velocity record with higher amplitude than 50°/sec. To extract the smooth pursuit component of the eye movement record, the saccades defined in this way were eliminated from the composite, raw eye movement record. The periods cut out were replaced with interpolated data. Proportion of smooth pursuit was calculated at the ratios of gain with and without saccades. It was found that proportion of smooth pursuit depended heavily on age and target speed. This can be seen in Fig. 3.1. The proportion of smooth pursuit increased substantially from 2 to 5 months of age. The effect of target velocity depended on age. At 2 months of age the proportion of smooth pursuit in the slowest condition (0.2 Hz and low amplitude) was almost twice as high as it was in the fastest condition (0.4 Hz and high amplitude). At 5 months of age, proportion of smooth pursuit was high in all conditions, approaching adult values.

The number of saccades did not decrease significantly with age in any of the two studies. There was, however, a significant increase in the number of saccades with increasing velocity of the target motion. This can be seen in Fig. 3.2. In contrast, Kremenitzer et al. (1979) found that in neonates pursuing a 12° target, the number of saccades (around 1.15/sec) was independent of target velocity in the interval 9 to 30°/sec.

The issue of how saccadic tracking is dependent on the size of the target may be illustrated by a case study from our laboratory of a 9-week-old boy tracking a

---

1   Von Hofsten and Rosander (1997) also used triangular motions but that data will not be considered here.

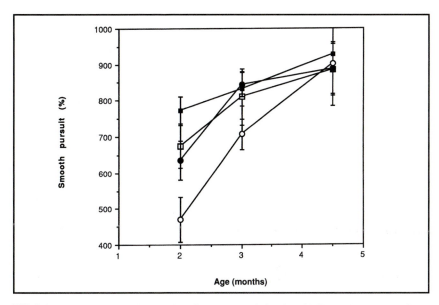

FIG. 3.1:   Mean and SEM of proportion of smooth pursuit for sinusoidally moving targets at the different amplitudes and frequencies and the different age levels studied in von Hofsten and Rosander (1997). (*circles* = 0.2 Hz; *squares* = 0.4 Hz; *open* = 10° amplitude; *filled* = 20° amplitude)

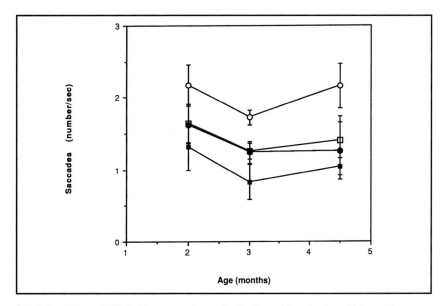

Fig. 3.2:   Mean and SEM of frequency of saccades for the tracking of a sinusoidally moving target at the different amplitudes and frequencies and the different age levels studied in von Hofsten and Rosander (1997). (*circles* = 0.2 Hz; *squares* = 0.4 Hz; *open* = 10° amplitude; *filled* = 20° amplitude)

target varying in size from a visual angle of 3.5 to 35°. The stimulus consisted of concentric black circles painted on a yellow background moving back and forth at a frequency of 0.25 Hz and with an amplitude of 34°. In Fig. 3.3, eye velocity gain is shown with or without saccades. First of all, Fig. 3.3 shows that tracking gain decreased dramatically below a minimum target size. Secondly, it suggests that the contribution of saccades is not linearly related to target size at this age. In this particular case, the largest contribution of saccadic tracking occurred at 7° and 14° of visual angle.

The temporal–nasal bias

During the first 2 to 3 months of life, smooth tracking is constrained in yet another way. At that age period, there is a bias for tracking targets moving from the temporal toward the nasal side of the monocular visual field as compared to targets moving in the opposite direction (Naegele & Held, 1982). This behavior might have deep biological roots. Animals with laterally placed eyes, like the rabbit, show the same temporal–nasal bias. There seems to be a functional reason for this. As the animal moves forward, there is a constant visual flow from the nasal toward the temporal part of the visual field which carries little information about important events in the world. However, movements towards the nasal part of the visual field are more important in this respect. In the young infant, the temporal–nasal bias has the

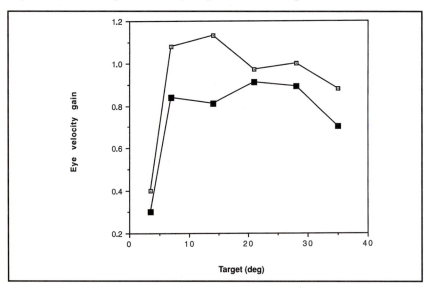

FIG. 3.3:   Eye velocity gain estimated with Fourier analysis as a function of target size of a 9-week-old boy. The target moved sinusoidally with an amplitude of 34° and a frequency of 0.25 Hz against a white background. *Filled squares* correspond to gain calculated from the raw eye movement data and *unfilled squares* correspond to gain calculated from the eye movement data after saccades had been removed. Note that the difference between the records is largest for targets of intermediate size.

consequence that both eyes tend to move toward the nose during visual tracking. If the target is oscillating back and forth in a horizontal path, the tracking eyes tend to end up in a rather strabismic configuration. The infant will then often close its eyes and as they reopen, they are once more aligned. The disappearance of the temporal-nasal tracking bias seems to be associated with the emergence of binocular vision (Atkinson & Braddick, 1981).

The emergence of predictive tracking

At what age does smooth pursuit start to become predictive? Aslin (1981) found that the smooth pursuit obtained for 10-week-old infants lagged the target but not always for 12-week-olds. At that age, the eyes often stayed on target or were even slightly ahead of it. In a somewhat different setting, Haith and associates (Haith et al., 1988; Canfield & Haith, 1991) showed that 3-month-old infants were able to predict where the next picture in a left–right sequence was going to be shown, by moving the eyes there before the picture appeared.

Von Hofsten and Rosander (1996;1997) calculated cross-correlations between eye velocity and target minus head velocity (hereafter called head slip). The results are shown in Fig. 3.4. It can be seen from Fig. 3.4 that the smooth eye tracking accomplished by the 1-month-old infants was associated with a substantial lag of almost 200msec. This lag was diminished to one third by 2 months of age and at 5 months of age the lag had turned into a lead.

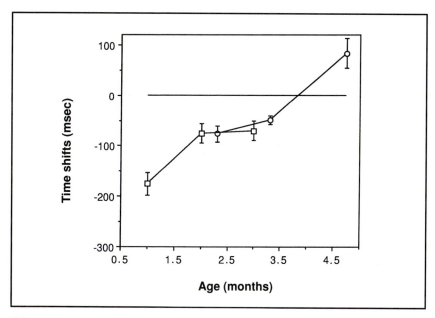

FIG. 3.4:   Lags of smooth pursuit tracking from the studies by von Hofsten and Rosander (1996;1997).

What kind of information might drive smooth tracking in young infants? Perceived target velocity could account for the tracking of the 1-month-olds, but not for the tracking of the older infants studied. The small lags of the 2- and 3-month-olds show that they also are able to extrapolate the change in velocity of the sinusoidal motions. The time lags are comparable to those obtained from adult experiments on visual tracking of pseudo-random motions where only local extrapolation processes are conceivable (Bahill & McDonald, 1983). The fact that smooth pursuit is not lagging at all at 5 months suggests further improvements in the prediction process at that age.

This is supported by von Hofsten and Rosander (1997). Apart from sinusoidal target motions, they also studied the tracking of targets with constant velocity which abruptly reversed at the turning points (triangular motions). The turns of such motions cannot be extrapolated from the direction, velocity, and acceleration of the target at any point in time. It has to be based either on the periodicity of the motion or on knowledge of where the target will turn. The 2- and 3-month-olds did not show such knowledge. Their eye movements lagged the triangular motions with around a quarter of a second. However, at 5 months the lag had decreased substantially.

Reaction time in the context of visual tracking is reflected by the latency time for onset of tracking. Infants up to at least 3 months of age show a significant variation in latency times. Several factors like attention and state variations may, however, considerably influence this measure. Data shown in Fig. 3.5 are evaluated from the study by von Hofsten and Rosander (1996). It was found that the latency time for the onset of tracking depended on age. In 1-month-old infants the mean was 0.9 sec (sd 0.7) and in 3-month-old infants 0.6 sec (sd 0.2). The corresponding value in adults is 0.15 sec (Carl & Gelman 1987). The latency was, however, not dependent on target velocity as it is in adults.

In the literature, two visual mechanisms for smooth tracking are described. One is assumed to be designed for tracking small moving objects, the smooth pursuit mechanism. It is supposed to be cognitively sophisticated so that it predicts the future motion of the target so that it properly adjusts the output of the oculomotor system. The other mechanism, called the opto-kinetic response (OKR), is assumed to be specialized in stabilizing gaze on the environment during self motion. It is considered a rather primitive reflex-like adjustment of eye direction. The reviewed developmental studies provide some support for the idea of two mechanisms because they show that smooth tracking of small stimuli, which is primarily associated with object motion. On the other hand, it is questionable whether the size effect is a sufficient argument for the existence of two separate mechanisms for visual tracking. Parsimony would actually argue for one single system (Kowler, 1990). Studies where the age of the infant and the size of the target are systematically varied are necessary to resolve this question. Such studies are in progress.

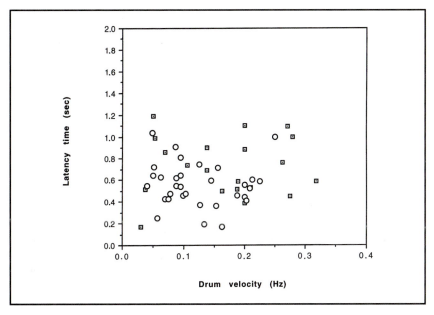

FIG. 3.5:   Latency time as a function of target velocity in 1- (*square*) and 3- (*circle*) month-old infants. The mean in 1 month is 0.86 and in 3 months 0.20 sec. (from von Hofsten and Rosander, 1996)

THE ROLE OF HEAD MOVEMENTS IN TRACKING

Little is known about the role of head movements in infant visual tracking. The reason is that, in most studies, infants have been restrained from moving their head. However, from the studies permitting free head movements, it is evident that from birth the head actively helps to direct gaze.

Neonates have rather poor control of their head but even then head movements contribute to visual tracking. Bloch and Carchon (1992) found that neonates tended to track as far into the periphery as possible before turning the head. With increasing control of the head, it is used more and more actively. Bloch and Carchon (1992) found that 30-day-old infants used the head significantly more than newborns in the tracking of a target. In a study of 5- to 52-weeks-old infants Roucoux et al. (1983) used targets of 2 to 10° of visual angle (velocity up to 40°/sec) and demonstrated well adapted tracking at 4 weeks based on head movements together with "small" saccades. Von Hofsten and Rosander (1996) showed that even in the 1-month-olds head movements contributed significantly to stabilizing gaze on the target. A tracking record from a 1-month-old infant where the head contributed significantly, is shown in Fig. 3.6.

Figure 3.6 shows that the gaze is better adjusted to the target motion than either single head or eye movements. Von Hofsten and Rosander (1996;1997) found that

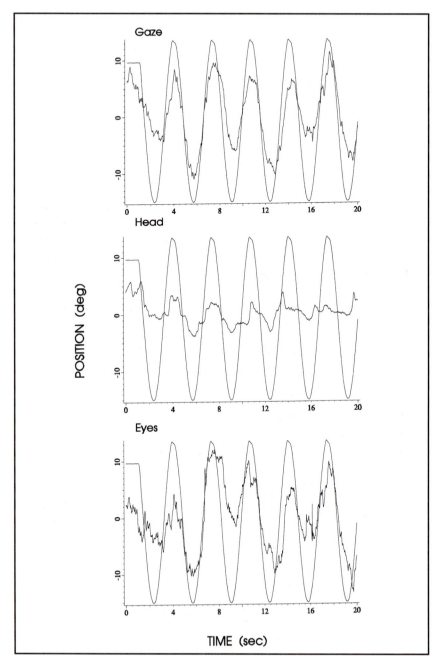

FIG. 3.6:   Records of eye, head, and gaze movements of a 1-month-old boy tracking a target covering the whole visual field. Note how head movements improve the tracking.

the contribution of head and eye movements improves considerably during the first few months of life. We found that some 5-month-old infants used almost entirely head movements in their tracking which can be seen in Fig. 3.7. The same developmental trend was observed by Daniel and Lee (1990).

Coordination of head movements and saccades in shifting gaze has earlier been studied in adults (e.g. Zangemeister & Stark, 1981) and in infants (e.g. Regal, Ashmead & Salapatek, 1983). When capturing a peripheral stimulus, infants present several strategies some of which are rarely seen in adults (Regal et al.,1983). In a review by Regal et al., (1983) various head-and-eye movements are demonstrated for infants' changing point of fixation: single and multiple eye and head movements are demonstrated as well as an example where a head movement precedes eye movement. Some examples of head and eye movements during tracking are shown in Fig. 3.8. It is seen that the relationship between head and eyes is very flexible. The movement of the head may lead as well as lag the saccadic eye movement. However, head movements are always compensated by appropriate compensatory eye movements and the resulting switching of gaze is quite steplike.

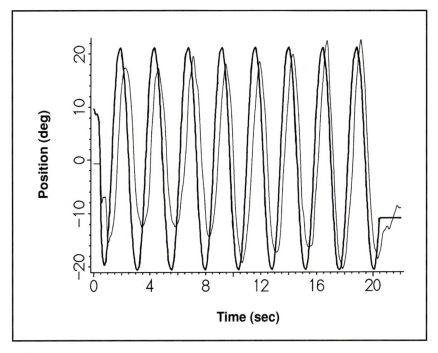

FIG. 3.7: An example of large head-tracking gain for a 5-month-old infant. The thicker line corresponds to the target motion and the thinner line to the head-tracking record. The head was lagging the target with 310msec.

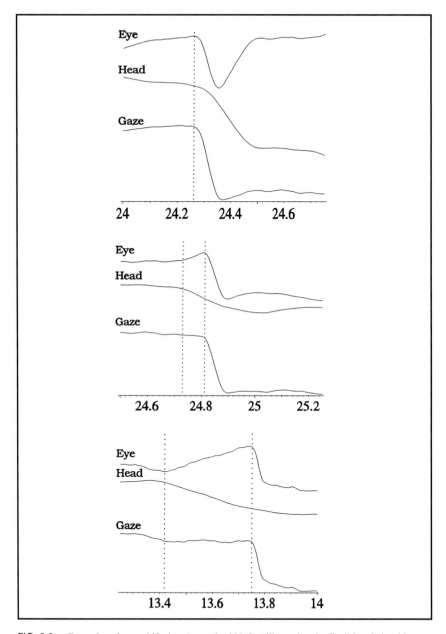

FIG. 3.8:   Examples of gaze shifts in a 1-month-old infant illustrating the flexible relationship between onset of head movement and the saccadic gaze shift. In the *upper* graph the head and the compensatory eye movement connected with it starts at the same time as the saccade. In the *middle* graph the saccade occurs in the middle of the head movement and in the *lower* graph the saccade occurs at the end of the head movement. The numbers indicate seconds.

COMPENSATING FOR HEAD MOVEMENTS UNRELATED TO THE LOOKING TASK

The head is not just a part of an active gaze system; it also moves for other reasons. In fact, any gross movement of the body will, in one way or another, cause the head to move. Most of these head movements are unrelated to the looking task and the eye movements must compensate for them. The problem is to know to what degree the performed head movements are part of the tracking of the target and to what degree they are unrelated to the tracking and should be compensated for.

Low-frequency movements

All visual tracking is confined to movements changing their velocity less than twice a second; i.e. 1 Hz. In fact, we start to have difficulties with tracking targets above 0.6 Hz. This upper limit of tracking, however, has very little effect on our ability to stabilize gaze on moving targets. Targets with inertia generally change their velocity at a much slower rate. Flying insects are one of the few examples of motions with a faster rate of change. This is why it is so difficult to stabilize gaze on them.

Gaze control within this region of the workspace (i.e. below 1 Hz) is determined in a flexible way by visual, proprioceptive and vestibular information. Visual information, however, is by far the most important one. The problem with proprioceptive and vestibular control is that both these senses are blind to where the target is, and therefore cannot contribute to tracking itself. In fact, by themselves, they cannot even solve the problem of stabilizing gaze on a stationary target during body movements. Vestibular or proprioceptive information must be supplemented with information about the distance to the target in order to scale the gaze adjustments appropriately. Large distances require small adjustments and small distances large adjustments.

From an early age both vestibular and proprioceptive information contribute to gaze stabilization during slowly changing passive head movements. It even seems that their influence is greater at a very young age and that vision gradually becomes more dominating during the first few months of life. While adults show incomplete compensations to whole body rotations in the dark, neonates have been reported to fully compensate for them (Schupert & Fuchs, 1988). In addition to the full-compensatory vestibulo-ocular response (VOR), Reisman and Anderson (1989) showed that infants have a significantly higher cervico-ocular reflex (COR) than adults. The gain of the COR was found to decrease between 2 and 4 months of age.

High-frequency movements

The head is not only subject to slowly changing movements which might interfere with visual fixation, but also to rapidly changing ones, like shaking or rattling. Such movements may originate from external perturbations of the head or the body but they may also be self-produced. In fact, the production of head movements themselves are subject to higher frequency modulations. For instance, in spite of the fact that the head is perturbed every time the foot hits the ground during walking, looking is unaffected.

The vestibular system is well designed to deal with these higher frequency changes of head position. It records acceleration and computes velocity. If head acceleration and velocity are known, compensatory eye movements can be monitored prospectively. Furthermore, the vestibular system is very closely connected to the oculo-motor system by two synapses separating them which gives minimum delays in the transmission of information.

In the interval between 1 and 6 Hz, adults' vestibularly controlled eye movements almost perfectly compensate for head movements. Benson (1970), Tomlinson, Saunders, and Schwartz, (1980), Hydén, Istl, and Schwartz (1982), and Jell, Stockwell, Turnipseed, and Guedry (1988) reported that the eyes compensate almost perfectly with no phase lag for head oscillations in the interval 1 to 6 Hz.

The VOR loop compensation for higher frequency head movements seems to be present at birth but has yet to be made functional and adjusted to its task. Von Hofsten and Rosander (1995) found that modulations of head velocity at frequencies between 1 and 6 Hz were consistently accompanied by reciprocal modulations of eye velocity in very young infants without any systematic lag. This can be seen in Fig. 3.9. Even at one month of age, the phase lag between eye velocity and head slip (target velocity minus head velocity) was found to be close to 0msec. However, eye and head movements were less well scaled to each other at that age but the fit improved considerably until 3 months of age.

Compensatory eye movements without a lag require prediction. Also the amplitude of the tracked motion must be predicted in order to have full compensation. During continuous head movements, vestibular information could, in principle, be used prospectively in both these respects for stabilizing gaze on the target. The timing problem is, however, relatively simpler than the scaling problem because the factors determining the various kinds of delays are relatively constant. When determining the amplitude of the compensatory eye movements the distance to the fixation target must also be taken into account.

The result of von Hofsten and Rosander (1996) also showed that the compensatory eye movements overlaid the tracking eye movements. In other words, young infants seem to be able to simultaneously perform tracking eye movements guided mainly by visual information, and to compensate for high-frequency head movements unrelated to the tracking. These two abilities seem to develop in parallel.

DISCUSSION

Developing an ability to stabilize gaze during looking involves the solution of a number of different problems. Different tasks have different requirements and an important part of development has to do with exploring and learning optimal ways of exploiting the system. First, the motor systems of the head and the eyes must become coordinated in order to utilize the advantages of each of these movable parts in an optimal and flexible way. The movements of the eyes and the head can be properly coordinated only if they are timed and scaled to each other which in turn presupposes a central administration of the efforts of each body part. Secondly, in order to stay on target, the gaze must anticipate how the target moves and how the subject moves relative to it. The problems to be solved are different for low-frequency movements which involve the tracking itself, and high-frequency movements which interfere with gaze stabilization.

From the behavior of the very young infant it is evident that the solution of some of the crucial problems of gaze stabilization have been facilitated during prenatal development. Neonates have an ability to smoothly turn their eyes to adjust to object and subject movements. Head movements may also be employed in this effort. They also seem to be able to utilize visual as well as vestibular and proprioceptive information to direct gaze. Thus, all the different parts of the gaze-directing system seem ready to be involved. On the other hand, there are serious restrictions on what the neonate can do. The amplitude of the smooth pursuit is insufficient for stabilizing gaze on a target and it is therefore intermixed with catch-up saccades

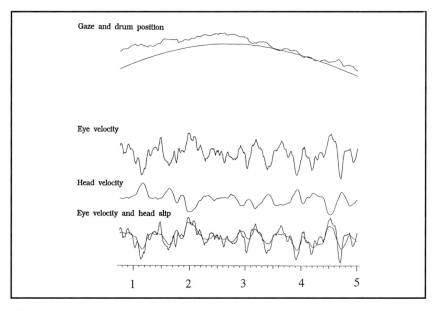

FIG. 3.9:   Example of a 3-month-old infant inspecting a 0.1 Hz oscillation of a wide angle (drum) stimulus. Records are shown of drum and gaze position superimposed, eye and head velocity, and eye velocity with head slip (difference drum and head velocity) superimposed. Peak cross-correlation was 0.84 at a lead of the eyes of 8msec. The numbers indicate seconds.

which are especially apparent for small targets. The head participates in tracking but its movements are noisy and the contribution small.

Actions are learnt through actions, and looking skills are learnt through the continuing attempts to direct gaze at interesting objects and events in the surroundings. It is clear that the acquisition of predictive skills in tracking is heavily dependent on experience with predictable visual events. This is probably also valid for developing an ability to compensate for high-frequency movements of the head. However, the neural patterns involved must also be sufficiently organized to provide minimum conditions for learning. For instance, the establishment of the middle temporal (MT) pathways are probably of crucial importance for the development of smooth pursuit and the synaptogenesis of the prefrontal cortex might be of importance for the development of predictive tracking.

The cerebellum is rarely discussed in the context of early skill development but recent research on the formation of predictive models has generally assumed the cerebellum to play a major role (Keeler, 1990; Miall, Weir, Wolpert & Stein, 1993; Kawato & Gomi, 1992). It may, in fact, play a crucial role in early sensory-motor development. At birth, the human cerebellar cortex has a well-established architecture with, for example, all Purkinje cells present. Prenatally, climbing fibers are connected to the surface of the cells (Rakic & Sidman, 1970).

The development of an ability to compensate for high-frequency head movements needs both reliable input about the acceleration and velocity of the head and a good model for calculating the compensatory eye movements which must be reciprocal and synchronous with the head movements and adequately scaled to them. The timing problem is relatively simpler than the scaling problem because the factors determining the various kinds of delays (receptor delays, processing delays, and mechanical delays) are relatively more constant than the factors determining the gains. These include the dynamic properties of muscles, tendons, and joints, and depend on fatigue, whether the performed movements are fast or slow, whether the normal load of the plant is altered etc. Therefore, timing is expected to be mastered before scaling which is in accordance with the results of von Hofsten and Rosander (1996). The high-frequency modulations of eye and head movements were actually poorly scaled to each other in the 1-month-old infants, the size of the eye movements being, on average, 4 times greater than the head movements. The results showed, however, that the scaling had improved considerably at 3 months of age.

Predicting voluntary head movements may be facilitated by also feeding the efferent signal to move the head to the oculomotor system. Such facilitation is known to be present in lower vertebrates. Stehouwer (1987) reported that isolated nervous systems of tadpoles generated organized activity in the oculomotor efferents (3rd and 6th cranial nerves) which were coordinated with activity in the spinal ventral roots during fictive swimming. The oculomotor signals were produced by purely central processes and were of a compensatory type. Such a central command system might also be present in higher mammals.

ACKNOWLEDGEMENTS

The authors gratefully acknowledge Dr Göran Westling, Department of Physiology, Umeå University, for the construction of the EOG amplifier. Mr Bäckström, Department of Physiology,Umeå University is thanked for help with his computer program, Fystat. This research was supported by the Tercentennial Fund of the Bank of Sweden.

REFERENCES

Aslin, R. (1981). Development of smooth pursuit in human infants. In D.F. Fischer, R.A. Monty, & W.J. Senders, (Eds.), *Eye movements: Cognition and visual perception* (pp.31–51).Hillsdale, NJ: Lawrence Erlbaum Associates Inc.

Atkinson, J., & Braddick, O. (1981). Development of optokinetic nystagmus in infants: An indicator of cortical binocularity? In D.F. Fischer, R.A. Monty, and J.W. Senders (Eds.) *Eye movements: Cognition and visual perception*. Hillsdale, NJ: Lawrence Erlbaum Associates Inc. pp. 53–64.

Bahill, T., & McDonald, J. (1983). Smooth pursuit eye movements in response to predictable target motions. *Vision Research, 23,* 1573–1583.

Benson, A.J. (1970). Interactions between semicircular canals and gravireceptors. In D. Dusbey & D. Reidel (Eds.) *Recent advances in aerospace medicine* (pp. 249–261). Holland: Dordrecht.

Bloch, H., & Carchon, I. (1992). On the onset of eye-head co-ordination in infants. *Behavioural Brain Research, 49,* 85–90.

Canfield, R.L., & Haith, M.M. (1991). Young infants' visual expectations for symmetric and asymmetric stimulus sequences. *Developmental Psychology, 27,* 198–208.

Carl, J.R., & Gelman, R.S. (1987). Human smooth pursuit: Stimulus-dependent responses. *Journal of Neurophysiology, 57,* 1446–1463.

Daniel, B.M., & Lee, D. (1990). Development of looking with head and eyes. *Journal of Experimental Child Psychology, 50,* 200–216.

Dayton, G.O., & Jones, M.H. (1964). Analysis of characteristics of fixation reflex in infants by use of direct current electrooculography. *Neurology, 14,* 1152–1156.

Haith, M., Hazan, C., & Goodman, G.S. (1988). Expectation and anticipation of dynamic visual events by 3.5-month-old babies. *Child Development, 59,* 467–479.

Hydén, D., Istl, Y.E., & Schwartz, D.W.F. (1982). Human visuo-vestibular interaction as a basis for quantitative clinical diagnosis. *Acta Otolaryngol., 94,* 53–60.

Jell, R.M., Stockwell, C.W., Turnipseed, G.T., & Guedry, F.E. (1988). The influence of active versus passive head oscillation, and mental set on the human vestibulo-ocular reflex. *Aviation, Space, and Environmental Medicine, 59,* 1061–1065.

Kawato, M., & Gomi, H. (1992) The cerebellum and VOR/OKR learning models. *Trends in Neuroscience, 15,* 445–453.

Keeler, J.D. (1990). A dynamical system view of cerebellar function. *Physica D, 42,* 396–410.

Kowler, E. (1990). The role of visual and cognitive processes in the control of eye movement. In E. Kowler, (Ed.), *Eye movements and their role in visual and cognitive processes: Reviews of oculomotor research, Vol.4* (pp.1-70). Amsterdam: Elsevier.

Kremenitzer, J.P., Vaughan, H.G., Kurtzberg, D., & Dowling, K. (1979). Smooth-pursuit eye movements in the newborn infant. *Child Development, 50,* 442–448.

Miall, R.C., Weir, D.J., Wolpert, D.M., & Stein, J.F. (1993). Is the cerebellum a Smith predictor? *Journal of Motor Behavior, 25,* 203–216.

Naegele, J.R., & Held, R. (1982). The postnatal development of monocular optokinetic nystagmus in infants. *Vision Research, 22,* 341–346.

Rakic, P. & Sidman, R.L. (1970). Histogenesis of cortical layers in human cerebellum, particularly the lamina dissecans. *Journal of Comparative Neurology, 139,* 473–500.

Regal, D.M., Ashmead, D.H., & Salapatek, P. (1983). The coordination of eye and head movements during early infancy: A selective review. *Behavioural Brain Research, 10,* 125–132.

Reisman, J.E., & Anderson, J.H. (1989). Compensatory eye movements during head and body rotation in infants. *Brain Research, 484,* 119–129.

Roucoux, A., Culee, C., & Roucoux, M. (1983). Development of fixation and pursuit eye movements in human infants. *Behavioural Brain Research, 10,* 133–139.

Salapatek, P., Aslin, R.N., Simonson, J., & Pulos, E. (1980). Infant saccadic eye movements to visible and previously visible targets. *Child Development, 51,* 1090–1094.

Schupert, C., & Fuchs, A.F. (1988). Development of conjugate human eye movements. *Vision Research, 28,* 585–596.

Stehouwer, D.J. (1987). Compensatory eye movements produced during fictive swimming of a deafferented, reduced preparation in vitro. *Brain Research, 410,* 264–268.

Tomlinson, R.D., Saunders, G.E., & Schwarz, D.W.F. (1980). Analysis of human vestibulo-ocular reflex during active head movements. *Acta Otolaryngol.* 90, 184–190.

Walls, G.L. (1962). The evolutionary history of eye movements. *Vision Research, 2,* 69-80.

Warren, W.H., & Hannon, D.J. (1990) Eye movements and optical flow. *Journal of the Optical Society of America, A7,* 160–169.

Wentworth, N., & Haith, M.M. (1992). Event-specific expectations of 2- and 3-month-old infants. *Developmental Psychology,28,* 842–850.

von Hofsten, C., & Rosander, K. (1996). The development of gaze control and predictive tracking in young infants. *Vision Research, 36,* 81–96.

von Hofsten, C., & Rosander, K. (1997). Development of smooth pursuit tracking in young infants, *Vision Research, 37,* 1799–1810.

Zangemeister, W.H., & Stark, L. (1981). Active head rotations and eye-head coordination. *Annals of the New York Academy of Sciences, 374,* 540–559.

PART II

Face Perception: Psychological and Neurological Models

CHAPTER FOUR

The Origins of Face Perception

Ian W.R. Bushnell
University of Glasgow, Scotland, UK

INTRODUCTION

Not all that long ago it was thought that the infant was born and then started to experience the world and very gradually attain competence. Initially the human infant was believed to have little visual functioning and to be capable only of restricted differentiation of blurred forms within a very restricted visual range. Such visual discrimination as did exist was thought by many to be based on quantitative differences in contrast at '"preferred" spatial frequencies since research on contrast sensitivity functions appeared to demonstrate that the human infant has limited if any capability to differentiate visual stimuli on qualitative terms. The underlying theme is that the infant does not really exist, function or develop in perceptual/cognitive terms until she can herself be seen after being born, and even then, the baby is considered essentially incompetent, relatively passive and with restricted capacity to process information or learn.

Much of the work on person recognition, including face perception research, has contributed to discrediting such a view of the human infant although the view still prevails that perceptual–cognitive development starts at or around birth. This chapter will discuss some of the research relevant to face perception and recognition in the first few days-of-life and for a broader perspective including attractiveness, gender, facial expression and imitation, reviews such as that of Slater and Butterworth (1997) should be examined.

Early learning capability

Should we expect very young infants to be able to process faces and use this information appropriately? Structural development of the visual system is far from complete at birth, but acuity and contrast sensitivity measures indicate that sufficient detail is potentially available from birth to individuate faces (Slater, 1993).

If we look at capability in other sensory modes, research indicates considerable early competence in terms of discriminating amongst complex stimuli including other people. For example, Hepper (1991) provides very interesting data on auditory prenatal learning in a study where auditory exposure to a tune experienced repeatedly when in the womb was linked to a preference for the same tune when the infant was tested in the first days of life. Early recognition of the mother from voice information is also well established now from a range of studies. The initial research evidence from DeCasper and Fifer (1980) that neonates prefer the sound of their mother's voice to that of a stranger has been further substantiated by Hepper, Scott and Shahidullah (1993) who used a movement measure with 2- to 4-day-olds to show that they prefer their mother's to a stranger's voice (and incidentally mother's normal speech to "motherese"). They even have evidence that the 36 week gestation foetus discriminates the mother's voice played through a loudspeaker on her abdomen from her voice when speaking naturally. In addition, Querleu, Lefebvre, Renard, Titran, Morillion and Crèpin (1984) tested infants less than 2-hours-old and with no postnatal auditory exposure, establishing that they preferred the voice of their mother to that of a set of 5 strangers.

This body of evidence therefore strongly supports pre- and postnatal learning of the mother and effective discrimination in the auditory domain, while other research also indicates early and comparable olfactory capability (MacFarlane, 1975; Russell, 1976; Schaal, Montagner, Hertling, Bolzoni, Moyse & Quichon, 1980)

Historical view of face perception research in early infancy

Faces are very special to adults. Our ability to differentiate amongst extremely large sets of faces and to recall specific faces is exceptional. Faces provide the main means of recognising others and of obtaining important social communications about feelings, moods and intentions. So important are faces and appropriate mutual gaze in adults, that deviation from the accepted norm within a culture is treated very seriously. For example, the amount and quality of eye contact of a candidate during a formal selection interview explains more variance in subsequent selection decisions than any other variable (Young & Beier, 1977).

When it comes to newborn and older human infants, we are equally concerned about faces, and parents spend considerable periods of time in close facial contact with their babies, often seeking to establish and maintain mutual eye contact. Also, because as adults we believe faces to be very special, we have an expectation that faces will be special for babies too.

An initial assessment of face perception research in infancy suggests that it is an area that has been quite well developed over the last few decades. Closer inspection of the research base, however, reveals that while there are a number of studies, not all have been well conceived or conducted.

Looking first at the question of when face discrimination and recognition are possible, many studies with single age samples point to the ability of infants over 3 months of age to discriminate amongst photographic representations of faces (Barerra & Maurer, 1981; Bigelow, 1977). Research with samples of younger infants has often failed to show reliable face discrimination (Caldwell, 1965; Cornell, 1974; Fagan, 1972; Haith, Bergman & Moore, 1977; Melhuish, 1982). Other studies that have taken a cross-sectional approach utilising the same stimuli and methodology across several ages have tended to show a progression in face discrimination capability although few studies reported discrimination earlier than 3 months. Examples of such work include the study by Fitzgerald (1968) who found discrimination between mother–stranger face pairs at 4 months but not at 1 or 2 months; Kaitz, Shaviv, Greenwald, Blum and Auerbach (1985) who discovered discrimination between mother–stranger face pairs by 3 months, but not as early as 1 week or 1 month; Nottle (1980) who reports discrimination between mother–stranger face pairs at 4 and 5 months but not at 1 month; and Sherrod (1979) who suggests discrimination between mother–stranger face pairs occurs at 5 months, but not at 1 month or 3 months.

However, another body of work supports the possibility of face discrimination in the early weeks of life, at least between dissimilar categories in terms of level of pre-exposure, such as mother and female stranger. Thus Bushnell (1982) and Maurer and Salapatek (1976) found discrimination between colour photographs of the faces of mothers and strangers in 5-week-olds, while a number of other studies found such discrimination in the first and second week of life with real faces (Carpenter, 1973, 1974; Carpenter, Tecce, Stechler & Friedman, 1970; Noirot, 1977). In this set of experiments, the Carpenter studies were not well controlled, the selection of stimulus faces in particular being rather suspect, while the Noirot study has not been reported in detail. The general picture from the research described is that infants show greater competence with more realistic stimuli and more suitable test procedures. For example, infant control procedures tend to provide far superior results to experimenter control procedures. In the former, stimulus presentation and removal are determined by the infant's attention level and the infant therefore "determines" how long the stimulus will be present, while in the latter, stimulus presentation and removal are determined by a schedule predetermined by the experimenter.

For a current statement about face perception in very young infants we can turn to three studies, starting with that of Field, Cohen, Garcia and Greenberg (1984). The principal result from this research with the real faces of mothers and strangers was that 45-hour-olds were able to demonstrate a mother preference when tested using a combination of the habituation and visual preference methods. The second study, that of Bushnell, Sai and Mullin (1989), used a paired-presentation, visual preference method and concluded that infants, average age 49 hours, were able to demonstrate a significant preference for their mother (See Fig. 4.1). This study adopted a number of controls not used in any of the preceding research, including ensuring that experimenters were blind to the identity of the mother and that olfactory information could not be used by the infant to orient towards the mother. In addition, mothers and strangers were partially matched for gross information such as hair colour and length.

In the third study, Walton, Bower and Bower (1992) made use of the high amplitude sucking technique to demonstrate greater sucking by infants aged 12–36 hours, when seeing a videotape of their mother's face was made contingent upon such sucking.

One criticism of the first two studies with real faces was that mothers may have actively elicited attention from their infants, despite instructions to the contrary. Bushnell, Sai and Mullin (1989) introduced a check where naive observers viewed videotapes of testing sessions and could not determine any difference in activity between mother and stranger, being unable to accurately decide which was the mother's face in each pair. It may then be argued that it could be micro-movements, phase-linked to the infant's movement pattern that underlie salience and these would not be detectable by an observer. However, Walton et al.'s study successfully used video stimuli and this clearly suggests maternal preference is not actively elicited by the mother.

MOTHER RECOGNITION AND FEATURE MANIPULATION

Once we know that infants as young as a few days old can discriminate between faces, the next question might be which features are infants using?

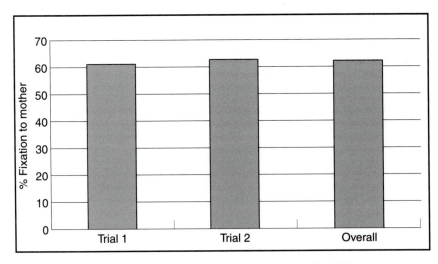

FIG. 4.1:   Summary of the preference data from Bushnell, Sai and Mullin (1989).

There are a few relevant studies in this area. For example, Bushnell (1982) used a cross-sectional approach with three groups of subjects, 5-, 12- and 19-week-olds using chromatic slides of faces. The features selected for analysis were the hair/face outline, the eyes and the mouth, with a final condition where eyes and hair were manipulated conjointly. The technique involved matching or standardising the feature across the pair of faces being used (the mother's for the habituation stimulus and that of a female stranger for the novel stimulus, matched for luminance flux). The results are shown in Fig. 4.2 where it can be seen that recovery of attention to the "novel" stimulus occurs when the eyes are standardised, but is lost when the hair or the eyes and hair together are standardised. Indeed it was not until 19 weeks that modifying the hair/face outline allowed recovery from habituation.

Whether these results hold true for younger infants needs to be determined. Bushnell et al. (1989) and Walton et al. (1992) matched mother and stranger quite closely for facial complexion, hair colour and length, but not style, yet discrimination was possible. A more direct empirical test of the importance of hair and eye information was carried out as a continuation of the series of studies summarised by Bushnell et al. (1989) and mentioned in passing in that report. A similar standardisation technique was used as in Bushnell (1982) where mother and stranger wore an identical wig (this time shoulder-length black hair) or a small pair of pince-nez lightly smoked glasses, but a visual preference method was employed rather than habituation.

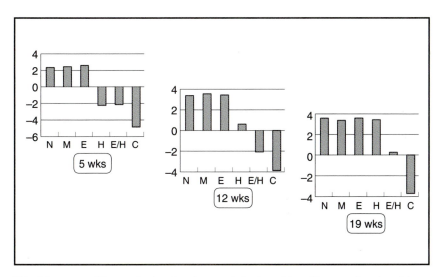

FIG. 4.2:   Mean difference fixation times in seconds for 6 conditions (N = normal, unaltered faces; M = mouth standardised; E = eyes standardised; H = Hair/face outline standardised; E/H = eyes and hair standardised; C = no change control).

A representation of the face stimuli in the two conditions is given in Figs. 4.3 and 4.4, while the visual preference data are provided in Fig. 4.5. The results show that standardising the eyes had no effect on recognition with nearly 60% of the infants' time being spent looking at the mother while standardising the hair prevented mother recognition.

Given the information we have about the importance of hair–face outline in face recognition with older infants, children and adults, it is perhaps not remarkable that standardising the hair of mother and stranger pairs has a major effect on mother recognition. Explaining this result is less clear. It can be argued that for infants to rely on hair information is evolutionarily unsound and that a less labile data set is

FIG. 4.3: Hair standardised by a wig.

FIG. 4.4: Eyes standardised by glasses.

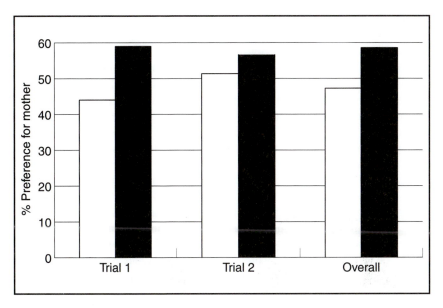

FIG. 4.5:   Typical preference when hair or eyes are standardised. ☐ hair ■ eyes

required. However, this probably overemphasises the variability of the hair–face outline in the short term as it does tend to stay fairly stable over periods of days and weeks though less so over months and years. Given the low spatial frequency information available from the outer parts of the face, a bias towards using this information may be expected and is consistent with work on older babies using schematic face stimuli (Maurer & Barrera, 1981).

However, there are methodological/interpretative problems with this kind of "standardisation" research, namely that one can never be certain what the reason is for a failure to discriminate or to show a preference. For example, it is possible that infants are attracted to the perceived change in the face and spend their time processing the changed feature, such as the hairline, and thus do not attend to the rest of the face. If they did attend to the rest of the face, it is conceivable that they could use this information to make discriminations and to recognise a specific face. They are thus distracted and not incompetent.

There are other fundamental problems with the kind of research designed to show that isolated "features" underlie the face discrimination/recognition process. Any change made to a single feature such as eyes or mouth also affects the spatial relations with the rest of the face. Conversely changing a relational property such as the internal spacing of component features also results in changes that could potentially be processed as distinct features (for example, the space between eyes and mouth). Far more research is required to establish the basis of early discrimination and recognition.

SPEED OF EARLY PERCEPTUAL LEARNING

It is quite evident from the previously mentioned research on antenatal auditory learning and from a range of studies on early postnatal learning in the auditory, olfactory and visual domains that the human infant is capable of learning from before birth and shows good short- and long-term memory in the early days of life. Research with visual stimuli indicates visual processing and memory are functional from minutes of age and thus it is to be expected that infants start to process and store visual information about their world and especially about the mother from the first contact.

Given that studies indicate the capacity to recognise the mother's face in the first 2 or 3 days of life, just how much opportunity to learn the mother's face does the average infant require? This question is particularly relevant because all the studies showing mother–stranger discrimination demonstrate a preference for the mother, the "familiar" stimulus. This result is quite different from most other infant perception research that shows a preference for novelty and thus greater attention to the mother is not an effect of habituation or of being familiarised to the mother for some time prior to being tested.

The best way to establish the amount of exposure required to establish a familiarity preference is to monitor exposure information and relate this empirically to mother–stranger discrimination performance. Some time ago, we completed a pilot study involving the observation of infants and mothers within the first few days of life on the maternity ward of a Glasgow hospital. This research provided some data on the typical exposure of infants to their mother, but did not test visual preference. A subsequent research project took this early work a stage further and gathered data using a time-sample methodology to determine: (1) how much contact was occurring; (2) when this contact occurred; and (3) what the nature of the contact was. The infants who were observed were then tested for mother recognition.

Mother–infant pairs were observed after leaving the labour suite from their point of arrival on the maternity wards for four 2-hour periods in every 24 hours following the point of first access by the observer on the maternity ward. This observation was continued for 3 days (72 hours) at which point the baby was tested on a mother–stranger discrimination using the visual preference method. Observation involved the use of a coding system that concentrated on face–face interaction. The principal aspects of this were: (1) caregiving, both physical (e.g. feeding, changing, cleaning) and mental (e.g. soothing); and (2) affective interaction (e.g. play; tickling, peek-a-boo, use of soft toys; talking; and singing). In total, 26 mother–infant pairs were successfully observed with the age at the start of observation ranging from 2 to 7 hours.

The main results are summarised in Fig. 4.6 where it can be seen that most of the time the babies were asleep, but when awake, the majority of the available time was spent with their mother. In addition, more time was spent awake in successive

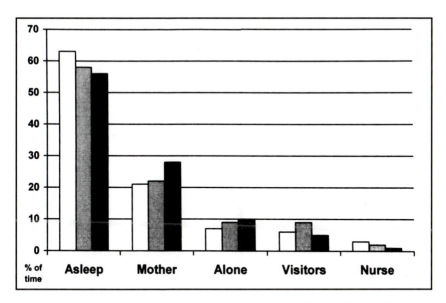

FIG. 4.6: Observed activity of babies over 3 days of observations. ☐ day 1 ▨ day 2 ■ day 3

24-hour periods, giving more opportunity for mother–infant interaction and visual learning of the mother. The amount of time spent in sleep is lower than that reported by Brown (1964), but there do seem to be very large individual differences (one of Brown's babies for example slept only 37% of the time) and thus there is considerable opportunity for sample variation.

When the extent of visual preference was subsequently correlated with the amount of exposure to the mother, the pattern of results in Fig. 4.7, indicated that about 11 to 12 hours of active exposure to the mother's face is required before infants showed a preference for the mother's face and this amount of exposure was easily being achieved within the first 3 to 4 days of life. This estimate is consistent with the previous research of Field et al. (1984) and Bushnell et al. (1989) where the average age of subjects at testing was 45 and 49 hours respectively, and probably fits with Walton et al.'s age range of 12 to 36 hours.

To what extent these results can be generalised to other infants in other situations remains to be seen. There are considerable differences in the structures and procedures associated with different maternity hospitals and the early experience of mothers and infants will therefore differ considerably.

DELAY AND RECOGNITION

When testing maternal face recognition there is always a delay between last exposure to the mother and preference testing. This can be very short when the

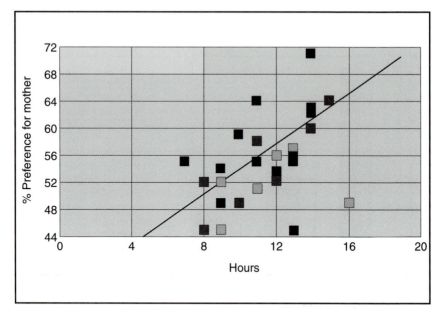

FIG. 4.7:   Preference for the mother plotted against number of active contact hours. r = 0.46

experimental set-up is well organised and the infants are "co-operative". Under other circumstances the delay may be far longer. Few researchers in the field seem to have paid attention to this issue and delays are not specified in experimental reports, yet any cognitive psychologist working with adult memory would be very aware of temporal factors in an experimental situation where memory is being assessed.

Probably the most common reason for a delay is difficulty in getting the subject settled and attentive, but where mothers and strangers are being used as subjects, getting these "stimuli" placed appropriately can also take some time.

A study was designed to directly compare two conditions of delay and the two intervals selected were <5 minutes and >15 minutes from the last sight of their mother's face to seeing their mother in the experimental situation as a stimulus. The visual preference method was used with two counterbalanced trials, where 20 seconds' fixation was accumulated per trial.

Short and long delay conditions were compared over both trials. In both short and long delay conditions the mother was preferred, but overall mother preference was stronger with the shorter delay (see Fig. 4.8). This suggests a clear effect of delay to weaken rather than remove the infants' ability to show a preference. A much longer delay may well be required to remove the recognition effect altogether. This suggests that mother learning is very stable and established as a long-term memory.

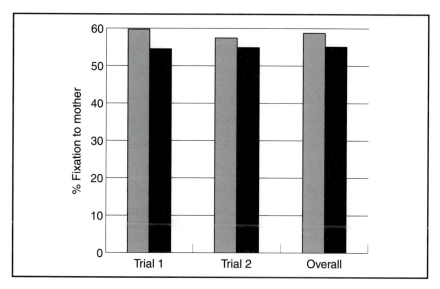

FIG. 4.8:   Preferences for the mother under two conditions of delay.
█ delay <5min ■ delay >15 min

FACES AS SPECIAL

A final question to be examined is whether or not faces are a special class of stimuli for the human neonate. Some of the most interesting research on face perception that suggests faces are special has come from work on an innate preference for the face-like configuration (Fig. 4.9). Goren, Sarty and Wu (1975) reported that infants only 9 minutes average age and with no prior experience of human faces, found a normal schematic face more salient than a "scrambled symmetric" or a "scrambled asymmetric" face, turning their eyes and head significantly more to pursue the normal configuration.

Subsequently these startling results were challenged on the basis that the baby holder and experimenter were not "blind" to the stimulus being presented, but the main result has since been replicated with appropriate controls in place. Johnson, Dziurawiec, Ellis and Morton (1991) used Goren et al.'s head-sized stimuli plus a blank and found that infants turned more to follow the normal than the scrambled than the blank stimulus. Johnson and Morton (1991) used this finding to bolster a claim that there exists a subcortically mediated mechanism they called Conspec whose sole function is to detect and orient infants towards faces. To this mechanism they added another—Conlern which was said to be a cortically mediated, general perceptual mechanism used by humans of all ages to make perceptual distinctions within sets of homogenous objects of which faces are obviously a particularly important class.

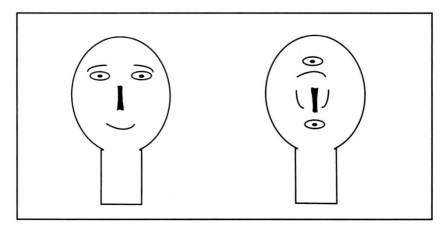

FIG. 4.9:   Examples of the two main stimuli in the Goren et al. 1975) study.

Johnson and Morton (1991) argued that evolution has established a mechanism that gives neonates a special interest in the human face. Accepting an evolutionary approach, it might well make sense to have a special face recognition system available to identify friend or foe and to take advantage of the benefits available from our complex social system. If one adds to this the considerable degree of homogeneity amongst the class of human faces, the brain can be seen to have a particularly difficult computational task for which a special processing system may have developed. There is some evidence for the existence of such a special mechanism including the existence of neural areas dedicated to face processing that when damaged can result in prosopagnosia (the specific inability to recognise faces; see de Renzi, 1986; Farah, 1996). However, to quote Rhodes (1995, p.47), "... the current consensus is that face recognition is not computationally special ... no evidence has been found for a processing system that deals exclusively with faces." In addition, "... the computations used to recognise faces are also used to recognise at least some other classes of stimuli that present a similar computational problem." Rhodes does not argue that all objects are recognised by the same general purpose recognition system. Basic object recognition relies on objects being decomposed into parts and their spatial relations which allows most basic objects to be differentiated since they have different parts or clearly different relations amongst parts (Tversky & Hemmenway, 1991). However, homogenous objects such as human faces that share parts and basic relations amongst parts can be identified as faces using basic object recognition, but clearly cannot be differentiated easily and specific exemplars recognised. Different computational processes are required that probably involve either second-order relational processing or perhaps "holistic coding" (Farah, 1990; Tanaka & Farah, 1993). These models imply that we have a specific system for coding the subtle variations in a shared configuration that allows differentiation within a class of homogenous objects, including faces. Rhodes (1995) also suggests an additional coding mechanism common to homogenous objects, that of norm-based coding which involves the coding of deviations from a spatial norm or average, or indeed a number of sub-category appropriate averages (for example, one for male faces and one for female faces). It is clear that at least by 2 or 3 months, human infants do establish face prototypes (Langlois, Roggman, Casey, Ritter, Rieser-Danner & Jenkins, 1987; Samuels & Ewy, 1985), but just how early this mechanism is in place remains to be assessed although Walton and Bower (1993) propose that newborns (average age 35 hours) can form some kind of face prototype within a minute of exposure to exemplars.

A prediction from these models would be that prosopagnosics who have a considerable familiarity with a class of objects other than faces would also show recognition failure within this other category and prosopagnosic ornithologists have indeed shown a loss in ability to recognise bird species (Bornstein, 1963) while prosopagnosic farmers have shown reduced ability to recognise their own animals (Bornstein, Stroka, & Munitz, 1969; Assal, Favre, & Anderes, 1984).

If we do not need to posit a special mechanism to discriminate and individuate faces in adults, do we need a special mechanism to attract infants towards faces? The answer is probably not and that a face-specific orientation system such as Conspec is superfluous. Following Bushnell et al. (1989, p.3), "... the face is not special *per se*, in the sense that the human neonate is genetically programmed to respond specifically to the human face, but rather that the human sensory systems are strongly attuned to aspects such as movement (both absolute and relative), to contrast, to objects of a particular size and proximity that make relatively high-pitched noises and can operate contingently". This argument is extended in the next section.

SENSORY–ECOLOGY MODEL

A model of early face perception is proposed, termed the *Sensory–Ecology Model.* (Fig. 4.10). The Sensory part of this model expands on the arguments just made and suggests that the human face is a particularly salient stimulus because it best matches the operation of human sensory, perceptual and cognitive mechanisms. The human face is a highly active and interactive stimulus with the capacity for a broad range of movements in three-dimensional space and for the independent movement of internal "features". It is also multidimensional and multisensory with texture, colour, shape, sound and smell all present. The Ecology part of the model stresses that in the environment in which the human infant is reared, the human face is probably the most commonly repeated stimulus to be presented during periods of alert, active attention. In the early days, the face of the mother is the most frequent visual stimulus within the appropriate close viewing distance and

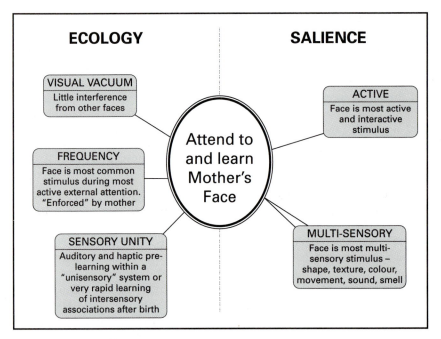

FIG. 4.10:   Sensory–Ecology Model of early face perception

this face appears in what might be considered a "visual vacuum" since there is little interference from other faces during periods of optimal arousal.

Far from needing evolution to have created a Conspec mechanism, it is more likely that evolution has relied on parents and especially the mother to "guide" the infant to attend to faces by actively seeking to manipulate the attention systems of the newborn and restricting the opportunity for alternative stimuli to attract attention. Infants are thus placed in an ecological framework that ensures they will attend strongly to faces and this framework is supported by the restricted range of operation of the visual system, especially its initial reliance on proximal input.

Does the configurational responding of newborns need further examination? Do we need to explain the ability of newborns to respond preferentially to face-like stimuli with no visual experience to base this on? It may at first seem a preposterous suggestion, but it is possible that the unborn infant does have prenatal "visual" experience of the human face. Of course it is not proposed that the baby can see faces outside the womb or even that the inside of the womb is sufficiently reflective to allow self-perception under conditions of bright light where the mother is unclothed and light may penetrate through the abdomen. What is worth considering is a follow-through of the concept of sensory integration or at its more extreme – "unimodality". If all the sensory systems have effective mappings onto each other or perhaps are one and the same at first and only gradually differentiate, then it is possible that experience of the face in an apparently different "modality" may allow pre-learning of the basic face configuration while still inside the womb. What might this process involve? Simply put, the foetus regularly moves hands to face and actively explores the face while frequently inserting a digit into the mouth. This haptic exploration over many weeks could lay down the basis for the finding of a configurational response just minutes after birth without having to define a Conspec mechanism with a pre-programmed face configuration. In addition, this early haptic learning may support the gaining of visual experience of the mother's face and allow very rapid early learning about facial characteristics. Some evidence for this kind of intersensory mapping (or perhaps a unisensory system?) comes from Meltzoff and Borton's (1979) paper demonstrating intermodal matching or equivalence of texture information between touch and vision and it also fits with the more coherent explanations of early infant imitation such as that of Meltzoff and Moore (1985).

CONCLUSION

Newborns have remarkable abilities to discriminate amongst a range of stimuli and in particular to discriminate amongst faces and recognise at least one significant face, that of the mother. The very rapid onset of these capabilities and their resistance to various experimental manipulations suggest preparedness. One form of preparation is the inherited sensory apparatus that is able to extract information of an appropriate nature (for example, certain wavelengths of light or auditory frequencies). Another form of preparation is that developed through appropriate experiences prior to birth. The latter can be readily understood in the auditory domain (and perhaps in the olfactory domain with a far more restricted range of stimulus input). Preparatory experience in the visual domain seems at first to be restricted to non-patterned light variation. However, if we can accept intersensory mapping or a unisensory system then visual preparedness becomes possible and a special system for face orientation and basic configurational encoding appears less relevant. In addition, when one considers the social environment into which infants are born, it becomes possible to conclude that infants are not so much attracted to faces as faces are attracted to infants.

REFERENCES

Assal, G., Favre, C., & Anderes, J.P. (1984). Non-reconnaissance d'animaux familiers chez un paysan: Zooagnosie ou prosopagnosie pour les animaux. *Revue Neurologique, 140*, 580–584.

Barerra, M.E., & Maurer, D. (1981). The perception of facial expressions by the three-month-old. *Child Development, 52*, 203–206.

Bigelow, A. (1977). *Infants' recognition of their mothers*. Paper presented at the biennial meeting of Society for Research in Child Development, New Orleans, LA, March.

Bornstein, B. (1963). Prosopagnosia. In L. Halpern (ed.), *Problems of Dynamic Neurology*. Jerusalem: Hassadah Medical Organisation.

Bornstein, B., Stroka, H., & Munitz, H. (1969). Prosopagnosia with animal face agnosia. *Cortex, 5*, 164–169.

Brown, J.L. (1964). States in newborn infants. *Merrill-Palmer Quarterly, 10*, 313–327.

Bushnell, I.W.R. (1982). Discrimination of faces by young infants. *Journal of Experimental Child Psychology, 33*, 298–308.

Bushnell, I.W.R., Sai, F., & Mullin, J.T. (1989). Neonatal recognition of the mother's face. *British Journal of Developmental Psychology, 7*, 3–15.

Caldwell, B.M. (1965). *Visual and emotional reactions of an infant to his mother and other adult females*. Paper presented to the Tavistock Study Group on Mother–Infant Interaction, London.

Carpenter, C.G. (1973). *Mother–stranger discrimination in the early weeks of life*. Paper presented at the meeting of the Society for Research in Child Development, Philadelphia.

Carpenter, C.G. (1974). Mother's face and the newborn. *New Scientist*, 21 March, 742–744.

Carpenter, C.G., Tecce, J.J., Stechler, G., & Friedman, S. (1970). Differential visual behaviour to human and humanoid faces in early infancy. *Merrill-Palmer Quarterly, 16*, 91–108.

Cornell, E.H. (1974). Infants' discrimination of faces following redundant presentations. *Journal of Experimental Child Psychology, 18*, 98–106.

DeCasper, A.J., & Fifer, W.P. (1980). Of human bonding: Newborns prefer their mothers' voices. *Science, 208*, 1174–1176.

de Renzi, E. (1986). Current issues in prosopagnosia. In H.D. Ellis, M.A. Jeeves, F. Newcombe & A. Young (eds.), *Aspects of face processing*. Dordrecht, NL: North Holland.

Fagan, J.F. (1972). Infants' recognition memory for faces. *Journal of Experimental Child Psychology, 14*, 453–476.

Farah, M.J. (1990). *Visual agnosia: Disorders of object recognition and what they tell us about normal vision*. Cambridge, MA: MIT Press.

Farah, M.J. (1996). Is face recognition special? Evidence from neuropsychology. *Behavioural Brain Research, 76*, 181–189.

Field, T.M., Cohen, D., Garcia, R., & Greenberg, R. (1984). Mother–stranger face discrimination by the newborn. *Infant Behavior and Development, 7*, 19–25.

Fitzgerald, H.E. (1968). Autonomic pupillary reflex activity during early infancy and its relation to social and non-social visual stimuli. *Journal of Experimental Child Psychology, 6*, 470–482.

Goren, C.C., Sarty, M., & Wu, P.Y.K. (1975). Visual following and pattern discrimination of face-like stimuli by newborn infants. *Pediatrics, 56*, 544–548.

Haith, M.M., Bergman, T., & Moore, M. (1977). Eye contact and face scanning in early infancy. *Science, 198*, 853–855.

Hepper, P.G. (1991). An examination of fetal learning before and after birth. *Irish Journal of Psychology, 12*, 95–107.

Hepper, P.G., Scott, D., & Shahidullah, S. (1993). Newborn and fetal response to maternal voice. *Journal of Reproductive and Infant Psychology, 11*, 147–153.

Johnson, M., Dziurawiec, S., Ellis, H.D., & Morton, J. (1991). Newborns' preferential tracking of face-like stimuli and its subsequent decline. *Cognition, 40*, 1–19.

Johnson, M., & Morton J. (1991). *Biology and cognitive development: The case for face recognition*. Oxford: Basil Blackwell.

Kaitz, M., Shaviv, E., Greenwald, M., Blum, M., & Auerbach, J. (1985). *At what age can a baby recognize mother's face?* Unpublished manuscript, Psychology Department, Hebrew University, Jerusalem, Israel.

Langlois, J.H., Roggman, L.A., Casey, R. J., Ritter, J.M., Rieser-Danner, L.A., & Jenkins, V.Y. (1987). Infant preferences for attractive faces: Rudiments of a stereotype?. *Developmental Psychology, 27*, 79–84.

MacFarlane, J.A. (1975). *Olfaction in the development of social preferences in the human infant*. Amsterdam: Elsevier.

Maurer, D., & Salapatek, P. (1976). Developmental changes in the scanning of faces by young infants. *Child Development, 47*, 523–527.

Maurer, D., & Barrera, M. (1981). Infants perception of natural and distorted arrangements of a schematic face. *Chid Development, 52*, 196–202.

Melhuish, E.C. (1982). Visual attention to mother's and stranger's faces and facial contrast in 1-month-old infants. *Developmental Psychology, 18*, 229–231.

Meltzoff, A.N., & Borton, R.W. (1979). Intermodal matching by human neonates. *Nature, 282*, 403–404.

Meltzoff, A.N., & Moore, M.K. (1985). Cognitive foundations and social functions of imitation and intermodal representation in infancy. In J. Mehler & R. Fox (eds.), *Neonate cognition: Beyond the blooming, buzzing confusion*. Hillsdale, N.J.: Lawrence Erlbaum Associates.

Noirot, E. (1977). *Social orientation and type of feeding in the human body*. Presented at the meeting of the International Society for the Study of Behavioral development, IVth Biennial Conference, Pavia.

Nottle, E. (1980). *Visual facial discrimination of mother and female stranger by young infants*. Unpublished honours thesis. Department of Psychology, Monash University, Clayton, Victoria.

Querleu, D., Lefebvre, C., Renard, X., Titran, M., Morillion, M., & Crèpin, G. (1984). Perception auditive et reativité du nouveau-né de moins de deux heures de vie à la voix maternelle. *Journal de Gynecologie, Obstetrique et Biologie de la Reproduction, 13*, 125–134.

Rhodes, G. (1995). Face recognition and configural encoding. In T. Valentine (ed.), *Cognitive and computational aspects of face recognition*. London: Routledge.

Russell, M.J. (1976). Human olfactory communication. *Nature, 260*, 520–522.

Sai, F., & Bushnell, I.W.R. (1988). The perception of faces in different poses by 1-month-olds. *British Journal of Developmental Psychology, 6*, 35–41.

Samuels, C.J., & Ewy, R. (1985). Aesthetic perception of faces during infancy. *British Journal of Developmental Psychology, 3*, 221–228.

Schaal, B., Montagner, H., Hertling, E., Bolzoni, D., Moyse, A., & Quichon, R. (1980). Les stimulation olfactives dans les relations entre l'enfant et la mere. *Reproduction, Nutrition et Dévelopment, 20*, 843–858.

Sherrod, L.R. (1979). Social cognition in infants: Attention to the human face. *Infant Behavior and Development, 2*, 279–294.

Slater, A.M. (1993). Visual perceptual abilities at birth: Implications for face perception. In B. de Boysson-Bardies, S. de Schonen, P. Jusczyk, P. McNeilage, & J. Morton (eds.), *Developmental neurocognition: Speech and face processing in the first year of life*. Dordrecht, Boston, London: Kluwer Academic Publishers.

Slater, A.M., & Butterworth, G. (1997). Perception of social stimuli: Face perception and imitation. In G. Bremner, A. Slater & G. Butterworth (eds.), *Infant development: Recent advances*. Hove, UK: Lawrence Erlbaum Associates.

Tanaka, J.W., & Farah, M.J. (1993). Parts and wholes in face recognition. *Quarterly Journal of Experimental Psychology: Human Experimental Psychology, 46*, 225–245.

Tversky, B., & Hemmenway, K. (1991). Parts and the basic level in natural categories and artificial stimuli: Comments on Murphy (1991). *Memory and Cognition, 19*, 439–442.

Walton, G.E., Bower, N.J.A., & Bower, T.G.R. (1992). Recognition of familiar faces by newborns. *Infant Behavior and Development, 15*, 265–269.

Walton, G.E., & Bower, T.G.R. (1993). Newborns form prototypes in less than 1 minute. *Psychological Science, 4*, 203–205.

Young, I.P., & Beier, E.G. (1977). The role of applicant nonverbal communication in the employment interview. *Journal of Employment Counselling, 14*, 154–165.

CHAPTER FIVE

Mechanisms Underlying Face Preference at Birth

Francesca Simion, Eloisa Valenza and Carlo Umiltà
Università di Padova, Italy

The human face is one of the most complex visual patterns to which human beings are exposed in either adulthood or infancy. Because of this, the study of face recognition has provided a meeting point for scientists from a wide variety of fields: neurophysiology, neuropsychology, cognitive psychology, and developmental psychology. Although the focus of the present chapter is on face processing in newborns, we will first briefly review the literature also from adult studies. A large part of this literature has been concerned with the issue of whether faces can be considered to be special visual patterns.

ARE FACES SPECIAL?

Hay and Young (1982) made the distinction between "uniqueness" and "specificity". Uniqueness implies that not only are faces handled by a system that is separate from that used for recognizing other objects, but that this system works in a different way from other visual recognition systems. Specificity implies that a separate system or module exists for face but that this system works in a similar way to systems used in processing other classes of visual stimuli.

In agreement with the specificity position, Ellis and Young (1989) suggested that evidence about the inversion effects in face recognition, the existence of specific cells in the monkey's brain that are dedicated to recognition of faces, and the syndrome of prosopagnosia in humans, provide support for the view that faces are special, but not unique, visual patterns.

Yin (1969) was the first to explore the specificity of face recognition in terms of inversion. He compared face recognition with recognition of other objects shown in the upright position and in the upsidedown position. The results demonstrated a significantly greater decrement (relative to the upright position) in recognition accuracy for faces than for other objects, such as houses and airplanes.

Scapinello and Yarmey (1970), using pictures of dogs, houses and faces found similar results. Based on these findings, Yin (1978) argued that face perception involves processes that are different from those involved in perceiving other classes of objects. More specifically, he assumed that face processing requires a different strategy in which holistic as opposed to distinctive features are extracted. Because inversion severely impairs configurational, but not componential perception, recognition of upsidedown faces is difficult. Face recognition is therefore special in that it involves more configurational processing than recognition of other objects.

However, a series of experiments by Diamond and Carey (1986) cast doubt on Yin's (1978) hypothesis. Diamond and Carey used pictures of dogs, as in Scapinello and Yarmey's (1970) study, but they tested subjects who could be considered to be highly experienced dog watchers. They predicted that dog experts would be as vulnerable to an inversion of dog pictures as recognition of human faces is for everyone else. Novices, on the other hand, should not be so affected. The results supported their predictions.

Diamond and Carey (1986) concluded that over the years one acquires expertise in the configurational recognition of upright faces. This expertise is useless when faces are inverted. However, acquisition of expertise for configurational recognition is not limited to faces, as evidenced by the fact that, in recognizing dogs, experts showed a greater inversion effect than novices. The inversion effect, therefore, seems to be characteristic of any complex, highly familiar class of similar stimuli whose configuration is altered by inversion.

Neurophysiological studies provided additional evidence in favor of the specificity of face processing. Gross, Rocha-Miranda, and Bender (1972) found that some cells in the temporal cortex of the monkey were selectively responsive to biologically important stimuli, such as hands and faces. These findings have subsequently been corroborated by several studies (see, e.g., Perrett, Mistlin, Potter, Smith, Head, Chitty, Broennimann, Milner, & Jeeves, 1986). In the temporal cortex of the macaque five different types of cells can be distinguished, each of which responds maximally to different facial characteristics (full face, profile, back of head, head up, and head down). Other cells respond selectively to one particular individual, regardless of pose, lighting, expression, and so on.

Data in support of the specificity of face processing originated also from neuropsychological studies. Prosopagnosia is a neuropsychological deficit characterized by inability to recognize familiar faces (see, e.g., de Renzi, 1982). Prosopagnosic patients can distinguish faces as a category quite easily from other visual objects, but have no idea to which individual a specific face belongs. In contrast, recognition of other visual objects remains relatively intact.

Damasio, Damasio and Van Hoesen (1982) argued that recognition of familiar faces differs from that of other objects in that it does not require a "generic" recognition of a class of objects, but rather the identification of a specific individual. The question is whether this impairment is unique to faces, or is merely an instance of a more general impairment in recognizing single items from a given class. However, cases of prosopagnosia have been reported, in which the ability to recognize single items belonging to other classes of objects was well preserved (de Renzi, 1986; de Renzi, Faglioni, Grossi, & Nichelli, 1991).

Gross and Sergent (1992) reasoned that it is impossible to demonstrate that prosopagnosia can occur in complete isolation, because it can never be certain that all possible deficits have been excluded. It is quite likely, on the other hand, that the lesion responsible for prosopagnosia is larger than would be necessary to produce the deficit. Therefore, the existence of associated deficits does not necessarily rule out the specificity of prosopagnosia.

On the basis of the available evidence, some authors (Ellis & Young, 1989; Humphreys & Bruce, 1989; Morton & Johnson, 1989) have concluded that there is no reason to believe that faces differ from other complex and familiar stimuli in the *manner* they are processed. However, the richness and diversity of the information that faces convey, renders it likely that faces are processed by a *separate system*.

OPERATIONS INVOLVED IN FACE PROCESSING

The ease with which faces are normally recognized should not mask the complexity of the operations involved in their processing. The choice of a specific task to examine the operations underlying face perception has important implications with respect to the particular processing requirements, as different tasks make different demands. In particular, tasks like face detection, face discrimination, and face recognition are likely to require different operations (Sergent, 1989).

Face detection involves a decision as to whether or not a given stimulus is a face, and it implies the capacity to detect the invariant characteristics (features and their relational properties) that define a face. Face discrimination (or simultaneous matching) involves a comparison between two simultaneously presented faces and a decision as to their sameness or difference. Face recognition (or delayed matching) involves a judgement of previous occurrence and, thus, whether a face has been seen earlier.

According to Sergent (1989), a configural or global process would be implied in face detection. This configural process would be based on the capacity to process the spatial relations among the component features of a face. In contrast, an analytic process would be responsible for face discrimination and face recognition. An analytic comparison implies that recognition operates on shape information determined by local features considered independently of one another. Therefore the spatial relations and interactions among the component features would not constitute the basis for face discrimination or for face recognition.

A number of functional models have been proposed for face processing (e.g., Bruce & Young, 1986; Ellis, Young, & Hay, 1987; Perrett, Mistlin, & Chitty, 1987; Rhodes, 1985). The one by Bruce and Young, which is the most influential, was implemented by using an interactive activation architecture (Burton, Bruce, & Johnston, 1990).

Bruce and Young's (1986) model is basically a three-stage, bottom-up model. In the first stage, called "structural encoding", the raw image undergoes those processes that are necessary for later perceptual processing. Any pattern that in the least corresponds to the basic facial structure is processed at this stage, which is fast, automatic, cannot be influenced by top-down processes and displays the quality of encapsulation that Fodor (1983) identified as a feature of modular systems.

The structural encoding provides data for the next stage, "the face recognition units". Each face recognition unit contains stored structural codes describing one of the faces known to a person. At this stage when a facial input makes contact with its representations, there are two kinds of outputs: a signal of familiarity, and a signal to the corresponding person node within semantic memory.

The last stage is called "person identity nodes". Its activity identifies who the person is, including his/her occupation and status. These person identity nodes may also be accessed via other, nonfacial information, such as name, voice, or gait.

Finally, the person identity node has access to the "name generator", which enables the perceiver to identify the person by name. Naming, however, is not a mandatory outcome of access to a given person identity node, as evidenced by the fact that one may recognize a given person, but cannot remember his/her name.

Bruce and Young (1986) assumed that face recognition is a sequential process, which takes place independently, in parallel to other processes, such as analysis of emotional facial expression, lip reading, and visual processing of specific facial features such as age and sex. For this reason, Bruce and Young assumed that, surrounding the core identification system, there are a number of satellite systems designed to process different kinds of facial information.

In Bruce and Young's (1986) view, therefore, face recognition is not a unitary event, because it involves the interaction of a number of different functional components. Each functional component processes a distinct type of information that can be derived from faces.

FACE PREFERENCE IN NEWBORNS

Morton and Johnson (1989) argued that a special function based on a separate system should have the following four properties: (1) the function would be present from birth (the innateness criterion); (2) it would be localized in a circumscribed area of the brain (the localization criterion); (3) the part of the brain that is responsible for the function would not be involved in any other function (the modularity criterion); and (4) the processing that subserves the function would differ in some respect from other processing (the uniqueness criterion).

The literature we have reviewed so far goes some distance toward showing that face processing meets the localization, modularity, and uniqueness criteria. In Morton and Johnson's view, however, only the innateness criterion is strictly necessary. Therefore, the experiments to be reported in the present paper were aimed at demonstrating that newborns possess an innate mechanism specifically devoted to processing faces.

In this context, the studies conducted on infants who are a few months old are scarcely relevant. Their performance is no doubt affected by learning, and thus cannot provide evidence concerning the possible innateness of face recognition. More convincing evidence comes from studies conducted on newborns, which demonstrated that a moving facelike pattern elicits greater following behavior than does a non-facelike pattern (Goren, Sarty, & Wu, 1975; Johnson, Dziurawiec, Ellis, & Morton, 1991; Maurer & Young, 1983). According to Johnson and Morton (1991; also see Morton and Johnson, 1991) these and related findings (Haaf & Bell, 1967; Kleiner, 1987; Kleiner & Banks, 1987) indicate the existence of a mechanism that contains information concerning the structure of facial features and their relative location in space. This mechanism would be available at birth without prior exposure to specific stimuli, and its function would be to orient the newborn to facial stimuli present in the environment by guiding an automatic orienting response that is presumably mediated subcortically.

Discrepant results were, however, obtained in studies that employed a preferential looking technique, which failed to obtain a preference for face with newborns (Hershenson, Kessen, & Munsinger, 1967; Slater, 1993). In view of these inconsistencies, the main purpose of the series of experiments reported in the present chapter is to elucidate which information is selected in facial processing by newborns. Before proceeding, we will briefly present the two hypotheses that have been proposed to explain face preference at birth; that is, the sensory hypothesis and the structural hypothesis.

The most recent version of the sensory hypothesis is based on the Linear System Model (LSM; e.g., Banks & Salapatek, 1981; Kleiner, 1987; Kleiner & Banks, 1987), according to which for any pattern, two functions may be derived: the amplitude spectrum, comprising the amplitude and orientation of the component spatial frequencies, and the phase spectrum, comprising the phase and orientation of the components. The attractiveness of a pattern is determined solely by the amount of effective energy of that pattern. The amplitude spectrum of the pattern is filtered through the Contrast Sensitivity Function (CSF) of the subject. In newborns, the CSF removes all information at frequencies greater than 2 cycles per degree. Therefore, newborn's visual preferences are for those stimuli that provide spatial frequency and contrast information that fit the visual window (i.e. the CSF), better than the pattern with which it is paired. Basically, the Linear System Model claims that newborn's preferences for visual patterns are determined solely by their visibility. Facelike patterns would not be different from other visual stimuli. They are preferred simply because they happen to have more appropriate sensory properties.

The original version of the LSM-based sensory hypothesis (Kleiner, 1987; Kleiner & Banks, 1987) stated that, for newborns, preferences for faces are entirely due to amplitude properties. Subsequently, Kleiner (1990, 1993) revised the hypothesis by proposing a sequential (hierarchical), two-stage model. In this new version, the sensory hypothesis states that stimuli are first compared for their amplitude, and then, if they do not differ on this property, their structure is compared. That is to say, the structure is deemed to produce preference for a facelike pattern only when the sensory characteristics of the stimuli are identical.

The structural hypothesis (Johnson & Morton, 1991; Morton & Johnson, 1991), instead, maintains that faces are special for the newborn because, at birth, the visual system possesses a device (i.e., Conspec), which contains structural information about the relative spatial location of elements within a face, like 3 high-contrast blobs in the correct relative locations for the eyes and mouth in a pattern of the size of a real human face.

Johnson and Morton (1991) also proposed that Conspec is subcortical, is located in the superior colliculus, receives information through the retinotectal pathway, and has the sole purpose to direct the newborn's gaze to any facelike patterns present in the visual field. Conspec would be functional at birth and would be replaced by a cortical mechanism, Conlern, by the time the infant is 2 months old.

In the rest of the chapter, we will report the results of a series of experiments conducted in our laboratory. A more complete description of the experiments can be found in Valenza, Simion, Macchi Cassia, and Umiltà (1996) and in Simion, Valenza, Umiltà and Dalla Barba (in press). In all the experiments, variants of the preferential looking task were employed. Basically, the task consisted in presenting newborns with two patterns, and in establishing if they looked longer at or oriented more frequently to one of them.

EMPIRICAL EVIDENCE

The first experiment was conducted to demonstrate that the preference for facelike patterns is present at birth. The regular preferential looking technique was used with newborn infants.

The stimuli (see Fig. 5.1) were head-shaped, head-sized, two-dimensional white forms, with blobs as features of a human face. The fundamental spatial frequency of the blobs was 0.06 cycles per degree. One stimulus had the blobs in the appropriate location for the eyes and the mouth. The other stimulus had an inverted position of the blobs.

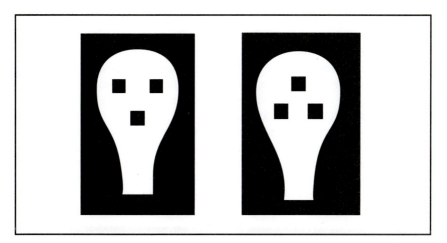

FIG. 5.1:   The two stimuli used in Experiment 1.

On every trial, as soon as the baby fixated the center light, the experimenter turned off the light and presented the two stimuli. Videotapes of the eye movements were subsequently analyzed to record the number of orienting responses, the duration of the first fixation, the duration of the longest fixation, and the total fixation time.

Analyses of variance were carried out on the 4 dependent variables. They indicated that on 3 of them (that is, duration of the first fixation, duration of the longest fixation, and total fixation time) the babies preferred the facelike over the non-facelike pattern.

If one considers that the two stimuli had been selected because they have nearly identical amplitude spectra, it is apparent that the results refuted the version of the sensory hypothesis that maintains that face preference at birth is solely determined by the sensory characteristics of the stimuli (Kleiner, 1987; Kleiner & Banks, 1987). In contrast, the results were in accord with the hypothesis that at birth preference responses are governed by structural information, because the newborn possesses a mechanism that is specifically tuned to respond to the structural information conveyed by a facelike pattern (Johnson & Morton, 1991; Morton & Johnson, 1991).

The results of this first experiment, however, did not refute the revised version that maintains that preference responses are emitted on the basis of the structural information when the sensory characteristics are identical (Kleiner, 1990, 1993).

In a subsequent experiment, the internal blobs of the stimuli were manipulated chosen to test the preference for the peak contrast sensitivity typical of newborns (i.e., between 0.1 and 0.2 cycles per degree, according to, e.g., Banks & Ginsburg, 1985; Slater, Earle, Morison, & Rose, 1985). It was predicted that the babies would prefer the stimulus with the optimal spatial frequency components.

Two pairs of stimuli were presented. Each stimulus had three square blobs in a triangular formation, arranged in the inverted locations for the eyes and the mouth. One pair of stimuli was formed by unframed blobs, whereas in the second pair the blobs were framed by the same head-shaped contour that had been employed in the previous experiment. In each pair, in one stimulus the blobs were completely black (0.06 cycles per degree), whereas in the other stimulus the blobs were black and white striped (0.19 cycles per degree).

The analyses of variance indicated that on three measures of preference (that is, number of orienting responses, duration of the longest fixation, and total fixation time) the babies preferred the stimulus with striped blobs over the stimulus with non-striped blobs. In view of the purpose of the final experiment to be discussed, it is also interesting to note that total fixation time was longer for the framed than the unframed pair.

The outcome of this experiment supported the sensory hypothesis, according to which newborns prefer the stimulus with the optimal spatial frequency components (i.e., 0.1–0.2 cycles per degree). In effect, visual preference was determined by the extent to which the physical properties of the stimulus matched those of the baby's sensory channels. Note, however, that the results were not at odds with the predictions of the structural hypothesis because facelike patterns were not presented in this experiment.

In the third experiment, one stimulus was a pattern with the structural configuration of a face but with non-salient physical properties (i.e., the preferred stimulus from the first experiment). The other stimulus was a non-facelike pattern with spatial frequency information that fitted the baby's CSF (i.e., the preferred stimulus from the second experiment).

The reasoning was that, if the sensorial factor was more important than the structural factor in producing response preference (Kleiner, 1990, 1993), newborns

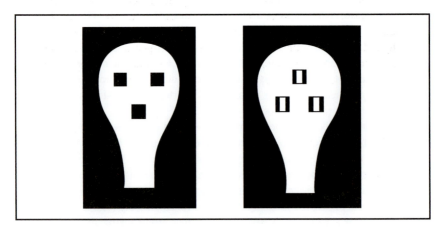

FIG. 5.2:   The two stimuli used in Experiment 3.

should show a preference for the stimulus that provided more salient visual information. If the structural factor was more important than the sensorial factor (Johnson & Morton, 1991; Morton & Johnson, 1991), newborns should show a preference for the facelike pattern.

The stimuli (see Fig. 5.2) were two head-shaped, head-sized white forms, with 3 square blobs inside. In one stimulus the blobs were completely black (0.06 cycles per degree) and were situated in the appropriate locations for the eyes and the mouth. In the other stimulus, the blobs were striped (0.19 cycles per degree) and were situated in the inverted locations for the eyes and the mouth.

The analyses of variance indicated that the babies preferred the pattern with a facelike structure over the stimulus with more salient blobs on number of orienting responses, duration of the longest fixation, and total fixation time.

It can be concluded that the facelike arrangement of the internal features can overcome the sensory preference that had emerged in the second experiment. Thus, it appears that, of the two factors that govern newborns' visual preference—that is, the structural factor and the sensorial factor—the former is more powerful than the latter.

It is important to note that the outcome of this experiment is at odds also with the revised version of the sensory hypothesis (Kleiner, 1990, 1993), which maintains that, regardless of the structure, the preferred stimulus is the one that contains the more salient spatial frequency components. Rather, even in the presence of a difference in visibility between the two stimuli, newborns preferred the one with the structural properties of a face. This is exactly what the structural hypothesis predicts (Johnson & Morton, 1991; Morton & Johnson, 1991).

As discussed earlier, Johnson and Morton (1991; Morton & Johnson, 1991) have proposed that newborns' preferential orienting to faces is primarily controlled by a subcortical mechanism (i.e., Conspec) containing a crude specification of the arrangement of the eyes and mouth. Cortical circuits specialized for processing faces (i.e., Conlern) would appear at around 2 months, as a result of the developing cortex being frequently exposed to faces due to the activity of Conspec.

This hypothesis concerning the neural basis of Conspec would be supported if face preference for faces showed a temporal–nasal asymmetry. A temporal–nasal asymmetry is evidence of retinotectal mediation (Johnson, 1990; Rafal, Henik, & Smith, 1991; Simion, Valenza, Umiltà, & Dalla Barba, 1995) because, when compared to the geniculostriate system, the retinotectal system has a greater crossed input from the contralateral eye (temporal hemifield) and a smaller direct input from the ipsilateral eye (nasal hemifield).

In the fourth experiment, newborns were tested monocularly. The most important departure from the procedure employed in the previous experiments was that the stimuli were presented one at a time in either the temporal or the nasal hemifield.

The stimuli were those shown in Fig. 5.1. One had the blobs in the appropriate locations for the eyes and the mouth regions. The other was identical but with an inverted position of the blobs. The stimulus pattern was placed in the temporal or nasal visual hemifield.

The analysis of variance was conducted on the number of orienting responses. The results showed that orienting responses were more frequent to the facelike than the non-facelike pattern. This difference, however, was present in the temporal hemifield and absent in the nasal hemifield.

If temporal–nasal hemifield asymmetry is a marker of the activity of the retinotectal pathway, the present results showed that in newborns the retinotectal pathway has the main role in controlling the visually guided behavior that is elicited by facelike patterns. This finding is no doubt congruent with the proposal that the mechanism that controls newborns' preferential orienting to faces is subcortical (Johnson & Morton, 1991; Morton & Johnson, 1991).

As might be remembered, the second experiment showed that total fixation time was longer for the framed than the unframed stimuli. This suggests that, besides the arrangement (and the saliency) of the internal features, the external contour also plays a role in producing visual preferences in newborns. The final experiment was aimed at investigating this issue further.

Two stimuli were simultaneously presented to the left and right of the center light and the procedure was that employed in the first three experiments.

Each of the two stimuli had 3 square black blobs (0.06 cycles per degree) in a triangular formation, arranged in either the normal or the inverted locations for the eyes and the mouth. The most relevant experimental manipulation concerned the type of contour (see Fig. 5.3). For a group of newborns, the blobs were framed by the same head-shaped contour that had been employed in the previous experiments. For another group, the frame had about the same size but its shape was square. For a third group, the blobs were presented without any frame.

The analysis of variance indicated that the infants spent more time looking at the facelike pattern when the component features were surrounded by either an oval contour or a square contour, whereas no preference was found when the contour was absent. Interestingly, whether the contour was oval or square did not seem to affect the preference for the facelike pattern.

The results of this experiment were important on two accounts. First, they showed that the external contour is crucial in producing the preference for facelike patterns over non-facelike patterns. Second, they showed that the contour need not have a specific shape in order to produce the preference. In fact, a square contour seemed to be as effective as a head-shaped one.

CONCLUSION

The series of experiments summarized in this chapter were devised to contrast the sensory hypothesis and the structural hypothesis as accounts of face preference in newborns. Supporting the structural hypothesis is important for the innateness issue.

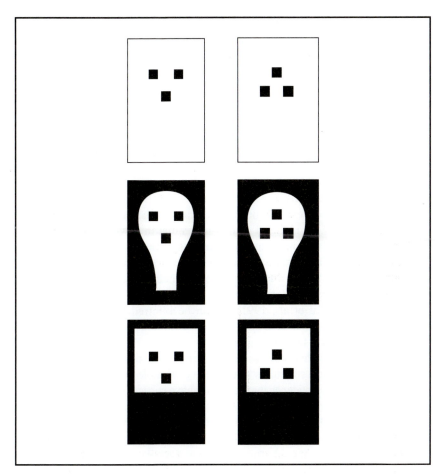

FIG. 5.3:   The stimuli used in Experiment 5.

This is because an innate mechanism for processing faces must be sensitive to the structure that characterizes a face. Merely showing that at birth there is a preference for some spatial frequencies, which belong to other stimuli besides to facelike patterns, would clearly be insufficient to claim that there is an innate mechanism specific for faces. In accord with the structural hypothesis, our results clearly demonstrated that newborns preferentially orient to faces and that this preference is based on the structural characteristics of the stimulus.

The structure of a face is mainly provided by the arrangement of the inner features. However, other facial features, besides the inner ones, may be necessary for newborns to recognize facelike patterns. The external contour, for example, is likely to be a basic feature of the face, because it is a part of the face newborns fixate, and a part that, based on their Contrast Sensitivity Function (CSF), should be easily visible (e.g., Maurer, 1985). In accordance with that, our results suggest that the preference for a facelike arrangement of the internal blobs may be contingent on the presence of a contour. Interestingly, it would seem that a square contour, not just a head-shaped contour, is sufficient to produce the preference for the facelike arrangement of the internal blobs.

In conclusion, the empirical evidence is in favor of the innateness criterion, which was proposed by Morton and Johnson (1989) as the main criterion for maintaining that face processing is a special function that is based on the activity of a separate system. This is because there can be little doubt, on the basis of our results, that newborns possess a mechanism that is specialized for processing the structural configuration of a face.

Johnson and Morton (1991; Morton & Johnson, 1991) also proposed that this mechanism, which they termed Conspec, is located in the superior colliculus. One of the experiments we conducted demonstrated that in newborns the preference for facelike patterns is strongly temporal–nasal asymmetric. That is to say, facelike patterns were more efficient than non-facelike patterns in summoning the newborn's gaze in the temporal hemifield but not in the nasal hemifield. If the temporal–nasal hemifield asymmetry is a marker of the activity of the retinotectal pathway (Johnson, 1990; Rafal et al., 1991), it can be inferred that in newborns the retinotectal pathway, and thus the superior colliculus, has the main role in controlling orienting to facelike patterns.

However, the claim that in newborns preferential orienting to faces is *exclusively* mediated by subcortical structures would be questionable for a number of reasons.

There appears to be evidence that newborns have cortical visual functions, albeit immature (e.g., Atkinson, Hood, Wattam-Bell, Anker, & Tricklebank, 1988; Slater, Morison, & Somers, 1988). There is no neurophysiological evidence to substantiate the notion that, in adult primates, collicular mechanisms in isolation are capable of processing configurational stimuli, such as facelike patterns (e.g., Schiller, 1985). Rather, the role of the colliculus may be limited to simple detection and orienting. In addition, it seems likely that, in adult primates, cortical mechanisms play a major role in integrating collicular functions (e.g., Stein & Meredith, 1994).

Finally, we found that face preference at birth was mainly indexed by dependent variables that implicate cortical mechanisms (i.e., total fixation time, duration of the first fixation, and duration of the longest fixation).

In the adult, spatial orienting depends on the posterior attentional system, which comprises the superior colliculus and the parietal cortex (e.g., Posner & Dehaene, 1994). The parietal cortex belongs to the dorsal stream, which processes spatial and pattern information for visually guided actions directed at objects (e.g., Goodale & Milner, 1992). Perhaps, the mechanism that governs orienting to faces in newborns (i.e., Conspec) depends on the combined functions of the superior colliculus and the parietal cortex. In contrast, Conlern, which matures much later, might depend on the functions of the ventral stream, which comprises the temporal cortex, and, in the adult, is devoted to perceptual identification of objects (Goodale & Milner, 1992).

AKNOWLEDGEMENTS

We thank Dr. Beatrice Dalla Barba, Ornella Crema and the nursing staff at the Pediatric Clinic of the University of Padua for their invaluable collaboration, and Sandro Bettella for writing the software. The experiments reported in the paper were supported by grants from MURST and CNR to F. Simion and C. Umiltà.

REFERENCES

Atkinson, J., Hood, B., Wattam-Bell, J., Anker, S., & Tricklebank, J. (1988). Development of orientation discrimination in infancy. *Perception, 17*, 587–595.

Banks, M.S., & Salapatek, P. (1981). Infant pattern vision: a new approach based on the contrast sensitivity function. *Journal of Experimental Child Psychology, 31*, 1–45.

Banks, M.S., & Ginsburg, A.P. (1985). Early visual preferences: a review and new theoretical treatment. In H.W. Reese (Ed.), *Advances in Child Development and Behavior* (Vol. 19), New York: Academic Press.

Bruce, V., & Young A. (1986). Understanding face recognition. *British Journal of Psychology, 77*, 305–327.

Burton, A.M., Bruce, V., & Johnston, R.A. (1990). Understanding face recognition with an interactive activation model. *British Journal of Psychology, 81*, 361–380.

Damasio, A.R., Damasio, H., & Van Hoesen, G.W. (1982). Prosopagnosia: anatomical basis and behavioral mechanism. *Neurology, 32*, 331–341.

de Renzi, E. (1982). *Disorders of space exploration and cognition.* Chichester: Wiley.

de Renzi, E. (1986). Current issues in prosopagnosia. In H.D. Ellis, M.A. Jeeves, F. Newcombe, & A.W.Young (Eds.) *Aspects of Face Processing.* Dordrecht: Martinus Nijhoff.

de Renzi, E., Faglioni, P., Grossi, D., & Nichelli, P. (1991). Apperceptive and associative forms of prosopagnosia. *Cortex, 27*, 213–221.

Diamond, R., & Carey, S. (1986). Why faces are and are not special: an effect of expertise. *Journal of Experimental Psychology: General, 115*, 107–117.

Ellis, H.D., & Young, A.W. (1989). Are faces special? In A.W. Young & H.D. Ellis (Eds.), *Handbook of Research on Face Processing.* Amsterdam: North Holland.

Ellis, H.D., Young, A.W., & Hay, D.C. (1987). Modelling the recognition of faces and words. In P.E. Morris (Ed.), *Modelling Cognition.* Chichester: Wiley.

Fodor, J.A. (1983). *The Modularity of Mind.* Cambridge, Mass: MIT Press.

Goodale, M. A., & Milner, A. D. (1992). Separate pathways for perception and action. *Trends in Neurosciences, 15*, 20–25.

Goren, C.C., Sarty, M., & Wu, P.J.K. (1975). Visual following and pattern discrimination of face-like stimuli by newborn infants. *Pediatrics, 56*, 544–549.

Gross, C.G., Rocha-Miranda, C.E., & Bender, D. B. (1972). Visual properties of neurons in inferotemporal cortex of the macaque. *Journal of Neurophysiology, 35*, 96–111.

Gross, C.G., & Sergent, J. (1992). Face recognition. *Current Opinion in Neurobiology, 2*, 156–161.

Haaf, R.A., & Bell, R.Q. (1967). A facial dimension in visual discrimination by human infants. *Child Development, 38*, 893–901.

Hay, D.C., & Young, A.W. (1982). The human face. In A.W. Ellis (Ed.), *Normality and Pathology in Cognitive Functions*, New York: Academic Press.

Hershenson, M., Kessen, W., & Munsinger, H. (1967). Pattern perception in the human newborn: a close look at some positive and negative results. In W. Wathen-Dunn (Ed.), *Models for the Perception of Speech and Visual Form.* Cambridge, Mass.: MIT Press.

Humphreys, G.W., & Bruce, V.(1989). *Visual Cognition*. Hillsdale, NJ: Erlbaum.

Johnson, M.H. (1990). Cortical maturation and the development of visual attention in early infancy. *Journal of Cognitive Neuroscience, 2*, 81–95.

Johnson, M.H., & Morton, J. (1991). *Biology and Cognitive Development: The Case of Face Recognition*, Oxford: Blackwell.

Johnson, M.H., Dziurawiec, S., Ellis, H., & Morton, J. (1991). Newborns' preferential tracking of face-like stimuli and its subsequent decline. *Cognition, 40*, 1–19.

Kleiner, K.A. (1987). Amplitude and phase spectra as indices of infants' pattern preferences. *Infant Behavior and Development, 10*, 49–59.

Kleiner, K. (1990). Models of neonates' preferences for facelike patterns: a response to Morton, Johnson, and Maurer. *Infant Behavior and Development, 13*, 105–108.

Kleiner, K. (1993). Specific versus non-specific face recognition device. In B. de Boysson-Bardies, S. de Schonen, P. Jusczyk, P. McNeilage & J. Morton (Eds.), *Developmental Neurocognition: Speech and Face Processing in the First Year of Life*. New York: Academic Press.

Kleiner, K., & Banks, M. (1987). Stimulus energy does not account for 2-months-olds' infants face preferences. *Journal of Experimental Psychology: Human Perception and Performance, 13*, 594–600.

Maurer, D. (1985). Infants' perception of facedness. In T.N. Field & N. Fox (Eds.), *Social Perception in Infants*. Norwood, NJ: Ablex.

Maurer, D., & Young, R. (1983). Newborn's following of natural and distorted arrangements of facial features. *Infant Behavior and Development, 6*, 127–131.

Morton, J., & Johnson, M.H. (1989). Four ways for faces to be special. In A.W. Young & H.D. Ellis (Eds.), *Handbook of Research on Face Processing*. Amsterdam: North Holland.

Morton, J., & Johnson, M.H. (1991). Conspec and Conlern: a two-process theory of infant face recognition. *Psychological Review, 98*, 164–181.

Perrett, D.I., Mistlin, A.J., Potter, D.D., Smith, P.A.J., Head, A.S., Chitty, A.J., Broennimann, R., Milner, A.D., & Jeeves, M.A. (1986). Functional organization of visual neurons processing face identity. In H.D. Ellis & M.A. Jeeves, F. Newcombe & A.W. Young (Eds.), *Aspects of Face Processing*. Dordrecht: Martinus Nijhoff.

Perrett, D.I., Mistlin, A.J., & Chitty, A.J. (1987). Visual neurones responsive to faces. *Trends in Neurosciences, 10*, 358–364.

Posner, M.I., & Dehaene S. (1994). Attentional networks. *Trends in Neurosciences, 17*, 75–79.

Rafal, R.D., Henick, A., & Smith, J. (1991). Extrageniculate contribution to reflex visual orienting in normal humans: a temporal hemifield advantage. *Journal of Cognitive Neuroscience, 3*, 351–358.

Rhodes, G. (1985). Lateralized process in face recognition. *British Journal of Psychology, 76*, 249–271.

Scapinello, K.I., & Yarmey, A.D. (1970). The role of familiarity and orientation in immediate and delayed recognition of pictorial stimuli. *Psychonomic Science, 21*, 329–330.

Schiller, P.H. (1985). A model for the generation of visually guided saccadic eye movements. In D. Rose & V.G. Dobson (Eds.), *Models of the visual cortex*. Chichester: Wiley.

Sergent, J. (1989). Structural processing of faces. In A.W. Young & H.D. Ellis (Eds.), *Handbook of Research on Face Processing*. Amsterdam: North Holland.

Simion, F., Valenza, E., Umiltà, C., & Dalla Barba, B. (1995). Inhibition of return in newborns is temporal–nasal asymmetrical. *Infant Behavior and Development, 18*, 189–194.

Simion, F., Valenza, E., Umiltà, C., & Dalla Barba, B. (in press). Preferential orienting to faces in newborns: a temporal–nasal asymmetry. *Journal of Experimental Psychology* (Human Perception and Performance).

Slater, A. (1993). Visual perceptual abilities at birth: implications for face perception. In B. de Boysson-Bardies et al. (Eds.), *Developmental Neurocognition: Speech and Face Processing in the First Year of Life*. New York: Academic Press.

Slater, A.M., Earle, D.C., Morison, V., & Rose, D. (1985). Pattern preferences at birth and their interaction with habituation induced novelty preferences. *Journal of Experimental Child Psychology*, *39*, 37–54.

Slater, A., Morison, V., & Somers, M. (1988). Orientation discrimination and cortical function in the human newborn. *Perception, 17*, 596–602.

Stein, B.E., & Meredith, M.A. (1994). *The merging of the senses*. Cambridge, Mass: MIT Press.

Valenza, E., Simion, F., Macchi Cassia, V., & Umiltà, C. (1996). Face preference at birth. *Journal of Experimental Psychology: Human Perception and Performance, 27*, 892–903.

Yin, R.H. (1969). Looking at upside-down faces. *Journal of Experimental Psychology, 81*, 141–145.

Yin, R.H. (1978). The parietal lobe and visual attention. *Journal of Psychiatric Research, 14*, 261–266.

CHAPTER SIX

About Functional Cortical Specialization: The Development of Face Recognition

Scania de Schonen, J. Mancini and Frederique Liegeois
Center for Research in Cognitive Neuroscience,
CNRS, Marseille, France

INTRODUCTION

Studying the relationship between the development of the brain and the emergence (or decline) of specific cognitive abilities is a useful way of approaching the links between brain and behaviour, in addition to what is being done in fields of investigation such as human adult neuropsychology and animal neurobiology. Anything that can be learned about how a competence functions in the early stages of its development will tell us something about how it will be organized in later life. A model for the way in which a competence works in adulthood would not be valid if it did not fit in with what is known about how that competence develops.

How does the brain manage during its postnatal maturation to sort out its surroundings into relevant categories of objects and events and to build up appropriate representations in such a way that even children living in quite different environments all seem to sort out the same categories of objects and events at approximately the same stage of infancy? What constraints having to do with the organization and functioning of the brain, and what constraints arising from the environment may interact so consistently that they shape the learning processes of all the members of the species (and possibly those of some other species) on the same lines, and so that the adult competences which eventually emerge are all organized in a very similar way?

This debate has been going on for a long time, but there are still so few relevant empirical data available that all we have at the moment are a few scenarios, the plausibility of which varies depending on the kind of cognitive competences under investigation.

The latest neuropsychological data argue in favour of the idea that some regions of the adult human brain may play a crucial role in the processing of specific classes of events. Some patients with brain damage, for instance, are able to recognize objects and to learn to recognize new items belonging to a known class of objects, but have irretrievably lost the ability to recognize familiar faces and to familiarize themselves with new faces. Others no longer recognize familiar faces but are able to recognize emotional expressions. It is therefore possible in adults for a brain lesion to wipe out a specific competence of one kind while sparing another competence which at some neural integrative level basically involves the same type of perceptual processing. On the other hand, some interindividual consistency can be said to exist as regards the location of the groups of neuronal networks involved in a given competence. Cortical lesions associated with prosopagnosia are localized in cortical regions where neural activation has been observed when famous faces are presented to normal subjects. How might this coarse localization possibly develop? How far can we assimilate localization and specialization?

Among the mechanisms possibly responsible for the coarse specialization of some cortical neural networks, it is worth mentioning the chain of events in the maturation of the brain, the differential timing of the development of various cortical networks, that of their inputs and their outputs, the selectivity of the connections resulting from the maturational patterns and the filtering effected on the inputs and outputs at various points in any given network during pre- and postnatal life. This is to say that the organizational constraints which, along with other factors, shape the patterns of neuronal connectivity during maturation might be sufficiently strong to push some groups of networks into one kind of processing function rather than another, and in this way, can be said to possibly determine what their function will be.

This idea is not incompatible with distributed processing if one takes this *a priori* kind of network specialization to be quite a rough process and the information to be distributed not over the whole cortex but just onto some small parts, due to limiting factors which are none other than the constraints operating during maturation about which we have just been speaking.

In this context, interindividual differences may be due either to timing discrepancies between the biological signals involved in building up the brain during pre- and postnatal life, or to systematic factors such as the effects of the sex hormones on the cortical tissues at some stages in the maturation process. These factors do not exclude the role of factors such as environmental events and the individual's own past history.

There is obviously no single, straightforward answer to the question as to whether or not there exists a system specializing in one specific competence, such as face processing. The data available so far on the network localizations, the dissociations between post-lesion deficits, and the post-lesion neuronal plasticity, all argue against the idea of a hard-and-fast system of cortical functional specialization.

One possible approach to this question consists of examining how competences which have been studied in adults develop, with a view to determining what factors are involved in building up the eventual adult picture as far as the functional specificities are concerned. What relationships may exist between the events in the postnatal maturation of the neuronal networks involved in a given adult competence on the one hand, and the development of the behaviour corresponding to this competence on the other hand? When and how is such and such a group of networks allotted to such and such a function, and up to when might they still be allotted to some other function, and so on? We have been asking questions of this kind about the development of face recognition in human infants. Faces are interesting objects to study, first because we know the exact date at which the ability to see shapes begins, namely at birth. Secondly, these complex biological objects play many social and cognitive roles in human societies. Lastly, a large body of data is available on the processing of faces and their recognition in adults.

Newborn infants' visual attention is spontaneously attracted towards a face-like pattern (Goren, Sarty & Wu, 1975; Johnson, Dziurawiec, Ellis & Morton, 1991; Johnson & Morton, 1991). The mechanism, possibly subcortical, underlying this attraction constitutes one of the earliest attentional constraints shaping the perceptual processes. An infant's gaze is attracted by faces for slightly longer periods than it is by other objects. Since infants' vision is not yet very keen, faces can be seen only under some conditions. They must for instance be quite near the subject (within a range of about 25cm). Now it so happens that people looking after infants tend to be at about this distance, when they turn their faces towards an infant and speak to him/her, which presumably reinforces the attraction exerted by the target face. In addition, infants as soon as they are born are known to react by turning their visual attention towards any source of noise. The conditions are therefore all highly favourable for infants to acquire a representation of faces. What information are they capable of processing so early in life? To what extent does their system of processing resemble that of adults?

PROCESSING AND MEMORIZING PATTERNS

Since an infant's gaze is attracted by the internal configuration consisting of the features of a face-like pattern, the question arises as to whether this mechanism might also serve to draw attention to the differences between two particular physiognomical configurations (between the mother's face and that of a stranger, for example). This question may seem perfectly absurd if one considers that the visual cortex is not even ready to function during the first few weeks of life (for a review, see Atkinson, 1984; Bronson, 1974, 1982; Johnson, 1990). The possibility cannot be ruled out, however, that some cortical networks may be functional at birth (Atkinson, Hood, Wattam-Bell, Anker & Tricklebank, 1988; Lewis, Maurer & Blackburn, 1985; Maurer & Lewis, 1979) or in the subsequent hours.

Are infants able to memorize visual episodes? The authors of three different studies have established that newborn infants can in fact learn something about individual faces, since, when confronted with their mother's and a stranger's face, they will preferentially look at the mother's face although all auditory, tactile and kinesthetic, temperature and olfactory information has been abolished and the two faces, placed side by side, remain quite motionless and expressionless (Bushnell, Sai & Mullin, 1989; Pascalis, de Schonen, Morton, Deruelle & Fabre-Grenet, 1995; Walton, Bower & Bower, 1992).

As early as a few days after birth, a memory can be said to exist for recognizing visual episodes; these episodes are recognized even when presented out of their usual context, since none of the information generally correlated with the arrival of the mother's head and face within an infant's visual field was present in the situation tested. Moreover a 4-day-old infant will still recognize her/his mother two or three minutes after seeing her (Bushnell et al., 1989, Pascalis et al., 1995; longer retention times were not tested). Likewise, a 4-day-old infant who has become familiarized with the photograph of a face will still recognize this face after an interval of two minutes when tested for visual preference between this photograph and that of another face (Pascalis & de Schonen, 1994). Now, amnesic patients no longer recognize a face or an object they have been shown when tested with a visual preference technique after an interval of only a few seconds (McKee & Squire, 1993). It can therefore be concluded that in addition to the habituation and operant conditioning memory, newborns are capable of memorizing visual episodes in some way, and thus of setting up a data base which might serve to shape the developing information processing system. This depends, however, on what kind of information the infant is able to encode about a face.

Might the mechanism whereby newborns distinguish between a facelike and a non-facelike configuration also serve to draw their visual attention towards the particular configuration of a given face, and thus shape the developing face-processing system? Newly born infants do not in fact seem to acquire sufficient information about a face as such when they are looking at one. We have investigated what information newborns actually process and encode when they recognize their mother's face (Pascalis et al., 1995). For this purpose, we changed the outer contour of the hair and the line separating the hair from the forehead by giving the mother and the stranger pale-coloured scarves to wear. If a newborn had learned the configuration of the mother's features (i.e. her actual physiognomy) he or she would presumably still show a preference for the mother's face versus that of a stranger. In this case, however, no preference was found to exist for either face. Newborns therefore seem to learn more about the shape of a head and that of the hairline than about the internal configuration consisting of the facial features. In this, they proceed in the same way as a prosopagnosic patient who has said that he recognizes people from the shape of their hair and their hairline (Davidoff, Matthews & Newcombe, 1986). It has furthermore been established in several studies that in healthy adults, the internal configuration is necessary to be able to recognize familiar faces, whereas when dealing with unfamiliar faces, the head contour is used as a cue in just the same way as the internal configuration formed by the features (Ellis, Sheperd & Davies, 1979; Endo, Takahashi & Maruyama, 1984; de Haan & Hay, 1986).

The fact that infants seem to discriminate between two individual faces on the basis of their outer contour and hairline during the first few weeks of life might of course be attributable to their poor visual acuity at this age. When photographs are filtered to remove the high and medium spatial frequencies, it is observed that it is still possible to learn to recognize these blurred faces and to distinguish between individuals on the basis of the inner configuration. In any case, individual face recognition during the first week of life does not involve processing the internal configuration of the facial features. Three studies have demonstrated, however, that a processing of this kind does take place between the end of the second month and the fourth month of life. Around the age of 6 to 8 weeks, an infant is able to recognize his or her mother's face, even when the mother and the stranger whose face is concomitantly presented are both wearing scarves (Bartrip, Morton & de Schonen, submitted). The face of the mother with her hair covered is recognized on a photograph and discriminated from that of a stranger at the age of 4 to 5 months, even with durations of presentation as short as 300 to 350msec (de Schonen, Gil de Diaz & Mathivet, 1986). Lastly, at the age of three months, after becoming familiarized with a face wearing a scarf which is presented successively from various angles, infants become able to recognize this face when it is presented from a new angle a few seconds and up to 24 hours later (Pascalis, de Haan, Nelson & de Schonen, in press).

In short, there seems to exist at birth one system which directs infants' visual attention slightly more frequently towards faces than towards other objects, and another system with which it is possible to learn visual patterns and in particular, to recognize a head but not a face (Pascalis et al., 1995); a few weeks later, either this second system becomes able to process physiognomies or a third system emerges (de Schonen & Mathivet, 1989). It is not possible to state as yet whether or not this later ability requires the other two to be functional, whether it derives from the second one, or whether it is simply a newly maturing, separate system and whether the first system, defined and called "Conspec" by Johnson and Morton (1991) acts only by orienting the infant's visual behaviour or also by some direct neural projections onto the cortex.

The system which serves to recognize a head might imaginably be the same system as that which enables newborns during the first week of life to learn visual patterns of any other kind (Slater, 1993). It is worth noting however that a newborn infant presented with a simple visual pattern with which he or she has been familiarized up to a given habituation criterion and with a new pattern will show a visual preference for the new pattern versus the familiar one (Slater, 1993). The visual preference found to exist for the mother's face (the familiar stimulus) might therefore seem to indicate the existence of a system dealing specifically with faces in general, or else it might have to do with the mother's special status and with the reinforcing context within which a newborn infant learns to recognize this particular face. Pascalis and de Schonen (1994) have observed, however, that once a 3-day-old infant has been familiarized with a frontal view of a woman's head and face, he or she will show a visual preference for a photograph of a novel face rather than for the familiarized face. When the head and face on the photograph are not those of the mother, newborns therefore react in the same way as they do towards simple patterns : they prefer novelty to familiarity. Their preference for the familiar head and face when they are those of the mother is therefore not based on a system dealing specifically with the learning of objects belonging to the "head and face" category. The reason why preference was given to the familiar stimulus in this case probably related more specifically to the circumstances under which this stimulus is generally learned than to the category of faces as such.

PROCESSING AND MEMORIZING INDIVIDUAL PHYSIOGNOMIES: THE EMERGENCE OF A SPECIALIZATION?

As mentioned above, the ability to process individual faces may emerge towards the end of the second month of life. Johnson and Morton (1991) and Morton and Johnson (1991) have put forward some convincing arguments in favour of the idea that an important change in the control of face processing occurs at the end of the second month. There exist some further arguments which are worth mentioning. The memory performances of 4-day-old newborns at recognizing a photograph of a head and face they were shown two minutes previously (Pascalis & de Schonen, 1994) becomes more difficult to demonstrate at the age of two months (Pascalis, unpublished data), but were recovered at three months (Pascalis et al., in press). On the other hand, the mode of visual face processing seems to change, since as we saw earlier, it is possible by this age to recognize a face even when the hairline and hairstyle are masked (Morton, 1993; Pascalis et al., 1995). In addition, infants at the age of three months become able to build up a single representation of a face from several views taken from different angles (Pascalis et al, in press). All these findings suggest that the face-processing ability undergoes a far-reaching change towards the end of the second month.

Morover, some of the anatomo-functional characteristics of adult face recognition have been found to exist by the age of 4 to 5 months (it has not yet been established whether or not they are already present at 3 months). The right hemisphere was distinctly better or faster than the left at recognizing a familiar face and discriminating between it and another face at about the age of 4–5 months (de Schonen & Mathivet, 1990). This right hemisphere advantage is all the more noteworthy in that it seems to be impossible for any information liable to facilitate recognizing and discriminating between two faces or two patterns to be transferred from the right hemisphere to the left (Deruelle & de Schonen, 1991; de Schonen

& Mathivet, 1990) until the age of 24–26 months (Liegeois & de Schonen, 1997). As soon as the ability develops to process the relevant physiognomical information among the various kinds provided by faces, an anatomo-functional feature present in adults—namely the right hemisphere advantage—can therefore be said to exist.

THE RIGHT HEMISPHERE ADVANTAGE AND THE VARIOUS MODES OF PROCESSING

In infants, as in adults, the left hemisphere is not completely incapable of encoding any information which can be used to distinguish and recognize physiognomies: but the information processed by the left hemisphere is not the same as that processed by the right for this purpose (Deruelle & de Schonen, 1991b; Deruelle & de Schonen, 1995; Deruelle & de Schonen, in press), and the information processed by the left hemisphere seems to be relevant to face recognition only under some conditions. The right hemisphere was found to be capable, for instance, of distinguishing and recognizing each of two faces which differed only in the size of the eyes or the orientation of the long axis of the eyes, but not in the shape of the eyes. When the two faces differed, however, only in the shape of their eyes and eyebrows while the length of the long axis and the orientation of the eyes were the same in both photographs, the right hemisphere was unable to learn to discriminate them, whereas the left hemisphere did so without any difficulty. The results of several studies have shown that there also exist interhemispheric differences of this kind in adults (Hillger & Koenig, 1991).

The finding that the right hemisphere advantage for face processing begins to emerge at the early age of 4 to 5 months and already shows some of the characteristics of adults' processing performances does not necessarily mean that the right hemisphere is equipped with a specific face-processing system. As a matter of fact, the difference between the kinds of information processed by the two hemispheres does not apply only to faces, but has also been pointed out in the case of geometrical pattern processing (Deruelle & de Schonen, 1991, 1995). The fact that the right hemisphere has a face-processing advantage might be due not so much to the existence of a specific face-processing system at an early stage of development, as to the information processed by the right hemisphere being particularly suitable (configural information) for representing and recognizing objects with properties as complex as those of individual human faces. The information processed by the left hemisphere (local information) may perhaps be invariant throughout a smaller number of transformations, or possibly ones of a different kind, but may more efficiently show up small local changes in patterns, such as the changes in the shape of the mouth which occur when a face is speaking (Campbell, Landis & Regard, 1986).

What can be said quite definitely is that the two hemispheres do not each extract the same information from the environment, or rather that they do not both put together in the same way the elementary information extracted by the low level processing systems. These hemispheric characteristics are obviously not imposed by the external environment. Nor do they result from the acquisition of writing, as some authors have suggested (Posner & Petersen, 1990; Rothbart, Posner & Boylan, 1990). They take shape because of the way in which the neuronal networks are organized, and not because of any direct environmental factors. We do not know yet what neuronal particularity may be responsible for these differences. Might they result from the differential timing of maturational events, and hence in particular from maturational lags between homologous cortical regions of the two hemispheres? Time lags of this kind might give rise for example to differences between the sizes of the receptor fields of the cells involved in the high-level processing of visual information.

SOME CONVERGENT FACTORS

We previously published a scenario (de Schonen and Mathivet, 1989) describing the events possibly leading to the development of the right hemispheric advantage for face recognition, which ran roughly as follows :

1. The associative cortical regions (those located in the temporal cortex) which receive the information about faces, objects and patterns might become functional at an earlier age in the right hemisphere than in the left counterparts (for a discussion, see de Schonen, 1989; de Schonen et al., 1993; de Schonen & Mathivet, 1989; Turkewitz, 1989, 1993).
2. When these regions become functional (at the age of about two months see next section), they receive visual information which is conveyed mainly by the low spatial frequency channels (Atkinson & Braddick, 1989; Banks & Dannemiller, 1987; Banks, Stephens & Hartmann, 1985).
3. The networks that receive the information sufficient for face processing (but not necessarily specialized in this task) may therefore first start doing so in the right hemisphere, mainly on the basis of low spatial frequency information.
4. Since we now know that the right hemisphere processes configural aspects, we can add that recognizing an object as complex as a face on the basis of low spatial frequencies alone might be possible only if the configuration (the spatial arrangement of the features, the orientation of their axis, the relative distances between them) of the physiognomy in question is encoded. Only configurations of this kind could be recognized from one presentation to another, whereas more local aspects such as the shape of a feature might be difficult to compare and might be wrongly encoded as differing from one presentation to another. Hughes, Fendrich and Reuter-Lorenz (1990) have observed that in adults, the priority given to global patterns (such as the global outer contour in their study)

in the processing of geometrical stimuli disappears when the low spatial frequencies are abolished.

5. By the time the corresponding parts of the left hemisphere have become functionally mature (during the second month of life), it may have become possible to process high spatial frequencies. The left brain regions might therefore begin by processing a wider range of frequencies than the right hemisphere began with. Since the patterns of connectivity will not be the same as those which were set up when these regions became functional in the right hemisphere, it is most unlikely that the structures on the left will carry out the same kind of processing as those on the right. It might therefore perform other kinds of processing. Even if the right hemisphere then begins to develop a face-processing system able to integrate high spatial frequencies, the previously established system will already have become stabilized.

Contrary to what was observed by Atkinson and Braddick (1989), and by Banks and Dannemiller (1987), Suter, Suter, Roessler, Parker, Armstrong and Powers (1994) have reported on the basis of evoked potential recordings that at the age of three weeks, the spatial frequency filtering system is qualitatively just as efficient as that of adults. It is nevertheless perfectly plausible that the maturational lag between the two systems we mentioned above might not involve the primary visual cortex, but might occur at some higher integrative level. This would help to understand the difference between the results of studies focusing on visual attention to patterns and those based on evoked potential recordings; the latter might require a lower level of integration than that involved in visual preference responses. This is in line with studies on adult performances (Christman, Kitterle & Hellige, 1991; Kitterle, Christman & Hellige, 1990; Kitterle & Selig, 1991; Sergent, 1983, 1985, 1987, 1989). It is also possible that visual limitations other than those attaching to spatial frequencies, such as contrast sensitivity, or sensitivity to spatio-temporal frequencies (Rebai, Bagot & Viggiani, 1994), might come into play.

EARLY REGIONAL SPECIALIZATION VERSUS OVERALL DIFFUSION OF SIGNALS AND PROCESSING SYSTEMS

We have established that by the age of 4 to 5 months, the face-recognition ability and some pattern-processing modes have already become lateralized, exactly as in adults. Within a single hemisphere, however, face processing may be taking place even during the first few months of life, either in networks occupying small areas which are identical to those which have been exactly mapped in adults, or in more widespread networks which might later on be gradually reduced either as the result of factors responsible for selecting the synaptic components (Changeux & Dehaenne, 1989) or as the result of neural factors related to learning processes. A positron emission tomography (PET scan) study was carried out using H2 015 as marker on two-month-old infants born with neurological deficits, with a view to developing a system of diagnosis and prognosis which would make it possible to apply suitable aid and rehabilitation procedures at an early age, before the onset of the behavioural signs (Tzourio, de Schonen, Mazoyer, Boré, Pietrzyk, Bruck, Aujard & Deruelle, 1992). These infants were no longer under medication at the time of the study and the neurological signs were mild at that time. The regional patterns of brain activation were compared in two situations. The first (control) situation involved a visual stimulus consisting of a small circular set of red and green diodes which lit up alternately, giving the impression of circular motion at a variable speed. In the second situation, some women's faces photographed frontally with neutral expressions (and wearing a scarf) were presented for 4 seconds each.

At the age of two months, the density of the synapses in the human cortex is increasing rapidly (Huttenlocher, 1993), the presentation of a ring of diodes and that of human faces might seem unlikely to give rise to any regional differences in the metabolic activity occurring in the associative cortex, nor might a visual stimulus such as a face seem likely to trigger anything other than a diffuse increase in the overall synaptic activity. Some authors have actually suggested that the intermodal responses recorded during the first few months of life might be due to some hyperconnectivity of the neuronal networks rather than to an intermodal processing properly speaking (Maurer, 1993).

In the first place, the results of our PET scan study showed the occurrence of a level of metabolic activity in the various cortices which was in line with that observed by Chugani and Phelps (1986) using a different marker, fluorine-18 labelled deoxyglucose (18 FDG). The latter authors established that between birth and the age of three months, the most active part of the cortex is the sensorimotor region; at the age of three months the overall activity in the occipital, temporal and parietal cortex increases, while the activity in the frontal cortex increases significantly at only about the age of 8 months. In our own study, the overall level of activity was found to be higher in the sensorimotor cortex than in the occipital, temporal and parietal cortices, and lower in the frontal cortex.

Despite these differences in the degree of maturation of the metabolic activity between the various regions and the fact that the level of activity is lower in the associative cortices, some regional activations were found to occur in associative cortices when faces were presented. Compared (by subtraction) to what occurred with the rotating circle of diodes, the face stimuli triggered an increase in the metabolic activity in some parts of the associative cortex only and no differences between the two situations could be detected in the primary visual cortex. The pattern of metabolic activity observed has some features in common with that recorded in adults in similar situations, but some differences are nevertheless present. In our study, the level of activity recorded in response to the faces (minus circle) was enhanced bilaterally in the superior and middle temporal gyrus, but not in the parietal cortex. A significant increase in the metabolic activity was also observed in the left orbito-frontal cortex and in the left Broca area. With a task involving attention to geometrical patterns, Corbetta, Miezin, Dobmeyer, Shulman and Petersen (1990) also observed in adults a bilateral increase in the metabolic activity recorded in the superior and middle temporal gyrus; the activity was also found to increase in the inferior and medial temporal cortex (an area which is known to be damaged in prosopagnosic patients) but since the data on these parts of the temporal cortex have not yet been analysed in our study, comparisons cannot be made in this respect. Likewise, posterior temporo-occipital activity was also triggered on the external surface in adults performing an unknown face comparison task, although the regions involved in adults were probably more posterior than in the infants we studied (Haxby, Grady, Horwitz, Ungerleider, Mishkin, Carson, Herscovitch, Schapiro & Rapoport, 1991). Magneto-encephalography (MEG) recordings obtained on adults presented with unknown faces showed that the activity was focused in the superior and middle temporal gyrus and at the occipito-temporal junction (Lu, Hämäläinen, Hari, Ilmoniemi, Lounasamaa, Sams, Vilkman, 1991). The temporal activity was significantly higher when faces were presented than when animals were presented.

The infant pattern can be said to fit the adult one in that the lateral temporal cortical regions found to be activated are also activated in adults presented with tasks involving attention to geometric shapes or unknown faces. The fact that the temporal cortex was activated but not the parietal cortex is perfectly in keeping with the fact that the visually perceived objects (faces) used as stimuli underwent a change of shape (the What pathway) but not of location (the Where pathway).

In another study, Sergent et al. (1992) recorded a pattern of activation occurring mainly in the medial parts of the temporal lobes and in the temporal poles during the performance of a recognition task where the subjects had to say which of the famous faces presented were those of actors. The data obtained in this situation and the control situation used (discriminating between the male and female faces) are obviously difficult to compare with the situations we used on our two-month-old subjects. It is worth noting in any case that the activation recorded in the left orbito-frontal cortex in response to the presentation of faces to infants occurred also in the study by Sergent et al. (1992) on adults both when recognizing famous faces and when categorizing objects. Despite the immaturity of the frontal cortex at the age of two months, activity associated with face presentation but not with a rotating circle was observed in this region. Now the increase in the metabolic activity occurring in Broca's region at the age of two months apparently has no equivalent in adults, and was not associated in infants with vocalization or buccal and/or laryngeal activity.

With both kinds of stimuli (circle and faces), the patterns of activity recorded in the two hemispheres were asymmetrical: there was more activity in the right lateral temporal and infero-frontal (homologous to Broca area) cortices than in the corresponding left hemispheric regions. One of the several possible explanations for this asymmetric pattern is that the rates of maturation of the associative cortices involved in visual activities may possibly differ between the two hemispheres (as predicted in our previous scenario, de Schonen & Mathivet, 1989; see earlier discussion; see also Scheibel, 1993).

At an age when the processing of information about faces is undergoing changes in infants, and when the cortical synaptogenesis is in its increasing phase, local patterns of activity occur which suggest that at this stage in development, the cortical maturation process does not encompass one large cortical region after another, but rather one group of networks after another, according to a scheme where the emphasis is a more functional one, as if cortical maturation proceeds by successive waves. Once again we are faced here with a set of data which argue both in favour of some progressive regional specialization, and against the idea that this regional specialization is likely to be strictly implemented.

The above findings are not incompatible with the idea that the organization of the cortical connectivity may first depend on factors other than experience, and that the subject's experience within the constraints previously set up (special linkages, maturational lags, etc.), might subsequently determine other aspects of the cortical functional scheme. It is therefore likely that experience interacts with inner developmental brain mechanisms, and therefore contributes to shape the effects of the successive waves of brain maturation that occur during infancy, childhood and adolescence.

REGULAR DAILY EXPOSURE TO FACES DOES NOT SUFFICE TO ACCOUNT FOR FACE-PROCESSING DEVELOPMENT

The possibility that early constraints on the neuronal organization of the asso-ciative cortices would no doubt explain why there is not much post-lesion func-tional plasticity as far as face and complex pattern processing is concerned. After unilateral perinatal brain lesions or malformation, the intact hemisphere might be expected to develop normal face-processing abilities. Since face pro-cessing develops at a very early age, this ability might call on neuronal resources which are reputedly still plastic during the whole first year of life; and face processing involves environmental stimuli of a kind which are present in abundance in the course of everyday life. It was established, however, in a study where various face recognition and pairing tasks were performed on faces, emotional expressions, lip gestures, etc., that children aged 6 to 12 years with perinatal brain damage had great difficulty in processing some of the information provided by faces, even though some of these children were under-going normal schooling and all of them were able to read (and therefore to process shapes of some kinds) (Mancini, de Schonen, Deruelle & Massoulier, 1994). Recent (unpublished) data by the same authors have confirmed this claim (see also Stiles & Thal, 1993).

CONCLUSION

Here we addressed the question as to whether adults' face-processing abilities might not develop within a system which progressively specializes in dealing with this particular kind of information. The data available on the development of face processing show that there exist several attentional and visual information-processing systems which are not specialized in face processing as such, but which jointly handle several of the components of face processing and memorizing.

From birth to about the age of 6 weeks, an elementary attentional mechanism is at work which introduces a slight visual preference for facelike patterns viewed from the front, while memory processes begin to memorize these visual patterns regardless of the plurimodal context in which they occur and the amount of interactive communication going on. The information processed at this stage seems, however, to include only the shape of the head and hair, in which case it might in fact be independent from the mechanism attracting the attention towards faces. It is actually only at the age of about two months that individuals' physiognomies (as opposed to their heads) and their differences begin to be efficiently processed. At that time, visual attention to faces is associated with an activity in associative cortical regions that are also known to be activated in adults under similar stimulations. It has by now become generally agreed that as far as the abilities involving the use of visual information are concerned, some crucial changes take place during this period.

Between 3 and 4 months of age, infants begin to process patterns and faces on similar lines to what occurs in adults: they become able to recognize a face viewed from various angles, even after a 24-hour delay, as well as a face wearing a scarf so that only the physiognomy properly speaking is visible. They therefore begin to be able to process configural information about faces, as well as some local information, although not enough of the latter kind to be able to recognize an individual on this basis alone. As in adults, the right hemisphere picks up the configural information and has an advantage for face processing, whereas the left hemisphere deals with the local information about the components of faces. This dissociation between the local and configural processing of faces and patterns can be due only to constraints which arise because of the way in which the brain is organized. At that age, however, the system is not yet in its adult state. For instance, it is not yet possible at this stage for the information acquired by the one hemisphere about individual physiognomies (and about patterns in general) to be transmitted to the other hemisphere, as it is in adults.

These systems and the underlying constraints determining the selection and filtering of information and the characteristics of the representations which are set up all seem to contribute in turn to shaping the successive development of the various face-related abilities. There exist moreover several aspects of face processing other than those we have been discussing here, such as the processing of the meaning of emotional expressions, the relationships between a person's face and what else is known about that person (such as his or her name, voice, manner, and status in relation to the observer). The ability to organize and establish relationships between these various kinds of knowledge at a particular time no doubt results from further constraints operating on the organization of the brain. The type of activity we carry out while dealing with faces is very different from that involving objects of other kinds. The existence of these differences in themselves implies that some constraints are present which result from both early cortical organization and experience.

The idea therefore gradually emerges that one of the main factors responsible for functional specialization might be the timing of the maturation of various networks, the connectivity (and other features) of which might be approximately determined by previous constraints. A specialized function develops in stages as the various modes of processing emerge either successively or at the same time. According to this point of view, the learning processes contribute to shaping the neuronal architecture and hence to determining the cortical functions, but these processes also depend themselves on structural constraints (such as the neuronal architecture, the patterns of connectivity, the type of synaptic transmission, timing factors, etc.) as well as on the order in which groups of networks become mature. As the result of all these constraints, it becomes possible at specific moments to acquire given representations of the environment, and either temporarily or permanently impossible to acquire others. This is what we mean when talking about specialized functional systems for acquiring representations of individual faces.

We still do not know of course whether exercising the abilities we have described as being acquired during the first few weeks of life, some of which (e.g., visual attentional preference for faces) might be controlled by sub-cortical structures, is a prerequisite for the subsequent sets of competences to emerge at the ages of about six weeks and two months. This is one of the questions we are working on at present.

Adult functional models alone cannot fully account for the specificity of the brain's processing systems, since they can show us only the final picture. In order to understand developmental brain pathologies such as those resulting from accidental brain damage with a view to taking appropriate measures (rehabilitation, brain grafts or specific biochemical therapy), it is necessary in the first place to elucidate the processes involved in the growth of the brain and the emergence of its functional specificities.

ACKNOWLEDGEMENT

This paper was supported partly by Grant RG-33/95B from the Human Frontier Science Program.

REFERENCES

Atkinson, J. (1984). Human visual development over the first six months of life: A review and a hypothesis. *Human Neurobiology*, *3*, 61–74.

Atkinson, J., & Braddick, O. (1989). Development of basic visual functions. In A. Slater and G. Bremner (Eds.), *Infant Development.* Hove, UK: Lawrence Erlbaum Associates.

Atkinson, J., Hood, B., Wattam-Bell, J., Anker, S., & Tricklebank, J. (1988). Development of orientation discrimination in infancy. *Perception, 17,* 587–595.

Banks, M.S., & Dannemiller, J.L. (1987). Infant visual psychophysics. In P. Salapatek and L. Cohen (Eds.), *Handbook of infant perception* (Vol. 1, pp. 115–184). Orlando: Academic Press.

Banks, M.S., Stephens, B.R., & Hartmann, E.E. (1985). The development of basic mechanisms of pattern vision: Spatial frequency channels. *Journal of Experimental Child Psychology, 40,* 501–527.

Bartrip, J., Morton, J., & de Schonen, S. (submitted). Infants responses to mother's face.

Bronson, G.W. (1974). The postnatal growth of visual capacity. *Child Development, 45,* 873–890.

Bronson, G.W. (1982). Structure, status and characteristics of the nervous system at birth. In P. Stratton (Ed.), *Psychobiology of the Human Newborn.* Chichester: Wiley.

Bushnell, I.W.R., Sai, F., & Mullin, J.T. (1989). Neonatal recognition of the mother's face. *British Journal of Developmental Psychology, 7,* 3–15.

Campbell, R., Landis, T., & Regard, M. (1986). Face recognition and lipreading: A neurological dissociation. *Brain, 109,* 509–521.

Changeux, J.P., & Dehaenne, S. (1989). Neuronal models of cognitive functions. *Cognition 33,* 63–109.

Christman, S., Kitterle, F.L., & Hellige, J.B. (1991). Hemispheric asymmetry in the processing of absolute versus relative spatial frequency. *Brain and Cognition, 16,* 62–73.

Chugani, H.T., & Phelps, M.E. (1986). Maturational changes in cerebral function in infants determined by FDG Positron Emission Tomography. *Science, 231,* 840–842.

Corbetta, M., Miezin, F.M., Dobmeyer, S., Shulman, G.L., & Petersen, S.E. (1990). Attentional modulation of neural processing of shape, color, and velocity in humans. *Science, 248,* 1556–1559.

Davidoff, J., Matthews, W.B., & Newcombe, F. (1986). Observations on a case of prosopagnosia. In H.D. Ellis, M.A. Jeeves, F. Newcombe & A. Young (Eds.), *Aspects of face processing* (pp. 279–290). Dordrecht: Martinus Nijhoff.

de Haan, E.H.F., & Hay, D.C. (1986). The matching of famous faces, given either the internal or the external features: A study on patients with unilateral brain lesions. In H.D. Ellis, M.A. Jeeves, F. Newcombe and A. Young (Eds.), *Aspects of face processing* (pp. 302–309). Dordrecht: Martinus Nijhoff.

de Schonen, S. (1989). Some reflections on brain specialisation in faceness and physiognomy processing. In A. Young and H.D. Ellis (Eds.), *Handbook of research on face processing.* Amsterdam: North Holland, pp. 379–389.

de Schonen, S., & Bry, I. (1987). Interhemispheric communication of visual learning: A developmental study in 3–6-month-old infants. *Neuropsychologia, 25,* 601–612.

de Schonen, S., Gil de Diaz, M., & Mathivet, E. (1986). Hemispheric asymmetry in face processing in infancy. In H.D. Ellis, M.A. Jeeves, F. Newcombe & A. Young (Eds.), *Aspects of face processing.* Dordrecht: Martinus Nijhoff Publishers, pp. 199–208.

de Schonen, S., & Mathivet, E. (1989). First come first served: A scenario about development of hemispheric specialization in face recognition during infancy. *European Bulletin of Cognitive Psychology (CPC), 9,* 3–44.

de Schonen, S., & Mathivet, E. (1990). Hemispheric asymmetry in a face discrimination task in infants. *Child Development, 61,* 1192–1205.

de Schonen, S., Deruelle, C., Mancini, J., & Pascalis, O. (1993). Hemispheric differences in face processing and brain maturation. In In B. de Boysson-Bardies, S. de Schonen, P. Jusczyk, P. MacNeilage & J. Morton (Eds.), *Developmental Neurocognition: Speech and Face Processing in the First Year of Life*. Dordrecht: Kluwer, 149–163.

Deruelle, C., & de Schonen, S. (1991). Hemispheric asymmetries in visual pattern processing in infancy. *Brain and Cognition, 16*, 151–179.

Deruelle, C., & de Schonen (1995). Pattern processing in infancy: Hemispheric differences in the processing of shape and location of visual components. *Infant Behavior and Development, 18,* 123–132.

Deruelle, C., & de Schonen, S. (in press). Do the right and left hemispheres attend to the same visuo-spatial information within a face in infancy? *Developmental Neuropsychology, 13*.

Ellis, H.D., Sheperd, J.W., & Davies, J.M. (1979). Identification of familiar and unfamiliar faces from internal and external features: Some implications for theories of face recognition. *Perception, 8*, 431–439.

Endo, M., Takahashi, K., & Maruyama, K. (1984). The effects of observer's attitude on the familiarity of faces: Using the difference in cue value between central and peripheral facial elements as an index of familiarity. *Tohoku Psychologica Folia, 43*, 23–34.

Goren, C.C., Sarty, M., & Wu, P.Y.K. (1975). Visual following and pattern discrimination of face-like stimuli by newborn infants. *Pediatrics, 56*, 544–549.

Haxby, J.V., Grady, C.L., Horwitz, B., Ungerleider, L.G., Mishkin, M., Carson, R.E., Herscovitch, P., Schapiro, M.B., & Rapoport S.I. (1991). Dissociation of object and spatial visual processing pathways in human extrastriate cortex. *Proceedings of the National Academy of Sciences USA, 88*, 1621–1625.

Hillger, L.A., & Koenig, O. (1991). Separable mechanisms in face processing: Evidence from hemispheric specialization. *Journal of Cognitive Neuroscience, 3*, 42–58.

Hughes, H.C., Fendrich R., & Reuter-Lorenz, P.A. (1990). Global versus local processing in the absence of low spatial frequencies. *Journal of Cognitive Neuroscience, 2*, 272–282.

Huttenlocher, P.R. (1993). Synaptogenesis, synapse elimination and neural plasticity in human cerebral cortex. In C.A. Nelson (Ed.), *Threats to optimal development: Integrating biological, psychological, and social risk factors*. (Minnesota Symposium on Child Psychology, Vol. 27). Hillsdale, NJ: Lawrence Erlbaum Associates Inc.

Johnson, M.H. (1990). Cortical maturation and the development of visual attention in early infancy. *Journal of Cognitive Neuroscience, 2*, 81–95.

Johnson, M.H., Dziurawiec, S., Ellis, H.D., & Morton, J. (1991). Newborns' preferential tracking of face-like stimuli and its subsequent decline. *Cognition, 40*, 1–19.

Johnson, M.H., & Morton, J. (1991). *Biology and Cognitive Development: The Case of Face Recognition*. Oxford: Blackwell.

Kitterle, F.L., Christman, S., & Hellige, J.B. (1990). Hemispheric differences are found in the identification, but not the detection, of low versus high spatial frequencies. *Perception and Psychophysics, 48*, 297–306.

Kitterle, F.L., & Selig, L.M. (1991). Visual field effects in the discrimination of sine-wave gratings. *Perception and Psychophysics, 50*, 15–18.

Lewis, T.L., Maurer, D., & Blackburn, K. (1985). The development of young infants' ability to detect stimuli in the nasal visual field. *Vision Research, 25*, 943–950.

Liegeois, F., & de Schonen, S. (1997). Simultaneous attention in the two visual hemifields and interhemispheric integration: A developmental finding on 20–26-month-old infants. *Neuropsychologia, 35*, 381–385.

Lu, S.T., Hämäläinen, M.S., Hari, R., Ilmoniemi, R.J., Lounasamaa, O.V., Sams, M., & Vilkman, V. (1991). Seeing faces activates three separate areas outside the occipital visual cortex in man. *Neuroscience, 43*, 287–290.

Mancini, J., de Schonen, S., Deruelle, C., & Massoulier, A. (1994). Face recognition in children with early right or left brain damage. *Developmental Medicine and Child Neurology, 36*, 156–166.

Maurer, D. (1993). Neonatal synesthesia: Implications for the processing of speech and faces. In B. de Boysson-Bardies, S. de Schonen, P. Jusczyk, P. MacNeilage, & J. Morton (Eds.), *Developmental Neurocognition: Speech and Face Processing in the First Year of Life.* (pp.109–124). Dordrecht: Kluwer.

Maurer, D., & Lewis, T.L. (1979). A physiological explanation of infants' early visual development. *Canadian Journal of Psychology, 33*, 232–252.

McKee, R.D., & Squire, L.R. (1993). On the development of declarative memory. *Journal of Experimental Psychology: Learning, Memory and Cognition, 19,* 397–404.

Morton, J., & Johnson, M.H. (1991). Conspec and conlern: A two-process theory of infant face recognition. *Psychological Review, 98,* 164–181.

Pascalis, O., & de Schonen, S. (1994) Recognition memory in 3- to 4-day-old human neonates. *Neuroreport, 5*(14), 1721–1724.

Pascalis, O., de Schonen, S., Morton, J., Deruelle, C., & Fabre-Grenet, M. (1995). Mother's face recognition in neonates: A replication and an extension. *Infant Behavior and Development, 18*, 79–85.

Pascalis, D., de Haan, M., Nelson, C., & de Schonen, S. (in press). Long term recognition memory for faces assessed by visual paired comparison in 3- and 6-month-old infants. *Journal of Experimental Psychology: Learning, Memory and Cognition.*

Posner, M.I., & Petersen, S.E. (1990). The attention system of the human brain. *Annual Review of Neuroscience, 13*, 25–42.

Rebai, M., Bagot J.D., & Viggiani, M.P (1993). Hemispheric asymmetry in transient visual evoked potentials induced by the spatial factor of the stimulation. *Brain and Cognition, 23*, 263–278.

Rothbart, M.K., Posner, M.I., & Boylan, A. (1990). Regulatory mechanisms in infant development. In J.T. Enns (Ed.), *The Development of Attention: Research and Theory* (pp. 47-66). Oxford: North Holland.

Scheibel, A. (1993). Dendritic structure and language development. In B. de Boysson-Bardies, S. de Schonen, P. Jusczyk, P. MacNeilage, & J. Morton (Eds.), *Developmental Neurocognition: Speech and Face Processing in the First Year of Life* (pp.51–62) Dordrecht: Kluwer,

Sergent, J. (1983). The role of the input in visual hemispheric processing. *Psychological Bulletin, 93*, 481–512.

Sergent, J. (1985). Influence of task and input factors on hemispheric involvement in face processing. *Journal of Experimental Psychology: Human Perception and Performance, 11*, 846–861.

Sergent, J. (1987). Failures to confirm the spatial-frequency hypothesis: Fatal blow or healthy complication? *Canadian Journal of Psychology, 41*, 412–428.

Sergent, J. (1989). Structural processing of faces. In A.W. Young and H.D. Ellis (Eds.), *Handbook of Research on Face Processing* (pp. 57-91). Oxford: North Holland.

Sergent J., Ohta, S., & MacDonald, B. (1992). Functional neuroanatomy of face and object processing: A positon emission tomography study. *Brain, 115*, 15–36.

Slater, A.M. (1993). Visual perceptual abilities at birth: Implications for face perception. In B. de Boysson-Bardies, S. de Schonen, P. Jusczyk, P. MacNeilage, & J. Morton (Eds.), *Developmental Neurocognition: Speech and Face Processing in the First Year of Life* (pp.125–134). Dordrecht: Kluwer.

Stiles, J., & Thal, D. (1993). Linguistic and spatial cognitive development following early focal brain injury: Patterns of deficit and recovery. In M. Johnson (Ed.). *Brain Development and Cognition: A Reader.* (pp. 643–664). Oxford: Blackwell.

Suter, P.S., Suter, S., Roessler, J.S., Parker, K.L., Armstrong, C.A., & Powers, J.C. (1994). Spatial-frequency-tuned channels in early infancy: VEP evidence? *Vision Research, 34*, 737–745.

Turkewitz, G. (1989). Face processing as a fundamental feature of development. In A. Young and H.D. Ellis (Eds.), *Handbook of research on face processing* (pp. 401–404). Amsterdam: North Holland.

Turkewitz, G. (1993). The origins of differential hemispheric strategies for information processing in the relationships between voice and face perception. In B. de Boysson-Bardies, S. de Schonen, P. Jusczyk, P. McNeilage & J. Morton (Eds.), *Developmental Neurocognition: Speech and Face Processing in the First Year of Life* (pp. 165–170). Dordrecht: Kluwer.

Tzourio, N., de Schonen, S., Mazoyer, B., Boré, A., Pietrzyk, U., Bruck, B., Aujard, Y., & Deruelle, C. (1992). Regional cerebral blood flow in two-month-old alert infants. *Society for Neuroscience Abstracts, 18*, 2, 1121.

Walton, G.E., Bower, N.J.A., & Bower, T.G.R. (1992). Recognition of familiar faces by newborns. *Infant Behavior and Development, 15*, 265–269.

CHAPTER SEVEN

Visual Sensory and Perceptual Abilities of the Newborn: Beyond the Blooming, Buzzing Confusion

Alan Slater
University of Exeter, UK

Scott P. Johnson
Texas A&M University, USA

INTRODUCTION

Until recent times the majority of theories of visual perception have emphasized the extreme perceptual limitations of the newborn and young infant. For example, the "father of modern psychology" William James claimed (1890, Vol. 1, p. 488), in one of the most memorable phrases in developmental psychology, that "the baby, assailed by eyes, ears, nose, skin and entrails at once, feels it all as one great blooming, buzzing confusion". Piaget (1953, 1954), and Hebb (1949) also argued that visual perception is exceptionally impoverished at birth and suggested that its development is a consequence of intensive learning in the months and years from birth. No-one would doubt that considerable learning about the visual world has to take place, but research over the last 30 years has given rise to conceptions of the "competent infant" who enters the world with an intrinsically organized visual world that is adapted to the need to impose structure and meaning on the people, objects and events that confront them.

Not surprisingly, though, the newborn infant's world is quite different from that of the adult, and in this chapter we outline some of the abilities and limitations of the newborn visual system, and of newborn visual perception. The chapter is in two major sections. In order to begin the business of making sense of the visual world, it has to be seen! Accordingly, considerable research has been carried out to describe the sensory capacities of the young infant, and an account of some of this research is given in the first section, headed SENSORY AND PERCEPTUAL FUNCTIONING: the subheadings are, *Eye movements, scanning and fixations*, and *Visual acuity, contrast sensitivity and colour vision*. In the next section,

VISUAL ORGANIZATION AT AND NEAR BIRTH, we discuss research that has investigated the intrinsic organization of the visual world, under the headings of *Cortical functioning at birth, Shape and size constancy, Form and object perception,* and *Perception of faces.*

SENSORY AND PERCEPTUAL FUNCTIONING

In order to perceive the visual world the perceiver needs a reasonable level of visual acuity (the ability to resolve detail), and the ability to distinguish the boundaries, colours, luminance levels, and textures of surrounding surfaces. Depth perception is necessary to discriminate surfaces against the background. The ability to track moving objects in the environment is important as well, because motion is often an important cue for segregation of visible surfaces. All of these skills depend on eye movements and efficient visual scanning, in order to foveate objects of interest (i.e., to focus the object's image on the fovea where visual acuity is highest).

Eye movements, scanning and fixations

Foveation consists of directing one's gaze to items of interest in the visual array. Foveation is most readily accomplished in humans via eye movements, although head and body movements also contribute. Even a neonate seems to foveate small objects, if he or she is motivated and the object is not too difficult to see (i.e., if it can be distinguished against the background and is close to the eyes).

However, there are limitations in very young infants' abilities successfully to produce certain eye movements. For example, until 8 to 10 weeks of age, infants rarely engage in smooth pursuit, or the tracking of a slowly moving small target (Aslin, 1981). Fig. 7.1 depicts eye movement records from two infants, aged 48 and 114 days, who attempted to follow an oscillating target. Note that the younger infant seemed to have difficulty staying on target, and her eye movements were much more "jerky". That is, they consisted of saccades, or fast eye movements — she did not track the object smoothly, nor anticipate its trajectory. In contrast, the older infant was better able to stay on target, tracking more smoothly.

Why do very young infants seldom engage in smooth pursuit? We do not know for sure, but it may have to do with the immaturity of the fovea at birth (Abramov, Gordon, Hendrickson, Hainline, Dobson, & LaBossiere, 1982). Although the peripheral retina is relatively mature at birth, the fovea undergoes considerable development in the first few postnatal months (for example, via receptor migration). Consequently, acuity is poor in neonates. Thus, when attempting to track a target, it may be difficult to follow its trajectory unless its image falls on extrafoveal regions, at which point foveation is again attempted. Alternatively, Johnson (1990) proposed that the emergence of smooth pursuit follows maturation of cortical pathways thought to be involved in nonsaccadic tracking.

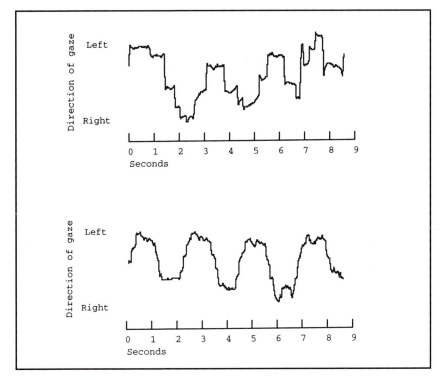

FIG. 7.1:   Eye movement recordings from two infants, aged 48 (top) and 114 days (bottom). The eye movements were recorded with electrooculography (EOG) which involves placing small sensors on the skin at the temples, to measure the difference in the skin's electrical potential caused by movements of the nearby eyeballs. The target consisted of a vertically oriented red rectangle, 8 by 23cm, rear-projected onto a dark screen, viewed from a distance of 1m. The target moved 92cm right and left, at a speed of about 71cm/s, and remained stationary for 1s at the endpoints to allow the infant's gaze to "catch up". The older infant's eye movements are characterized by a much higher incidence of smooth pursuit.

Very young infants may also be limited in their ability to scan stationary patterns effectively. Bronson (1990, 1991) has used the corneal-reflection technique to investigate changes in visual scanning with development. This method involves recording eye movements on film, onto which the stimulus is later superimposed to gauge scanning accuracy. The measure of interest is where individual infants fixate on the stimulus, and for how long. Older infants are thought to encode stimulus attributes more effectively, in a shorter amount of time, than do younger infants, as revealed by more efficient scanning patterns (Fig. 7.2). It should be noted, however, that there are large individual differences within age groups. Aslin (1987) cites other potential problems with the interpretation of such results, such as the assumption that the scan path accurately reflects foveation of desired targets, and the possibility that fixation does not necessarily mean that the stimulus was

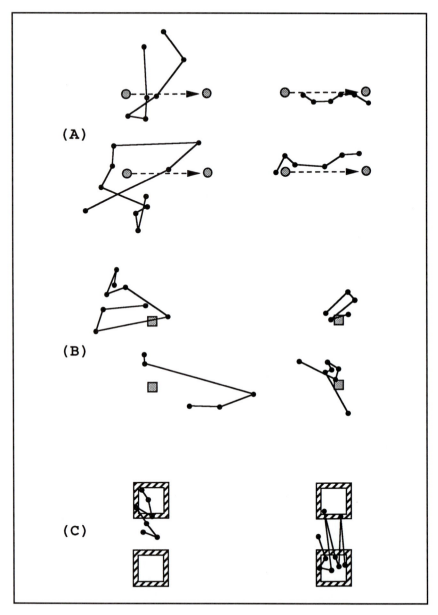

FIG. 7.2:   Examples of young infants' inefficient (left) and efficient (right) scanning patterns. Each dot represents a brief fixation; lines connecting dots represent saccades. (A) *A small target, moving horizontally*; (B) *A small stationary target*; (C) *A pair of targets*. Very young infants, around 2 to 5 weeks of age, more often engage in "unguided" scans, away from stimulus contours. Older infants more often engage in scanning patterns marked by brief fixations, more widely scattered across the stimulus (adapted from Bronson, 1990).

encoded. Nevertheless, there are clear differences between age groups in scanning patterns and, most likely, differences in scanning quality, perhaps reflecting some of the ways in which the visual abilities of very young infants might undergo considerable and rapid improvement over the first few months.

A third way in which very young infants' scanning abilities improve is via control over reflexive eye movements. Examples of reflexive eye movements include optokinetic nystagmus (OKN) and the vestibuloocular reflex (VOR). These describe the visual system's ability to maintain fixation to large-field stimuli during motion of the field itself, or the individual, or both. For example, imagine riding in a train, gazing out of the right window. Your eyes may scan rightward, briefly following the terrain outside, then "snap" to the left, follow to the right, snap left, and so on in a repeating fast–slow eye movement cycle. This cycle is optokinetic nystagmus. For an example of vestibuloocular reflex, read this sentence while you move your head from side to side (either rotate or translate your head). Notice that your eyes have no difficulty staying on target. Now, try to read the text while you move the page left and right at the same rate. This is much more difficult, even though the relative motions of eye and page may be similar. In the former case, your eyes are able to compensate precisely for head movements – this is the vestibuloocular reflex. A combination of optokinetic nystagmus, vestibuloocular reflex, and smooth pursuit is responsible for adults' ability to move around the world while effortlessly maintaining fixation on targets (whether moving or stationary) of choice (Aslin & Johnson, 1996).

Even neonates have been found to engage in optokinetic nystagmus (Kremenitzer, Vaughan, Kurtzberg, & Dowling, 1979) and to show the vestibuloocular reflex (Laurence & Feind, 1953). However, the ability to suppress optokinetic nystagmus and the vestibuloocular reflex is necessary for controlled eye movements under conditions of self-motion (in our train example above, you would suppress optokinetic nystagmus when inspecting a fly on the window). Can very young infants overcome the reflexive tendency to engage in these eye movement patterns to large-field stimuli, volitionally to foveate small targets? The answer seems to be no. Aslin and Johnson (1994; 1996) found that at 2 and 4 months of age, infants were proficient at suppressing both optokinetic nystagmus and vestibuloocular reflex in response to small, (presumably) interesting targets. However, 1-month-olds displayed little if any suppression, although both optokinetic nystagmus and vestibuloocular reflex were observed in this age group. These findings imply that very young infants lack the ability to maintain effective fixation on objects as they themselves move.

In summary, neonates seem to be limited in visual scanning skills, although attempts at foveation have been noted at birth. How would this affect perception? If scanning is limited, whether scanning stationary or moving targets, or under conditions of self-motion, then opportunities for visual abstraction of object properties will also necessarily be limited. If neonates learn about object properties primarily by visual inspection, scanning limitations might have detrimental effects on this process, because neonates spend a fair amount of their waking hours in motion (e.g., being transported, or moving their heads while seated or reclining). In what ways the development of visual perception is concomitantly limited as a result is presently unknown. However, these scanning limitations are largely overcome by the fourth month of life (see also Gilmore & Johnson, this volume).

Visual acuity, contrast sensitivity and colour vision

As noted earlier, foveation has been observed even in the youngest infants. However, this does not mean that when newborn infants foveate they see what adults see. Neonates are limited in visual acuity, contrast sensitivity, and colour perception. That is, they are less able to discriminate fine detail in visual patterns, and they are less able to discriminate differences in luminance contrast (i.e., shades of grey), and between colours, than are older infants and adults.

Visual acuity in infants has been tested with the forced-choice preferential looking (FPL) procedure (Teller, 1979). The neonate is seated and shown a pair of stimuli, at a distance of some 20 to 40cm from the eyes. One stimulus is a homogeneous grey, whereas the other consists of vertical black-and-white stripes (a square wave grating; see Fig. 7.3). Infants tend preferentially to fixate the member of a stimulus pair they find more salient or interesting, and stripes are more interesting than a grey field, so if the stripes can be resolved, the infants more often look to that side than the other. If the stripe width is too small, however, the detail will not be visible, and no preference is observed. The infant's looking to each side is recorded by an observer, watching through a peephole or on a video monitor, and the smallest stripe width that is reliably preferred to the grey is taken as the estimate of acuity.

An alternative method for assessing visual acuity, and other visual functions, is measurement of visually evoked potentials (VEP). This consists of recording

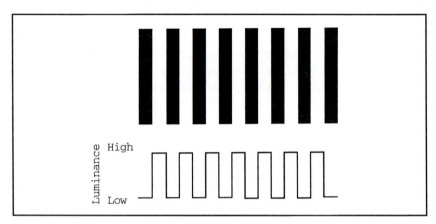

FIG. 7.3:   A square wave grating, so called because a plot of its luminances resembles a square wave. The stimulus is high in contrast, its edges sharply defined.

activity in the visual cortex (at the back of the skull) via electrodes placed on the skin. When a stimulus such as a grating or checkerboard is presented, it is repeatedly phase-reversed (i.e., its dark elements switch to light as its light elements switch to dark). If the stimulus is registered by the visual system, the evoked potential signal should have a frequency component that matches the frequency of phase reversal.

Preferential looking studies suggest that neonate visual acuity is poor, about 1 to 2 cycles per degree, which is around 20/600 Snellen (Allen, 1978; cited in Banks & Dannemiller, 1987; see also Slater, 1995). (Adult visual acuity is typically around 30 cycles per degree, or 20/20 vision.) Thus, a neonate could resolve black and white stripes about 2.5cm wide at a distance of 30cm. Use of the visually evoked potential gives a more optimistic estimate, but only by a few cycles per degree (Sokol, 1978). Acuity improves rapidly. The evoked potential technique suggests acuity is nearly adultlike by 6 months of age (Sokol, 1978), but the preferential looking method indicates that more development in acuity occurs after this time (Banks & Dannemiller, 1987). The reasons for the discrepancy between the two procedures remain unclear (Banks & Dannemiller, 1987).

Visual acuity is assessed in infants with stimuli of maximum contrast, such as black and white stripes (gratings) or checkerboards. However, most of the objects we see in the world do not have surfaces that are either maximally dark or light. Rather, surfaces typically have widely varying contrast levels. The infant must detect these differences in contrast in order to discriminate accurately between surfaces. This is known as contrast sensitivity, and is described in terms of the contrast sensitivity function (CSF), which is defined as detection of the minimum contrast required to detect a sine wave grating (Fig. 7.4). The contrast sensitivity function is linked to acuity. Contrast sensitivity is maximal for adults at intermediate stripe widths, about 3 to 4 cycles per degree. At coarser and finer stripe widths,

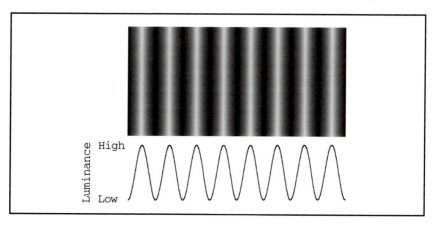

FIG. 7.4:   A sine wave grating, so called because a plot of its luminances resembles a sine wave. The stimulus varies gradually in contrast, its edges blurry or fuzzy.

contrast sensitivity falls off. Both preferential looking and visually evoked potentials have been used to assess contrast sensitivity in young infants, their outcomes agreeing more closely than is the case with acuity. Fig. 7.5 depicts contrast sensitivity functions for infants and adults. Note that improvement occurs rapidly over the first few months postnatal, in like manner to acuity.

As with acuity and contrast, neonates have been found to be limited in their abilities to detect colour. A common misperception is that neonates are "colour-blind", but this is not quite correct. Use of the preferential looking procedure, with colour vs. achromatic stimuli, has revealed that few neonates discriminate blue, green, and yellow from grey patches matched in luminance (14%, 36%, and 25%, respectively). However, 74% of the neonates apparently discriminated red from grey (Adams, Courage, & Mercer, 1994). Thus, there is some evidence of colour perception in neonates, most strongly for red. Colour perception improves rapidly. With the same technique, 3-month-olds were found to discriminate all four colours tested, with 1- and 2-month-olds showing intermediate patterns of performance (Mercer, Courage, & Adams, 1991).

VISUAL ORGANIZATION AT AND NEAR BIRTH

We have seen that scanning abilities, acuity, contrast sensitivity, and colour discrimination seem to be limited in neonates. However, despite these limitations

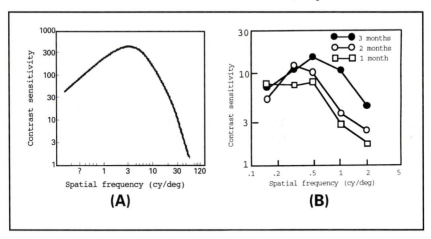

FIG. 7.5: (A) *Top*: stimulus illustrating the relation between stripe width and contrast sensitivity. In this stimulus, contrast is maximal at the bottom, and minimal at the top. Note how the stripes are best distinguished at medium width. *Bottom*: the contrast sensitivity function for adults. Note that contrast sensitivity is maximal for medium stripe widths. (B) The contrast sensitivity function for young infants. Note that infant CSFs have the same general shape as the adult function, although the placement of the peak is different. (A) from Banks and Salapatek, 1981, reprinted by permission; (B) adapted from Banks and Salapatek, 1981.

the visual system is functioning at birth, and in this section several types of visual organization that are found in early infancy are discussed. Many parts of the brain, both subcortical and cortical, are involved in vision, but it is reasonable to claim that visual perception, in any meaningful sense, would not be possible without a functioning visual cortex, and this is discussed in the next section.

Cortical functioning at birth

The cortex is responsible for humans' memory, reasoning, planning, and many visual skills. Without a functioning visual cortex the visual world would be one of fleeting snapshots, each lasting the duration of a fixation which is typically less than a second, and then immediately forgotten. The ability to foveate and to discriminate detail is also mediated by the visual cortex, and we have already presented evidence, which suggests that newborns can foveate stimuli. However, it has been proposed (Bronson, 1974) that the visual cortex is not functional at birth, and that the visual behaviours of infants for around the first 2 months from birth are mediated by subcortical structures such as the *superior colliculus*, which is particularly involved in the control of eye movements.

At the time that Bronson produced his account there were already several reports of habituation and subsequent preferences for novel stimuli to be found (i.e., Friedman, 1972), which implies memory formation for the "familiar" stimulus. However, Bronson interpreted these reports in terms of retinal adaptation rather than memory: he suggested that when the newborn fixates the "familiar" stimulus, cells in the retinae adapt, making the stimulus less detectable, and the apparent habituation (decline of visual attention) that results is actually sensory adaptation rather than memory formation. The apparent dishabituation, or recovery of visual attention to a novel stimulus, results from the activation of a new population of retinal cells. The two eyes work independently, such that if one eye is adapted, the other is unaffected. This independence means that the experiment to test Bronson's model was quite simple: Newborns were habituated to a simple stimulus with one eye as the "viewing eye", while the other was covered by a gauze patch, and when they reached the criterion of habituation, the viewing eye was changed (by reversing the patching) and paired presentation of novel and familiar stimuli followed. In two experiments we found significant novelty preferences for a novel colour and a novel shape (Slater, Morison & Rose, 1983).

These findings suggest that a retinal adaptation model of newborn habituation can be ruled out, but since they do not show the neural basis of the effects they do not demonstrate that the visual cortex is functional. A critical test of cortical functioning is discrimination of orientation. In primates, orientation discrimination is not found in subcortical neurons, but it is a common property of cortical cells, and orientation selectivity is therefore an indicator of cortical functioning. We carried out a study to test for orientation discrimination in newborns (Slater, Morison & Somers, 1988). In this, newborn infants were habituated to a black and white stripes pattern (grating), presented in an oblique orientation, and on subsequent test trials they clearly gave a preference for the same grating in a novel orientation (the mirror-image oblique of the familiarized stimulus).

This finding, which was replicated by Atkinson, Hood, Wattam-Bell, Anker and Tricklebank (1988), is an unambiguous demonstration that at least some parts of the visual cortex are functioning at birth. Later accounts have attempted to describe which parts may be more functional than others (Atkinson, 1984; Johnson, 1990). However, even if the visual cortex is immature, it is difficult to know in what ways this imposes limitations on visual perception: as Atkinson and Braddick (1989, p. 19) have put it, "we do not really have any idea how little or how much function we should expect from the structural immaturity of new-born visual cortex". Certainly, as will be described in the next sections, it has become clear that the newborn infant is possessed of many ways in which to begin to make sense of the visual world.

Shape and size constancy

As objects move, they change in orientation, or slant, and perhaps also their distance, relative to an observer, causing constant changes to the image of the objects on the retina. However, we do not experience a world of fleeting, unconnected retinal images, but a world of objects that move and change in a coherent manner. Such stability, across the constant retinal changes, is called *perceptual constancy*. Perception of an object's real shape regardless of changes to its orientation is called *shape constancy*; and *size constancy* refers to the fact that we see an object as the same size regardless of its distance from us. If these constancies were not present in infant perception the visual world would be extremely confusing, perhaps approaching James's "blooming, buzzing confusion", and they are a necessary prerequisite for many other types of perceptual organization.

The first person to report systematic experimental evidence for the presence of constancies in infant perception was Tom Bower (1966). He used a head-turn conditioning procedure, from the results of which he concluded that infants as young as 8 weeks of age responded to objects' real, rather than retinal, shapes and sizes. Other researchers were unable to find evidence for size constancy at such an early age, and in a review of the literature Ross Day (1987, p.85) concluded that "size constancy is operative at 18 weeks", but left open the question as to whether it is present in earlier infancy. There was thus some uncertainty as to when these constancies were present in infant perception. E.J. Gibson expressed the critical question with respect to size constancy, but her remarks are equally applicable to shape constancy: "Does this mean that no learning is involved in the development of size constancy? Definitely not, since even eight weeks gives a lot of opportunity for visual experience" (1970, p.104). However, more recent experiments have given clear evidence that these constancies are present at birth, and these are discussed next.

In a study of shape constancy, Slater and Morison (1985) described two experiments. In the first (a preferential looking procedure, PL) two paired stimuli, the outline shapes of a square and a trapezium, were shown side by side to infants who averaged just over 2 days of age. The trapezium was always shown in frontal plane, but the square varied in its slant, and a highly systematic effect was found, such that the more the square was oriented away from the frontal plane, the less time the babies spent looking at it. This demonstrated that newborn infants detect, and respond systematically to, changes in objects' slants. The second experiment was to find if newborns could respond to an object's real shape, regardless of its slant. Newborns were presented with a single shape (either the trapezium or the square) during six familiarization trials, shown at a different slant during each trial: each infant thus viewed the same shape in different orientations. On the test trials that followed, the infants saw the square and trapezium paired together, the familiar one in a different slant from any shown earlier, and every one of the 12 newborns tested looked more at the novel shape. These results demonstrate that newborn babies have the ability to extract the constant, real shape of an object that is rotated in the third dimension: that is, they have shape constancy.

In a study of size constancy, Slater, Mattock, and Brown (1990) also used PL and familiarization procedures. A newborn infant being tested in a size constancy experiment is shown in Fig. 7.6. In the PL experiment they presented pairs of cubes of different sizes at different distances, and it was found that newborns preferred to look at the cube which gave the largest *retinal size*, regardless of its distance or its real size. These findings are convincing evidence that newborns can base their responding on retinal size alone. However, in the second experiment each infant viewed either a small cube or a large cube during familiarization trials: each infant was exposed to the same-sized object shown at different distances on each trial. After familiarization, the infants were shown both cubes side by side, the small cube nearer and the large cube farther, such that their retinal images were identically sized (Fig. 7.7). The infants looked longer at the cube they were not familiarized with (consistent with the novelty preferences commonly observed in habituation studies). This indicates that the neonates differentiated the two cube sizes despite the similarities of the retinal sizes, and abstracted the familiar cube's real size over changes in distance.

In conclusion, the findings described above demonstrate that shape and size constancy are organizing features of perception that are present at birth.

Form and object perception

The terms "figure", "shape", "pattern" and "form" are often used interchangeably, and as long ago as 1970 Zusne (p.1) commented that "Form, like love, is a many-splendored thing ... there is no agreement on what is meant by form, in spite of the tacit agreement that there is". However, the most often used stimuli in studies of form perception are static, achromatic, two- or three-dimensional figures with easily detectable contours that can stand as figures in a figure–ground relationship, and

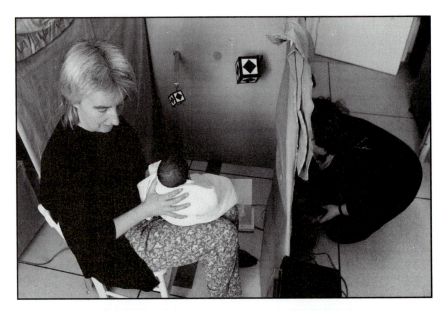

FIG. 7.6: A newborn infant being tested in a size constancy experiment.

FIG. 7.7: The stimuli shown to the infants on the post-familiarization test trials. This photograph, taken from the babies' viewing position, shows the small cube on the left at a distance of 30.5cm, and the large cube on the right at a distance of 61cm.

it is primarily with reference to these that most theories of form perception have been concerned.

One of the most intractable issues in the study of form perception in early infancy is whether or not such figures or patterns are innately perceived as parts or as wholes. This can be illustrated with respect to the newborn infant's perception of simple geometric shapes. We know that newborns discriminate easily between the outline shapes of simple geometric forms such as a square, circle, triangle and cross, but the basis of the discrimination is unclear since these shapes differ in a number of ways, such as the number and orientation of their component lines, and as was mentioned earlier newborns can discriminate on the basis of orientation alone.

One experiment which suggests that there is a change in the way form is perceived in early infancy was by Cohen and Younger (1984). Six- and 14-week-old infants were habituated to a simple stimulus consisting of two connected lines which made either an acute (45°) or an obtuse (135°) angle, similar to those shown in Fig. 7.8. On subsequent test trials the 6-week-olds dishabituated to a change in the orientation of the lines (where the angle remained unchanged), but *not* to a change in angle alone, while the 14-week-olds did the opposite in that they recovered attention to a change in angle, but not to a change in orientation. These findings suggest that 4-month-olds are able to perceive angles, and therefore perceive simple shapes as wholes, whereas form perception in infants 6 weeks and younger may be dominated by attention to lower-order variables such as orientation.

An experiment was reported by Slater, Mattock, Brown and Bremner (1991) which tested this claim with newborn infants. Each infant was shown either an obtuse or an acute angle, but the angle changed its oriention on each of six habituation or familiarization trials. On the test trials the babies now gave a strong preference for the novel angle, when this was shown paired with the familiar one: the stimuli shown on the familiarization and test trials are shown in Fig. 7.8.

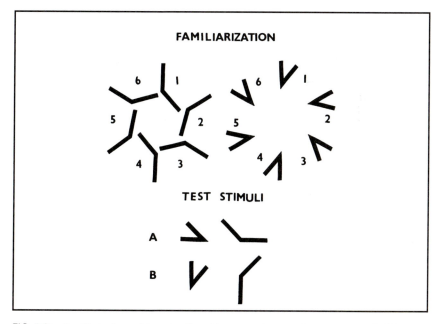

FIG. 7.8:   Familiarization and test stimuli used in an experiment on form perception. Half the infants were familiarized to the six variations of the acute angle (upper right), half to the obtuse angle. On test trials the newborns looked more at the novel angle.

One interpretation of these findings is that newborn infants are able to respond both to low-order variables of stimulation, such as orientation, and also to higher-order variables, such as form (i.e., angles), and that the variable to which they respond depends on the experimental manipulation. When orientation was made irrelevant to the discrimination, by varying it during familiarization trials, the newborns showed that they could respond on the basis of the higher-order invariant of angle size. A different interpretation was offered by Cohen (in Slater et al., 1991, p. 405), who argued that "the discrimination between acute and obtuse angles shown by newborns might be interpreted in terms of differences in the relative sizes of the 'blob' at the apex of the angles, rather than on the angular relationship between the two line segments"—in other words, the newborns might still have been responding to a low-order variable of stimulation, the "blob" at the apex. At present we do not have experimental evidence to discriminate between these interpretations.

All visual stimuli are stimulus compounds in that they contain separate features that occur at the same spatial location, and which the mature perceiver "binds together" as a whole. With such an ability we see, for example, a green circle and a red triangle, while without it we would see greenness, redness, circularity and triangularity as separate stimulus elements. Evidence suggests that newborn infants perceive stimulus compounds. In an experiment by Slater, Mattock, Brown, Burnham, and Young (1991) newborns were familiarized, on successive trials, to two separate stimuli. For half the infants these were a green vertical stripe and a red diagonal stripe; the other babies were familiarized to green diagonal and red vertical stipes. In the former case there are two novel combinations, these being green diagonal and red vertical, and on post-familiarization test trials the babies were shown one of the familiar compounds paired with one of the novel ones, and they showed strong novelty preferences. Note that the novel compounds consisted of stimulus elements that the babies had seen before, and the novelty preferences are therefore clear evidence that the babies had processed and remembered the colour/form compounds shown on the familiarization trials.

A clear difference has been found in infants' perception of partly occluded objects in the age range birth to 4 months. Kellman and his colleagues (Kellman & Spelke, 1983; Kellman, Spelke & Short, 1986) habituated 4-month-olds to a stimulus (usually a rod) that moved back and forth behind a central occluder, so that only the top and bottom parts of the rod were visible (as in the upper part of Fig. 7.9). When adults are shown this display they perceive the rod to be complete, or whole, behind the occluder, and Kellman et al.'s findings demonstrated that 4-month-olds do as well. On the post-habituation test trials the infants were shown two test displays, one being a complete rod, the other being the top and bottom parts of the rod, with a gap where the occluder had been (as in the lower part of Fig. 7.9), and the babies recovered attention to the rod pieces, but not to the complete rod, suggesting that they had been perceiving a complete rod during habituation.

However, when newborn babies were tested with a similar display they looked longer on the test trials at the *complete* rod (Slater, Morison, Somers, Mattock,

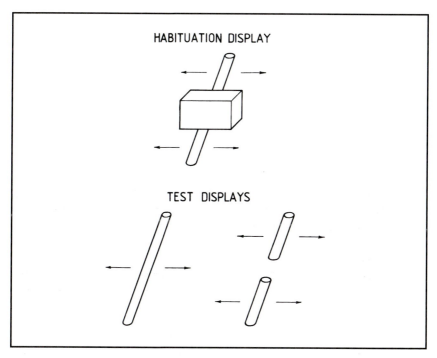

FIG. 7.9:   Habituation and test displays shown to infants to test perception of object unity. During habituation the rod, and during test trials the rod and rod parts, moved back and forth undergoing common motion.

Brown, & Taylor, 1990). Thus, neonates appear not to perceive partly occluded objects as consisting of both visible and nonvisible portions. Rather, they seem to respond only to what they see directly. This finding was recently replicated with newborn infants, with displays that were quite rich in visual cues, such as a large depth difference between the rod, occluder, and background, small occluder size, and textured (i.e. patterned) background, all designed to heighten the contrast between the objects, and thus facilitate perception of object unity. The neonates did not seem to take advantage of the extra visual information in the displays, still finding the complete rod novel after habituation (Slater, Johnson, Brown, & Badenoch, 1996; Slater, Johnson, Kellman, & Spelke, 1994). Recent findings suggest that an understanding of the completeness, or unity, of partly occluded objects begins around 2 months from birth (Johnson & Aslin, 1995; Johnson & Náñez, 1995).

The findings described above show that newborn infants have a range of perceptual abilities and limitations. These are discussed further after the next section, which considers whether infants come into the world able to perceive the human face.

Perception of faces

Newborn infants have been found to learn individual faces very rapidly, distinguishing real faces from one another. The most likely candidate for a quickly learned face is, of course, the mother, and mother's face is discriminated within days from birth (Bushnell, Sai, & Mullin, 1989; Bushnell, this volume): in Bushnell et al.'s procedure 4-day-old neonates consistently looked longer at their mother's face than at a female stranger's, where the stranger's face was similar to the mother's in terms of hair colour and skin tone. Apparently, this recognition is not dependent solely on facial features. The effect disappears if the women's hairlines are covered with a scarf (Pascalis, de Schonen, Morton, Deruelle, & Fabre-Grenet, 1995). Thus, attention to outer contours seems to contribute to neonates' face recognition abilities.

This rapid learning about the mother's face is perhaps another example of the newborn infant's remarkable learning capacity, which may not be specific to faces. However, there are three lines of evidence which suggests that newborns enter the world with a preference for, and awareness of the structure and organization of the face.

Figure 7.10 depicts stimuli that have been shown to neonates (Johnson, Dziurawiec, Ellis, & Morton, 1991). The infants were seated on an experimenter's lap, who held each stimulus at midline about 18 to 25cm from the infant's eyes, and then moved it from side to side until the infant no longer tracked it. The infants tracked the face-like stimulus further than any of the others, indicating the ability to discriminate the stimuli, as well as an innate preference for faces.

The second line of evidence relates to infants' preferences for attractive faces. Samuels and Ewy (1985) showed pairs of black and white slides of same-gender faces (equal numbers of male and female faces were used) to 3- and 6-month-old infants. The slides were constructed so that the two members of a pair were as

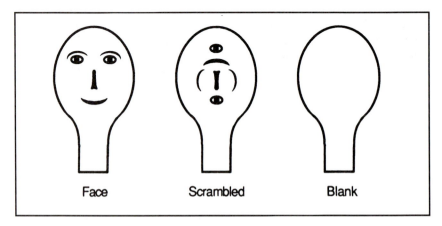

FIG. 7.10:   Stimuli presented to neonates in a face perception experiment (from Johnson and Morton, 1991).

similar as possible in gross physiognomic appearance, but they differed in attractiveness as rated by adults. Both age groups looked longest at the attractive faces, and this was true for all of the 12 pairings used: the preference was extremely strong with the attractive face eliciting 70% of the total looking. This finding was replicated with slightly younger infants (2- to 3-month-olds) by Langlois et al. (1987) who used colour slides of female faces only. More recently, Langlois et al. (1991) found that the effect held with faces from different races than the infants tested, and for young and old faces: the effect is therefore replicable and general.

There seem to be at least two interpretations of this effect. The one offered by Samuels and Ewy (1984) is that it is an example of an unlearned aesthetic appreciation at birth. In order to test this it would be necessary to find out whether infants have an aesthetic appreciation of objects that differ along non-face-like dimensions, but as yet such a test has not been carried out (Samuels et al., 1994, describe additional investigations, and interpretations of this effect).

A second interpretation is in terms of a facial prototype. If several faces of the same sex are averaged together (usually this is done using computer-averaging procedures) the resulting "average" face is seen as very attractive (Langlois & Roggman, 1990, illustrate this in their article entitled "Attractive faces are only average"!). We know that for many psychological categories the average exemplar is seen as more representative of the category than an extreme example (for example, a mongrel dog is perceived as more "dog-like" than some of the more exotic species). Thus, it can be argued that infants prefer the more attractive of a pair of faces, simply because it looks more face-like and they prefer to look at faces.

The third line of evidence that suggests that newborns have an innate representation of the face is the finding that they will imitate some of the facial gestures they see adults perform: in this literature the gestures most commonly produced by adults (and imitated by infants!) are tongue protrusion and mouth opening. The finding that newborns can innately imitate was first reported by Maratos (1973), and studied systematically by Meltzoff and Moore (1977), and since then there have been many more reports (i.e., Meltzoff & Moore, 1983, 1992, 1994; Reissland, 1988). These findings, and their theoretical implications, are complex, and a detailed discussion of infant facial imitation is beyond the scope of this chapter (but see Maratos, this volume). The point we wish to make is that such imitation indicates that the newborn infant appears to enter the world with an innate representation of the human face, on which he/she can match their own facial gestures.

CONCLUSION

In the first section of this chapter we presented evidence that scanning abilities, acuity, contrast sensitivity, and colour discrimination are limited in neonates. However, as Hainline and Abramov (1992, pp. 40-41) put it, "While infants may not, indeed, see as well as adults do, they normally see well enough to function effectively in their roles as infants." Thus, despite their sensory limitations, it is clear that newborn infants have several means with which to begin the business of making sense of the visual world. The visual cortex, while immature, is functioning at birth. Newborn infants can clearly remember what they see, and demonstrate rapid learning about this world. It seems to be the case that newborn infants possess at least rudimentary form perception, in the sense of perceiving wholes rather than only separate elements of two-dimensional stimuli, and perceiving colour/ orientation compounds rather than processing these elements separately. It is clear, though, that important changes occur in the first few months as a propensity to respond to low-order variables of stimulation, or parts, is replaced by response to higher-order variables.

One prerequisite for object knowledge is distinguishing proximal from distal stimuli. The proximal stimulus is the sensory stimulation— in this case, the pattern of light falling on the retina. The distal stimulus consists of what is represented by the pattern of stimulation—the object itself. Neonates distinguish proximal from distal stimuli when they demonstrate size and shape constancy: the object is perceived accurately, despite changes to its retinal image.

Inevitably, some types of visual organization take time to develop. An appreciation of the underlying unity, coherence and persistence of occluded objects is not present at birth, and a proper understanding of the physical properties of objects emerges only slowly as infancy progresses. However, other visual abilities appear to be remarkably advanced at birth. Several lines of evidence converge to suggest that infants are born with an innate preference for, and representation of the human face.

The picture of newborn visual perception that is emerging is complex: some aspects of visual perception are very immature, whereas others appear to be well developed. Nevertheless, it is clear that the newborn infant's visual world is, to a large extent, structured and coherent as a result of the intrinsic organization of the visual system. However well organized this world may be, it lacks the familiarity, meaning, and associations that characterise the world of the mature perceiver: as development proceeds, the innate and developing organizational mechanisms are added to by experience, which assists the infant in making sense of the perceived world.

ACKNOWLEDGEMENTS

The first author's research has been supported by research grants RC00232466 and R000235288 from the Economic and Social Research Council.

REFERENCES

Abramov, I., Gordon, J., Hendrickson, A., Hainline, L., Dobson, V., & LaBossiere, E. (1982). The retina of the newborn human infant. *Science, 217*, 265–267.

Adams, R.J., Courage, M.L., & Mercer, M.E. (1994). Systematic measurement of human neonatal color vision. *Vision Research, 34*, 1691–1701.

Aslin, R.N. (1981). Development of smooth pursuit in human infants. In D.F. Fisher, R.A. Monty, & J.W. Senders (Eds.), *Eye movements: Cognition and visual perception* (pp. 31–51). Hillsdale, NJ: Erlbaum.

Aslin, R.N. (1987). Motor aspects of visual development in infancy. In P. Salapatek & L. Cohen (Eds.), *Handbook of infant perception: Vol 1. From sensation to perception* (pp. 43–113). London: Academic Press.

Aslin, R.N., & Johnson, S.P. (1996). Suppression of the optokinetic reflex in human infants: Implications for stable fixation and shifts of attention. *Infant Behavior and Development, 19*, 235–242.

Aslin, R.N., & Johnson, S.P. (1994, May). *Suppression of vestibuloocular reflex by human infants*. Poster presented at the Association for Research in Vision and Ophthalmology conference, Sarasota, Florida.

Atkinson, J. (1984). Human visual development over the first six months of life: A review and a hypothesis. *Human Neurobiology, 3*, 61–74.

Atkinson, J., & Braddick, O. (1989). Development of basic visual functions. In A. Slater and G. Bremner (Eds.), *Infant development*. Hove, UK: Erlbaum.

Atkinson, J., Hood, B.M., Wattam-Bell, J., Anker, S., & Tricklebank, J. (1988). Development of orientation discrimination in infancy. *Perception, 17*, 587–595.

Banks, M.S., & Dannemiller, J.L. (1987). Infant visual psychophysics. In P. Salapatek & L. Cohen (Eds.), *Handbook of infant perception: Vol 1. From sensation to perception.* (pp. 115–184). London: Academic Press.

Banks, M.S., & Salapatek, P. (1981). Infant pattern vision: A new approach based on the contrast sensitivity function. *Journal of Experimental Child Pschology, 40*, 1–45.

Bower, T.G.R. (1966). The visual world of infants. *Scientific American, 215*(6), 80–92.

Bronson, G.W. (1974). The postnatal growth of visual capacity. *Child Development, 45*, 873–890.

Bronson, G.W. (1990). Changes in infants' visual scanning across the 2- to 14-week age period. *Journal of Experimental Child Psychology, 49*, 101–125.

Bronson, G.W. (1991). Infant differences in rate of visual encoding. *Child Development, 62*, 44–54.

Bushnell, I.W.R., Sai, F., & Mullin, J.T. (1989). Neonatal recognition of the mother's face. *British Journal of Developmental Psychology, 7*, 3–15.

Cohen, L.B., & Younger, B.A. (1984). Infant perception of angular relations. *Infant Behavior and Development, 7*, 37–47.

Day, R.H. (1987). Visual size constancy in infancy. In B.E. McKenzie & R.H. Day (Eds.), *Perceptual development in early infancy: Problems and issues*. Hillsdale, NJ: Erlbaum.

Friedman, S. (1972). Habituation and recovery of visual response in the alert human newborn. *Journal of Experimental Child Psychology, 13*, 339–349.

Gibson, E.J. (1970). The development of perception as an adaptive process. *American Scientist, 58*, 98–107.

Hainline, L., & Abramov, I. (1992). Assessing visual development: Is infant vision good enough? In C. Rovee-Collier & L.P. Lipsitt (Eds.), *Advances in infancy research* (Vol. 9, pp. 39–102). Norwood, NJ: Ablex.

Hebb, D.O. (1949). *The organization of behavior*. New York: Wiley.

James, W. (1890). *Principles of psychology*. New York: Henry Holt.

Johnson, M., & Morton, J. (1991). *Biology and cognitive development: The case of face recognition*. Oxford: Blackwell.

Johnson, M.H. (1990). Cortical maturation and the development of visual attention in early infancy. *Journal of Cognitive Neuroscience, 2*, 81–95.

Johnson, M.H., Dziurawiec, S., Ellis, H., & Morton, J. (1991). Newborns' preferential tracking of face-like stimuli and its subsequent decline. *Cognition, 40*, 1–19.

Johnson, S.P., & Aslin, R.N. (1995). Perception of object unity in 2-month-old infants. *Developmental Psychology, 31*, 739–745.

Johnson, S.P., & Náñez, J.E. (1995). Young infants' perception of object unity in two-dimensional displays. *Infant Behavior and Development, 18*, 133–143.

Kellman, P.J., & Spelke, E.S. (1983). Perception of partly occluded objects in infancy. *Cognitive Psychology, 15*, 483–524.

Kellman, P.J., Spelke, E.S., & Short, K.R. (1986). Infant perception of object unity from translatory motion in depth and vertical translation. *Child Development, 57*, 72–86.

Kremenitzer, J.P., Vaughan, H.G., Kurtzberg, D., & Dowling, K. (1979). Smooth-pursuit eye movements in the newborn infant. *Child Development, 50*, 442–448.

Langlois, J., & Roggman, L.A. (1990). Attractive faces are only average. *Psychological Science, 1*, 115–121.

Langlois, J.H., Roggman, L.A., Casey, R.J., Ritter, J.M., Rieser-Danner, L.A., & Jenkins, V.Y. (1987). Infant preferences for attractive faces: Rudiments of a stereoptype?. *Developmental Psychology, 23*, 363–369.

Langlois, J.H., Ritter, J.M., Roggman, L.A., & Vaughn, L.S. (1991). Facial diversity and infant preferences for attractive faces. *Developmental Psychology, 27*, 79–84.

Laurence, M., & Feind, C. (1953). Vestibular responses to rotation in the newborn infant. *Pediatrics, 12*, 300–306.

Maratos, O. (1973). *The origin and development of imitation during the first 6 months of life*. Unpublished doctoral dissertation. University of Geneva, Switzerland.

Meltzoff, A.N., & Moore, M.K. (1977). Imitation of facial and manual gestures by human neonates. *Science, 198*, 75–78.

Meltzoff, A.N., & Moore, M.K. (1983). Newborn infants imitate adult gestures. *Child Development, 54*, 702–709.

Meltzoff, A.N., & Moore, M.K. (1992). Early imitation within a functional framework: The importance of person identity, movement, and development. *Infant Behavior and Development, 15*, 479–505.

Meltzoff, A.N., & Moore, M.K. (1994). Imitation, memory, and the representation of persons. *Infant Behavior and Development, 17*, 83–99.

Mercer, M.E., Courage, M.L., & Adams, R.J. (1991). Contrast/color card procedure: A new test of young infants' color vision. *Optometry and Vision Science, 68*, 522–532.

Pascalis, O., de Schonen, S., Morton, J., Deruelle, C., & Fabre-Grenet, M. (1995). Mother's face recognition by neonates: A replication and an extension. *Infant Behavior and Development, 18*, 79–85.

Piaget, J. (1953). *The origins of intelligence in the child*. London: Routledge & Kegan Paul.

Piaget, J. (1954). *The construction of reality in the child*. New York: Basic Books.

Reissland, N. (1988). Neonatal imitation in the first hour of life: Observations in Rural Nepal. *Developmental Psychology, 24*, 464–469.

Samuels, C.A., Butterworth, G., Roberts, T., & Graupner, L. (1994). Babies prefer attractiveness to symmetry. *Perception, 23*, 823–831.

Samuels, C.A., & Ewy, R. (1985). Aesthetic perception of faces during infancy. *British Journal of Developmental Psychology, 3*, 221–228.

Slater, A. (1995). Visual perception and memory at birth. In C. Rovee-Collier and L. Lipsitt (Eds.), *Advances in infancy research* (Vol. 9, pp.107–162). Norwood, NJ: Ablex.

Slater, A., Johnson, S.P., Brown, E., & Badenoch, M. (1996). The roles of texture and occluder size on newborn infants' perception of partly occluded objects. *Infant Behavior and Development, 19*, 145–148.

Slater, A., Johnson, S.P., Kellman, P.J., & Spelke, E. S. (1994). The role of three-dimensional depth cues in infants' perception of partly occluded objects. *Early Development and Parenting, 3*, 187–191.

Slater, A., Mattock, A., & Brown, E. (1990). Size constancy at birth: Newborn infants' responses to retinal and real size. *Journal of Experimental Child Psychology, 49*, 314–322.

Slater, A., Mattock, A., Brown, E., & Bremner, J.G. (1991). Form perception at birth: Cohen and Younger revisited. *Journal of Experimental Child Psychology, 51*, 395–405.

Slater, A., Mattock, A., Brown, E., Burnham, D., & Young, A.W. (1991). Visual processing of stimulus compounds in newborn infants. *Perception, 20*, 29–33.

Slater, A., & Morison, V. (1985). Shape constancy and slant perception at birth. *Perception, 14*, 337–344.

Slater, A., Morison, V., & Rose, D. (1983). Locus of habituation in the human newborn. *Perception, 12*, 593–598.

Slater, A., Morison, V., & Somers, M. (1988). Orientation discrimination and cortical function in the human newborn. *Perception, 17*, 597–602.

Slater, A., Morison, V., Somers, M., Mattock, A., Brown, E., & Taylor, D. (1990). Newborn and older infants' perception of partly occluded objects. *Infant Behavior and Development, 13*, 33–49.

Sokol, S. (1978). Measurement of infant acuity from pattern reversal evoked potentials. *Vision Research, 18*, 33–40.

Teller, D.Y. (1979). The forced-choice preferential looking procedure: A psychological technique for use with human infants. *Infant Behavior and Development, 2*, 135–153.

Zusne, L. (1970). *Visual perception of form.* New York: Academic Press.

PART III

Perception, Action and Communication

CHAPTER EIGHT

Neonatal, Early and Later Imitation: Same Order Phenomena?

Olga Maratos
University of Athens, Greece

The issue of infant imitation has been alive for almost a century. The works of Guillaume (1926), Valentine (1930) and Piaget (1935, 1946) have been important milestones in the theoretical and experimental study of it. Nearly forty years ago, the French psychologist Zazzo (1957) had reported that 15-day-old infants imitated tongue protrusion; he dismissed the finding as he failed to reproduce it. Zazzo's anecdotal evidence was not immediately followed up because theories of child development could not accommodate such findings. Learning, psychoanalytic and Piagetian theories about human cognitive and affective development have focussed on the study of the ability of the newborn human organism to perceive and represent external reality. They have, however, mostly compared this ability with similar abilities in the older infant. They all described the newborn as an impotent, dependent organism who lives in a state of adualism in relation to the external world. Early imitation was thought to be an "archaic" reflex and the fact that it was not possible to evoke imitation of tongue protrusion in relatively older infants strengthened this belief.

In the last three decades the special interest of infant psychologists in the mental functioning of the newborn and the young infant has been revived. Sophisticated experiments have thrown new light on the way scientists approach the study of the first year of life and have led to a review of most basic developmental theories. Imitation has been a privileged area of research as the act of imitating presupposes certain abilities that touch upon sensory, mental and emotional functioning: (1) sensory and perceptual discrimination of the model; (2) sensorimotor and possibly intermodal coordination, at least as far as the imitation of some models is concerned; (3) representational capacity—even if in an emerging state; (4) ability to relate and communicate with the other person; and (5) maybe intention to reproduce the model.

The purpose of this chapter is two-fold: (1) to address the phenomenon of neonatal imitation by commenting on the mechanisms involved and on the kind of perceptual, cognitive and representational abilities the newborn must possess in order to imitate; and (2) to try to answer the question whether neonatal and early attempts at imitation (between birth and six months of age) of certain models is the same phenomenon, governed by the same mechanisms, as later imitation (from the end of the first year onwards).

NEWBORN AND EARLY IMITATION

Twenty-six years ago, Gardner and Gardner (1970) published an article reporting the observation of imitation of tongue protrusion on their 6-week-old son.[1] Maratos (1973,1982) was among the first to follow up the phenomenon in an attempt to bring together cognitive and affective aspects of infant psychological functioning. In a longitudinal study, twelve infant girls were examined fortnightly, from the age of 1 month to the age of 6 months. They were presented with nine models for imitation: tongue protrusion, mouth opening, head shaking, finger movements (perceived visually), recorded crying of a newborn baby, recorded vocalizations of a 4-month-old infant, the vocalizations "aa-aa", "agh" and "ma-ma" pronounced by the adult (perceived acoustically), and active rhythmical movement of their legs moved by the experimenter (perceived kinaesthetically). The main findings of this research were that infants at one month imitate three visually perceived models (tongue protrusion, mouth opening, head shaking). Recorded crying elicits an automatic response described as "contagious crying". Finger movements and the other two vocal models were first imitated at 2 months.[2]

The finding that newborn babies (during the first month of life) can imitate was confirmed by Meltzoff and Moore (1977, 1983), Jacobson (1979), Field, Woodson, Greenberg and Cohen (1982), Fontaine (1984), Kugiumutzakis (1985, in press), Vinter (1985) and others.[3] Few researchers (e.g. Anisfeld, 1979 and Hayes and Watson, 1981) reported that they could not elicit imitation in newborns and some (e.g. Masters, 1979) were critical of the experimental procedures that were followed

---

1   Between the Zazzo finding and the Gardner & Gardner report, there were some isolated references to observations of early imitation, i.e. Brazelton and Young (1964).

2   The most interesting finding of this research proved to be the different fate of the various imitative responses, i.e. different developmental curves during the age span examined (the first 6 months of life). This is commented upon in the second section of this chapter.

3   There will be no attempt in this chapter to give an exhaustive list and to critically review all literature on early imitation. The reader is referred to the important review articles of Kugiumutzakis (1993) and Meltzoff and Moore (1994).

in early research. The discussion about methodological issues highlights the difficulties involved in research with very young infants. Apart from choosing the optimal physiological state – which is alert and quiet – the most important precaution in doing research with newborns and very young infants is to register the individual baseline activity of each infant before any model is presented but also during the presentation of models that involve the human face, as babies interacting naturally with their mothers' faces tend to move parts of their own face and body.

The fact that neonates less than 72 hours old (Meltzoff and Moore, 1983), at 36 hours (Field, Woodson, Greenberg and Cohen, 1982) and even at 30 minutes after birth (Kugiumutzakis, in press) can imitate rules out the possibility that imitative responses are learned responses. The newborn infants tested in the aforementioned experiments imitated mainly facial gestures: mouth opening and tongue protrusion in the Meltzoff and Moore study; differential facial expressions of happiness, sadness and surprise in the Field et al. study and tongue protrusion, mouth opening and the sound "aa" in the Kugiumutzakis study. Studies of imitation stress the infant's preference for facial gestures and head movement during the first month of life. Differential attention between face and hand movements and to various vocalizations and imitation of the corresponding models are reported later in age. This preferential attention of the newborn baby for stimuli coming from the human face is to be noted and will be commented on later in the chapter. The phenomenon of neonatal imitation of certain models is currently widely accepted and not challenged any more, and the still-animated theoretical discussions concern its meaning and importance for developmental psychological theories.

Developmental approaches to imitation

Maratos (1973), Pawlby (1977), Jacobson (1979), Abravanel and Sigafoos (1984), Fontaine (1984), Kugiumutzakis (1985) and Vinter (1985) have conducted developmental studies on imitation of infants between 15 days and 10 months of age. Pawlby saw the infants between 4 and 10 months, Vinter between birth and three months and the other experimenters between 15 days or 1 month and 6 months; Abravanel and Sigafoos, Fontaine and Jacobson used the cross-sectional method whereas Kugiumutzakis, Maratos, Pawlby and Vinter saw the infants longitudinally. They have all (except Pawlby)[4] reported a progressive decline in imitative responses to tongue protrusion and mouth opening after the first 2 or 3 months.[5] At the same time, imitative responses to sounds, vocalizations, hand and

---

4 Pawlby's study was focussed on spontaneous imitative interaction between the mother and the infant in a situation where they could both imitate each other interchangeably. She did not specifically study imitation of mouth opening and tongue protrusion, but she found that imitative interaction showed an overall increase between 4 and 10 months.

5 The phenomenon is so remarkable that one could superimpose developmental curves obtained in different studies and reach an almost perfect match.

finger movements show smoother developmental patterns; these models are imitated more frequently and with a better accuracy as the infant gets older.

This very interesting finding (i.e. the temporary disappearance of successful imitation of certain face movements) has not been interpreted in a satisfactory way. Some researchers failed to elicit imitation in very young infants and criticized the methodological approaches of the early studies (i.e. Anisfeld, 1979 and Masters, 1979). Some interpreted early imitation as pseudo-imitation; Abravanel and Sigafoos (1984) suggested that tongue protrusion may be a potential "social" reflex and Fontaine tried to explain the phenomenon of early imitation by relating it to the evolution of motor competences. Others (e.g. Jacobson & Kagan, 1979) maintained that neonatal imitation of tongue protrusion is mediated by releasing mechanisms and is not real imitation. None of the aforementioned researchers discussed the remarkable finding of the neonate's capacity for differentially imitating mouth opening and tongue protrusion.

This finding is strong enough evidence that early imitation is not reflexive, nor is it a fixed action pattern as are innate releasing mechanisms. Furthermore, not all infants imitate tongue protrusion and mouth opening and there are different individual patterns in the way they imitate; this is yet another argument against early imitation being either a reflex or an innate releasing mechanism. Maybe newborn imitation is still a puzzling problem which cannot be accommodated in existing developmental theories; it is however a fact and the mechanisms involved in it should be explored, as should the phenomenon of temporary disappearence of this early capacity.

LATER INFANT IMITATION

Piaget (1946), Uzgiris (1981), Maratos (1973) and Meltzoff (1985) have conducted cross-sectional or longitudinal research with older infants (from 9 months to the end of the second year of life). Piaget was interested in individual development and based his theory of imitation on the observation of his three children; he tried to accommodate his findings in his more general theory of cognitive development. Killen and Uzgiris (as reported in Uzgiris, 1981) and Meltzoff's more recent research with older infants were conducted once neonatal and early infant imitation were not challenged any more.

Maratos,[6] in a pilot study (unpublished) tried the facial and head movement models of her original work (i.e. tongue protrusion, mouth opening and head shaking) with ten infants ranging between 9 and 11 months of age and obtained imitative responses by all of them. The interest of this study lies in the fact that the infants had stopped imitating these models between 3 and 6 months when they

---

6   Some reference to this pilot work is included in Maratos' Ph.D. thesis, 1973.

were tested longitudinally (Maratos 1973, 1982). Furthermore, the imitative responses to all three movements (two face and one head) that were presented as models differed from the imitative responses obtained at the earlier age (between birth and 3 months).

At the *earlier age*, the 1- or 2-month-old infant reacts after a relatively long latency, following repeated presentation of the models. Her[7] movements are rapid, of small amplitude and of short duration. In the case of successful imitation of the tongue protrusion model the tongue is often just barely apparent outside the lips and this response has been called by Vinter (1985, p. 75) "half protrusion" and by Abravanel and Sigafoos (1984, p. 385) "partial tongue protrusion". Once the infant starts protruding her tongue, or opening her mouth, she tends to go on repeating the movement several times. Mouth opening is accordingly imitated after a relatively long latency, often during the presentation of the model with hesitant and almost constant movements of the area around the mouth, including swallowing, until one sees the final response with the mouth open wide. In the case of the head-shaking model, the infant continues the original movement of the head that is necessarily made in order to follow the model's head-shaking movement and what was scored as a successful imitative response of this particular model was in fact the continuation of the same movement once the presentation of the model had ended. The duration of the imitative response lasted less than 5 seconds and the movement was never spontaneously repeated by the infant without a new presentation of the model.[8]

At the *later age*, the 9- or 10-month-old infant reacts immediately after the very first presentation of the models. The response is given only once and is a much more accurate match of the model_a clear tongue protrusion with the tongue well visible between the lips, wide mouth opening or well controlled head shaking that reproduces correctly even the rhythmical aspect of the model. None of these responses is followed by any accompanying movements as happens with the younger infant. Furthermore, the older infant often has an amused expression on the face, thus sending us the message that the act is intentional. Another difference in the behaviour of the older infant, when compared with that of the younger one, is the fact that she waits for the experimenter to present the next model for imitation without moving the area around the mouth between model presentations as the younger infant so often tends to do. Finally, the older infant tries to imitate "new" models, i.e. models that

---

7   The female form is chosen because the subjects were all girls. As there is no evidence of sex differences in early or even later imitation (around the end of the first year of life), the reader can substitute he for she.

8   This response is described in Piaget's second stage "sporadic imitation" as a typical example of the infant's attempt to accommodate a sensorimotor scheme to an external stimulus. According to his explanation, the imitation that ensues is simply a continuation of the infant's original reaction and is not yet international.

involve movements which are not produced spontaneously. In the case of the Maratos pilot study this was illustrated by presenting the infants with the following model: an exaggerated and noisy inhalation with accompanying lip protrusion and lifting of the nose; the 9-month-olds tried immediately to repro-duce the model, laughing at the same time, whereas the younger ones either ignored it or moved their mouths while looking intensely at the experimenter's face; they did not succeed in imitating the model.

The aforementioned differences in: (1) motor activity around the mouth area that accompanies the act of imitation; (2) control of buccal and tongue movements; (3) reaction time;   and (4) the pleasure that is obviously experienced in the successful reproduction of the models do not allow us to consider the two imitative reactions (of the 1- or 2-month-old and of the 9- or 10-month-old infant) as identical or even governed by the same mechanisms.

There are, in my view, two possible lines to follow in order to approach and understand neonatal and early imitation and at the same time take into consideration the phenomenon of temporary "disappearance" of some early imitative responses: the first is the nature of the relations between imitation, cognition and representation; and the second is the motivational, affective framework of intersubjective communication. In other words, one has to consider simultaneously the cognitive and the affective–social aspect of an imitative act.

IMITATION, COGNITION AND REPRESENTATION

Piaget is the only cognitive developmental psychologist who had a distinctive theory about the development of imitation in the first two years of life. In his detailed and interesting account, using the method of "critical observation" on his own three children, Piaget considered imitation as a function of sensorimotor intelligence and has traced its development in six sub-stages that are parallel to the stages of sensorimotor intelligence. Piaget placed the origin of representation in imitation and saw in the imitative act of the infant the primacy of accommodation over assimilation within the frame of the action scheme. This approach may be a problem in view of the recent findings of early imitation in newborn infants; if the capacity for representation is a necessary precondition for imitation to occur, then it should developmentally precede successful imitation of invisible parts of the body. If such is the case then Piaget's hypothesis was wrong, as according to him, it is through imitation that one traces the genesis of differentiated signifiers which are essential elements of the symbolic function. Piaget's account of the development of imitation in his early work (1946), but also in his later elaborations on the subject (Piaget & Inhelder, 1966) includes the following three important features: (1) a detailed description of the psychogenesis of imitation; (2) a discussion of the function of imitation; and (3) emphasis upon the importance of imitation in symbolic and cognitive functioning.

Psychogenesis of imitation

The six stages of imitation Piaget described are the following: preparation through reflex (up to 4 weeks); sporadic imitation (1 to 4 months); systematic imitation of known sounds and acts visible on own body (5 to 8 months); imitation of acts invisible on own body (8 to 11 months); systematic imitation of new models (11 to 16 months); and deferred or representative imitation (from 16 months onwards). Piaget believed that imitation does not depend on an instinctive or hereditary technique but that the child learns to imitate; he considered imitation as a continuation of the effort at accommodation and maintained that it occurs when accommodation has primacy over assimilation. As imitation is closely related to the development of sensorimotor intelligence his observations of successful imitative acts are explained in terms of circular reaction, assimilations and reproduction of total schemes of action as distinguished from reproductions of the final result of a perceived act. The culmination of psychogenetic development of imitation is deferred or delayed imitation of new acts which is observed around 16 or 18 months.

Function of imitation

According to Piaget, imitation is internalized by the end of the second year of life and is no longer dependent upon actual action. The role of imitation in mental development is of paramount importance because of its relations with representation. Deferred imitation coincides with the beginnings of the use of signs and symbols. Deferred imitation, language and mental image emerge almost simultaneously in the second half of the second year of life. The mental image (defined as the symbol which is an internalized copy of the object) is the product of internalized imitation. When accommodation involves visible gestures, actual imitation of models occurs, but when accommodation is virtual or internal, then there is mental image or internalized imitation. In Piaget's cognitive theory the imitative act, as the origin of mental image, is thus given a special place in the semiotic function together with oral and written language, drawing, symbolism, etc. Imitation is also recognized by Piaget as playing an important role in the development of memory.

Representation

According to Piaget, representative processes are based on imitation. He maintained that imitative accommodation could account for the formation of signifiers which are necessary to representative activity (Piaget, 1946). In later formulations (Piaget & Inhelder, 1966) imitation, together with perception and image, is viewed as a figurative mechanism (or as a figurative instrument) involved in mental development, a function that does not transform the object but tends to imitate it; figurative mechanisms are opposed to operative mechanisms which transform the objects by the actions performed on them. The fact that Piaget places all representative processes of the infant mind at the end of the second year of life is, in my view, the most controversial idea in Piaget's account of sensorimotor intelligence. I believe the finding of an early imitative capacity at birth and its course during sensorimotor development calls for a review of the relations between imitation and representation. Some psychologists have already criticized Piaget on this issue (see Butterworth, 1981).[9] Piaget maintains that representation, in its narrow sense, is the mental image, or the mnemonic image, that is the symbolic evocation of absent reality; according to his theory, representation is the association between a signifier which provokes the evocation, and the signified which is provided by sensorimotor intelligence. The signifiers of the sensorimotor stage are mainly signs and perceptual indices. The development of imitation in the first 16 or 18 months of life leads to the formation of mental images and to symbolic function. Piaget, along with Wallon (1942), did not believe that there is a capacity for either representation or symbolic functioning during the first stages of sensorimotor development (in the first year of life). But unless one postulates some kind of representational capacity from very early on it is not possible to accommodate the phenomenon of early imitation in any developmental theory. Bruner (1966), Bower (1979), Mounoud (1971) and Meltzoff (1981) have all formed hypotheses on the development of representation; however, only Mounoud (1971) and Meltzoff (1981) had in mind the data on early imitation when their hypotheses were formulated.

Bruner (1966) defines representation as *a set of rules in which one conserves one's encounters with events* and he postulates three forms of representation: (1) *enactive*, which is the most primitive: the infant's perception is defined by his acts; (2) *iconic*, which functions around 12 months: there is a new organization of perceptual forms in iconic or imagery forms; *iconic* representation comes about by the gradual separation of perceptions from acts; and (3) *symbolic*, which comes about at the end of the second year of life. Both Piaget and Bruner place the origin of representational activity in the infant's act; however, Bruner postulates an iconic representation much earlier in development than Piaget but there was no controversy between them as to the fact that deferred imitation appears towards the end of the second year of life. According to Piaget, fully operational deferred imitation exists only in the absence of the model, as he illustrates in his observations nos. 52–55 (Piaget, 1946, pp. 64–65).[10] Bruner, on the other hand, would explain both imitation of parts invisible on own body (e. g. imitation of tongue protrusion) and deferred imitation by the mechanism of iconic representation.

Bower (1979) thinks that perception *per se* is a process of representation which develops separately from action and movement. He maintains that there are

---

9 See especially Part III: The development of representation; chapters by A. Bullinger, pp. 173–199, P. Mounoud and Annie Vinter, pp. 200–235, A.N. Meltzoff, pp. 85–114 and G. Butterworth, pp. 137–169.

10 These observations were made on his own children at the age of 16 and 17 months.

representations since birth and they are the internal descriptions of events and of external objects. These first representations are abstract; that is, they maintain only the most general and universal qualities of reality and they become more specific as the infant develops, by integrating the unique qualities of events and objects. Bower thinks that the first representations use abstract symbols and the later ones use images. It is obvious that Bower postulates the development of representation going in the opposite direction to the one Bruner and Piaget describe. It is difficult to see how this approach could account for early imitation which is limited and specific to the reproduction of certain face movements and it certainly does not appear to be governed by any abstract representation but, if any, by a very concrete one, namely the representation of the human face. It is also worth stressing at this point that newborns do not imitate movements of inanimate objects or human acts on objects.

Mounoud (1971) and Vinter (1985)—adopting Mounoud's theory on representation—define representation as the result of acts of trial and analysis and as the correlation of different aspects and variations of real objects and events. They think that representations serve as models or memories, which structure internally the content of reality, so that they interfere in mental acts, such as the identification of objects, recognition and evocation. Representations in this theoretical approach can be defined according to the code which they use in order to arrange the structure of their content. Mounoud and Vinter mention four such codes: (1) the sensory code that exists at birth; (2) the perceptual code which develops during the sensorimotor stage; (3) the conceptual code which brings about a new organization of data; and (4) the formal code which is characteristic of representations during formal intelligence. These systems of representation (sensory, perceptual, conceptual and formal) are not mutually exclusive, nor do they succeed one another, but they can co-exist. Representations by each code system are successively global, then partial, then total and rigid, and finally total and adaptable or expandable. This theoretical formulation could, in my view, explain the phenomenon of early imitation by the use of sensory and perceptual codes and in that the representation using these codes is originally selective and global; i.e. it reproduces only movements that are related to the human face.

Meltzoff's AIM hypothesis (Active Intermodal Mapping) postulates that "... neonates can ... apprehend the equivalence between body transformations that they see and body transformations of their own that they feel themselves make" (Meltzoff, 1985, p. 15). Furthermore, he has tested the infant's capacity to tactually and visually discriminate between different shapes, and he hypothesizes the possible storage of some representation of tactually perceived shapes which are then related and recognized visually. He concludes that this capacity is innate. Meltzoff's AIM hypothesis certainly explains the mechanisms involved in early successful imitation of parts of the face of the other, parts that are not visible on the baby's own body, but does not explain the phenomenon of "disappearance" of this particular capacity for some months before it appears again at the age of 9 months.[11] Meltzoff and Moore's (1994) more recent work with older infants has led them to formulate the hypothesis of an innate capacity to represent the invisible as an important capacity towards baby's understanding of people. Furthermore, Meltzoff and Moore (1995, p.73) propose that *"... infants differentiate self from nonself and also recognise the commonality between themselves and other people, starting from birth."* This is a provocative hypothesis, but still premature and not fully supported by evidence from the total psychological/mental functioning of the infant. The notion of "self" should be well defined before such a claim can be made. Which "self" is differentiated by the newborn—the sensory, the perceptual, the preverbal, the verbal, the ecological, the conceptual, the social (see Neisser, 1994, and Stern, 1985)?

THINKING AND AFFECT IN PSYCHOANALYTIC THEORIES

Imitation was examined in the previous section from the point of view of the infant's cognitive functioning, leaving out the emotional aspect; i.e. motivational issues and affect accompanying the imitative act. Psychoanalytic theories have always been concerned with the very first relationship of the infant with his mother (or caregiver), which is the frame within which imitation takes place. Their hypotheses may, in my view, be helpful in advancing our theories about early imitation.

It is to be noted that the main representatives of the four psychoanalytic theoretical streams (Drive, Object, Ego and Self psychological theories) have addressed the issue of how thought is originated in human psychological development.[12] Thus Freud (1911) had already proposed that when the state of psychical rest is disturbed, whatever is thought or wished for is simply presented in the mind in a hallucinatory manner. As satisfaction does not come about by hallucination, this attempt is abandoned and *"... instead of it, the psychical apparatus has to decide to form a*

---

11 It should be stressed at this point that "disappearance" of imitative capacity concerns exclusively the imitation of tongue protrusion, a model that is not imitated between the ages of 3 and 8 or 9 months approximately. Imitation as a general tendency and capacity does not disappear at any time during development; on the contrary, the infant between birth and two years becomes more proficient at imitating various models.

12 It is obviously not possible within the limited space of this chapter to cover all relevant psychoanalytic literature on the subject; the references chosen (Freud's as representative of Drive theory and Bion's as representative of Object Relations theory) are in my opinion the most relevant views for the sake of the argument that follows and are limited only to what could be useful in understanding early imitation within an interactional situation. It should, however, be noted that there are many and very rich psychoanalytic ideas about mechanisms involved in early infant development concerning the mental life of the infant as well as the development of "self" and the relation to other people.

conception of the real circumstances in the external world ... A new principle of mental functioning is thus introduced... the reality principle which proves to be a momentous step" (Freud, 1911, p. 219). Although Freud does not indicate the age at which he supposes this principle is at work, we can assume that attempts at hallucinatory satisfaction may take place the very first time the infant is not fed immediately when he feels hungry and once he has already been fed and has had the chance to associate satisfaction with the breast; in other words, the reality principle may be at work very soon after birth. This approach is helpful as it stresses the possibility of the existence of an early form of mnemonic traces immediately after the infant has come into contact with the external world. Also Freud, in his attempt to explain how mental representations are formed, and in his effort to find psychophysical parallelisms, chose the term "presentation" instead of representation, with the prefix sensory-, object-, thing-, word- in order to strengthen his argument in favour of this parallelism (Freud, 1915, pp. 199–215). It is as if Freud had already in 1915 postulated different forms of representation operating in what he had termed in his psychoanalytic theory the "preconscious", i.e. the system in which, among other things, the presentations of things are associated with the presentations of words.

Bion (1967), in the formulation of his theory of thinking, postulates an inborn expectation of the breast, the *a priori* knowledge of the breast, and he maintains that when the infant comes into contact with the breast itself the pre-conception of the breast is combined with the awareness of the realization and this is the moment a conception or thought is born and starts to develop. Bion states *"... thoughts are classified according to their developmental history as pre-conceptions, conceptions or thoughts and finally concepts..."* (Bion, 1967, p. 111). Most important is Bion's idea that conceptions or thoughts are constantly combined with an emotional experience of satisfaction or frustration; that is, with an affective tone; frustration is experienced when the pre-conception is not met with a realization, when for instance there is no breast available.

Neither Freud nor Bion use the term "representation", but I believe in both conceptions – i.e. in Freud's idea of the importance of the failure of "hallucinatory satisfaction" in the genesis of thinking and in Bion's idea of the importance of the meeting of a pre-conception with its realization — the concept of representation is implied. Furthermore, in both Freud and Bion's formulations but also in most psychoanalytic literature, every experience, right from birth, is thought to have an emotional and a cognitive component. Continuing this line of thought, I believe that we can postulate an early capacity for some form of representation of the absent object which is not however any kind of object. It is specifically a representation of the human face.

The special importance of the human face

The human face is rightly recognized by psychoanalytic and developmental theories as a privileged stimulus for the newborn and the young infant. Even Piaget (1936,

p. 82),[13] who was not specially interested in motives and affects gives his own version of it:

> In other words the human figure presents this almost unique property in the universe of the baby, to lend itself to a totality of simultaneous assimilations... In the case of the other person's face and voice, we can talk of a general total assimilation and not of a connection between different assimilations, and this naturally explains why smile is much more frequent to people rather than to objects... The infant is searching, in a certain sense, to hear the face and to see the voice.

What a beautiful example of intermodal functioning! However, in spite of this early recognition, neither Piaget nor Freud could expand on this very important assumption, Piaget because of his exclusive interest in the cognitive aspect of development and Freud because he considered the baby's "psychical organ" as initially governed exclusively by unconscious Id-impulses and primary process. Psychoanalysts who were particularly interested in child development, under the influence of Freud's idea of the baby as an impotent and inadequately functioning human being, have initially postulated an adualism, a symbiosis or a fusion between mother and infant interacting within the dyad. These views have in the last decade been modified within the different theoretical currents. Special reference should be made to the contribution of the Kleinian School and of its formulations: (1) on the existence of an early Ego (the part of the psychical apparatus that comes into contact with the external world); and (2) on the concept of innate unconscious fantasies (as proof of a capacity for a rich mental life right at birth). Some of these ideas stem from direct infant observation, a practice that was originally instituted by Esther Bick and is today included in psychoanalytic training offered by some psychoanalytic Institutes. The relevant concepts are further discussed within the psychoanalytic theoretical framework and modified in the light of data coming from experimental infant psychology research.

Stern's (1985) account of the phases of development of the self is an interesting and successful example of the effort psychoanalysts make to review their theories and to initiate a dialogue with infant psychologists. Stern describes developmental phases from the perspective of the sense of the self, postulating it as the primary organizing principle in infant development. For the earliest period of life (the first two months) he infers the sense of an emergent self, from two months onwards the sense of a core self, from six months onwards the sense of a subjective self and from 15 months onwards the sense of a verbal self. He also discusses development from the important viewpoint of relatedness of self to other. His theory is important as it stresses the fact that every infantile action that takes place within a social context has cognitive and affective components. The "vitality affects" (Stern, 1985,

---

13 My translation from the 3rd French edition.

pp. 54–55) which characterize the early phases of development may be the newborn's expression of affect matching, the affective counterpart of the earliest imitative attempts that are behaviourally observable.

Finally, it is important to report that Trevarthen has since 1979 postulated an innate capacity to make contact with another human being; he suggested the term "innate intersubjectivity" to describe a function that helps the infant to evaluate and to define the quality of contact with his mother. He calls this function "primary intersubjectivity" during the first months of life and "secondary intersubjectivity" thereafter, when play, handling of objects and action games can be undertaken by the communicating partners. During the early phase the encounter between the mother and the infant is described as "protoconversation" and he uses musical terms to describe what goes on: *"... standards of rhythm, tonality and melody to confirm a harmony of moods"* (Trevarthen & Logotheti, 1987, p. 77). The expression of emotion by both partners is essential during protoconversations. Early imitative capacity is considered by Trevarthen (1985, p. 25) to be *"... a by-product of an inborn ability to generate basic forms of expressive movement..."*.

CONCLUSION

Bion's theory of thinking may serve as an inspiration for trying to explain newborn imitation of facial movements and grimaces. As the newborn seems to respond more readily and preferentially to the human face and voice, and this is a fact stressed by all developmental scientists, I propose that there is a preconception of the special facial configuration and of the human voice of the other person; in other words, of the human characteristics of our species. This pre-conception is recognized the moment the newborn comes into contact with a moving human face and he tends to imitate it. The movements the newborn baby does during the imitative act are all part of the repertoire of movements the newborn performs spontaneously. In order to match the model the infant must be able to function intermodally so that he can translate what he perceives visually to something he knows tactually and kinaesthetically; Meltzoff and Moore's proposition of a capacity for active intermodal mapping already operating at birth seems to be justified. The next question is: do we need a hypothesis of an innate fully developed representation of the body? It is my opinion that this is not necessarily a precondition and it is certainly not supported either by data on early imitation or from the course of development of these early imitative responses. The newborn does not succeed in matching any movement that he perceives visually on the other person's body nor does he attempt novel movements that he does not perform spontaneously.

However, in order to perform the matches that have been reported in neonatal imitation the newborn must possess at least some form of representation of the face both of the other person's and of the baby's own — both human after all — and this is a prerequisite for understanding this act of imitation. What still remains open to discussion is what kind of representation is present at birth. I do not think our data support the hypothesis that there is only one kind of representation and that this is already present at birth. On the contrary, data on imitation suggest that there are different kinds of representation, and it seems that Mounoud and Vinter's hypothesis of different codes of representation is justified. A type of representation is operative at birth using the sensory code. The perceptual code would be operative later during sensorimotor development, in the case of imitation at around 8 or 9 months when non visible parts of the body are imitated again and when new models that were never performed spontaneously before by the infant are imitated. Neonatal imitation can be explained by the concepts of pre-conception of the human face, active intermodal mapping and representation using the sensory code.

Furthermore, early imitation is intentional, not as an imitative act, but as a form of relating and as an effort to communicate. Acting similarly with the other person enhances understanding and interpreting the other's emotional state and intention. The difficulty in imitating models that are not monitored visually between the third and the eighth month coincides with the appearance of other more efficient relational and communicative skills that catch the attention of adults and are reinforced maybe because they make more sense to them; e.g. smiling, mutual vocal imitation, playful behaviour and acts on inanimate objects. Imitation as a form of relating and communicating between adult and baby never disappears; what seems to go through a temporary recess are the earliest forms of imitation which are highly selective and concern exclusively the human face.

Trevarthen's musical terms in the description of early interaction are very well chosen as they convey the emotional climate in which early interactions take place; the message conveyed is that the infant comes into the world equipped with special skills both for discriminating cues from the human face and for relating and communicating with the other person. Stern is also right in viewing development in phases during which earlier phases are included in the new perspectives of later ones, and in discussing relatedness of self with others rather than communication. It seems that analysing the young infant's different acts and expressions separately from the emotional setting in which they take place may lead to inadequate and unsubstantiated conclusions. The fact is that empathy, emotional resonance and affect attunement are present and important in every adult–baby encounter right from the beginning of life. My suggestion is that imitation as part of this very special situation happens already at birth because of the pre-conception of the human face which exists in the infant.

REFERENCES

Abravanel, E., & Sigafoos, A.D. (1984). Exploring the presence of imitation during early infancy. *Child Development, 55*, 381–392.

Anisfeld, M. (1979). Interpreting "imitative" responses in early infancy. *Science, 205*, 214–215.

Bion, W.R. (1967, 1984). A theory of thinking. In W.R. Bion, *Second thoughts* (Chapter 9). London, Maresfield Reprints, 1984.

Bower, T.G.R. (1979). The origins of meaning in perceptual development. In A. Pick (Ed.) *Perception and its development*. Hillsdale, NJ, Lawrence Erlbaum.

Brazelton, T.B., & Young, G.C. (1964). An example of imitative behavior in a nine-week-old infant. *Journal of the American Academy of Child Psychiatry, 3,* 53–67.

Bruner, J.S. (1966). The growth of representational processes in childhood. In J.M. Anglin (Ed.) *Beyond the information given*. London, Allen & Unwin.

Bullinger, A. (1981). Cognitive elaboration of sensorimotor behaviour. In G. Butterworth (Ed.) *Infancy and epistemology* (pp. 173–199). Brighton, Harvester Press.

Butterworth, G. (Ed.) (1981). *Infancy and epistemology: An evaluation of Piaget's theory*. Brighton, Harvester Press.

Butterworth, G. (1981). Object permanence and identity in Piaget's theory of infant cognition. In G. Butterworth (Ed.) *Infancy and epistemology* (pp.137–169). Brighton, Harvester Press.

Field, T.M., Woodson, R., Greenberg, R., & Cohen, D. (1982). Discrimination and imitation of facial expressions by neonates. *Science, 218,* 179–181.

Fontaine, R. (1984). Imitative skills between birth and six months. *Infant Behavior and Development, 7,* 323–333.

Freud, S. (1911, 1974). Formulations on the two principles of mental functioning. *Standard Edition*, (Vol. 12, pp. 215–224). London, Hogarth Press.

Freud, S. (1915, 1974). The unconscious. *Standard Edition* (Vol. 14, pp. 159–215). London, Hogarth Press.

Gardner, J., & Gardner H., (1970). A note on selective imitation by a six-week-old infant. *Child Development, 41,* 1209–1213.

Guillaume, P. (1926/1971). *L'imitation chez l'enfant*. Paris Libr. Felix Alcan (1926); Engl. transl, *Imitation in children*. Chicago, University of Chicago Press (1971).

Hayes, L.A., & Watson, J.S. (1981). Neonatal imitation: Fact or artifact? *Developmental Psychology, 17,* 655–660.

Jacobson, S.W. (1979). Matching behavior in young infants. *Child Development, 50,* 425–430.

Jacobson, S.W., & Kagan, J. (1979). Interpreting "imitative" responses in early infancy. *Science, 205,* 214–215.

Kugiumutzakis, G. (1985). *Development of imitation during the first six months of life*. Unpublished Ph.D. thesis, University of Uppsala, Report no. 377.

Kugiumutzakis, G. (1993). Intersubjective vocal imitation in early mother–infant interaction. In J. Nadel & L. Camaioni (Eds.) *New perspectives in early communicative development* (pp. 23–47). London, Routledge.

Kugiumutzakis, G. (in press). Neonatal imitation in the intersubjective companion space. In S. Braten (Ed.) *Intersubjective communication and emotion in ontogeny*. Cambridge, Cambridge University Press.

Maratos, O. (1973). *The origin and development of imitation in the first six months of life*. Unpublished Ph. D. thesis, University of Geneva.

Maratos, O. (1982). Trends in the development of imitation in the first six months of life. In T.G. Bever (Ed.) *Regressions in mental development: Basic Phenomena and Theories* (pp. 81–101). Hillsdale, NJ, Erlbaum.

Masters, J.C. (1979). Interpreting "imitative" responses in early infancy. *Science, 205,* 215.

Meltzoff, A.N. (1981). Imitation, intermodal co-ordination and representation in early infancy. In G. Butterworth (Ed.) *Infancy and epistemology* (pp. 85–114). Brighton, Harvester Press.

Meltzoff, A.N. (1985). The roots of social and cognitive development: Models of man's original nature. In T.M. Field and N. Fox (Ed.) *Social perception in infants* (pp. 1–30). Norwood, NJ, Ablex.

Meltzoff, A.N., & Moore, M.K. (1977). Imitation of facial and manual gestures by human neonates. *Science, 198*, 75–78.

Meltzoff, A.N., & Moore, M.K. (1983). Newborn infants imitate adult facial gestures. *Child Development, 54*, 702–709.

Meltzoff, A.N., & Moore, M.K. (1994). Imitation, memory and the representation of persons. *Infant Behavior and Development, 17*, 83–99.

Meltzoff, A.N., & Moore, M.K. (1995). A theory of the role of imitation in the emergence of self. In P. Rochat (Ed.) *The self in early infancy* (pp. 73–93). New York, North-Holland-Elsevier.

Mounoud, P. (1971). Développement des systémes de représentation et de traitement chez l'enfant. *Bulletin de Psychologie, 296*, 261–272.

Mounoud, P., & Vinter, A. (1981). Representation and sensorimotor development. In G. Butterworth (Ed.) *Infancy and epistemology* (pp.200–235). Brighton, Harvester Press.

Neisser, U. (1994). *The perceived self: Ecological and interpersonal sources of self knowledge.* Cambridge, Cambridge University Press.

Pawlby, S.J. (1977). Imitative interaction. In H.R. Schaffer (Ed.) *Studies in mother–infant interaction* (pp. 203–224). London, Academic Press.

Piaget, J. (1935). Les théories de l'imitation. *Cahiers de pédagogie expérimentale et de psychologie de l'enfant, No. 6*, 1–13.

Piaget, J. (1936). *La naissance de l'intelligence chez l'enfant.* Neuchâtel and Paris, Delachaux et Niestlé.

Piaget, J. (1946/1962). *La formation du symbole chez l'enfant.* Neuchâtel and Paris, Delachaux et Niestlé (1946). Engl. transl., *Play, dreams and imitation in childhood.* London, Routledge (1962).

Piaget, J., & Inhelder, B. (1966/1971). *L'image mentale chez l'enfant.* Paris, Presses Universitaires de France (1966). Engl. transl., *Mental imagery in the child.* London, Routledge (1971).

Stern, D.N. (1985). *The interpersonal world of the infant.* New York, Basic Books.

Trevarthen, C. (1979). Communication and cooperation in early infancy. A description of primary intersubjectivity. In M. Bullowa (Ed.) *Before speech: The beginnings of human communication.* Cambridge, Cambridge University Press.

Trevarthen, C. (1985). Facial expressions of emotion in mother–infant interaction. *Human Neurobiology, 4*, 21–32.

Trevarthen, C., & Logotheti, K. (1987). First symbols and the nature of human knowledge. [Ch. 3 in Symbolisme et conaissance]. *Cahiers de la fondation archives Jean Piaget, No. 8*, 65–92.

Uzgiris, I.C. (1981). Two functions of imitation during infancy. *International Journal of Behavioral Development, 4*, 1–12.

Valentine, C.W. (1930). The psychology of imitation with special refence to early childhood. *British Journal of Psychology, 21*, 2, 8–132.

Vinter, A. (1985). *L'imitation chez le nouveau-né.* Neuchâtel and Paris Delachaux et Niestlé.

Wallon, H. (1942). *De l'acte a la pensée.* Paris, Flammarion.

Zazzo, R. (1957). Le problème de l'imitation chez le nouveau-né. *Enfance, 10*, 135–142.

CHAPTER NINE

Initial Capacities for Speech Processing: Infants' Attention to Prosodic Cues for Segmentation

Josiane Bertoncini
Laboratory of Cognitive and Psycholinguistic Sciences,
Paris, France

In the past 30 years, the study of cognitive development has greatly advanced. Newborn infants are now recognized as being very efficient perceptual processors. They can discriminate various stimuli on the basis of minimal distinctive features. They are able to categorize different kinds of stimuli, indicating that they can extract some common property shared by different items. All these processes have been well documented, if as yet not completely understood, in the visual domain as well as in the auditory domain, especially that of speech perception. However, the auditory processing of speech has certain specific characteristics beyond the general properties common to any system of information processing. It is the aim of the present chapter to focus on some specific aspects of speech processing and of its development.

SOME CHARACTERISTICS OF SPEECH DEVELOPMENT

First of all, there is clear evidence that speech development is a process by which universal abilities progressively narrow down to specialized, language-specific abilities. We are born equipped with a universal ability to acquire language in a very efficient way. Subsequent exposure to one (or two) specific language(s), however, makes us so proficient and specialized in our native language that we lose most of this primary ability. This process offers a kind of elegant "natural experiment" for studying one of the most crucial questions in developmental psychology, namely, how the environment shapes perceptual processing. By means of the cross-linguistic study of speech perception, we aim to define: (1) how the initial processing system deals with different kinds of linguistic input; and (2) how it converges progressively towards a language-specific processor.

Thus, by comparing how infants process various speech stimuli taken from different languages, or by comparing the performance of infants from different linguistic environments, it becomes possible to establish the nature of the primary universal abilities to process speech, and then to trace early effects of experience on the development of speech perception.

Another characteristic of speech processing concerns the sequential nature of the auditory input. One of the main problems for psycholinguists is to establish how linguistically relevant units such as words are retrieved from the speech signal. This so-called segmentation problem stems from the absence of a one-to-one correspondence between the phonetic segment and the acoustic signal. The signal is continuous and there are no obvious pauses between individual meaningful units, such as words. Under normal circumstances, we tend to ignore that segmentation can be a problem. Our automatic and specialized mechanisms operate smoothly, from the low-level acoustic analysis of the speech signal to the integration of a meaningful message. Segmentation can be achieved by the joint operation of both lower-level and higher-level mechanisms, the latter of which rely on phonological, lexical and syntactic knowledge. Such a process becomes clear only when we are confronted with distorted or non-prototypical speech. For instance, when listening to a non-native speaker of our own language we suddenly become aware of possible failures of our segmentation process, and we need to really pay attention just to retrieve the words that are being spoken. The higher-level processes that adults may rely on are obviously out of reach for infants who have yet acquired any lexical knowledge. Since this is in fact precisely what they must acquire, it becomes even more crucial that they segment correctly the continuous signal, with only the help of basic acoustic mechanisms.

FROM UNIVERSAL TO LANGUAGE-SPECIFIC: THE PROBLEM OF SEGMENTATION

The aim of our research is to understand the innate abilities to segment the speech stream and to retrieve the *units* that are linguistically functional in the language.

Previous studies have shown that adult listeners do not use a universal strategy when it comes to segmenting speech into words, but rather one that is related to the phonological, especially rhythmical, properties of their native language (Cutler, Mehler, Norris & Segui, 1983). For example, English speakers use the alternations of stressed and unstressed syllables to locate potential word boundaries (Cutler & Norris, 1988; Cutler & Butterfield, 1990; 1992). In contrast, native speakers of French, a language with a syllable-based rhythm, seem to rely mainly on the syllable to segment and access spoken words (Mehler, Dommergues, Frauenfelder & Segui, 1981; Cutler, Mehler, Norris & Segui, 1986). This series of data has been extended to another language, Japanese, which is mora-timed. Accordingly, experimental results suggest that for Japanese listeners the mora acts as the perceptual segmentation unit (Otake, Hatano, Cutler & Mehler, 1993). Taken together, such data indicate that the perceptual strategies developed by speakers to extract linguistically relevant units from the continuous speech stream are language-specific. Moreover, even perfectly fluent bilingual speakers of French and English do not seem to switch strategy from one language to the other (Cutler, Mehler, Norris & Segui, 1989).

These results suggest that the development of a segmentation strategy might originate in the very early stages of language acquisition. This idea receives some support from evidence showing that neonates do not process multisyllabic utterances as irreducible entities, but that they are able to detect structural properties related to the number of components in these strings (Bijeljac-Babic, Bertoncini & Mehler, 1993). In this study and those that will be briefly described later, the basic idea was to present newborns with complex utterances and to test their sensitivity to the number of components that constitute these utterances. If infants can extract such a property shared by phonetically varied utterances, they should be able to discriminate two sets of utterances that differ only on this dimension. When discrimination is obtained, it is taken as an indication that infants can analyse and use some information about components. In other words, their processing system would seem to be prepared to start tackling the segmentation problem.

The results obtained by Bijeljac-Babic et al. (1993) showed that neonates discriminate varied sets of 2-CV (Consonant-Vowel) from 3-CV French pseudo-words. Moreover, this effect holds regardless of whether there was a difference in duration between the 2-CV and the 3-CV utterances. These results suggest that newborns represent complex utterances in terms of syllables. Note that we are not claiming that the represented syllables are fully specified. It is possible that a primary pattern of representation involves only *syllable-like* units, not necessarily finely specified around the vowel nuclei. In fact, infants failed to discriminate between 4-phoneme and 6-phoneme bisyllabic utterances (CVCV, VCCV, CVVC... vs. CCVCCV, CVCCVC, VCCCVC...) although the 6-phoneme utterances contained more consonants, and therefore more complex syllabic structures, than the 4-phoneme utterances (Bijeljac-Babic, et al., 1993; see also Bertoncini, Bijeljac-Babic, Jusczyk, Kennedy & Mehler, 1988).

From these results one can infer that syllables, or syllable-like units, constitute what we could call a *good* speech pattern, in that it fits infants' initial processing proclivities. But an alternative hypothesis deserves to be considered. The rhythmical structure of French is based on syllables. We know that young infants are highly sensitive to the prosodic information that characterizes speech (Cooper & Aslin, 1990; Kemler-Nelson, Hirsh-Pasek, Jusczyk & Wright Cassidy, 1989), and that they are sensitive to rhythmical structure in music (Trehub & Thorpe, 1989). It is thus possible that infants only apply their universal ability to pick up rhythmical properties for French as they would do for any kind of rhythm used in a natural language. In this case, syllables would emerge as an inherent property of French utterances, as other rhythmical units would naturally emerge from languages that are not syllable-timed, but mora-timed or stress-timed instead.

In any case, the infant must acquire one particular processing strategy because we know that adult listeners use neither a universal strategy to segment speech, nor a specific strategy suited to each language they hear, but rather only the one determined by their native language. Thus, even if the syllable acts as a universal primary unit of representation, it is necessary that any other unit can be derived from it in case the native language is not syllable-timed. On the other hand, if infants are initially sensitive to any kind of unit, this universal sensitivity is expected to narrow down to just the one unit which is suited to process the native language.

ARE INFANTS SENSITIVE TO ANY KIND OF SPEECH UNIT?

The question of whether the initial processing system is sensitive to any kind of unit can be addressed by testing neonates' reaction to various types of linguistic input. The Japanese language offers us a unique opportunity to dissociate two kinds of units, i.e. the *mora* and the *syllable*, within the same linguistic material. In Japanese (Tokyo standard), syllables can be composed of either one mora (V, CV), or two morae. There are different types of bimoraic syllables: long vowels (VV), CVVs, and closed syllables (V or CV followed by a nasal consonant (N), or by the first part of a geminate consonant (represented as Q)). Morae are rhythmic units, in that it has been shown that the duration of a word is a function of the number of its moraic components (Hoequist, 1983; Port, Dalby and O'Dell, 1987), and each mora receives a pitch value (High or Low).

Thus, using Japanese words composed of monomoraic and bimoraic syllables allowed us to compare infants' sensitivity to syllabic and sub-syllabic rhythmical units. The infants were presented with two large sets of phonetically varied Japanese words. In one experiment, *bisyllabic* words like *mika, buke, kago, seki* were contrasted with *trisyllabic* words like *hekiga, kokesi, erika*. In another experiment, bisyllabic-*bimoraic* words were to be discriminated from bisyllabic-*trimoraic* words like *kaNgo, mikaN, seQki, buuke* . If infants represent Japanese words in terms of both syllables and morae, they should discriminate in both cases, i.e. when there is a change either in the number of syllables or in the number of morae. In contrast, if they represent words exclusively in terms of syllables, they should notice a change in the number of syllables but not in the number of morae. The results were interpreted in support of the second hypothesis. That is, newborns reacted to the change from bisyllabic to trisyllabic words, but not to the change from bimoraic to trimoraic words (Bertoncini, Floccia, Nazzi & Mehler, 1995).

These results suggest that not all rhythmic units are equally salient to newborns. One possibility is that infants represented both bimoraic and trimoraic words as being composed of two syllables regardless of whether they were simple CVs, or more complex syllables, including bimoraic ones. On this view, the perceptual representation, at least in a context of phonetically varied bisyllabic words, would merely include information about the vocalic nucleus without finer details about the internal structure of the syllable. This possibility is in accordance with the hypothesis that syllables are only globally represented (Bijeljac-Babic et al., 1993; Jusczyk, Jusczyk, Kennedy, Schomberg & Koenig, 1995). To conclude, then, infants do not seem to represent trimoraic words as containing one more unit than bimoraic words. When differences in word rhythm are carried by non-syllabic elements, i.e. without a vowel nucleus, they appear not to be perceived by infants.

PROSODY AND SPEECH SEGMENTATION

It is patently obvious that our native language models our articulatory system in such a fashion that our native accent persists even after years of total immersion in a second language. However, only relatively recently we have come to realize that our perceptual system is also strongly tuned by our native language (Werker & Tees, 1984). Although the "segmentation process is so basic to human language comprehension that psycholinguists long assumed that all speakers would do it in the same way" (Cutler et al., 1989, p. 229), it appears now that various segmentation strategies are likely to develop under the early influences of different types of linguistic input. As we said earlier, segmentation seems to accord with the prosodic, especially rhythmical, properties of the native language.

Some prosodic regularities have been shown to contribute to word segmentation (Cutler, 1990). English-speaking adults tend to assume that a stressed syllable corresponds to the onset of a word, which is an efficient strategy because the most frequent prosodic pattern for multisyllabic English words is of the form Strong–Weak (SW) or trochaic (the syllable in initial position receives the main stress, and is followed by a weaker syllable(s)). Recently, several studies by Jusczyk and his colleagues have demonstrated that, by the second half of the first year of life, infants also make use of English stress pattern regularities in segmenting words from fluent speech. Seven-and-a-half-month-olds have been shown to segment more efficiently SW words than WS words. Indeed, the infants relied so strongly on the most probable SW pattern that they could be misled into grouping the last Strong syllable of WS words with a following Weak syllable into a "false" SW word. For example, when presented with sentences containing sequences like "guitar is", infants segmented the possible SW word "taris" (Newsome & Jusczyk, 1995).

In several elegant experiments, Morgan and his colleagues investigated, among other factors, the role of rhythmic properties in the way infants separate and cluster syllables within an utterance. For 8-month-old infants, it was found that rhythmic cues facilitate the grouping of syllables into word-like units (Morgan, 1994). In addition, comparing 9-month-old and 6-month-old infants, Morgan and Saffran (1995) showed that, while older infants grouped syllables according to both syllable order and rhythmic pattern, younger infants relied exclusively on prosodic cues.

ARE NEONATES SENSITIVE TO PROSODIC CUES FOR SEGMENTATION?

Prosody not only involves information about the rhythmical characteristics of a language, but also provides some indication of what can be a word in the language. Certain prosodic structures, at the level of sentences or clauses, seem to be used in most languages; however, there is a remarkable diversity among the prosodic patterns that characterize words in different languages. In English, most multisyllabic words begin with a strong syllable followed by a weaker one(s), containing a reduced vowel. In French, where there is no vowel reduction, all syllables are fully realized, with prominence on the final syllable of a word. In Japanese, the accentual pattern is principally given by the pitch variations, pitch accent being carried by the last High (syllabic) mora before a Low mora (Shibatani, 1990). If infants were sensitive to this kind of prosodic variation, this would stand them in good stead for segmenting and grouping speech units into coherent word-like patterns.

We have seen that neonates are particularly sensitive to the syllabic composition of utterances, and that the resulting representations may merely include information about vowels (Bijeljac-Babic et al., 1993; Bertoncini et al., 1988; Jusczyk, Bertoncini, Bijeljac-Babic, Kennedy & Mehler, 1990). Moreover, vowels are the principal bearers of prosodic variation. From this, it could be hypothesized that infants' primary representations, though not phonetically specified, integrate not only information about vowels but also some indication as to their inherent prosodic variations with respect to amplitude, duration and pitch movement. A similar view has been proposed by Mehler, Dupoux, Nazzi and Dehaene-Lambertz (1996) which specifically relates to vowel durational cues that infants would use in the discrimination of different languages (Nazzi, 1996).

Several recent studies offer converging evidence that neonates are sensitive to fine prosodic variations at the word level. In a series of experiments, Sansavini, Bertoncini and Giovanelli (1997) demonstrated that neonates are able to discriminate stress patterns in Italian words like *mAma* vs. *mamA*, or *tacAla* vs. *tAcala*, as well as to categorize stress patterns across phonetically varied words like *dAga*, *nAta*, *mAra*, *lAma*… vs. *dagA*, *natA*, *marA*, *lamA* …(A represents the stressed vowel). In another experiment, I found that neonates discriminate sets of Japanese bisyllabic words that were phonetically similar, but different in pitch contour (High–Low words vs. Low–High words). Moreover, neonates appear to be able to pick up fine prosodic differences associated to word boundaries. Christophe, Dupoux, Bertoncini & Mehler (1994) showed that 3-day-old neonates discriminate between two types of 2-CV strings that were either constituted of 2 syllables taken from within a word (e.g., *mati* extracted from mathé*mati*quement), or composed of the last syllable of one word and the first syllable of a following word (e.g. *mati* extracted from panora*ma ty*pique), i.e. including a prosodic word boundary.

These results support the hypothesis that, at the word level, neonates represent prosodic information including variations in vowel duration, amplitude and pitch movements. In addition, there are some indications that vowels and prosodic variation are genuinely linked in infants' processing of word patterns. For instance, Sansavini et al. (1997) showed that neonates can categorize stress pattern in sets of words including varied consonants like *daga, nata, mara*. However, in another study, Sansavini (in press) reported that, in similar conditions, infants failed to discriminate stress patterns when they were presented with sets of words that varied also in their constituent vowels (e.g. *baco, peri, cibo, pote*..). Of course, negative results should always be cautiously interpreted. Nevertheless, these data seem to suggest that information about vowels and stress variations might be difficult to dissociate, in tasks that require subjects to store the relevant (to be discriminated) information and to ignore irrelevant variations when they are both carried by the same segments. Related findings in adults suggest that segmental and suprasegmental information remain interconnected at some level of speech processing (Wood, 1974; Miller, 1978). Bertoncini (1993) reported similar findings suggesting that infants can extract information about the number of constituents only when presented with consistent prosodic patterns. While neonates distinguished ascending (L–H) from descending (H–L) Japanese words, and 2-CV from 3-CV Japanese words within each contour category, they failed to discriminate 2-CV from 3-CV words when they were presented with sets of words that included both types of prosodic contours.

Although we cannot exclude the possibility that these results merely reflect general limitations of infants' processing abilities, we propose that they could in fact be typical of the initial processing system. Our suggestion is, therefore, that representation and segmentation of complex utterances into units would firstly depend on prosodic information. Accordingly, infants would perceive utterances as being composed of different units by mainly relying on prosodic variations between constituents. Moreover, by merely representing multisyllabic utterances as sequences of vowels (or syllable-like units) along with their prosodic variations, infants would have access to the rhythmical and intonational properties that roughly define the word-like patterns in what is to become their native language.

CONCLUSION

In acquiring a language one of the main problems is to segment appropriately fluent incoming speech into meaningful units that can subsequently contribute to the construction of a mental lexicon. We presented evidence that infants display a keen sensitivity to both the syllabic composition of utterances and some associated prosodic properties. This sensitivity would allow infants to start processing speech by firstly relying on prosodic properties associated with syllable-like constituents of utterances. The resulting representations would then consist of a vocalic template conveying the accentual pattern of the word-like utterance. Moreover, infants seem to perceive differences in number of components, either in stress pattern or in intonational contour, only when they are carried by syllables, i.e. by units containing a vocalic nucleus. Such results suggest that the syllable, thus defined, may be the primary unit upon which initial speech processing would be universally based.

This first *universal* stage of speech processing would be affected by the native language input, since it has been shown in adult listeners that their native language determines which strategy they use for segmenting speech, and probably which information may be incorporated in their lexical entries. Word-like patterns provided by suprasegmental information, along with characteristics of the rhythmical structure of the language, could be used by infants to start lexicon acquisition. Which prosodic features will be maintained or discarded in the process of building the lexicon would depend upon the native language. For English, the sensitivity to contrasts between stressed and unstressed syllables will be maintained, sharpened up and integrated into automatic processing. While these contrasts are lexically relevant in English, they never come to be lexically functional for French learners whose sensitivity to stress differences is therefore expected to decline. During the first six months of life, infants may acquire the prosodic patterns that characterize the words in their native language, and before the end of the first year they might use appropiate segmentation strategies. Further cross-language comparisons will help to understand how initial sensitivity to prosodically varied syllables allows infants to develop language-specific solutions for the inescapable problem of segmentation.

ACKNOWLEDGMENTS

This research was supported by grants from the Human Frontier Scientific Program, the European Communities Human Capital Program and the CNET (Convention 837BD28 00790 9245 LAA/TSS/CMC). I would like to thank Brit van Ooijen for her very helpful comments on earlier versions of this chapter.

REFERENCES

Bertoncini, J. (1993). Infants' perception of speech units, primary representation capacities. In B. de Boysson-Bardies, S. de Schonen, P.W. Jusczyk, P.F. MacNeilage & J. Morton (Eds.), *Developmental Neurocognition: Speech and Face Processing in the First Year of Life* (pp. 249–257). Dordrecht: Kluwer Academic Publishers B.V.

Bertoncini, J., Bijeljac-Babic, R., Jusczyk, P.W., Kennedy, L., & Mehler, J. (1988). An investigation of young infants' perceptual representations of speech sounds. *Journal of Experimental Psychology: General, 117*, 21–33.

Bertoncini, J., Floccia, C., Nazzi, T., & Mehler, J. (1995). Morae and syllables: Rhythmical basis of speech representation in neonates. *Language and Speech, 38*, 311–329.

Bijeljac-Babic, R., Bertoncini, J., & Mehler, J. (1993). How do four-day-old infants categorize multisyllabic utterances? *Developmental Psychology, 29*, 711–721.

Christophe, A., Dupoux, E., Bertoncini, J., & Mehler, J. (1994). Do infants perceive word boundaries? An empirical approach to the bootstrapping problem for lexical acquisition. *Journal of the Acoustical Society of America, 95*, 1570–1580.

Cooper, R.P., & Aslin, R.N. (1990). Preference for infant-directed speech in the first month after birth. *Child Development, 61*, 1584–1595.

Cutler, A. (1990). Exploiting prosodic probabilities in speech segmentation. In G.T.M. Altmann (Ed.) *Cognitive Models of Speech Processing: Psycholinguistic and Computational Perspectives* (pp. 105–121). Cambridge, MA: MIT Press.

Cutler, A., & Butterfield, S. (1990). Durational cues to word boundaries in clear speech. *Speech Communication, 9*, 485–495.

Cutler, A., & Butterfield, S. (1992). Rhythmic cues to speech segmentation: Evidence from juncture misperception. *Journal of Memory and Language, 31*, 218–236.

Cutler, A., Mehler, J., Norris, D., & Segui, J. (1983). A language-specific comprehension strategy. *Nature, 304*, 159–160.

Cutler, A., Mehler, J., Norris, D., & Segui, J. (1986). The syllable's differing role in the segmentation of French and English. *Journal of Memory and Language, 25*, 385–400.

Cutler, A., Mehler, J., Norris, D., & Segui, J. (1989). Limits on bilinguism. *Nature, 320*, 229–230.

Cutler, A., & Norris, D. (1988). The role of strong syllables in segmentation for lexical access. *Journal of Experimental Psychology: Human Perception and Performance, 14*, 113–121.

Hoequist, C. (1983). Syllable duration in stress-, syllable- and mora-timed languages. *Phonetica, 40*, 203–237.

Jusczyk, P.W., Bertoncini, J., Bijeljac-Babic, R., Kennedy, L.J., & Mehler, J. (1990). The role of attention in speech perception by young infants. *Cognitive Development, 5*, 265–286.

Jusczyk, P.W., Jusczyk, A.M., Kennedy, L.J., Schomberg, T., & Koenig, N. (1995). Young infants' retention of information about bisyllabic utterances. *Journal of Experimental Psychology: Human Perception and Performance, 21*, 822–836.

Kemler-Nelson, D.G., Hirsh-Pasek, K., Jusczyk, P.W., & Wright Cassidy, K. (1989). How the prosodic cues in motherese might assist language learning. *Journal of Child Language, 16*, 55–68.

Mehler, J., Dommergues, J.Y., Frauenfelder, U., & Segui, J. (1981). The syllable's role in speech segmentation. *Journal of Verbal Learning and Verbal Behavior, 20*, 298–305.

Mehler, J., Dupoux, E., Nazzi, T., & Dehaene-Lambertz, G. (1996). Coping with linguistic diversity: The infant's viewpoint. In J.L. Morgan & K. Demuth (Eds.), *Signal to syntax: Bootstrapping from speech to grammar in early acquisition* (pp. 101–116). Mahwah, NJ: Lawrence Erlbaum Associates Inc.

Miller, J.L. (1978). Interactions in processing segmental and suprasegmental features of speech. *Perception and Psychophysics, 24*, 175–180.

Morgan, J.L. (1994). Converging measures of speech segmentation in preverbal infants. *Infant Behavior and Development, 17*, 389–403.

Morgan, J.L,. & Saffran, J.R. (1995). Emerging integration of sequential and suprasegmental information in preverbal speech segmentation. *Child Development, 66*, 911–936.

Nazzi, T. (1996, April). Role of prosody in the discrimination of foreign languages by newborns. Poster presented at the XXVIIIth Stanford Child Language Research Forum, Stanford University, CA.

Newsome, M., & Jusczyk, P.W. (1995). Do infants use stress as a cue for segmenting fluent speech? In D. MacLaughlin & S. McEwen (Eds.), *19th Boston University Conference on Language Development, 2* (pp. 415–426). Somerville, MA. Cascadilla Press.

Otake, T., Hatano, G., Cutler, A., & Mehler, J. (1993). Mora or syllable? Speech segmentation in Japanese. *Journal of Memory and Language, 32*, 258–278.

Port, R.F., Dalby, J., & O'Dell, M. (1987). Evidence for mora timing in Japanese. *Journal of the Acoustical Society of America, 81*, 1574–1585.

Sansavini, A. (in press). Neonatal perception of the rhythmical structure of speech: The role of stress patterns. *Early Development and Parenting*.

Sansavini, A., Bertoncini, J., & Giovanelli, G. (1997). Newborns discriminate the rhythm of multisyllabic stressed words. *Developmental Psychology, 33*, 3–11.

Shibatani, M. (1990). *The Languages of Japan*. Cambridge, Cambridge University Press.

Trehub, S.E., & Thorpe L.A. (1989). Infants' perception of rhythm: Categorization of auditory sequences by temporal structures. *Canadian Journal of Psychology, 43*, 217–229.

Werker, J.F., & Tees, R.C. (1984). Cross-language speech perception: Evidence for perceptual reorganization during the first year of life. *Infant Behavior and Development, 7*, 49–63.

Wood, C.C. (1974). Parallel processing of auditory and phonetic information in speech discrimination. *Perception and Psychophysics, 15*, 501–508.

CHAPTER TEN

What is Special About Pointing in Babies?

George Butterworth
University of Sussex, UK

INTRODUCTION

Index-finger pointing is a species-specific means of reference that is intimately connected with communication through gesture and language. In pointing, the index finger and arm are typically extended in the direction of the interesting object, while the remaining fingers are curled under the hand, with the thumb held down and to the side (Fig. 10.1). Manual pointing, as a means of redirecting the attention of another member of the same species, is specific to humans and it is a basic means of making reference to things. Pointing is both a specialised orienting response of the body and a gesture with universal significance. The development of pointing will be considered here as an aspect of joint visual attention. It will be argued that pointing is the royal road from pre-verbal communication into spoken language. This chapter will only briefly review the precursors of pointing in joint visual attention, since that literature has been recently considered elsewhere (Messer, 1994; Butterworth, 1995; Moore & Corkum, 1994). Here the main discussion will be on alternative conceptualisations of joint visual attention in early development and on the causes and consequences of manual pointing.

JOINT VISUAL ATTENTION AS A PRECURSOR OF POINTING

Joint visual attention may be defined simply as looking where someone else is looking. In recent years there has developed a controversy over whether babies

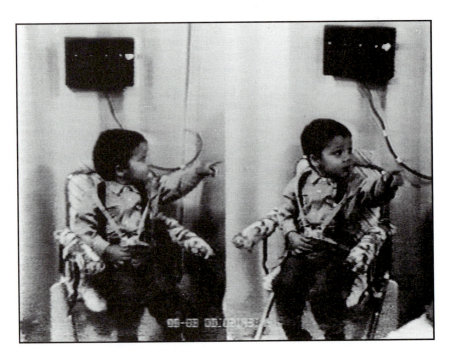

FIG. 10.1:   Human infant pointing.

first comprehend signals given by changes in the orientation of another's head and eyes and only then begin to comprehend pointing, or whether both pointing and head and eye movements are understood simultaneously, relatively late in the first year. Some favour the hypothesis that joint visual attention is not possible until the end of the first year of life and that it is more or less coincident with the comprehension of pointing (Moore & Corkum, 1994; Corkum & Moore, 1995; Morissette, Ricard & Gouin-Decarie, 1995). Others, however, have consistently claimed that joint visual attention can be observed at least as early as 6 months, long before there is evidence for comprehension of pointing (Scaife & Bruner, 1975; Butterworth & Cochran, 1980; Butterworth & Jarrett, 1991; D'Entremont, Hains & Muir, in press). This is an important issue because: (1) an apprenticeship in comprehension of gaze direction may contribute to comprehension of pointing; and (2) it is quite possible that joint attention at different ages may be mediated by different cognitive processes.

Scaife and Bruner (1975) claimed that two-month-old infants follow a change in the orientation of gaze of an adult. In their study, babies followed the direction of gaze, to left or right, into an empty visual field. In a more recent study, D'Entremont, Hains and Muir (in press) reported evidence for joint attention in babies aged under 4 months. Babies would look in the direction of a change of gaze of the experimenter, toward a doll carefully placed to be within the baby's visual field. These results suggest that a form of joint visual attention is available long before the end of the first year.

To some extent, differences of opinion about the time of onset may be explained by differences in experimental procedures. For example, the angular distance of targets from the infant is an important factor determining whether joint attention will be observed both in looking and in pointing (see later). It is very likely that joint attention places demands on the ability of the infant to integrate information over space and time. The infant may be able to comprehend a change in a partner's postural orientation as a signal that there is something of interest but she may be limited in the capacity to bridge the gap in space between the adult's signal and that object. Thus, D'Entremont et al. (in press) were successful in demonstrating that very young babies can look in the same direction as an adult because they ensured that target objects were directly in front of the baby, just to left and right, within the span of apprehension of four-month-old infants. It is important to note, however, that the requirement for success at this most elementary developmental level is that the infant need only look in the appropriate direction to left or right. The precision with which infants can localise a particular target among other identical ones within the same visual hemifield is not assessed. By assessing accuracy of target localisation the possibility that different mechanisms may be involved at different ages can be investigated.

Many other factors influence the likelihood of observing joint visual attention in babies under one year of age. The number of targets in the visual field influences the probability of a response, with two targets reliably eliciting more responses than just one (Grover, 1988). This suggests that joint attention depends, at least in part, on resolving uncertainty. It may be that the greater the number of potential targets, the greater the uncertainty as to which is the referent, and thus the more informative the signal. The question of resolving uncertainty also raises the issue whether there are links between social referencing and affective processes. This issue will not be discussed here but it is an important one for any theory of origins of early human communication (Campos et al., 1983, Baldwin & Moses, 1996).

Although Grover (1988) found that the likelihood of the infant making a response increased with the number of targets , the accuracy of the infant's response was not a simple function of uncertainty. This depends on other ecological factors, such as whether the correct target is in motion. Furthermore, the characteristics of the signal (change in head orientation with eye movements or eye movements alone, or pointing plus head and eye movements) also influence the incidence of infant responses (Butterworth & Jarrett, 1991; Butterworth & Grover, 1988, 1989). This might be because a signal depending on eye movements alone can specify only a relatively broad region of space for an observer, to the left or right (and perhaps in the vertical plane) whereas the larger scale orienting movements involving head, hand and eye may be less ambiguous. This hypothesis is considered in greater detail later.

The limitation on the spatial informativeness of another's eye movements may explain why it is relatively difficult to find evidence for eye movements alone being effective in joint attention before about 18 months, (Corkum & Moore, 1995; Butterworth & Jarrett, 1991). In fact, even among adults, eye movements are not as effective as eye and head movements in allowing an observer to localise a specific target. Itakura and Butterworth (1997) found that adults were as accurate to a signal of a head and eye movement when the experimenter was wearing sunglasses as when the eyes were visible. Findings such as these suggest that the eyes are not necessarily the primary source of information in joint visual attention tasks (see e.g. Baron-Cohen, 1995; Povinelli & Eddy, 1996a,b).

Differences in scoring procedures may also influence whether experimenters find joint attention to be possible in the period before comprehension and production of pointing begins. Where the scoring procedure distinguishes between spatially incorrect responses (i.e. looking in the opposite direction to that being signalled) and simple failure to respond, there is evidence that babies from 6 months look in the correct direction significantly more often than they look in the incorrect direction (Butterworth & Jarrett, 1991). Where responses in the incorrect direction are summed with all other incorrect responses, the first evidence for a significant majority of correct responses to a change in gaze comes at about 12 months and this is as equally often before as after the baby comprehends pointing (Morissette, Ricard & Gouin-Decarie, 1995).

These methodological factors may therefore explain, at least in part, why different results have been obtained in different laboratories in assessing the onset of joint visual attention. In summary, there is research which demonstrates that joint visual attention is possible before comprehension of pointing. These studies control for the spatial demands of the task on the infant's capacity to bridge the spatial gap between a signal and its referent.

The fundamental developmental question, however, concerns the mechanisms which operate in joint attention at different ages. The argument to be pursued here is that additional, cognitive mechanisms come to serve joint visual attention after the comprehension and production of pointing. How does a baby, who does not yet understand pointing, look where someone else is looking? Butterworth and Jarrett (1991) reported evidence for three successive mechanisms of joint visual attention in the age range between six months and eighteen months. At six months, babies look to the correct side of the room, as if to see what the adult is looking at but they cannot tell which of the two identical targets on the same side of the room is correct, unless it happens to move or in some way be the more attention-worthy. Grover (1988), showed that adding movement to one or the other of two alternative targets on the same side of the field of view raised the accuracy of babies, even when both targets were simultaneously in motion. It was as if motion in the target helped the child to direct attention to the periphery. It would appear therefore that the change in the adult's orientation of head and eyes conveys information as to the direction in which to look (i.e. to the left or right in the baby's visual field) but the precise location for joint attention is specified by the object itself.

This earliest process has been called the "ecological" mechanism of joint visual attention (Butterworth & Jarrett, 1991). It depends on the differentiated structure of the natural environment, so that what initially attracts the adult's attention and leads her to turn, (thus providing the baby with information about *spatial direction* through the change in her postural orientation) is also likely, in the natural environment, to capture the attention of the infant (thus providing information about *spatial location* through the object's intrinsic properties). The ecological mechanism enables a "meeting of minds" in the self same object. Such a mechanism is quite consistent with the possibility that there may be joint attention at 6 months, or even earlier, by the participants in an interaction at least under the spatial and object constraints which apply at that age.

Between twelve and eighteen months, however, the infant begins to localise the target correctly, even when this requires the baby to ignore the first of two identical targets along the scan path (Butterworth & Jarrett, 1991). This new "geometric" mechanism may require extrapolation of an invisible line between the mother's head orientation and the referent of her gaze. Babies may first alight on the wrong target before looking further into the periphery but by correcting themselves, they reveal that they are aware that the more peripheral of the two targets was intended as the referent. The adult's change of gaze now signals both the direction and the location in which to look. This is a new mechanism which is perhaps analogous to Piaget's (1954) Stage V mechanism for perceiving invisible displacements of objects. At Stage V of Piaget's sensori-motor progression (around twelve months) babies become able to infer an object's invisible trajectory between successive locations.

The comprehension of pointing is more or less coincident with the appearance of this geometric mechanism. The implication is that a cognitive developmental change has occurred which leads to understanding pointing. The geometric mechanism specifies more precisely the location within the hemifield of visual space where the interesting object is located. In real life, of course, ecological and geometric mechanisms may interact in the service of reducing ambiguity of reference.

Another important finding has been that joint visual attention is limited by the boundaries of the babies' visual space, even to 18 months of age and the theoretical implications of this have not been fully explored. The spatial limitation is suggested by the fact that infants localise only the targets within the visual space in front of them that is bounded by the limits of the visual field (Butterworth & Jarrett, 1991). If the mother looks at a target behind the baby, the infant either fixates a target in front or does not respond (Butterworth & Cochran, 1980). Joint visual attention therefore appears to depend on the infant's sharing a visual spatial frame of reference with others. Furthermore, there are implications for auditory aspects of reference since it seems possible that the space behind the infant is initially specified auditorily. Certainly, babies have no difficulty orienting to a sound behind them but in joint attention studies, the space behind the infant is normally silent. Thus, the problem for the infant may be to comprehend that the adult's visual signal has made reference to auditory space. It is noteworthy that a similar inability to search at locations out of view of the infant has been demonstrated in a manual search task involving rotation of the infant relative to objects that were first hidden in the field of view (Landau & Spelke, 1988). The space behind the infant is inaccessible on the basis of visual information alone, whether the task is to search on the basis of social, joint attention cues or whether only manual search is required.

By eighteen months, although babies do not search behind them when there are targets in the field of view, they will do so if the visual field is empty. Thus, infants are able to access the invisible portion of space at eighteen months (but not at twelve months) so long as there is no competition from locations within the visible space. The infant is visually dominated but a "representational" spatial mechanism is nevertheless available, which serves to integrate the "visual" space in front of the baby with the "auditory" space behind. Thus, once the representational mechanism is available, one might theorise that a visual signal will implicitly carry auditory significance.

In summary, as far as the comprehension of gaze is concerned, there is evidence in the first eighteen months of life that three successive mechanisms are involved in "looking where someone else is looking". The earliest, "ecological mechanism", is available well before there is comprehension of pointing but it may encode from the adult's signal only the general spatial direction and is completed by the intrinsic, attention—capturing properties of objects. At around twelve months, there is evidence for the beginning of a new mechanism, a "geometric" process, whereby the infant from her own position extrapolates from the orientation of the mother's head or gaze the intersection of a line with a relatively precise zone of visual space. This mechanism develops at about the same time as the baby begins to comprehend and produce manual pointing; i.e. towards the end of the first year. It seems unlikely that the long apprenticeship in gaze monitoring is sufficient to account for this developmental change. Rather, it has many of the qualities of a stage transition within a process of cognitive development. There is a further stage in the development of joint attention to a "represented" space, which surrounds the infant and other objects, like a container. This represented "amodal" space serves to link visual signals to the silent "auditory" space behind the baby. The series of stage transitions suggests that a simple apprenticeship, based just on comprehension of gaze in the absence of cognitive development, is insufficient to account for changes in the capacity for joint visual attention in the first eighteen months of life.

COMPREHENSION OF POINTING IN BABIES

As is the case for studies of language, researchers have distinguished between processes involved in the comprehension and production of manual pointing. Many studies agree that the comprehension of pointing, at about 10 months, slightly precedes its production (Butterworth & Grover, 1989; Franco & Butterworth, 1996; Leung & Rheingold, 1981; Messer, 1994). There is also evidence that the spatial conditions of testing influence whether infant's comprehend pointing or not. An early study by Lempers (1976) for example, found that babies of 9 months comprehend pointing to nearby targets and by 12 months they comprehend pointing to more distant targets (when the targets are on the same side of the room as the pointing hand). Morissette, Ricard and Gouin-Decarie (1995) in a longitudinal study also found that comprehension of manual pointing to relatively distant targets begins at about 12 months. They found that the angle subtended by the targets, relative to the baby, influenced the probability of comprehension. Targets at 20 degrees from the midline and 0.85 metres distance were localised at 12 months, before targets at 70 degrees and 2.11 metres which were localised at 15 months. Again, the most frequent error of babies was to look at the pointing hand rather than at the designated target. Perhaps related is the finding, by Murphy and Messer (1977), that pointing comprehension was earlier (9 months) for targets on the same side of the room as the pointing hand than when the point was into the contralateral half of the infant's visual space, across the body midline of the adult (12 months).

Butterworth and Grover (1988, 1989) showed that pointing was understood by 12 months. By contrast, infants at 6 or 9 months were as likely to fixate the pointing hand as the designated target. If babies at 6 and 9 months succeeded in fixating the target, they did so in a two-step manner, pausing first at the adult's hand, then alighting on the target, whereas 12-month-babies looked to the target rapidly and smoothly. Indeed, it has sometimes been noted that mothers go to a great deal of trouble, with exaggerated hand movements, to lead the young infant's gaze from her hand onto the target (Murphy & Messer, 1977). This may be a component in learning to interpret the manual pointing signal between the ages of 9 and 12 months. Grover (1988) showed that the infant's latency to fixate the correct target significantly decreases between 9 and 12 months. She also showed that manual pointing is a more potent signal than a simple change in head and eye orientation. Babies at 12 months were significantly more likely to respond when the signal included a point and more likely to fixate a target further into the periphery of vision, even if this meant ignoring an identical target seen earlier along the scan path.

Ecological factors also influence the form and incidence of the infant's response to pointing. The likelihood of a response to pointing increased from 69% to 80% of trials when the number of targets in the field of view was increased from one to two. When the salience of the targets was experimentally manipulated, by setting them into motion, either singly or in pairs, the infant's response to pointing increased to ceiling level. Target motion was sufficient to eliminate hand fixation in 9-month-old infants, although babies then went on to fixate only the first target along their scan path from the adult's hand. By 15 months however, babies did alight on the second, more peripheral target, in a sequence of fixations. Thus, infants are not merely fixating the first object they encounter along the line of gaze from the adult's hand when they comprehend pointing. Rather, they appear to be extrapolating an angular trajectory through space to intersect with a potential target, as would be expected if the mechanism is "geometric", and in doing so, they tend to favour targets in the periphery of vision.

Butterworth (1989) carried out a series of studies of pointing comprehension which controlled for the angular separation and distance of targets from the baby. Infants were 6 months, 12 months and 16 months old, and the accuracy with which they could locate a target was compared at angular separations between pairs of identical targets ranging from 10 degrees to 47 degrees. The targets were presented in pairs, with one target always at 10 degrees from the baby (the first along the scan path) and the second at a more peripheral position, on a semicircular distribution at 2.76 metres from the infant. The experimenter either looked at the target (with head and eye movements) or looked and pointed at the target. In all three age groups there was little evidence that babies would accurately select the more peripheral of the pair just on the basis of head and eye movements. However, from 12 months manual pointing had a significant effect on the accuracy of the response and by 15 months there was a clear advantage to pointing (Fig. 10.2). The added effect of manual pointing may be simply explained in terms of the "lever" formed by the arm. For any given spatial separation between a pair of targets, the angular excursion of a long lever, like the arm, will be greater than that of a shorter lever, like the head, or a pair of very short levers, like the eyes. Thus, a part of the body, the arm and pointing hand , may have become specialised for referential communication because it is particularly useful in disambiguating which of several alternatives is actually the focus of a person's attention. This hypothesis requires to be tested by comparative evidence and is discussed further later.

In summary, these data therefore suggest that the earliest comprehension of pointing may depend on the infant being able to see the pointing hand and the target close by, simultaneously in visual space. With development, greater angular distances can be bridged between the hand and the target. Certainly, the angular distance of the targets is important in assessing when pointing compre-hension actually begins with estimates varying between 10 and 15 months, depending on the conditions of testing. The pointing signal is not only more likely to elicit a response in the baby than a simple change of head and eyes but also it allows the baby more accurately to locate the target, in the periphery. There may be an advantage in using the extended arm and index finger to refer to objects for joint attention because it offers a less ambiguous signal, all else being equal, than a simple change in eye gaze, head orientation or whole body posture.

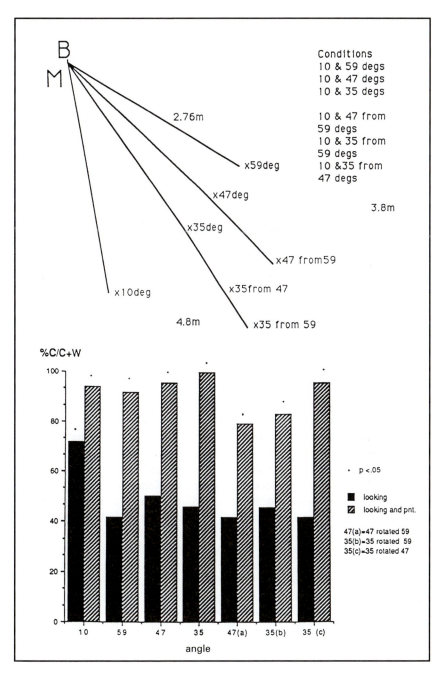

FIG. 10.2:   Pointing increases accuracy of 15-month-old infant's comprehension when targets are at small angular separations in a large scale space.

PRODUCTION OF POINTING IN BABIES AND CHIMPANZEES

That comprehension of pointing may precede production is possible, but differential timing may simply reflect our relative lack of knowledge about the antecedents of pointing production. Canonical pointing (extended arm and index finger) emerges by 14 months, although babies as young as 8.5 months have been observed to point (Schaffer, 1984; Butterworth & Morissette, 1996). Possible antecedents of pointing have been observed in the isolated extension of the index finger of the three-month-old baby which occur in close association with "speech-like" sounds in the infant engaged in social interaction (Fogel & Hannan, 1985; Masataka, 1995). Thus it is possible that components of the pointing gesture which are particularly closely linked to syllabic vocalisation can be observed very early in development and that pointing production is developing in parallel with comprehension. At a basic level, jointly shared attention is essential for communication in many species. When animals show a sudden change in body posture, or an intense and sustained gaze in a particular direction, this will often act as a signal to the location of an interesting event. For example, the pointer, which is a type of hunting dog, will signal by standing stock still, so that the orientation of the dog's body from nose to tail, is aligned with the prey. This type of orienting movement involves the whole body, whereas the argument to be advanced here is that humans have evolved pointing as a species-specific mechanism for redirecting attention, using a part of the body, the arm and index finger, to carry the signal. The question is: is there anything special about pointing in humans, or is it just one among many widely available behaviours for indicating? Is pointing inherently different from other means of indicating, such as extending the flat hand, or simply flexing the index finger, or extending the arm with a closed fist in the direction of an interesting object?

Chimpanzees comprehend humans pointing but they attend mainly to the information provided by bodily orientation rather than to the spatial direction as specified by the extended arm. In fact, adding pointing to the signal may actually decrease the accuracy with which they locate the object of interest (Povinelli & Eddy, 1996b). It seems likely that pointing will prove to be a specialised human adaptation. Franco and Butterworth (1996) found there was no significant correlation between incidence of pointing and incidence of other indicative gestures in babies aged 12 to 18 months. Butterworth et al. (1997) found that pointing accounted for 55% of all gestures made by babies whereas indicative gestures with the open hand extended, or arm extended and fist closed, or just the index finger extended, accounted for only 18% of gestures. These gestures co-exist in the repertoire and do not replace each other. Index finger pointing is the baby's preferred means of referring to objects, and other indicative gestures are not nearly so frequent. Open-handed indicative gestures (and other non-pointing means of indicating) are infrequent in babies and appear to be independent of pointing.

The precise definition of the pointing gesture is rather important in evaluating comparative evidence from higher primates. Chimpanzees and orang-utans are capable of signalling with manual indicative gestures in which the arm, open hand and extended fingers, are oriented in the direction of an interesting sight (Fig. 10.3). The question is should such open handed indicative gestures in chimpanzees be considered equivalent to human pointing or does their relative lack of precision imply a different origin and function? It is important for the theory to be proposed that higher primates generally give no prominence to the index finger (Blaschke & Ettlinger, 1987; Menzel, 1974; Call & Tomasello, 1995). One factor that may limit index-finger pointing in apes is that the anatomy of the hand, with its relative lack of functional specialisation of the index finger, does not readily allow it (Butterworth, 1991; Povinelli & Davis, 1994).

It has recently been shown that chimpanzees (*Pan troglodytes*) are capable of signalling with an index finger (Leavens, Hopkins & Bard, 1996). The clearest evidence came from a chimpanzee named Clint, aged 14 years, who made the pointing gesture (with left and right hand) apparently as a request to the experimenter for food which had fallen from a reward dispenser. Index-finger pointing occurred on 38 occasions and whole-hand indicative gestures on 102 occasions. That is, the ratio of indicative gestures to pointing was opposite to that which has been observed in human infants (Franco & Butterworth, 1996). Pointing was mainly used by Clint as a proto-imperative for food items (i.e. *give me that food*) and it is possible that his index-finger pointing gesture may have been learned as a particular consequence of social contact with humans. It is interesting that Clint was never observed to use the index-finger pointing gesture with conspecifics. Nevertheless, some of his index-finger points were accompanied by vocalisation and checking back and forth with the experimenter. Also, as in the human case his pointing gesture required an audience, since he pointed only when the experimenter was facing him.

Assuming that pointing is possible in chimpanzees, there are still many details of contrast with humans. Pointing in babies seems to be used as a pro-todeclarative (i.e. *look at that*, Franco & Butterworth, 1996) and it is highly unlikely to be socially transmitted from adult to child, (although it may be socially reinforced by adults, Kaye, 1982). Pointing is made for conspecifics whereas it has never been observed to occur between chimpanzees. It would be very interesting to know whether chimpanzees in the wild communicate by means of indicative gestures. Leavens et al. (1996) speculate that pointing would be unnecessary in the wild, since chimpanzees can locomote to obtain food, whereas infant humans cannot. The assumption seems to be that the imperative aspect of the gesture has primacy, which may not actually be the case in humans.

Perhaps the question whether chimpanzees point should no longer be expressed simply in terms of whether the ability is present or absent. The more appropriate question is why index-finger pointing is relatively infrequent and very difficult to observe in chimpanzees? More progress in understanding the functional significance of index-finger pointing might be made if it could be ascertained why

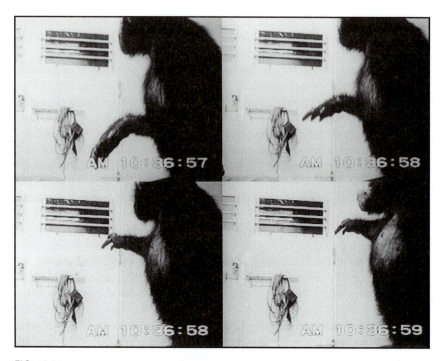

FIG. 10.3:   Chimpanzee making an indicative gesture.

indicative gestures generally take the whole-hand open form in chimpanzees, but generally involve index finger extension in humans with the other fingers flexed?

ARE THE ORIGINS OF POINTING IN PREHENSION OR IN COMMUNICATION?

Franco and Butterworth (1996) suggested that index-finger pointing is a species-typical gesture specialised for human social communication. They compared the incidence of pointing and reaching gestures in 14-month-old babies in declarative and imperative communicative contexts. Pointing was never confused with reaching gestures. It occurred only under conditions where a social partner was available for communication (i.e. there was an audience available), even when the partner was another baby (Franco, Perruchini & Butterworth, 1992). Pointing occurred primarily to distal targets and was accompanied by checking with the partner, thus revealing communicative intent. This evidence runs against traditional views of the origins of pointing which stress either that pointing develops out of prehension (Vygotsky, 1988) or that it is initially performed primarily for the self rather than for purposes of social communication (Werner & Kaplan, 1963). That is, these results suggest that the pointing gesture in humans initially serves a protodeclarative purpose (i.e. *look at that*) rather than a protoimperative purpose (i.e. *give me that*).

That is not to say that pointing has nothing at all to do with prehension but the argument to be advanced here is that pointing and the pincer grip are co-evolved but different aspects of hand function. A clue to the reasons for the morphology of the human pointing gesture comes from the specific adaptation of the hand. The human hand is highly flexible, with a very great capability for precision based on the fully opposable index finger and thumb which is considered one of the key features differentiating man from other primates. Napier (1960, 1970) argued that only humans are capable of the pincer grip because the relative proportion of thumb to index finger (the opposability index) sets limits on the extent to which the thumb can be abducted against it. He gave values for the opposability index of 0.65 for man and 0.43 for chimpanzees, a difference due to the relatively short thumb of the chimpanzee positioned low down the wrist.

Two studies have recently reported that the pincer grip is in fact available in the repertoire of the chimpanzee. In one experiment, 80 captive chimpanzees *(Pan troglodytes)* aged from 1 to 25 years were observed picking up raisins measuring 1.0 to 1.5 cm from the cage floor. A human-like pattern of pincer grip was observed at 2 years, which reached a peak of 10% of all responses at 6 years, (Tonooka & Matsuzawa, 1995). The same study showed that males were more likely than females to use the pincer grip once they were over 10 years of age. A second study of 13 captive chimpanzees *(Pan troglodytes)* aged from 2 to 5 years showed that precision grips involving the thumb and index finger at or below the first, distal joint occurred on 25% of trials (Jones-Engel & Bard, 1996). The pincer grip with thumb pad to finger pad abduction occurred on 2% of trials.

These studies suggest that chimpanzees are capable of a degree of precision, notwithstanding the well-attested morphological differences with human hands (Jouffroy, 1993), but they do not establish how precision grips develop. In human infants the pincer grip and imprecise opposition of the index finger and thumb above the first distal joint (the inferior forefinger grip) can already be observed at 8 months. The pincer grip is systematically selected by 15 months to grip cubes of 0.5 cm. Power grips, where the object is held between flexed fingers and palm, without thumb opposition, are rarely used by human infants with objects of these sizes after 15 months (Butterworth, Verweij & Hopkins,1997).

Butterworth and Itakura (in press) studied eleven captive chimpanzees *(Pan troglodytes)* aged from 4 to 20 years who were video recorded grasping cubes of apple measuring, 0.5, 1.0 and 2.0 cm. This study confirmed that chimpanzees do have precision grips in their repertoire, at least from the age of 2 years, where the object is held between thumb tip and at or below the first joint of the index finger. Precision grips increase in frequency slowly, until chimpanzees are adult, and they are not systematically selected on the basis of object size at any age. Power grips are commonly selected in chimpanzees to the age of 8 years, even when grasping small objects. This new developmental evidence, which covers the age range from juvenile to adult chimpanzees, shows that lack of systematic selection of precise grips for small objects extends across the age range. Although there is index finger–thumb opposition, the whole index finger is selected and the exact position of opposition of the thumb is relatively uninfluenced by object size. Furthermore, the pincer grip is more likely to be observed in adult male chimpanzees and may simply be a function of changes in hand size, which enable the long index finger more readily to be bent toward the thumb.

The contrast with human infants is revealing since the chimpanzee makes a developmental transition to precision grips, very much later than is observed in babies. In human infants, there is an early transition (between 8 and 15 months), when power grips which do not involve the thumb are eliminated and the precision pincer grip is systematically selected by object size (Butterworth et al., 1997). In chimpanzees a similar range of grips appears to be in the repertoire, but there is little evidence for systematic selection, except for the relative decrease in power grips after 8 years. Thus, just as for pointing and indicative gestures, the repertoire of precise grips in chimpanzees overlaps that of humans but the rapid rate of development in humans ensures that precision grips will be used consistently from the end of infancy. By contrast, precise grips are infrequent, not consistently selected and more typical of adult chimpanzees.

The importance of this new evidence is that the characteristic hand posture observed in human pointing may be related to the pincer grip but as its "antithesis". Darwin (1904) first proposed the principle of antithesis to explain how animal communication often exploits visual signals which accompany behaviour to convey information. For example, an animal may signal readiness to attack by making "intention movements" which are preparatory to fighting. After a fight, the subdued posture of the defeated dog signals submission because the muscles are activated in the opposite configuration, or antithesis, to those involved in aggression (Marler, 1959).

In the case of pointing the opposition of the tip of the index finger and thumb in the pincer grip has pointing as its postural antithesis. This contrast in relative positions of index finger and thumb also involves a change in the focus of visual attention. In manual activities with tools, focal attention is on the hand, the tool and the object, in the service of precise control of manipulation. In pointing, by contrast, attention is outer directed and serves rather precisely to reorient the attention of another person, so that an object at some distance can become a focus for shared experience.

The principle of antithesis also explains why chimpanzees make whole-hand indicative gestures more readily than they perform index-finger pointing while the opposite is true for humans. It also explains why the two gestures are uncorrelated in the repertoire of human infants (Franco & Butterworth, 1996). On this Darwinian hypothesis, the typical chimpanzee indicative gesture (whole hand open) is the antithesis of a power grip, (in which the fingers are simply flexed against the palm) whereas the index-finger point is the antithesis of the pincer grip (which requires precise opposition of the index-finger and thumb, with the other fingers usually tucked out of the way). If this argument is correct then it might be expected that the index finger pointing gesture, in its purpose of precise gestural communication, may be rather closely linked to the development of spoken language. Pointing serves in human pre-verbal communication to single out an object of interest for joint attention.

POINTING AND THE TRANSITION TO LANGUAGE

The link between pointing and language is becoming clearer through studies which suggest that babies depend on the adult's referential acts, including pointing, for the comprehension of speech. A variety of studies have implicated pre-verbal referential communication to language acquisition (e.g. Baldwin, 1991, 1993). There is evidence that the amount of pointing at 12 months predicts speech production rates at 24 months (Camaioni, Castelli, Longobardi & Volterra, 1991). Links between pointing onset and comprehension of object names have also been established, with infants understanding their first categorical object name in the same week as they point (Harris, Barlow-Brown and Chasin, 1995).

Butterworth and Morissette (1996) studied the relation between age of pointing onset and the subsequent comprehension and production of speech and gestures. A longitudinal study was carried out linking pointing, handedness and onset of the pincer grip to early verbal and gestural communication as measured by the MacArthur infant language inventory (Fenson et al., 1994). Canonical pointing began 22 days earlier in girls than in boys, about one month after the pincer grip was systematically selected for small objects. The pincer grip was invariably in the repertoire when pointing was observed. The earlier the age of onset of pointing, the greater were the number of different gestures (including pointing) and the greater the amount of speech comprehension at 14.4 months. Girls showed consistent right-handedness in tasks requiring only one hand and they showed more right-handed pointing than boys. The amount of right-handed pointing, and the relative balance of pincer grips between the left and right hands (a measure of lateralised fine motor control) predicted speech comprehension and production at 14.4 months. At this age boys had relatively few words in production (about 3) whereas girls had on average 12 words. By 16 months the sex difference in speech production is marked (the MacArthur norms show females have 95 words in production, and males 25 words; Fenson et al., 1994). Thus, earlier onset of pointing, earlier right-handed pointing and more rapid development of speech in girls suggests that there is a link between pointing and the development of language and that there may be sex differences in this process.

Little is known about the mechanisms of selective attention involved in the production of pointing. Manual pointing depends on vision since it is not observed in the untutored congenitally blind but it is present in the congenitally deaf which suggests that auditory experience is not necessary for the pointing gesture (Fraiberg, 1979; Feldman, Goldin-Meadow & Gleitman, 1978). However, other evidence suggests that pointing may be influenced by auditory factors, by gender differences and by hemispherical asymmetries usually associated with language. For example, all else being equal, pointing favours the right side of visual space when there is a conflict between targets on the left and right (Butterworth et al., 1997). When doll-like targets which "speak" and move their arms and legs are used, (but not when the targets lack auditory qualities) girls of 15.6 months point right-handed to the right and as far as 15 degrees into the left side of their visual space. Further into the left periphery they are ambidextrous. Boys at the same age point with the left hand to the left periphery (50 degrees), with the right hand to the right periphery and they are ambidextrous from 15 degrees right to 15 degrees left of the midline (Butterworth et al., 1997). It seems possible that these sex differences may imply different rates of transition from an undifferentiated system of communication through both gestures and vocalisation, to a lateralised symbolic language system favouring speech (Thatcher, Walker & Giudice, 1987).

There is independent evidence that pointing may be linked to asymmetries in perception of auditory–visual space. Adults with lesions to the left anterior parietal lobe have difficulty pointing right-handed to sounding targets located in the left visual field (Pinek et al., 1989). It seems possible, therefore, that sex differences in the onset time and dominant use of the right hand for pointing are involved in the transition from communication through gestures, (which may be bilaterally organised initially) to a lateralised speech system favouring the auditory-vocal mode (Witelson, and Nowakowski, 1991). Furthermore, combinations of pointing and a word are produced consistently at 16 months, just before the child makes the transition to two-word speech. Such combinations of speech and gesture maximise communicative opportunities at a time when vocabulary and other linguistic resources may be limited, (Volterra and Iversen, 1995).

CONCLUSION

The chapter began by asking whether human index-finger pointing is special. It can be concluded that it is. What is special about pointing is that, although it is a simple, social means of re-orienting attention, it is also intimately connected with species-typical handedness of humans and with the acquisition of language. Although it shares some characteristics with the indicative gestures of other species it also differs in that it serves very precisely to refer to objects, perhaps because it makes use of the same anatomical adaptations and attentional mechanisms which serve precise tool use through the pincer grip. Pointing, through the geometric and representational aspects of joint visual attention, can serve to link a visual referent to the concurrent sound stream and thereby authorise the link between the object, language and culture from the baby's perspective. Pointing, in a sense, authorises visual objects to take on auditory qualities and this is an early means for the infant to learn that objects have names. Pointing is special; it is the royal road to language.

ACKNOWLEDGEMENTS

I am grateful to Elvidina Adamson-Macedo for her assistance with the research in the Butterworth (1989) report, and to the Economic and Social Research Council of Great Britain who funded many of the studies.

REFERENCES

Baldwin, D. (1991). Infants' contribution to the achievement of joint reference. *Child Development, 62*, 875–890.

Baldwin, D. (1993). Early referential understanding: Infants' ability to recognise referential acts for what they are. *Developmental Psychology, 29* (5), 832–843.

Baldwin, D.A., & Moses, L.J. (1996). The ontogeny of social information gathering. *Child Development, 67*(5), 1915–1913.

Baron-Cohen, S. (1995). The eye direction detector and the shared attention mechanism: Two cases for evolutionary psychology. In C. Moore & P.J. Dunham (Eds.) *Joint attention: Its origins and role in development*. Hillsdale, NJ, Erlbaum.

Blaschke, M., & Ettlinger, G. (1987). Pointing as an act of social communication by monkeys. *Animal Behaviour, 35*, 1520–1525.

Butterworth, G.E. (1987). Some benefits of egocentrism. In J.S. Bruner & H. Weinreich-Haste (Eds.) *Making sense of the world: The child's construction of reality* (pp. 62–80). London, Methuen.

Butterworth, G.E. (1989). *The geometry of pre-verbal communication*. Final report: Economic and Social Research Council of Great Britain (Grant no 000232311). British Library.

Butterworth, G.E. (1991). The ontogeny and phylogeny of joint visual attention. In A. Whiten (Ed.) *Natural theories of mind* (pp. 223–232). Oxford, Blackwell.

Butterworth, G.E. (1995). Origins of mind in perception and action. In C. Moore & P.J. Dunham (Eds.) *Joint attention: Its origins and role in development* (pp. 29–40). Hillsdale, NJ, Erlbaum.

Butterworth, G.E., & Cochran, E. (1980). Towards a mechanism of joint visual attention in human infancy. *International Journal of Behavioural Development, 3*, 253-272.

Butterworth, G.E., & Franco, F. (1993). Motor development, communication and cognition. In A.F. Kalverboer, B. Hopkins & R. Geuze (Eds.) *Motor development in early and later childhood: Longitudinal approaches* (pp. 153–165). Cambridge, Cambridge University Press.

Butterworth, G.E., & Itakura, S. (in press). *Development of precision grips in chimpanzees*. Paper submitted for publication. *Developmental Science, 1*.

Butterworth, G.E., Franco, F., McKenzie, B., Graupner, L., & Todd, B. (1997). *Dynamic aspects of visual event perception and the production of pointing by human infants*. Paper submitted for publication.

Butterworth, G.E., & Grover, L. (1988). The origins of referential communication in human infancy. In L. Weiskrantz (Ed.) *Thought without language* (pp. 5-25). Oxford, Oxford University Press.

Butterworth, G.E., & Grover, L. (1989). Joint visual attention, manual pointing and preverbal communication in human infancy. In M. Jeannerod (Ed.) *Attention and Performance XII* (pp. 605–624). Hillsdale, NJ, Erlbaum.

Butterworth, G.E., & Jarrett, N.L.M. (1991). What minds have in common is space: Spatial mechanisms for perspective taking in infancy. *British Journal of Developmental Psychology, 9*, 55–72.

Butterworth, G.E., & Morissette, P. (1996). Onset of pointing and the acquisition of language in infancy. *Journal of Reproductive and Infant Psychology, 14,* 219–231.

Butterworth, G.E., Verweij, E., & Hopkins, B. (1997). The development of prehension in infants: Halverson revisited. *British Journal of Developmental Psychology, 15*, 223–236.

Call, J., & Tomasello, M. (1994). The production and comprehension of referential pointing by orang-utans *(Pongo pygmeaus)*. *Journal of Comparative Psychology, 108,* 307–317.

Camaioni, L., Castelli, M.C., Longobardi, E., & Volterra, V. (1991). A parent report instrument for early language assessment. *First Language, 11,* 345–360.

Campos, J. J., Barrett, K.C., Lamb, M.E., Hill, H., Goldsmith, H., & Stenberg, C. (1983). Socio-emotional development. In P. Mussen (Ed.) *Handbook of Child Psychology, 4,* New York, Wiley.

Corkum, V., & Moore, C. (1995). The origins of joint visual attention. In C. Moore and P.J. Dunham (eds.) *Joint attention: its origins and role in development* (pp. 61–83). Hillsdale, NJ, Erlbaum.

Darwin, C. (1904). *The expression of the emotions in men and animals.* London, John Murray.

D'Entremont, B., Hains, S.M.J., & Muir, D.W. (in press). A demonstration of gaze-following in 3-to-6-month-olds. *Infant Behaviour and Development.*

Feldman, M., Goldin-Meadow, S., & Gleitman, L. (1978). Beyond Herodotus: The creation of language by linguistically deprived deaf children. In A. Lock, (Ed.) *Action, gesture and symbol: The emergence of language.* (pp. 351–414). London, Academic Press.

Fenson, L., Dale, P.S., Reznick, L., Bates, E., Thail, D., & Pethick, S. J. (1994). Variability in early communicative development. *Monographs of the Society for Research in Child Development, 59*, 5.

Fogel, A., & Hannan, T.E. (1985). Manual actions of nine- to-fifteen-week-old human infants during face to face interaction with their mothers. *Child Development, 56,* 1271–1279.

Fraiberg, S. (1977). *Insights from the blind.* New York, Basic Books.

Franco, F., & Butterworth, G.E. (1996). Pointing and social awareness: Declaring and requesting in the second year of life. *Journal of Child Language, 23*, 307–336.

Franco, F., Peruchinni, P., & Butterworth, G. (1992). *Pointing for an age mate in 1-2 year olds.* Paper presented at the VIth European Conference on Developmental Psychology, Seville, Spain.

Grover, L. (1988). *Comprehension of the pointing gesture in human infants.* Unpublished Ph.D. thesis. University of Southampton, England.

Harris, M., Barlow-Brown, F., & Chasin, J. (1995). Early referential understanding. *First Language, 15*, 1 43 19-34.

Itakura, S. & Butterworth, G.E. (1997, April). *The roles of head, eyes and pointing in joint visual attention between adults.* Poster presented to the Meeting for Research in Child Development, Washington, DC, USA.

Jones-Engel, L.E., & Bard, K.A. (1996). Precision grips in young chimpanzees. *American Journal of Primatology, 39,* 1–15.

Jouffroy, F. (1993). Primate hands and the human hand: The tool of tools. In A. Berthelet & J. Chavaillon (Eds.) *The use of tools by human and non-human primates* (pp. 6–33). Oxford, Oxford University Press.

Kaye, K. (1982) *The mental and social life of babies: How parents create persons*. Chicago, University of Chicago Press.

Kimura, D. (1992). Sex differences in the brain. *Scientific American, 267* (3), 81–87.

Landau, B., & Spelke, E. (1988). Geometric complexity and object search in infancy. *Developmental Psychology, 4*, 512–521.

Leavens, D.A., Hopkins, W.D., & Bard, K.A. (1996). Indexical and referential pointing in chimpanzees (*Pan troglodytes*). *Journal of Comparative Psychology, 110*(4), 346–353.

Lempers, J.D. (1976). *Production of pointing, comprehension of pointing and understanding of looking behaviour in young children*. Unpublished doctoral dissertation. University of Minnesota.

Leung, E.H.L., & Rheingold, H.L. (1981). Development of pointing as a social gesture. *Developmental Psychology, 17*(2), 215–220.

Marler, P. (1959). Developments in the study of animal communication. In P.R. Bell (Ed.) *Darwin's Biological Work*. Cambridge, Cambridge University Press.

Masataka, N. (1995). The relation between index-finger extension and the acoustic quality of cooing in three-month-old infants. *Journal of Child Language, 22*, 247–257.

Menzel, E.W., Jr. (1974). A group of young chimpanzees in a one-acre field. In A. Schrier & F. Stollnitz (Eds.) *Behaviour of non-human primates: Modern research trends*. San Diego, Academic Press.

Messer, D.J. (1994). *The development of communication: From social interaction to language*. Chichester, Wiley.

Moore, C., & Corkum, V. (1994). Social understanding at the end of the first year of life. *Developmental Review, 14*, 349–372.

Morissette, P., Ricard, M., & Gouin-Decarie, T. (1995). Joint visual attention and pointing in infancy: A longitudinal study of comprehension. *British Journal of Developmental Psychology 13*(2), 163–177.

Murphy, C.M., & Messer, D.J. (1977). Mothers, infants and pointing: A study of gesture. In H. R. Schaffer (Ed.) *Studies of mother–infant interaction*. London, Academic Press.

Napier, J. (1970). *The roots of mankind*. London, Allen and Unwin.

Napier, J. (1960). Studies of the hands of living primates. *Proceedings of the Zoological Society of London, 134*, 647–657.

Piaget, J. (1954). *The construction of reality in the child*. New York, Basic Books.

Pinek, B., Duhamel, J.R., Cave, C., & Brouchon, M. (1989). Audio-spatial deficits in humans: Differential effects associated with left versus right hemisphere parietal damage. *Cortex, 25*, 175–186.

Posner, M.I., & Rothbart, M.K. (1980). The development of attentional mechanisms. In J. H. Flowers (Ed.) *Nebraska Symposium on Motivation* (pp. 1–51). Lincoln, NE, University of Nebraska Press.

Povinelli, D.J., & Eddy, T.J. (1996b). What young chimpanzees know about seeing. *Monographs of the Society for Research in Child Development, 61*, Serial No. 247.

Povinelli, D.J., & Davis, D.R. (1994). Differences between chimpanzees (*Pan troglodytes*) and Humans (*Homo sapiens*) in the resting state of the index finger. *Journal of Comparative Psychology, 108*(2), 134–139

Povinelli, D.J., & Eddy, T.J. (1996a). Factors influencing young chimpanzees' (*Pan troglodytes*) recognition of attention. *Journal of Comparative Psychology, 110*(4), 336–345.

Scaife, M., & Bruner, J.S. (1975). The capacity for joint attention in the infant. *Nature, 253*, 265–266.

Schaffer, H.R. (1984). *The child's entry into a social world*. New York: Academic Press.

Thatcher, R.W., Walker R.A., & Giudice W.S. (1987). Human cerebral hemispheres develop at different rates and ages. *Science, 236*, 1110–1113.

Tonooka, R., & Matsuzawa, T. (1995). Hand preferences of captive chimpanzees (*Pan troglodytes*) in simple reaching for food. *International Journal of Primatology, 16*(1), 17–23.

Volterra, V., & Iversen, J.M. (1995). When do modality factors affect the course of language acquisition? In K. Emmorey & J. Reilly *Language, gesture and space* (pp. 371–391). Hillsdale: NJ, Erlbaum.

Vygotsky, L.S. (1988). Development of the higher mental functions. Reprinted in Richardson, K. & Sheldon, S. *Cognitive development to adolescence* (pp. 61–80). Hove, UK, Erlbaum.

Werner, H., & Kaplan, B. (1963). *Symbol formation: An organismic-developmental approach to language and the expression of thought.* New York, Wiley.

Witelson, S.F., & Nowakowski, R.S. (1991). Left out axons make men right: A hypothesis for the origins of handedness and functional asymmetry. *Neuropsychologia, 28*, 327–333.

CHAPTER ELEVEN

Human Handedness: Developmental and Evolutionary Perspectives

Brian Hopkins
Lancaster University, UK

Louise Rönnqvist
Umeå University, Sweden

INTRODUCTION

Contemporary estimates of righthandedness in adults range from 70% to 90% depending on cultural background and the criteria used to determine the preferred hand (Porac & Coren, 1981). In Western countries, values range from 85% to 95% (Brackenbridge, 1981). These figures raise two general questions: why do the majority of humans show a righthand preference and much less than half of any population a lefthanded one? In turn, we can ask whether a population bias for the right hand is unique to humans and if a lefthand preference constitutes a pathological deviation from the dextral norm. These questions seem to touch on the very essence of what it is to be human. As a consequence, they sometimes elicit strong emotional reactions. One of us, a lefthander forcibly converted in childhood to using the right hand for writing and other tasks, can attest to this fact.

Given the long history of interest in handedness, it is surprising that until the last two decades the quest to understand this phenomenon was not informed by appropriately designed developmental studies. Rather, the development of handedness has been studied as an epiphenomenon of language acquisition and only recently in its own right. The same applies to the evolution of human handedness. On both time scales, handedness has been treated as a late-occurring trait without any prelinguistic origins. One of the aims of this contribution is to show that these assumptions are incorrect. Thus, we argue that a proper understanding of the development of handedness can be attained only when it is theoretically divorced from issues surrounding the origins and acquisition of language.

THE PAST AND ITS LEGACY

Scientific interest in how humans acquire a hand preference probably begins with Aristotle (384–322 BP) and his mentor Plato (428–348 BP). In his *Dialogues*, Plato contended that symmetry is the natural condition of all living things. For him, asymmetries in the structure and functioning of humans arose as a consequence of misguided attempts to educate young children. Aristotle in his *De Partibus Animalium* took a stance that was diametrically opposed to his teacher in holding that asymmetry was a universal state that could not be altered by environmental influences. To bolster his stance, Aristotle proposed a theory based on the temperature of the blood: humans are predominantly righthanded because the blood supply to the right side of the body is warmer and more pure. Traces of this theory can be found in contemporary research on handedness (e.g., Dabbs, 1980). In addition, Aristotle has been proved correct in claiming that nature is fundamentally asymmetrical at all levels of organisation (Hegstrom & Konepudi, 1990).

The contrasting viewpoints of Aristotle and Plato led to speculations about the origins of handedness being cast into two schools of thought—the nativists and nurturists—and thus the loss of a true (i.e., epigenetic) developmental perspective. In an erudite historical overview, Harris (1983) documented swings of opinion in both nativist and nurturist accounts. Prior to Broca (1824–1880), nativists focused on differences in the size and weight of muscles, bones and viscera as determinants of handedness. Following Broca's clinical evidence presented in 1864, of a link between cerebral asymmetries, hand preference and the control of speech, attention shifted to the brain as a locus of all functional asymmetries. This shift still continues to permeate current theories and research on the origins and development of handedness while at the same time inextricably linking them both to the acquisition of language (see Springer & Deutsch, 1985). In general, Broca's findings led to two distinct, but related, brain theories: one that hand preference emerges as a result of differences in the growth gradients of the two hemispheres and the other that it arises from differential development of more specific bilateral structures in the brain.

Nurturist accounts have led to a convincing body of evidence that a hand preference for writing and tool use in general can be changed by particular forms of training. In perhaps the earliest study to demonstrate this fact, Shaw (1902) subjected two righthanded infants to a regime in which objects were placed only in the left hand. They soon adopted a lefthand preference that later could be changed back to a righthanded one. For lefthanders, the world around them exerts subtle, covert pressures for assuming a righthand preference on certain tasks—a fact of life incorporated into the *right sided world hypothesis* of Porac and Coren (1981). Also included in this hypothesis are more overt pressures stemming from culturally determined beliefs about the functional status of the left hand and which are expressed in many of the world's languages. That such beliefs have served in the past as a vehicle for channelling children's hand preferences towards the dextral norm is beyond doubt. According to Harris (1980), they are still potent sources of influence for suppressing a lefthanded preference in some European countries (Germany, Italy, Russia), Japan and many African countries where Islam is practised. This fascinating topic, which has been generally neglected by developmental psychologists interested in handedness, is beyond the scope of this contribution. Interested readers can find informative overviews in Coren (1992), Fincher (1977), Porac and Coren (1981) and Fabbro (1994).

The relevance of nurturist accounts such as the *right sided world hypothesis* for understanding the development of handedness is expressed by Porac and Coren (1981, p. 94; italics in original) as follows: "That handedness *can* be learned indicates only that it maintains a certain degree of plasticity, not that hand preference originally emanates from a learning process".

How then have nurturists accounted for the origins of a hand preference? There appear to have been at least two explanations offered during the nineteenth century —one based on prenatal experience and the other on early postnatal influences involved in the act of nursing (Harris, 1983). The first concerns the intrauterine position of the fetus that is determined by asymmetries in the uterus such that the fetal head is positioned on the left side of the mother. This prenatal bias is then reinforced by the tendency to hold the infant on the left arm when nursing. This later explanation was put forward by, for example, Baldwin (1890) although others such as Stanley Hall (1891) contended that infants were nursed predominantly on the right arm. Once again, we find these explanations continue to be influential in contemporary research on the developmental origins of handedness. Thus, by the beginning of this century both the theoretical and empirical agenda for unravelling the mechanisms by which a hand preference develops had been articulated in general outline. While a nativist–nurturist dichotomy can still be discerned, some current theoretical efforts attempt to frame the development of handedness within an epigenetic perspective.

Perhaps one of the reasons why the development of handedness has attracted scientific attention for so long is that a hand preference appears to be a readily observable trait throughout most of the lifespan. Consequently, it would seem to lend itself to addressing some of the fundamental issues about development such as gene- and brain-behaviour relationships, constancy versus change and whether or not there are detectable sensitive periods. Recent deliberations on the nature of handedness emphasise that it is far from being a simple phenotypical expression open to easy measurement. In practice, defining handedness proves to be a tricky business. We need to do so if only to identify what it is that develops.

THE ONTOLOGY OF HANDEDNESS

Handedness is typically taken to be synonymous with hand preference. This has led to defining handedness as the preferred or consistent use of one hand on unimanual tasks, which is then labelled the dominant hand. On closer inspection, it appears that there are few, if any, truly unimanual tasks. Take, for example, handwriting. Most of us prefer the right hand for this task. But note what your left arm and hand are doing: the left arm provides support for your upper body to adopt an appropriate writing posture while the left hand secures the paper on which you are writing. Writing is thus a bimanual task in which it makes little sense to talk about a dominant hand. Rather, the right hand is more proficient at one thing and the left hand at another. The distinction between preference and proficiency has been stressed by a number of authors (e.g., Annett, 1972; Benton et al., 1962; Satz et al., 1967; Todor & Doane, 1977). It has even been claimed that proficiency and preference are separate dimensions of handedness (Porac & Coren, 1981). This claim is based on two findings with adults. Firstly, proficiency measures assume a normal distribution while those for preference follow a bimodal, J-shaped curve. Secondly, preference and proficiency scores are not perfectly correlated.

It is still a point of debate as to whether preference and proficiency measure the same thing or two different dimensions of handedness. Contrary to Porac and Coren (1981), Bishop (1989) describes a model that treats them as reflecting common underlying processes. It also supports the contention that preference is determined by a number of components of proficiency (e.g., speed, strength and precision). This debate emphasises the need for using a range of tasks in studying the development of handedness so that the emerging relationships between hand preference and proficiency can be charted. Few studies concerned with infants have used this strategy.

A related distinction is between hand preference and manual specialisation (Young, 1977). As before, a hand preference refers to the consistent use of one hand on simple and familiar tasks (i.e., primary actions such as feeding, hammering, throwing and writing). Manual specialisation is defined as lateralised usage on more complex, less practised tasks that may involve either hand. How then does a developing hand preference become incorporated into actions requiring some degree of manual specialisation? Put another way, how does a hand preference become integrated with bimanually coordinated actions? There is a stunning lack of answers to this question, particularly for the period of infancy. Developmentally, of course, the problem with this distinction is to know when tasks can be considered familiar.

Having dealt with the problem of defining and measuring handedness, we turn to speculations about the origins of what now should be regarded as a complex, multidimensional trait. We begin by considering the controversial issue of the evolutionary origins of human handedness.

THE EVOLUTIONARY ORIGINS OF HANDEDNESS

Reconstructing our evolutionary past derives from two main sources: the (hominid) fossil record and comparative studies within the primate order. Both sources have revealed information relevant to the evolution of handedness that continues to be hotly debated. The nub of the debate concerns the evolutionary depth of human handedness. Was it established before the pongoid-hominid divergence, before the acquisition of language or before the establishment of habitual bipedal locomotion? In answering these questions, we need to bear in mind the distinction between hand preference and manual specialisation, something that is not always done in studies addressing the evolutionary origins of human handedness.

Figure 11.1 presents a hypothetical reconstruction of hominid phylogeny based on the fossil evidence. The evidence to date does not permit the derivation of a phylogenetic tree, but only a reconstruction in terms of times of first appearance and survival durations. It should be emphasised that these times and durations are speculative and others are possible. Nevertheless, they represent the considered opinions of most contemporary palaeoanthropologists.

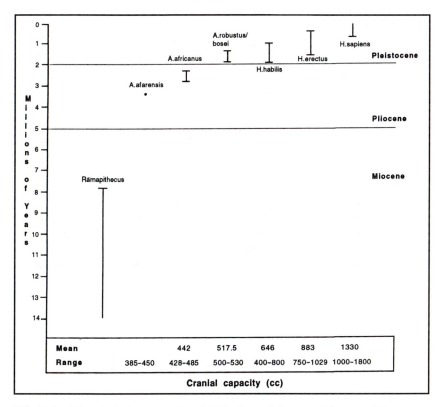

FIG. 11.1: Chronological summary of hominid fossil record. At present it is not possible to reconstruct an adequate phylogenetic tree based on this record. The values for *H. erectus* are *H. erectus erectus*. The mean and range for *H. erectus pekensis* are higher, being 1043cc. and 915–1225cc. respectively.

A major problem in evaluating the evolutionary depth of human handedness is the scarcity of hominid hand bones. Another problem is that artifacts indicative of tool use in the earliest hominids may have been made from wood and thus they are not preserved in the fossil record. Much of the relevant evidence dates from the Lower/Middle Pleistocene epoch and one hominid in particular: *Homo habilis*, which roughly translated means 'handy man' (Leakey et al., 1964).

Endocranial casts of a *H. habilis* specimen (KNM-ER-1476) dated at 2 million years BP have shown hemispherical asymmetries (Tobias, 1981). Specifically, the inferior frontal and parietal lobules were larger in the left hemisphere. The former corresponds to Broca's area and the latter to Wernicke's area. The partial hand bones of *H. habilis* (Olduvai Hominid 7) led to the conclusion that this hominid was perhaps the first toolmaker (Tobias, 1987). The bones, which share many anatomical features with modern humans, are more curved and robust suggesting a hand well suited for power grips. Compared to earlier hominids, the vascular and nerve supply to the finger tips is more abundant, thus implying improved abilities for performing pincer grips. These findings, indicative of some form of manual specialisation, are complemented by the analysis of artifacts from about 2 million years BP (Toth, 1985). Flakes produced by stone tools of the Oldovan type indicate not only bimanual control, but also that the majority of toolmakers (57:43%) were righthanded.

If bipedalism was the prime mover for the establishment of manual specialisation in hominid evolution as originally suggested by Darwin (1871), then handedness may have an even greater evolutionary age than *H. habilis*. The hominid *Australopithecus afarensis* has been dated at 3–5 million years BP (Johanson, 1985). It had an upright posture and the ability to locomote bipedally based on the anatomical features of the pelvic girdle. The hands, intermediate in configuration between chimpanzees and modern humans, suggest the potential for a variety of power and precision grips. While the hands would seem to exclude a fully abducted pincer grip, this does not rule out the potential for manual specialisation. The lack of any artifacts associated with this hominid does, however, hinder any firm conclusions as to whether *A. afarensis* possessed manual specialisation together with a hand preference.

This brief overview of the palaeological evidence puts the evolutionary origins of human handedness at somewhere between 3.5 and 2.0 million years BP. Such an evolutionary depth suggests that handedness and language did not co-evolve, but rather that the former preceded the latter in human evolution. In fact, it may be the case that the evolution of handedness was an important agency through which our linguistic abilities were acquired. We turn now to comparisons between human and nonhuman primates. If it can be shown that nonhuman primates possess human-like characteristics of handedness, then this would push the evolutionary origins to a still older age.

Estimates for the timing of the divergence between humans and the great apes are dependent on one of three approaches. These are classical morphology, multivariate morphometrics and biomolecular analyses of extant primate species (Oxnard, 1982). The latter has been termed quantitative molecular anthropology (Washburn, 1978) and involves four main methods: amino acid sequencing, electrophoresis, immunological reactions and DNA hybridisation (see Tanner, 1981, for a helpful introduction to these methods). The classical approach has provided estimates for the human–great apes split ranging from 40 to 4 million years BP with most being closer to the older age. Molecular anthropology together with multivariate morphometrics consistently arrives at estimates of 5 to 4 million years BP. It is now generally accepted that these two approaches lead to more valid estimates for divergence times in primate evolution.

What then do comparisons of existing primates tell us about the evolutionary origins of human handedness? In short, if it can be established that non-human primates have a righthanded bias at the population level, they can tell us three things. Firstly, that this bias was present before the appearance of the first hominid. Secondly, if one or more of the great apes show such a bias, then it has an evolutionary depth of at least 5 to 4 million years BP. Thirdly, its presence in New or Old World monkeys would suggest a depth of 40 to 35 million years BP (based on divergence times obtained from molecular anthropology). As we shall see, none of these suppositions can be fully supported by the available evidence. Nevertheless, primate studies of handedness are beginning to converge on to some testable theoretical perspectives that have reawakened an interest in its evolutionary origins.

One of the earliest, systematic observations of hand preference in nonhuman primates was carried out by William Ogle (1871), an English physician and translator of Aristotle's *De Partibus Animalium*. He studied 23 monkeys (species not mentioned) at the London Zoological Gardens and reported that 20 of them consistently used the right hand in reaching for bits of food. He also noted that hand preference could change as a consequence of reaching distance. Ogle concluded that monkeys, just like humans, were righthanded. In line with Aristotle's thinking, he speculated the dominant right hand had something to do with the transport of the blood around the body. More specifically, it was due to the greater supply of blood vessels to the left hemisphere. Ogle's forthright opinions on primate handedness and the relationship between anatomical and functional asymmetries were subsequently washed away by apparently contradictory evidence. Up to, and even beyond, the 1960s the received view was that the primate brain was essentially symmetrical (e.g., von Bonin, 1962; Smith, 1966) and a dextral bias pertained only to humans (e.g., Warren, 1977; 1980). The first part of this view began to collapse with Geschwind and Levitsky's (1968) finding of a larger planum temporale in the left hemisphere, a finding subsequently replicated for the chimpanzee (Yeni-Komshian & Benson, 1976). The second part has proved more obdurate and controversial. It was not really challenged until MacNeilage et al. (1987a) proposed a model of primate handedness founded on a re-evaluation of the existing literature. Later christened the *postural origins theory* (MacNeilage,

1991), it has generated a new wave of research into the origins of human handedness.

What MacNeilage et al.'s theory challenged was the long-held claim that hand preference in humans assumes a J-shaped distribution while that for nonhuman primates is U-shaped. Such a bimodal distribution means that monkeys and apes may show individual, but not population-level, preferences. The *postural origins theory* holds that a hand preference was an established feature in ancestral populations of prosimians (thus giving an evolutionary depth of about 60 million years BP). In ancestral prosimians there was a lefthand preference for "bug snatching" (i.e., visually directed reaching to capture fast-moving insects) with the right forelimb providing the necessary postural support. The change from vertical clinging and leaping in prosimians to quadrupedal locomotion in more terrestrial primates resulted in the right side of the body becoming more dominant in environmental interactions. Concordant with this conjecture is the finding that lowland gorillas have a righthand preference in reaching for food when they adopt a bipedal, but not a quadrupedal, posture (Olson et al., 1990). In comparison with other apes, these gorillas are markedly terrestrial and tend to restrict the use of their hands to processing food.

With the advent of pseudo-opposable and opposable prehensile thumbs, this rightsided postural superiority evolved into a righthand preference and superiority for fine, sequential manipulative movements, particularly in the context of bimanual coordination. Thus, according to the evolutionary scenario hypothesised by MacNeilage et al., there was a shift from a left handed/right hemisphere dominance in prosimians to a righthanded/left hemisphere one for manipulation in monkeys and apes. If this was the case, then the dextral bias typical of most humans was established before the onset of persistent bipedalism, an inference contrary to previous evolutionary scenarios.

After reviewing and re-analysing more than 30 studies covering prosimians, New and Old World monkeys and apes, MacNeilage et al. (1988, p. 743) concluded "... the findings ... put the existence of handedness in nonhuman primates beyond reasonable doubt". How well have studies since the original target article conformed to the predictions of their theory? Table 11.1 provides some answers based on a selective overview of 34 studies.

Clearly, the studies on prosimians (A) support the theory. Those involving New World monkeys (B) are less supportive and sometimes contradict each other. The studies of Old World monkeys (C) are in general compliant with the theory's predictions while those with apes as subjects (D) are less so. A more detailed perusal of Table 11.1 reveals that findings with monkeys and apes are more theory-friendly when the tasks involve tool use and experimental manipulations rather than simple reaching for food. This outcome is predicted by Mac-Neilage et al. in maintaining that handedness in monkeys and apes is task-dependent. An elaboration of this theme is that complex (i.e., high level) novel tasks requiring spatiotemporal coordination are more likely to reveal

TABLE 11.1A
Prosimians

Author	Species	Task	Findings	Support for theory
1. Forsythe & Ward (1988)	33 black lemurs (*Lemur macaco*)	Simple food processing	20 LH, 12 RH, 1NP	+
2. Forsythe et al. (1988)	5 black and white ruffed lemurs (*Varecia variegata variegata*)	3 food reaching conditions requiring different postures	LH preference, particularly in tripedal stance. RH for food manipulation between hand and mouth.	+
3. Milliken et al. (1989)	13 ringtailed lemurs (*Lemur catta*)	Food reaching and manipulation	LH preference for reaching. RH for postural support. LH reachers less bimanual manipulation than RH and NP reachers. More males LH	+
4. Masataka (1989)	22 ringtailed lemurs (*Lemur catta*)	4 types of spontaneous behaviours (pick-up; push; reach, grasp)	20 LH for manipulation, RH for postural support	+
5. Larson et al. (1989)	10 lesser bushbabies (*Galago senegalensis*)	8 food reaching conditions manipulating posture, visibility and reach angle	7 LH, 3 RH. Only bipedal posture effective in increasing LH use	+
6. Ward et al. (1990)	194 lemurs distributed over 6 species	Simple food reaching	LH preference, particularly in males. Changes in preference with age (RH bias increased)	+

KEY: Studies of handedness in nonhuman primates published since MacNeilage et al. (1987). Studies cover (A) prosimians; (B) New World monkeys; (C) Old World monkeys; and (D) apes.
R = right, L = left; H = hand preference; NP = no preference;
+ = findings support theory; − = findings do not support theory; ? = unclear how to interpret findings in terms of theory.

TABLE 11.1B
New World Monkeys

Author	Species	Task	Findings	Support for theory
1. Costello & Fragaszy (1988)	6 capuchins (*Cebus apella*) squirrel monkeys (*Samiri sciureus*) Capuchins have precision grip, squirrel monkeys do not	Reaching and manipulation	Tendency for RH manipulation in both species. RH capuchins more likely to use precision grip, LH ones just as likely to use power grip	–
2. Fragaszy & Mitchell (1990)	7 capuchins (*C. apella*). While capuchins have precision grip, opposition between thumb and 1st finger different from Old World primates	Spontaneous activities (feeding, searching, grooming) and uni- and bimanual experimental tasks	No population bias, but preferences more evident in experimental tasks (faster responses with preferred hand)	–
3. Masataka (1990)	24 black-backed capuchins (*C. apella*), 4 white-throated capuchins (*C. capucinus*) 3 white-fronted capuchins (*C. albifrons*)	Picking up scattered bits of food	25 RH, 4 LH, 2 NP	+
4. Matoba et al. (1991)	46 adult and 23 infant marmosets (*Callithrix juchus*)	Picking up scattered bits of food	Adults: 20 LH, 11 RH, 15 NP Infants: 9 LH, 8 RH, 6 NP	+
5. Aruguete et al. (1992)	13 squirrel monkeys (*S. sciureus*)	Manipulative touching	RH and foot for body touching, but not environmental touching	?
6. Westergaard (1991)	5 capuchins (*C. apella*)	Dipping branches, sticks and straw into containers of sweet syrup	3–4 LH depending on component of task	+
7. Westergaard & Suomi (1993)	40 capuchins (*C. apella*)	Using stones to crack open walnuts	4 RH, 8 LH, 5 NP. 67% of lateralised subjects had LH preference	+
8. Roney & King (1993)	30 squirrel monkeys (*S. sciureus*), 14 cotton-top tamarins (*Saguinus oedipus*)	Food reaching in different postures	No population bias in either species. Preferences intensified in upright posture	–

TABLE 11.1C
Old World Monkeys

Author	Species	Task	Findings	Support for theory
1. Vauclair & Fagot (1987)	18 baboons (*Papio papis*)	Variety of spontaneous uni- and bimanual activities in field situation	5 RH, 2 LH, 11 NP on unimanual activities. Changes in preference with age (younger subjects more LH on bimanual activities)	−
2. Kuhl (1988)	± 30 rhesus monkeys (*Macaca fuscata, M. mulatta, M. mulatta, M. nemestrina*)	Discrimination of speech sounds by pressing or releasing centrally-located telegraph key and monitoring lights signalling trial and response onsets	RH responding for all subjects	+
3. Fagot & Vauclair (1988a)	25 baboons (*P. papis*)	Simple reaching and complex (visuospatial) tasks	Consistent LH preference for complex tasks, bimodal distribution for simple ones	+
4. Hopkins et al. (1989)	2 rhesus monkeys (*M. mulatta*)	Joystick manipulation to track target on monitor with cursor; reaching for food reward	RH preferences for manipulating, joystick; no preferences for reaching	+/−
5. Fagot et al. (1991)	29 rhesus monkeys (*M. mulatta*)	Haptic and visual discriminations	21 LH for haptic task. Strongest in vertical 3-point hanging position or in sitting; weakest in visual task or in tripedal posture	+
6. Westergaard (1991)	4 lion-tailed rhesus monkeys (*M. silenius*)	Dipping branches, sticks and straw into containers of sweet syrup	2 LH depending on component of task	+
7. Hauser et al. (1991)	277 free-ranging monkeys (*M. mulatta*)	Lifting/holding lid of chow dispenser to remove food	Predominant LH preference for lifting, RH for holding, LH for food retrieval	+

TABLE 11.1D
Apes

Author	Species	Task	Findings	Support for theory
1. Fagot & Vauclair (1988b)	8 lowland gorillas (*Gorilla gorilla*)	Simple reaching and complex (visuospatial) tasks	Consistent LH preferences for complex tasks, no preference for simple one	+
2. Hopkins (1989)	3 chimpanzees (*Pan troglodytes*)	Joystick manipulation to track target on monitor with cursor, reaching for food reward	RH preference for manipulating joystick; no preferences for reaching	+/–
3. Stafford et al. (1990)	8 siamangs (*Hylobates syndactylus*), 7 white-chequed gibbons (*H. concolor*), 4 white-handed gibbons (*H. lar*)	Food reaching and brachiation	All older females RH for reaching, but not younger females or males in general. No preference for R or L limb leading off brachiation for those who showed these behaviours. Changes in preference age	+
4. Olson et al. (1990)	12 gorillas (*G. gorilla*) 13 orangutans (*Pongo pygmaeus*) 9 gibbons (*H. lar*)	a. retrieving raisins on floor b. collecting raisings above head height c. unfastening metal hook	No preference for a. and c. For b.: All gibbons RH, 10 gorillas RH, orangutans bimodal distribution	+/–
5. Annett & Annett (1991)	31 lowland gorillas (*G. gorilla*)	Spontaneous food reaching	No population bias	–
6. Boesch (1991)	67 wild chimpanzees (*P. troglodytes*)	Naturally occurring forms of tool use	RH preference for wadge dipping. Changes in preference with age (more RH in younger subjects)	+/–
7. Byrne & Byrne (1991)	44 wild mountain gorillas (*G. gorilla berengei*)	6 naturally occurring feeding activities	No population bias. Females stronger preferences	–
8. Aruguete et al. (1992)	27 chimpanzees (*P. troglodytes*)	manipulative touching	RH preference for environmental touching, but not for body touching	?
9. Hopkins et al. (1993)	11 pygmy chimpanzees (*P. paniscus*)	7 behaviours including food reaching with postural manipulation	Greater RH preference in reaching from bipedal posture. RH preference for feeding when LH holding food. Changes in preference with age (older subjects stronger RH bias)	+

TABLE 11.1D (continued)
Apes

Author	Species	Task	Findings	Support for theory
10. Sugiyama et al. (1993)	18 wild chimpanzees (*P. troglodytes*)	Food picking and nut cracking	No population bias, but LH preference more prevalent in adults	–
11. Hopkins (1994)	140 chimpanzees (*P. troglodytes*)	Bimanual feeding	RH bias in those with significant hand preference. Sub-adult less lateralised than adults. No sex differences	+
12. Colell et al. (1995)	31 chimpanzees (*P. troglodytes*), 2 pygmy chimpanzees (*P. paniscus*), 3 orangutans (*P. pygmaeus*)	4 types of spontaneous behaviours (food reaching; drinking water with hand; waking currents in water; throwing objects)	No population bias in any species for food reaching and throwing. RH preference for drinking and waking currents. (LH for postural support) for those who showed these behaviours. Changes in preference with age	+
13. Tonooka & Matsuzawa (1995)	80 chimpanzees (*P. troglodytes*)	Food reaching	No population bias	–
14. Hopkins & de Waal (1995)	10 pygmy chimpanzees (*P. paniscus*)	7 behaviours including food reaching	Similar to Hopkins et al. (1993). Differences: RH bias in marking gesture; LH bias for body touching	+
15. Jones-Engell & Bard (1996)	13 chimpanzees (*P. troglodytes*)	Retrieving food from plexiglass box	No population bias for either precision or power grips	–
16. Rogers & Kaplan (1996)	43 semi-wild orangutans (*P. pygmaeus*)	5 types of spontaneous behaviour (body touching; food manipulation; touching conspecifics; finger/foot sucking)	LH preference to touch face or head when finger flexed. RH preference for food manipulation in older females, especially in propped or sitting position	+/–

population-based handedness than simple (i.e., low level) well-practised tasks (Fagot & Vauclair, 1991). In contrast, it has been proposed that simian species may have a "soft" form of handedness that is intermediate between population-level ("hard") handedness and no preference (Roney & King, 1993). On this view, "soft" handedness may prevail when an already low intensity preference is increased by a more demanding task, once again stressing the fluid, task-specific nature of manual biases in nonhuman primates.

Two other generalisations can be drawn from Table 11.1: sex and age differences, which sometimes have been shown to interact as in humans (D3, D15). Unfortunately, both sorts of differences when reported are not very consistent across studies. It is highly probable that the lack of consistency reflects task differences between studies such that one study involves tool use (e.g., D6) and the other food manipulation (e.g., D9). None of the studies in Table 11.1 was explicitly developmental in nature, most of them involving juvenile or adult subjects or both. This perhaps accounts for why so few age-related trends are reported. We shall consider the relevance of the few developmental studies on nonhuman primates in subsequent sections.

In conclusion, the *postural origins theory* does a relatively good job of accounting for similarities and differences between human and other primate species in mature forms of handedness. Other evolutionary accounts have implicated, for example, tool use (Corballis, 1983) and throwing (Calvin, 1983) as the means by which handedness became a feature of primate phylogeny. In these accounts, handedness arose as a consequence of quantitative changes in some function. The MacNeilage et al. account is different in stressing that patterns of handedness evolved with qualitative changes in postural control and structure — lefthanded reaching with the prehensile prosimian hand and righthanded manipulation with the opposable simian thumb. The continuing plausibility of their theory will depend on showing more consistent findings within and between monkeys and apes, and between them and humans. There are at least three ways in which this can be achieved. Firstly, the use of the same measures of handedness for both human and nonhuman primates, something that has hardly ever been done. When it is done, there are considerable similarities between species such as a stronger righthanded preference for females (Seltzer et al., 1990). Secondly, the use of both preference and performance measures. The *postural origins theory* implicates benefits in performance accruing from the use of the preferred hand, especially if the preference is associated with a neural asymmetry (see also Corballis, 1989). Only three studies listed in Table 11.1 (B2, C5, D4) have expressly addressed the functional relationship between preference and performance. Thirdly, comparisons between captive and feral subjects. The majority of studies in Table 11.1 concern caged animals who are known to acquire behavioural stereotypes as a consequence of occupying one corner in a cage (Box, 1977). In such a situation, one hand may become artificially restricted leading to the stereotypical use of the other. Further improvements in testing the theory could be gained from:

1. Better control of age, sex and practice levels as well as task difficulty.
2. The inclusion of a variety of tasks involving unimanual, bimanual and multicomponent manipulation.
3. Improved criteria for classifying individuals as being right- , left- or ambihanded (typically most studies on humans and other primates classify left- and ambihanders into a "non-righthanded" group thereby obscuring potentially important information).

We consider next the ontogenetic origins of handedness in humans. As we shall see, posture is once again assigned an important formative role. Moreover, cross-species comparisons of infants within the primate order are essential to a proper understanding of how handedness originates in ontogenetic development. If handedness preceded the appearance of habitual bipedal locomotion and tool use in hominid evolution, as we have claimed, then we would predict that its purported functional precursors should also be demonstrable in other primate species.

THE DEVELOPMENTAL ORIGINS OF HUMAN HANDEDNESS

Contemporary theorising about the developmental origins of handedness can be grouped into five models, all of which can trace their roots to at least the nineteenth century: *the biased oocyte, the biased gene, the biased brain, the biased head,* and *the biased uterus* model. Each of the models can be, and have been, applied to questions about the evolutionary origins of handedness. And because each of them has a particular focus, none can provide a comprehensive explanation for the origins of handedness. On this issue, it has been questioned whether such explanations are desirable as by their very size and complexity they may not be open to falsification (McManus & Bryden, 1991). Where possible, we will attempt to show links between the models. Most attention is devoted to the *left-otolithic dominance hypothesis* (Previc, 1991), which amounts to an integration of the biased head and uterus models.

The biased oocyte: the left-to-right maturational gradient model

The biased oocyte model can be traced back to Broca (1865) who explained the hemispheric lateralisation of language in terms of a left–right gradient. The basic assumption in its current form is that structural or chemical asymmetries at the cellular level are governed by a left-to-right maturational gradient (Corballis & Morgan, 1978; Morgan & Corballis, 1978). This gradient is coded in the cytoplasm of the unfertilised egg rather than in the nuclear genes. Another assumption is that these asymmetries give rise to lateralised structures in the developing brain, which in turn are responsible for functional asymmetries such as handedness. The unique feature of the model is the inclusion of maternal effects that do not rely on an interaction between maternal cytoplasmic factors and nuclear genes from both parents. Thus, the gradient is established during oogenesis by factors intrinsic to the cytoplasm (e.g., asymmetrical distribution of mitochondria in a cell) and not the nuclear genes. However, the actual expression of an asymmetry during development ultimately depends on nuclear genes and susceptibility to environmental (chemical) influences.

The gradient model, which favours faster development on the left side and a subsequent takeover by the right side, accounts for some initial asymmetries in brain and behaviour development as we shall see. In accounting for why some individuals become lefthanded, the model would hold that the gradient is absent in some of these cases, thus enabling environmental asymmetries to play a role. While the model can produce such plausible explanations, it suffers from a number of shortcomings. Perhaps the main one is the lack of evidence showing that asexual cytoplasmic inheritance plays a role in vertebrates. Another problem is that neural asymmetries do not relate in any simple way to functional asymmetries, thereby intimating that they are not derived from the same maturational gradient. Furthermore, studies on the growth of embryological structures do not consistently demonstrate left–right gradients, but rather right–left gradients (Best, 1988) and even cyclical or fluctuating asymmetries (Mittwoch, 1978). In reality, there may be at least three embryological growth gradients in addition to a lateral one (Best, 1988): anteriorposterior, posterioranterior and ventrodorsal gradients. The lateral gradient interacts with the other three to give a three-dimensional growth vector. This vector induces a counterclockwise torque in the shape of the developing brain such that the left hemisphere is twisted backwards and the right hemisphere forwards. Certain cerebral asymmetries, in particular left–right differences in the positions and angles of fissures, can be accounted for by such a growth vector.

The next model is diametrically opposed to that of Corballis and Morgan in maintaining that lateralised traits are inherited.

The biased gene: the right shift gene model

At the functional level, the biased gene model treats handedness as a continuously varying gradient distributed along a normal curve, rather than as a discrete variable (Annett, 1972;1978;1985). Consequently, there are degrees of preference that, according to the model, are systematically related to performance differences between the two hands. The model itself rests on two components: one is genetic and the other environmental or accidental. The majority of individuals inherit a right shift gene (RS+) that predisposes them to a dominant left hemisphere for the control of speech. This in turn increases the likelihood of righthandedness. When this gene is absent (RS-), cerebral dominance for speech and hand preference are determined at random. Such individuals will become left- or righthanded with equal likelihood. In summary, this model proposes a genetic tendency towards righthandedness in humans, but not for lefthandedness, which arises as a consequence of randomness in the absence of the RS+ gene.

An important consequence of the Annett and other genetic models (e.g., Levy & Nagylaki, 1972) is that they direct attention to the neglected role of familial handedness in the development of hand preference. In comparison with the two-gene (4 allele) model of Levy and Nagylaki (1972), Annett's single gene (2 allele) model makes better predictions in this respect. For example, Annett's more probabilistic model accounts quite well for the high percentage (60%) of individuals who become righthanded despite being born to two lefthanded parents. Given that these individuals lack the RS+ gene, the model predicts about 50% would be righthanded. The fact that the figure is slightly higher than the predicted 50% could be explained by covert and overt pressures to conform with a righthanded world. However, to qualify as a valid model for the developmental origins of handedness, the right shift gene model needs to be applied to the distribution of neonatal functional asymmetries purported to be precursors of later hand preference. The data Annett has gathered to bolster her model are derived from children older than 2 years and adults.

Despite its elegant parsimony and predictive validity, the right shift gene model is based on a number of questionable assumptions. To begin with, there is no theoretical or empirical support that both dominant and recessive alleles are present in the population each with a frequency of 50%. Nor is there unequivocal support for the assumption that preference and performance covary in the way predicted by Annett (see Porac & Coren, 1981). Support for the assumption that human handedness evolved as a secondary consequence of cerebral lateralisation for speech is also lacking. As we have seen, the evidence from studies of nonhuman primates suggests a lefthanded preference may have preceded a righthanded one, both being present in ancestors who did not possess speech. Implicit in Annett's model is that random dominance is typical of nonhuman primates. Thus, righthandedness and left hemisphere dominance have a recent evolutionary origin. This assumption contrasts with the evidence drawn upon by the next model. In its most recent form, this model purports to be epigenetic rather than genetic in explaining how neural asymmetries arise.

The biased brain model

Gross cerebral asymmetries in the adult human, particularly on the upper surface of the temporal lobe, were first identified more than 120 years ago. At this level, it has been shown that in most righthanded subjects the left hemisphere is larger, heavier, has more convolutions and more grey than white matter (Gur et al., 1994). Some asymmetries have been found in hominid endocasts and nonhuman primates, indicating their great evolutionary depth. In addition to the planum temporale mentioned earlier, these include a longer Sylvian fissure and larger occipital petalia (skull indentions) on the left side (Holloway & LaCoste-LareyMondie, 1982; LeMay, 1976). Both these asymmetries are probably a consequence of the hominid brain having a counterclockwise torque (Chui & Damasio, 1980). In human development, the planum temporale can be observed as early as 29 weeks postconception (Wada et al., 1975). However, supramarginal, angular and transverse temporal (Heschl) gyri are larger and more common on the right side of the fetal brain (Chi et al., 1977), a finding that speaks against the left–right gradient model.

The appearance of cerebral asymmetries as early as the second trimester of pregnancy is problematic on two counts. Firstly, it is unknown whether they arise during embryogenesis or during later stages of brain development (viz., neurogenesis, neuronal migration or maturation). Secondly, the processes by which they occur are poorly understood: do they reflect suppression of development on one side, an enhanced development on the other, or some combination of both processes? According to the *neuronal loss hypothesis* (Galaburda et al., 1987), the cerebral hemispheres initially have an equivalent rate of development followed by involution (i.e., shrinkage) on one side. Thus, there is an initial period of symmetrical (over) production of neurons, axons and synapses that are then pruned down on one side by epigenetic factors leading to that side (typically the right) becoming smaller. While there is initial equivalence between the two hemispheres, the right one subsequently leads during fetal development. The left hemisphere has a slower rate of development, but eventually becomes the dominant partner. In keeping with a general embryological principle (Jacobson, 1978), its slower rate implies a greater vulnerability to epigenetic factors that may interfere with development. One such factor is the male sex hormone testosterone. Its purported effects on the prenatal development of the left hemisphere resulted in the *testosterone or Geschwind-Behan-Galaburda (GBG) hypothesis* to account for individuals who do not develop a righthand preference among other things (Geschwind & Behan, 1982; 1984; Geschwind & Galaburda, 1985; Geschwind & Galaburda, 1987).

The GBG hypothesis has been described as "arguably the most massive (and untidy) theory ... in the history of neuropsychology" (Previc, 1994, p. 174). The starting point for this outcome was the clinical observation that immune disorders such as allergies and migraine are more frequent in dyslexic (mainly male) children who are lefthanders. Given the sex-related nature of these disorders, it was reasoned that overproduction or an increased sensitivity to testosterone in the fetus was the responsible agent. Specifically, it was proposed that testosterone, or some factor related to it, retards the growth of specific regions in the more vulnerable left hemisphere. Homologous regions in the right hemisphere would be less affected and its normally occurring involution could thus be prevented. The end state could be a symmetrical, rather than an asymmetrical, brain in which there was a shift to the right hemisphere participation in handedness and language. In terms of handedness, the outcome is an anomalous (nonstandard) pattern dominance. Anomalous dominance is perhaps the most important construct in the GBG hypothesis and it does not consist of just frank lefthandedness (McManus &

Bryden, 1991). Instead, it represents graded asymmetries along a continuum varying from reversed (left) handedness through reduced handedness to standard (right) handedness. Individuals with symmetrical brains resulting from left hemisphere delays should have random handedness as do those lacking the RS+ gene in Annett's model. Thus, frank handedness will only constitute a minority of the anomalous dominance group, the rest having patterns that deviate from the standard form.

An important corollary of the GBG hypothesis is that patterns of handedness will depend on when in development the effects of testosterone are most potent. If the (unknown) substrate for handedness in the left hemisphere develops before testosterone can affect it, then standard dominance will be the outcome. A subsequent increase in testosterone levels or sensitivity may disrupt the left cortical cytoarchitecture associated with language rather than for handedness. While these sorts of differential timing effects are a plausible addition to the hypothesis, they have yet to be empirically demonstrated. This is a problem because it introduces an unfalsifiable element " ... providing additional free parameters in the model" (McManus & Bryden, 1991, p. 247).

The GBG hypothesis has other problems. One is the fact of large differences in prenatal testosterone levels between males and females while the hypothesis proposes only slightly elevated numbers of males with atypical handedness (Bishop, 1989). Another is the definition of anomalous dominance. As McManus and Bryden (1991) rightly point out, the multiple criteria used to pin it down lead to the risk of committing Type II errors due to multiple testing of its separate (6) components (atypical handedness, atypical language dominance and atypical visuospatial dominance where atypical refers to either reversed or weakened dominance). Furthermore, the hypothesis continues to be dogged by a lack of clear-cut empirical support. Part of the problem here is that the hypothesis is in fact an enormous concatenation of seemingly disparate variables bridging many different levels of organisation. With this degree of complexity, it is not surprising that it has spawned conflicting findings. Nevertheless, the hypothesis is perhaps the first general theory of cerebral lateralisation stressing "bottom-up", rather than "top-down" determinants of handedness (Previc, 1994). In addition, its explicit developmental and epigenetic slant should eventually provide some important insights into the origins of deviations of handedness from the rightsided norm. To achieve this, the unwieldy hypothesis will have to be reduced to a set of coherent postulates — a task that has already begun (see McManus & Bryden, 1991).

The incursion of noninvasive, in vivo brain-imaging techniques into brain-behaviour research have confirmed and sometimes contradicted the older findings derived from autopsy material and invasive techniques such as ventriculography, angiography and computer-assisted tomography. However, to date the use of nuclear magnetic resonance imaging (MRI) and functional MRI to investigate the neural correlates of handedness have been restricted to adults (e.g., see Kertesz et al., 1990; Kim et al., 1993; Steinmetz et al., 1991). MRI, particularly the functional variant, has limited application to developmental research because it requires subject cooperation to keep the head still. Nevertheless, in clinical cases requiring sedation it could be used to test some of the predictions made by the GBG hypothesis about the neuroanatomical origins of handedness. In general though, MRI (and postmortem) studies have tended to focus on cerebral asymmetries that are more related to speech lateralisation than to hand preference, the Kim et al. (1993) study being an exception to the rule. Thus, what is needed is more information about the development of asymmetries in structures known to be involved in motor control of the limbs, particularly at the sub-cortical level.

In a study of 18 normal brains, some of them as young as 28 weeks gestation, 16 had a larger globus pallidus on the left side. This asymmetry was found in some brains before the age of 18 months and in all brains younger than 4 years (Kooistra & Heilman, 1988). This, and other nuclei of the basal ganglia (caudate nucleus, putamen), contain higher concentrations of dopamine on the left side in postmortem adult brains (Glick et al., 1982). This neurochemical asymmetry may be greater than anywhere else in the brain. It has been suggested that it may account for functional biases observed in infants up to the age of 3 months (Liederman, 1988). Asymmetries in other neurotransmitters have been found in the thalamus and the temporal lobe (Amaducci et al., 1985; Oke et al., 1978).

To date none of these pharmacological asymmetries have been related to differences in the patterning of handedness. Moreover, the precise function of each nucleus of the basal ganglia continues to be a controversial topic (see Goldman-Rakic & Selemon, 1990, and associated papers). This controversy apart, the basal ganglia receive indirect contralateral projections from the vestibular system that are functional (e.g., in ipsilateral turning and postural control). As we shall see, the bilateral labyrinth has been implicated as a substrate for the origins of handedness.

Do the corticospinal tracts show asymmetries and can they be related to handedness? The answer is yes they do, but they have not yet been shown to be unambiguously associated with hand preference or any of its purported functional precursors. It has been known for some time that the direct corticospinal system, ultimately responsible for contralateral control of the fingers, decussates more completely from left to right than the other way round in most fetal brains (Yakovlev & Rakic, 1966). If so, then it is possible that corticospinal fibres destined to innervate the small number of muscles of the right hand may be more numerous than for the left one. Such a differential pattern of innervation would create a dextral bias in hand preference. In adults, this asymmetry in decussation does not predict hand preference (Kertesz & Geschwind, 1971). However, the small number of lefthanders in this study (7/158) probably accounts for this outcome. Across a wide variety of species, variations in mammal dexterity are closely related to where the corticospinal fibres terminate in the spinal cord (Heffner & Masterson, 1983). This finding suggests that the inferior rather than the superior end of the corticospinal tracts is the place to look for the structural correlates of hand preference

(Harris & Carlson, 1988). The spinal cord itself is larger on the right side in most adults (Nathan et al., 1990). This asymmetry might arise from more corticospinal fibres crossing from left to right. Nothing is known about the developmental timing of this differential decussation in humans.

What can we conclude about neuroanatomical asymmetries and the developmental origins of handedness? Firstly, they appear during prenatal development, most of them during the first half of pregnancy. Secondly, most of those identified are cerebral asymmetries and as such are better predictors of speech lateralisation than hand preference. Thirdly, they are typically defined in terms of some measure of difference in size, but the functional implications of such a measure have a questionable status in neurophysiology (Passingham, 1979). Fourthly, the processes by which neuroanatomical asymmetries express themselves in particular functional asymmetries have so far escaped satisfactory specification. This criticism applies to GBG hypothesis and with even more force to the gradient and genetic models. The next two models have been combined in an attempt to arrive at a process-oriented account of how a dextral preference becomes established in development.

The biased head and uterus models

When placed in a supine position, most healthy fullterm newborns maintain a characteristic posture with the head positioned to the right (Gesell, 1938). A turning bias has also been consistently observed when the head is released from a midline position, the majority of newborns assuming a position to the right (Liederman, 1983). In both cases, there is similar dextral bias to that found for hand preference in adults. Thus, about 70% to 80% of newborns assume and maintain a rightsided preference. This similarity has led to the suggestion that the lateralised head position of the newborn is a functional precursor of a later hand preference (Gesell & Ames, 1947).

This suggestion lay dormant for a number years before being taken up by Michel and colleagues in a series of carefully controlled studies. In general, they found both the assumption (Michel & Goodwin, 1979; Goodwin & Michel, 1981) and maintenance (Coryell & Michel, 1978) of a lateralised head position predicted the arm used in initial attempts at reaching. In addition, it was shown that these early functional asymmetries were predictive of hand preference at 60 weeks (Michel, 1981) and 74 weeks (Michel & Harkins, 1986).

Michel (1987) recapitulated a plausible and testable explanation for how "headedness" might be related to later manual specialisation. The basic idea is that a head position preference to the right or left in the newborn induces a lateral asymmetry in hand regard and activity. Greater visual experience with one hand leads to it being preferred for reaching, which in turn ensures that it will become specialised for fine motor abilities. Thus, as each functional asymmetry appears it is transferred to a subsequent ability, not because they stem from a common neural mechanism but because there is a continuity in visual experience of one hand rather than the other. On this view then, the developmental origin of handedness resides in greater visual experience of one hand created by the lateralised head position preference of the newborn.

There are a number of reasons for qualifying this epigenetic account:

1. The newborn data really only predict right arm and hand preference at older ages. For example, in the Goodwin and Michel (1981) study, the majority (74%) of newborns who assumed a head right position had a right arm preference for reaching at 19 weeks. In contrast, just less than half (46%) of those with a leftward assumption had a left preference for reaching. This outcome is in line with the predictions of the right shift gene model given that there was no relationship between familial lefthandedness and either head or arm preference (see also Coryell, 1985; Liederman & Kinsbourne, 1980).

2. A lateralised head position preference in the newborn does not appear to be a robust phenomenon. When the head is held in a midline position for up to 15 min., a rightsided bias in head turning is reduced or even temporarily lost (Roberts & Smart, 1981; Turkewitz & Creighton, 1974). If biomechanical constraints on head turning are lifted, then the newborn maintains the head more in the midline position, but there is still a greater right- than leftsided preference (Rönnqvist & Hopkins, 1996). Together with more midline crossings (see Fig. 11.2), these findings strengthen the claim that neonatal "headedness" reflects a neural asymmetry (Liederman, 1983;1988) while at the same time indicating that its influence is modulated by biomechanical factors (e.g., a heavy head) acting on weak anti-gravity muscles of the neck.

3. A lateralised head position is only consistently present for 2–3 months after birth, following which there is a preference to maintain the head in the midline (Cornwell et al., 1985; Hopkins et al., 1990). This is an inordinately short space of time for acquiring the rudiments of a hand preference, unless one treats it as a sensitive period for this trait.

4. Given Michel's explanation assumes differential visual experience of the two hands, one would expect infants born without sight should develop patterns of hand preference that differ from the normal population. This possibility does seem to be borne out by the few relevant studies. For example, blind children between the ages of 6 and 14 years did not differ from sighted counterparts in the direction and degree of hand preference across a range of tasks (Ittyeral, 1993). And congenitally-blind adults have a righthanded bias in reading braille (Bradshaw et al., 1982; Fertsch, 1947) and a postural bias to the right (Cernacek & Jagr, 1972).

While these qualifications, and in particular the latter two, speak against the explanation offered by Michel, they do not entirely negate it. Perhaps there are other posturally based asymmetries in the newborn period that do not have such an obligatory link to vision and which persist beyond the age when a head midline

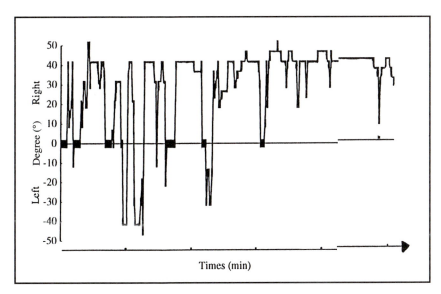

FIG. 11.2:   A five-minute registration of head movements plotted sec.by sec. in a 2-day-old newborn during State 4. The head is supported in a specially designed holder that allows the head to move freely from side to side. There is a general preference to maintain the head to the right. But note also the number of midline crossings and the presence of periods when the head is maintained in the midline (■). These two features of head control in the supine position do not normally become evident until 2–3 months later.

position becomes dominant. One such candidate might be found in hand–mouth contacting, a behaviour that does not seem to be under visual control in the newborn (Butterworth & Hopkins, 1988).

In newborns one hour after birth, hand–mouth (but not hand–face) contacting was highly lateralised: all of them contacted the mouth with the hand ipsilateral to the head position and most did it with the right hand (Hopkins et al., 1987). Interestingly, the same rightsided bias has been reported for chimpanzee infants up to 3 months of age (Bard et al., 1990; Hopkins & Bard, 1993). In the human, the ipsilateral synergy between head and hand seems to dissolve between 2 and 3 months of age such that the infant is just as likely to contact the mouth with either hand regardless of head position (Hopkins, 1994). By 18 weeks though, the earlier hand preference was re-established, but now with the head in the midline. Furthermore, the preferred hand at 3 weeks of age predicted hand preference during the toddler period. The left handers at 3 weeks had either left or mixed preferences as toddlers and at least one instance of familial lefthandedness. This finding appears to contravene Annett's model. However, there were only 4/15 children who had a left- or mixed hand preference—a typical fate of small-scale studies of handedness that use aselect samples. What the study does suggest is that something more than a biased visual experience of the hands should be part of the necessary conditions for later hand preference, namely, spontaneous differential usage of the hands during early infancy.

If newborns show postural asymmetries that may bias the development of handedness, what is the origin of such asymmetries? One proposal has to do with the position of the fetus in the last few weeks of pregnancy. It is a well-established obstetrical fact that there is a direct correspondence between fetal position in the last few weeks of pregnancy and birth position (Hughey, 1985). Moreover, two-thirds of fetuses born in a left vertex presentation (the most common position at birth) lie with their backs towards the mother's left side some 3 to 4 weeks before a fullterm delivery (Dunn, 1976. See Fig. 11.3). This position can be either left occiput anterior (LOA) or transverse (LOT). There are two relevant suppositions associated with this, and other, positions. One is that when the fetus is in the LOA/LOT position, with the right side of the head facing outwards, movements of the left arm are restricted by the pelvis and backbone of the mother (Moss, 1929). The other is that in LOA/LOT deliveries the brain will be subjected to asymmetrical forces that induce the counterclock-wise torque mentioned previously, which leads to larger neuroanatomical asym-metries on the left (Grapin & Perpère, 1968). ROA/ROT positions should have the opposite set of effects.

Given the asymmetrical consequences of these mechanical restrictions and forces, it was asked if the LOA/LOT–ROA/ROT distinction predicted neonatal "headedness" and hand preference (Goodwin & Michel, 1981; Michel & Goodwin, 1979). The outcomes have a familiar ring to them. The left vertex presentation was significantly associated with a rightsided head and hand preference. For ROA/ROT deliveries, head and hand preferences were randomly distributed rather than leftsided as predicted. This again fits in with Annett's model and indicates that these infants may have had a history of familial lefthandedness. Furthermore, asymmetries in mechanical forces during passage through the birth canal would appear to be irrelevant, based on a report about head position preference in infants delivered by Caesarian section (Turkewitz, 1977). These infants had a population-level rightsided bias. This leaves fetal position in some way implicated in head position asymmetries after birth. But how? To answer this question requires posing another: why do fetuses assume a lateralised position with the right side of the head facing outwards?

One answer is that placental location determines the position of the fetus (Hoogland & de Haan, 1980). The majority of anterior placentas are located on the right side of the uterus (thus inducing a LOA/LOT position) while most posterior ones are on the left (thus inducing a ROA/ROT position). These relationships have been discounted in an ultrasound study of fetal position (Ververs et al., 1994a,b). Another answer refers to the fact that in most pregnancies the uterus has a torsion to the right resulting in the maternal bladder and rectum being positioned to the right (Taylor, 1976). With this uterine asymmetry, there is more room for the head and body when the fetus is in a left vertex position. How this position is associated with a head-right preference has been addressed by Previc (1991) in his *left-otolithic dominance hypothesis*.

This hypothesis, which is a direct competitor of the GBG hypothesis, involves relating the position of the fetus in the last trimester of pregnancy to the biomechanics of maternal walking. The action of the mother walking forwards can be decomposed into two phases: an acceleration phase when the trailing leg is

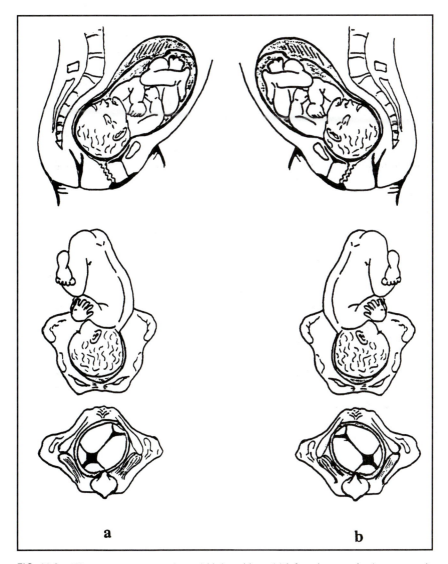

FIG. 11.3:   The two most common (vertex) birth positions: (**a**) left occiput anterior (or transverse) and (**b**) right occiput anterior (or transverse) (drawn by Louise Rönnqvist).

swung forwards and a deceleration phase at heel strike. While the acceleration phase is slightly longer (300ms) than the deceleration phase (200ms), the latter provides a sharper form of stimulation for the fetus. This is because the deceleration phase involves braking and thus an inertial force travelling backwards. In a left vertex presentation, the fetus is moved sideways to the right when the mother walks forwards. When this happens, forward acceleration is registered by the right otolith (i.e., utricle) of the fetus and the more prominent backward inertial force due to deceleration by the left otolith (Fig. 11.4a). In short, there is an unequal shearing of the hair cells in the two otoliths resulting in a left-otolith dominance.

How is the maternally induced asymmetry responsible for the head position preference of the newborn? Impulses from the maculae of the utricles travel centrally to both the brain stem and cerebellum. In the brain stem they terminate on the vestibulospinal tract. Almost all of the fibres of this tract are uncrossed and most end on interneurons in the spinal cord. The main function of this tract is ipsilateral control of extensor muscles. For head turning, the most important muscle is the bilateral sternocleidomastoid—the left of which is activated to turn the head to the right (see Fig. 11.5). Thus, a left-otolithic dominance should be related to a leftsided activation of the muscle and thereby to a rightsided head preference.

The left-otolithic dominant hypothesis is one of two hypotheses that together form a more general model on the prenatal origins of cerebral lateralisation (Previc, 1991). The other is the *auditory lateralisation hypothesis* used to account for the origins of left hemisphere dominance for speech perception and language. A starting point for this hypothesis is that two-thirds of newborns have a right ear advantage (REA) in a dichotic listening task (e.g., Bertoncini et al., 1989). How does the REA originate? According to Previc, it arises from craniofacial asymmetries acquired prenatally. In the adult population about two-thirds of individuals have a slight enlargement of the left side of the face. A smaller right craniofacial region means a shorter middle (right) ear conduction time and thus an aural sensitivity advantage for the right ear, particularly for sounds in the midfrequency (i.e., speech) range. The REA then biases the left hemisphere for speech and language.

With these two hypotheses, Previc's general epigenetic model succeeds in disassociating questions about the developmental origins of handedness from those about language. It does so by proposing independent mechanisms for the origins of a rightsided motor dominance (the left-otolithic dominance hypothesis) and a right-ear sensitivity (the auditory lateralisation hypothesis). Previc also tries to account for his opinion that nonhuman primates lack hand preferences at the population level that are similar to humans. This is due to a different cephalic lie in the nonhuman primate fetus that results in a left–right symmetrical stimulation of the utricles by inertial forces when the mother locomotes quadrupedally (see Fig 11.4b). The logical consequence of this difference with humans is that a population-based dextral bias arose with the change from a quadrupedal to a

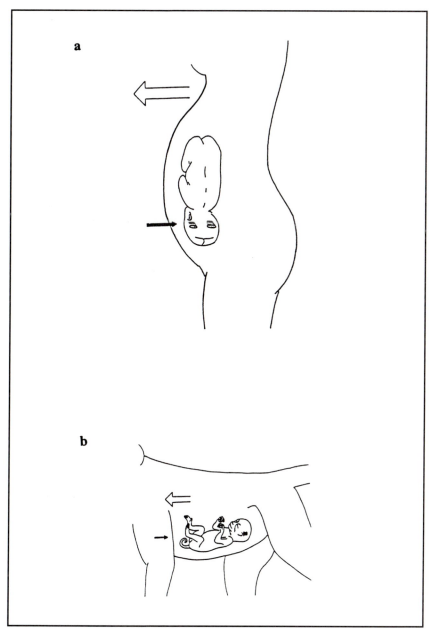

FIG. 11.4:   The position of the fetus in the last trimester of pregnancy: (a) in humans; and (b) in nonhuman primates. Indicated are forward acceleration (open arrow) and the resultant backward inertial force (dark arrow) during species-characteristic maternal locomotion (Previc, 1991). Reprinted by permission of Fred Previc.

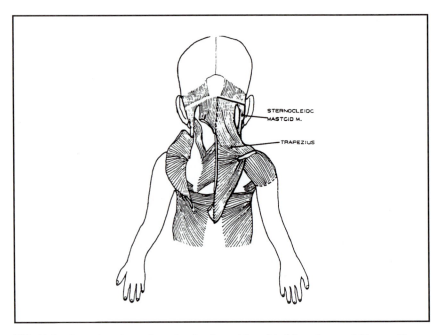

FIG. 11.5:   Rear view of a newborn showing the position of the bilateral sternocleidomastoid muscle relative to the bilateral trapezius muscle. The contralateral sternocleidomastoid muscle is active when the head is turned to the right or left.

bipedal gait in the early hominids. As we have seen, recent findings across a range of (pro)simian species run counter to the notion of bipedal locomotion being a prime mover in the evolution of human handedness. There are other assumptions upon which the left-otolithic dominance hypothesis is built that require studies designed specifically to test them. In no particular order of priority they are as follows:

1. An asymmetry in third trimester fetal position is a crucial event in establishing a head position preference in the fullterm newborn and later handedness. Studies of preterm infants born before the third trimester would be relevant here as they should not develop a consistent head and hand preference to the right. This prediction receives some support for neonatal head position (Gardner et al., 1977; Kurtzberg et al., 1979) and hand preference at 4 years (O'Callaghan et al., 1987). There are, however, a number of other findings that challenge this assumption: (i) healthy preterm infants born before 32 weeks gestational age had a rightsided bias for the maintenance, but not the assumption, of a head position at 35 weeks (Geerdink et al., 1993). It is difficult to know how to reconcile these differences in performance with Previc's hypothesis; (ii) healthy fetuses did not develop a predominant head position to the right until 36–38 weeks gestational age (van Gelder et al., 1990; Ververs et al., 1994a), but there

was considerable intra- and interindividual variability. In addition, there was a lack of evidence for the fetal vertebral column being to the mother's left side during the last trimester (Ververs et al., 1994b). This means that the fetal head to the right did not consistently face outwards. Once again, these findings are difficult to reconcile with Previc's hypothesis. He now believes that asymmetrical shearing of the otoliths may not require a constant lateral position during the third trimester, but rather a much narrower window of time around 30–32 weeks (personal communication, 14 June, 1995); and (iii) in an ultrasound study of thumb-sucking in the fetus, there was a clear bias for sucking on the right thumb as early as 15 weeks of gestation (Hepper et al., 1991). No relationship was found between fetal position and thumb sucking preference. What was found was that, out of 28 right-thumb suckers, 23 turned the head to the right. Three of the four classified as left-thumb suckers had a left turning bias. It was concluded that thumb sucking initiates development of brain lateralisation, rather than the interaction between fetal position maternal walking. The challenge of this study is that if the fetus sucks on the right thumb so early in pregnancy, then the theoretical link between 'headedness' and handedness may reside in a more fundamental asymmetry appearing many weeks before a lateralised fetal position.

2. Another crucial event is maternal walking. If this is so, then fetuses whose mothers have to take a protracted period of bedrest during the last trimester may not develop a clear lateral bias in head position, due to a lack of vestibular stimulation arising from the immobile mother. Previc (1991) counteracts this possibility by suggesting differential stimulation of the otoliths when the mother lies in the supine position. In this position, common in later pregnancy, the left utricle lies underneath the right one, which may result in its being more stimulated. But, as Previc admits, this stimulation will consist of sustained shearing of the hair cells, rather than the more potent transient shearing that accompanies maternal walking. If this is the case, then one would expect maternal bedrest to be associated with a reduction in the degree, rather than the direction, of lateral biases after birth.

3. "... the origins of vestibular asymmetry in man lie in a *neural* rather than structural imbalance favoring the left utricle" (Previc, 1991, p. 318). The vestibular system is structurally mature early in prenatal life (Humphrey, 1964), but there is no evidence that it is functional before birth. Experiments with neonatal guinea pigs revealed that the system is functionally inhibited by the low levels of oxygen tension that typify the situation *in utero* (Schwartze & Schwartze, 1977). In the human, shaking the maternal abdomen from side-to-side failed to change the heart rate pattern or induce movements in the near-term fetus (Visser et al., 1983). Such effects would be expected if the vestibulum was functional prior to birth. It is unlikely, therefore, that any movements of the endolymphs and hair cells in the fetal otoliths would be registered centrally in terms of action potentials. A more likely scenario is that a structural imbalance

is induced by the differential stimulation of the two otoliths, which then exerts its neural effects after birth. This view does not fit in with Previc's current opinion that the vestibular system may directly influence prenatal positioning rather than the other way round as maintained in his original hypothesis (personal communication, 14 June, 1995).

So far, we have dealt with some of the hypothesised preconditions for establishing a hand preference at some later point in development. The main point is that functional precursors to later handedness are already evident by the third trimester of pregnancy, if not somewhat earlier. They are further consolidated in the newborn period through interactions with a caregiving environment that is essentially asymmetrical. How then does handedness develop beyond the newborn period?

THE DEVELOPMENT OF HANDEDNESS: THE NEWBORN AND BEYOND

The age at which a consistent, adult-like hand preference is attained has not been a point of general consensus. For some it is as early as 13 months (Bates et al., 1986) or 18 months (Gottfried & Bathurst, 1983). For others it may not be until 2 years (Giesecke, 1936; Hildreth, 1949), 3 years (Annett, 1970) or after 8 years (Connolly & Elliott, 1972; Gesell & Ames, 1947). In addition, there is a lack of agreement about the nature of the developmental course that eventuates in the end state and the role played in it by task and subject variables. Finally, there is a neglect of how hand preference and bimanual coordination coalesce in the performance of complex tasks requiring the use of both hands. Such issues undoubtedly reflect different methodologies, but ultimately deep-seated divisions about the underpinning of a theory accounting for the development of handedness defined in terms of reaching and grasping.

In the ensuing part of this section, we will concentrate on these interrelated issues to the exclusion of trying to provide an exhaustive review of relevant studies. We do so because the available evidence is fragmentary and sometimes contradictory. The aforementioned claims about when the mature state is achieved should have forewarned us that this is the case. Due to space restrictions, we are not able to deal with the development of bimanual coordination and how it relates to the emergence of a hand preference.[1] Thus, we focus mainly on the development of unimanual handedness.

Stability versus instability
Associated with this issue is the question whether a lefthand preference appears before a rightsided one. Both Gesell and Ames (1947) and Seth (1973) found an initial leftsided bias for reaching, which would be in agreement with the

maturational gradient model. However, both studies have been criticized on methodological (e.g., no object absent condition) and statistical grounds (Annett, 1978; Young, 1977). More recent and better controlled studies have not resolved this question. One reported no initial side preference for newborn hand movements (Rönnqvist & von Hofsten, 1994), others an initial rightsided preference for arm movements (e.g. von Hofsten, 1982; Ottaviano et al., 1989), while others found a leftsided preference appearing before or around 3 months (e.g., Coryell & Michel, 1978; DiFranco et al., 1978; McDonnell, 1979). A similar lack of agreement is apparent when infants in about the same age range were required to grasp a rattle placed in the hand. Three studies found in favour of the right hand (Caplan & Kinsbourne, 1976; Hawn & Harris, 1983; Petrie & Peters, 1981) while a fourth could not find any bias (Yu-Yan et al., 1983).

The majority of studies on handedness during infancy have been cross-sectional in design. The lack of longitudinal data has meant that there is no clear consensus whether infants show a consistent hand preference over age. In one longitudinal study from 3 to 8 weeks, the majority (14/15) of infants showed a consistent leftsided bias for reaching towards a target presented at different positions from the body midline (McDonnell et al., 1983). In another study, there was a stable rightsided preference for the first half year (Michel & Harkins, 1988). For closely spaced intervals around 6 months, others reported large changes in the classification of hand preference (McCormick & Maurer, 1988). The same picture of fluctuating asymmetries was found in a truly longitudinal study covering 6 to 12 months (Carlson & Harris, 1985). Beyond the first year, longitudinal research points to the majority of infants attaining a consistent righthand preference across a range of tasks (Archer et al., 1988; Bates et al., 1986; Gottfried & Bathurst, 1983).

The stability–instability issue raises two important observations about studying the development of handedness during infancy. The first is the widespread use of reaching movements as indicative of handedness during the first year. In other words, it is assumed that the arm preferred for reaching will be ipsilateral to hand preferred for prehension at older ages. It is known that the ventromedial system, which includes the vestibulospinal tracts, develops earlier than the direct corticospinal system (Kuypers, 1985). The vestibulospinal tract projects bilaterally to the spinal cord and controls the proximal muscles of the arm. Thus, when reaching first appears it would involve ipsilateral control. Subsequent manipulative abilities are dependent on the direct corticospinal tracts that provide contralateral control of the fingers. As this system develops, infants could display more consistent *hand* preferences. The point to be made is that the early forms of reaching should be treated as an indication of *arm* preference. The question then is how an arm

---

1   Relevant studies on the development of bimanual coordination include Bresson et al. (1977), Cornwell (1991), Fagard (1987), Fagard & Jacquet, (1989), Goldfield & Michel (1986a,b), Michel et al., (1986), Ramsay (1980), Ramsay et al. (1979), Ramsay & Weber (1986), Ramsay & Willis, (1984), and Thelen et al. (1993).

preference for reaching can be reconciled with a hand preference or prehension. Put another way, how can a bias in the functioning of the ventromedial system induce one in the corticospinal system? Answers to this question account for dominant hand use and not for the superiority of the left hand in visuospatial abilities. However, they warn us that the assessment of handedness involving goal-directed arm movements will be based on different motor systems at different ages. It is the process of the developmental integration of the vestibulospinal and corticospinal tracts that may create inconsistent hand preferences across age, leading to what Palmer (1964) referred to as undifferentiated handedness.

The second observation is that we tend to view development as a stable process with any variability being treated as unnecessary "noise". It is now abundantly clear that normal motor development can be better characterised as having a high degree of inter- and intraindividual variability (Beek et al., 1993; Thelen & Smith, 1995; Touwen, 1978). Handedness, as we have seen, appears to fluctuate, especially during the first year. For "headedness" there are too few longitudinal studies to give us confidence as whether it is also a fluctuating asymmetry. For hand–mouth contacting, we noted a high degree of variability in hand preference up to 18 weeks. What we want to emphasise here is that a strong lateralised and consistent preference to the left *or* to the right for any functional asymmetry may be indicative of underlying neuropathology. This view challenges models proposing only leftsided or ambiguous functional asymmetries as a manifestation of a pathological state (e.g., Bakan, 1971; Satz, 1972).

Task variables: intrinsic and extrinsic properties of objects

For adults it is well known that hand preference depends on the tasks employed (e.g., Steingrueber, 1975; van der Staak, 1975). In studies on infants, task effects may arise from introducing variations in the extrinsic (position, distance) and intrinsic (size, shape, texture) properties of objects. As we have mentioned, reaching is the typical performance measure of handedness during early infancy. It does not figure as a measure of hand preference in adults.

The one study to compare infants and adults on reaching using the same procedure varied the position, distance and size of the object (Harris & Carlson, 1993). The infants, the same as those in the Carlson and Harris (1985) study, used the arm ipsilateral to the object to reach towards it. As found by others, infants at all ages from 6 to 12 months sometimes made reaching movements to a laterally positioned object with the contralateral hand (see also Butterworth et al., in press). That they did so, once again demonstrates the need to do away with the notion that young infants have a midline barrier preventing them from reaching into the contralateral space (Bruner, 1969).

The adults, like the infants, reached more often with the same-side hand to objects in the lateral position. Their reaches to objects in the midline position were made most often with the (self-reported) dominant hand. The same position resulted in outcomes requiring qualification for the infants as we shall discuss under

Subject variables. For both adults and infants, there were no effects for distance on the side used for reaching. However, object size influenced adults, but not infants, in rather subtle ways: its effect was present only for the midline position and then only for the right handers who tended to reserve the dominant hand for the smaller object. This finding contradicts those on self-reported hand preference in adults obtained from questionnaires and serves to re-emphasise the task-specificity of performance assessments.

It is undoubtedly the case that task parameters are increasingly taken into account during the development of hand use. Our hunch is that the extrinsic properties of objects will be more influential in the first 6 months and their intrinsic properties thereafter based on what is known about the development of prehension (e.g. see Bushnell & Boudreau, 1993; von Hofsten & Rönnqvist, 1988).

Subject variables: familial handedness and sex

We have seen familial handedness accounts for individual differences in neonatal "headedness". How does it relate to the development of handedness? In adults, familial lefthandedness is associated with a less consistent pattern of hand preference than those with a history of familial righthandedness (Beukelaar & Kroonenberg, 1983). A similar lack of consistency has been noted in the reaching movements of familial lefthanded infants between 6 and 12 months (Carlson & Harris, 1985). In contrast, for infants assessed three times around 6 months of age, those with familial lefthandedness had more consistent preferences than their familial righthanded counterparts (McCormick & Maurer, 1988). Things become more complicated with a finding from cross-sectional study of female infants from 9 to 20 months of age (Cornwell et at., 1991): most of the familial righthanded infants had a righthand preference versus only 50% of those with a familial history of lefthandedness who were themselves lefthanded, but this difference applied only to bimanual manipulation in the oldest age group.

The sex of the infant has been infrequently accounted for in research on functional asymmetries. Across a range of functions, it is well known that females develop faster than males. In addition, adult females have a more pronounced preference for the right hand (Bryden, 1977). Consequently, it can be presumed that girls will develop a consistent arm or hand preference earlier than boys. This presumption was confirmed in a cross-sectional study (Humphrey & Humphrey, 1987) and subsequently replicated in a longitudinal one (Humphrey & Humphrey, 1988). In both studies, younger females (5–8 months) had more right-arm reaches, while at the older ages (9–12 months) both sexes were rightsided. The longitudinal study also revealed that by 24 months of age, girls showed a more consistent righthanded preference in executing a pincer grasp.

Finally, we must consider the possibility that the development of handedness may involve complex interactions between subject variables (and between them and task variables). Only the Carlson and Harris (1985) study has addressed this level of complexity. They found that while familial righthanded boys and girls increased the incidence of rightsided reaches from 6 to 9 months, the girls had a more consistent right arm preference. From about 6 months onwards, the familial righthanded boys had a left arm preference and no bias by 12 months. In contrast, neither the familial lefthanded boys nor girls had a lateral preference at 6 months, which was then followed by a right to left trend up to 12 months, the shift occurring later for boys than girls. When the object was presented in the midline, familial righthanded boys had a leftsided preference and the familial righthanded girls a rightsided one regardless of age. For the lateral position, the familial righthanded boys and girls differed yet again, the boys having more left to right and the girls more right to left midline crossings.

These findings run counter to any notion of a simple maturational gradient and cannot be reconciled straightforwardly with Annett's model. However, the fluctuating trend of the familial lefthanded infants is in accordance with her model as presumably they lacked the right shift gene making them more susceptible to variations in environmental influences. The best conclusion that can be drawn from this and other studies that have catered for subject variables is that familial righthanded girls develop a lateral preference for reaching earlier than the other three groups derived from a sex by familial handedness classification. Moreover, this preference appears to be more readily maintained over variations in object position and size than in males.

CONCLUDING REMARKS

In this contribution, we have made the following claims. *Firstly*, handedness in humans has a greater evolutionary depth than speech and language and perhaps even habitual bipedalism. *Secondly*, the developmental origins of handedness are based on different mechanisms than for speech and language. *Thirdly*, there is no simple task (e.g., reaching) that will provide a valid index of handedness during the first year. *Fourthly*, studies on the development of handedness need to be more sensitive to the roles of task and subject variables. *Fifthly*, the development of handedness should be addressed by models that incorporate hand preference into different modes of bimanual coordination. In order to pursue these claims further, future research should involve the following sorts of investigations:

1. *Studies designed explicitly to test the predictions of the postural origins theory* (MacNeilage et al., 1987a,b). The problem here is to find tasks other than reaching that can be used with human and nonhuman primates. Testing should also include longitudinal studies that chart the developmental course of handedness, particularly in the great apes. Such studies should incorporate assessments of functional asymmetries prior to the occurrence of a hand preference for manipulating objects. In this regard, it would be of great value

to be able to make ultrasound recordings of fetal movements (e.g. thumb sucking) and posture (e.g. head position) as already has been done for humans.

2. *Studies designed explicitly to test the left-otolith dominance hypothesis* (Previc, 1991). Of all the models concerned with the developmental origins of handedness, we consider this to be the most promising, if only because it provides a process-oriented explanation that delivers readily testable predictions. Its main problem is a lack of convincing evidence that ROA/ROT fetal lies predict left-sided biases in head position after birth. This shortcoming could in part be overcome by the inclusion of pregnant mothers who are frank left handers. The offspring of these mothers should assume ROA/ROT lies in the last trimester of pregnancy and after birth show about equal numbers with a left- or rightsided head position preference.

3. *Longitudinal studies derived to examine whether early motor asymmetries and late handedness have stable or fluctuating developmental trends.* Fluctuating asymmetries may: (1) apply to only a subset of infants (e.g. familial lefthanded boys); (2) signal an upcoming transition in which there is a shift from one patterning of handedness to another or from bilateral reaching to bimanual actions. Criteria are now available from both catastrophe theory (Gilmore, 1981) and synergetics (Haken, 1977) for detecting the presence of such non-equilibrium phase shifts (see van der Maas & Molenaar, 1992 and Wimmers et al., in press for developmental applications); and (3) reflect changes in task variables from one age to the next. Certainly, a continued over-reliance on reaching movements as an index of handedness is only going to result in more evidence for fluctuating trends. Consistency between ages maybe a more subtle phenomenon that can be found by using a range of performance measures at each age. Another possibility is that infants may show fluctuating trends for some measures and consistency in others. Fluctuating asymmetries may constitute naturally occurring means for exploring the properties of the external world while any consistencies ensure developmental pathways that eventuate in the acquisition of population-level biases.

4. *Studies in which the roles of hand preference in the development of bimanual coordination are elucidated.* We consider this to be the most pressing need at the present moment. In addition, we need to know when and how infants become able to combine or assemble different modes of bimanual coordination in achieving some desired outcome. Unfortunately, we currently lack a requisite theoretical perspective that would enable us to test both developmental enterprises in a principled way. This may be achieved by incorporating symmetry-breaking principles operative in open dissipative systems into our theorising about how the two hands achieve a cooperative division of labour in tasks that are essentially asymmetrical in nature (see Hopkins & Butterworth, 1997 for applying these dynamical systems principles to the development of action in general).

Finally, in terms of theory, we need to re-examine two persistent but contradictory views as to their continuing usefulness for understanding the development of handedness. One is the notion of progressive lateralisation (Lenneberg, 1967). Its basic assumption is that the newborn's brain is asymmetrical or equipotential in both structure and function and that lateral biases emerge gradually with the development of language abilities. The discovery of neural asymmetries in the fetal brain and motor asymmetries in healthy newborns effectively undermines this view. The same discoveries helped to propagate the opposite view that the brain is functionally lateralised from birth and remains relatively invariant throughout subsequent development (Kinsbourne & Hiscock, 1977). One prediction of assuming such age-invariant lateralisation is that functional asymmetries in the newborn are intimately connected with hemispheric specialisation for handedness and language. As we have seen, this connection is far from intimate and the mechanisms involved poorly understood. Furthermore, both views rest on at least two questionable assumptions: one that neural asymmetries directly determine functional asymmetries; and the other that handedness is an epiphenomenon of hemispheric specialisation for language. Our view is that such neurogenic language-biased theories are inadequate for describing and explaining the developmental course of handedness at the functional level. While we have some testable models for the origins of motor asymmetries, we still lack appropriately powerful models for linking early lateral biases to later forms of hand preference and manual specialisation via a tractable set of processes. Thus, what we need is a theory based on the premise that asymmetrical actions and the experiences they generate beget further asymmetrical actions. Such a theory will have to account for the nonlinear nature of development in general and for the role of subject and task variables in particular.

ACKNOWLEDGEMENT

We wish to thank Kim Bard and William D. Hopkins (Yerkes Primate Center) for their help in tracing references dealing with handedness in non-human primates.

REFERENCES

Amaducci, L.A., Sorbi, S., Bracco, L., Morandi, A., & Piacentini, S. (1985). Chemical asymmetries in human brain. *Abstracts XIIIth World Congress of Neurology*, Hamburg, p. 97.

Annett, M. (1970). The growth of manual preference and speed. *British Journal of Psychology, 61,* 303–321.

Annett, M. (1972). The distribution of manual asymmetry. *British Journal of Psychology, 3,* 343–358.

Annett, M. (1978). Throwing loaded and unloaded dice. *Behavioral and Brain Sciences, 1,* 278–279.

Annett, M. (1985). *Left, right, hand and brain: the right shift theory.* Hillsdale, NJ: Erlbaum.

Annett, M., & Annett, J. (1991). Handedness for feeding in gorillas. *Cortex, 17*, 269–276.

Archer, L., Campbell, D., & Segalowitz, S.J. (1988). A prospective study of hand preference and language development in 18- to 30-month olds: I. Hand preference. *Developmental Neuropsychology, 4*, 85–92.

Aruguete, M.S., Ely, E.A., & King, J.E. (1992). Laterality in spontaneous motor activity of chimpanzees and squirrel monkeys. *American Journal of Primatology, 27*, 177–188.

Bakan, P. (1971). Handedness and birth order. *Nature, 229*, 195.

Baldwin, J.M. (1890). The origin of left-handedness. *Science, 16*, 247–248.

Bard, K.A., Hopkins, W.D., & Fort, C.L. (1990). Lateral bias in infant chimpanzees (*Pan troglodytes*). *Journal of Comparative Psychology, 104*, 309–321.

Bates, E., O'Connell, B., Vaid, J., Sledge, P., & Oakes, L. (1986). Language and hand preference in early development. *Developmental Neuropsychology, 2*, 1–15.

Beek, P.J., Hopkins, B., & Molenaar, P.C.M. (1993). Complex systems approaches to the development of action. In: G.J.P. Savelsbergh (Ed.), *The development of coordination in infancy*. Amsterdam: North-Holland, pp. 497–515.

Benton, A.L, Meyers, R., & Pobler, G.J. (1962). Some aspects of handedness. *Psychiatric Neurology, 144*, 321–337.

Bertoncini, J., Morais, J., Bijeljac-Babic, R., McAdams, S., Peretz, I., & Mehler, J. (1989). Dichotic perception and laterality in neonates. *Brain and Language, 37*, 591–605.

Best, C.T. (1988). Early human development: a literature review and a neuroembryological model. In: D.L. Molfese, & S.J. Segalowitz, (Eds.), *Brain lateralization in children: developmental implications*. New York: Guilford Press, pp. 5–34.

Beukelaar, L.J., & Kroonenberg, P.M. (1983). Towards a conceptualization of hand preference. *British Journal of Psychology, 74*, 33–45.

Bishop, D.V.M. (1989). Does hand proficiency determine hand preference? *British Journal of Psychology, 80*, 191–199.

Boesch, C. (1991). Handedness in wild chimpanzees (*Pan troglodytes*). *International Journal of Primatology, 12*, 541–558.

Box, H.O. (1977). Observations on spontaneous hand use in the common marmoset (*Callithrix jacchus*). *Primates, 18*, 395–400.

Brackenbridge, C.J. (1981). Secular variation handedness over ninety years. *Neuropsychologia, 19*, 459–462.

Bradshaw, J.L., Nettleton, N.C., & Spehr, K. (1982). Braille reading and left and right hemispace. *Neuropsychologia, 20*, 493–500.

Bresson, F., Maury, L., Pieraut-LeBonniec, G., & de Schonen, S. (1977). Organization and lateralization of reaching in infants: an instance of asymmetric functions in hands collaboration. *Neuropsycholgia, 15*, 311–320.

Broca, P. (1865). Sur le siége de la faculté de langage articulé. *Bulletins de la Societé d'Anthropologie de Paris, 6*, 377–393.

Bruner, J.S. (1969). Eye, hand and mind. In: D. Elkind & J.H. Flavell (Eds.), *Studies in cognitive development*. Oxford: Oxford University Press, pp. 223–236.

Bryden, M.P. (1977). Measuring handedness with questionnaires. *Neuropsychologia, 13*, 617–624.

Bushnell, E.M., & Boudreau, J.P. (1993). Motor development and the mind: the potential role of motor abilities as determinants of aspects of perceptual development. *Child Development, 64*, 1005–1021.

Butterworth, G.E., & Hopkins, B. (1988). Hand mouth coordination in the new-born baby. *British Journal of Developmental Psychology, 6*, 302–314.

Butterworth, G., Verweij, E., & Hopkins, B. (in press). The development of prehension in infants: Halverson revisited. *British Journal of Developmental Psychology*,

Byrne, R.W., & Byrne, J.M. (1991). Hand preference in the skilled gathering tasks of mountain gorillas (*Gorilla gorilla berengei*). *Cortex*, *27*, 521–546.

Calvin, W.H. (1983). *The throwing madonna: essays on the brain*. New York: McGraw-Hill.

Caplan, P.J., & Kinsbourne, M. (1976). Baby drops the rattle: asymmetry of duration grasp by infants. *Child Development*, *47*, 532–534.

Carlson, D.F., & Harris, L.J. (1985) Development of the infant's hand preference for visually directed reaching: preliminary report of a longitudinal study. *Infant Mental Health*, *6*, 158–174.

Cernacek, J., & Jagr, J. (1972). Posture, vision and motor dominance. *Aggressologie*, *13C*, 101–105.

Chi, J.E., Dooling, E.C., & Gilles, F.H. (1977). Gyral development of the human brain. *Annals of Neurology*, *1*, 86–93.

Chui, H.C., & Damasio, A.R. (1980). Human cerebral asymmetry evaluated by computed tomography. *Journal of Neurology, Neurosurgery and Psychiatry*, *43*, 873–878.

Colell, M., Segarra, M.D., & Sabater, P.J. (1995). Hand preferences in chimpanzees (*Pan troglodytes*), bonobos (*Pan paniscus*) and orangutans (*Pongo pygmaeus*) in food reaching and other daily activities. *International Journal of Primatology*, *16*, 413–434.

Connolly, K., & Elliott, J. (1972) The evolution and ontogeny of hand function. In: N. Blurton-Jones (Ed.) *Ethological studies of child behaviour*. Cambridge: Cambridge University Press, pp.329–383.

Corballis, M.C. (1983). *Human laterality*. New York: Academic Press.

Corballis, M.C. (1989). Laterality and human evolution. *Psychological Review*, *96*, 492–505.

Corballis, M.C. & Morgan, M.J. (1978). On the biological basis of human laterality: I. Evidence for a maturational left–right gradient. *Behavioral and Brain Sciences*, *1*, 261–269.

Coren, S. (1992). *The left-hander syndrome: the causes and consequences of left-handedness*. London: Murray.

Cornwell, K., Barnes, C., Fitzgerald, H.E., & Harris, L.J. (1985). Neurobehavioral reorganization in early infancy: patterns of head orientation following lateral and midline holds. *Infant Mental Health Journal*, *6*, 126–136.

Cornwell, K.S., Harris, L.J., & Fitzgerald, H.E. (1991). Task effects in the development of hand preference in 9-, 13-, and 20-month-old infant girls. *Developmental Neuropsychology*, *7*, 19–34.

Coryell, J. (1985). Infant rightward bias asymmetries predict right-handedness in childhood. *Neuropsychologia*, *23*, 269–271.

Coryell, J.F., & Michel, G.F. (1978). How supine postural preferences of infants can contribute toward the development of handedness. *Infant Behavior and Development*, *1*, 245–257.

Costello, M., & Fragaszy, D. (1988). Prehension in *Cebus* and *Saimiri*: 1. Grip type and hand preference. *American Journal of Primatology*, *15*, 235–245.

Dabbs, J.M. (1980). Left-right differences in cerebral blood flow and cognition. *Psychophysiology*, *17*, 548–551.

Darwin, C. (1871). *The descent of man*. London: Murray.

DiFranco, D., Muir, D., & Dodwell, P. (1978). Reaching in very young infants. *Perception*, *7*, 385–392.

Dunn, P.M. (1976). Congenital postural deformities. *British Medical Bulletin*, *32*, 71–76.

Fabbro, F. (1994). Left and right in the bible from a neuropsychologial perspective. *Brain and Cognition*, *24*, 161–183.

Fagard, J. (1987). Bimanual stereotypes: bimanual coordination in children as a function of movements and relative velocity. *Journal of Motor Behavior*, *19*, 355–366.

Fagard, J., & Jacquet, A.Y. (1989). Onset of bimanual coordination and symmetry versus asymmetry of movement. *Infant Behavior and Development*, *12*, 229–235.

Fagot, J. (1993). Ontogeny of object manipulation and manual lateralization in the Guinea Baboon: preliminary observations. In: J.P. Ward & W.D. Hopkins (Eds.), *Primate laterality: current behavioral evidence of primate asymmetries*. New York: Springer, pp. 235–250.

Fagot, J., & Vauclair, J. (1988a). Handedness and manual specialization in the baboon. *Neuropsychologica*, *26*, 795–804.

Fagot, J. & Vauclair, J. (1988b). Handedness and bimanual coordination in the lowland gorilla. *Brain, Behavior and Evolution*, *32*, 89–95.

Fagot, J., Drea, C.M., & Wallen, K. (1991). Asymmetrical hand use in rhesus monkeys (*Macaca mulatta*) in tactually and visually regulated tasks. *Journal of Comparative Psychology*, *105*, 260–268.

Fagot, J., & Vauclair, J. (1991). Manual lateralization in nonhuman primates: a distinction between handedness and manual specialization. *Journal of Comparative Psychology*, *109*, 76–89.

Fertsch, P. (1947). Hand dominance in reading braille. *American Journal of Psychology*, *60*, 335–349.

Fincher, J. (1977). *Sinister people*. New York: Putnam.

Fischer, R.B., Meunier, G.F., & White, P.J. (1982). Evidence of laterality in the lowland gorilla. *Perceptual and Motor Skills*, *54*, 1093–1094.

Forsythe, C., Milliken, G.W., Stafford, D.K., & Ward, J.P. (1988). Posturally related variations in the hand preferences of the ruffed lemur (*Varecia variegata variegata*). *Journal of Comparative Psychology*, *102*, 248–250.

Forsythe, C., & Ward, J.P. (1988). Black lemur (*Lemur macaco*) hand preference in food reaching. *Primates*, *29*, 369–374.

Fragaszy, D.M., & Mitchell, S.R. (1990). Hand preference and performance on unimanual and bimanual tasks in capuchin monkeys (*Cebus apella*). *Journal of Comparative Psychology*, *104*, 275–282.

Galaburda, A.M., Corsiglia, J., Rosen, G., & Sherman, G. (1987). Planum temporale asymmetry, reappraisal since Geschwind and Levitsky. *Neuropsychologia*, *25*, 853–868.

Gardner, J., Lewkowicz, D., & Turkewitz, G. (1977) Development of postural asymmetry in premature human infants. *Developmental Psychobiology*, *10*, 19–23.

Geerdink, J., Hopkins, B., & Hoeksma, J.B. (1993). The development of head position preference in preterm infants beyond term age. *Developmental Psychobiology*, *27*, 153–168.

Geschwind, N., & Behan, P. (1982). Left-handedness: association with immune disease, migraine, and developmental learning disorder. *Proceedings of the National Academy of Science*, *79*, 5097–5100.

Geschwind, N., & Behan, P. (1984). Laterality, hormones, and immunity. In: N. Geschwind & A.M. Galaburda (Eds.), *Cerebral dominance: the biological foundations*. Cambridge, MA: Harvard University Press, pp. 211-224.

Geschwind, N., & Galaburda, A.M. (1985). Cerebral lateralization: Biological mechanisms, associations and pathology: I. A hypothesis and a program for research. *Archives of Neurology*, *42*, 428-459.

Geschwind, N., & Galaburda, A.M. (1987). *Cerebral lateralization*. Cambridge, MA: MIT Press.

Geschwind, N., & Levitsky, W. (1968). Left/right asymmetries in temporal speech region. *Science*, *161*, 186–187.

Gesell, A., & Ames, L.B. (1947). The development of handedness. *Journal of Genetic Psychology*, *70*, 155–175.

Gesell, A. (1938). The tonic neck reflex in the human infant. *Journal of Pediatrics, 13*, 455–464.

Gesell, A., & Ames, L.G. (1947). The development of handedness. *Journal of Genetic Psychology, 70*, 155–175.

Giesecke, M. (1936). The genesis of hand preference. *Monograph of the Society for Research in Child Development, 1*, (Serial No. 5), 1–102.

Gilmore, R. (1981). *Catastrophe theory for scientists and engineers.* New York: Wiley.

Glick, S.D., Ross, D.A., & Hough, L.B. (1982). Lateral asymmetry of neurotransmitter in the human brain. *Brain Research, 234*, 53–63.

Goldfield, E.G., & Michel, G.F. (1986a). The ontogeny of infant bimanual reaching during the first year. *Infant Behavior and Development, 9*, 81–89.

Goldfield, E., & Michel, G.F. (1986b). Spatio-temporal linkage in infant interlimb coordination. *Developmental Psychobiology, 19*, 259–364.

Goldman-Rakic, P.S., & Selemon, L.D. (1990). New frontiers in basal ganglia research. *Trends in Neurosciences, 13*, 241–244.

Goodwin, R., & Michel, G.F. (1981). Head orientation position during birth and in infant neonatal period, and hand preference at nineteen weeks. *Child Development, 52*, 819–826.

Gottfried, A.W., & Bathurst, K. (1983). Hand preference across time is related to intelligence in girls. *Science, 221*, 1074–1076.

Grapin, P., & Perpère, C. (1968). Symétrie et latéralisation du nourrison. In: R. Kourilsky & P. Grapin (Eds.), *Main droite en main gauche: Norme et lateralite.* Paris: Presses Universitaires de France, pp. 83–100.

Gur, R.C., Ragland, J.D., Resnick, S.M., Skolnick, B.E., Jaggi, J., Muenz, L., & Gur, R.E., (1994). Lateralized increases in cerebral blood flow during performance of verbal and spatial tasks: relationship with performance level. *Brain and Cognition, 24*, 244–258.

Haken, H. (1977). *Synergetics: an introduction.* Heidelberg: Springer.

Hall, G.S. (1891). Notes on the study of infants. *Pedagogical Seminary, 1*, 128–138.

Harris, L.J. (1980). Left-handedness: early theories, facts, and fancies. In: J. Herron (Ed.), *Neuropsychology of left-handedness.* New York: Academic Press, pp. 3–78.

Harris, L.J. (1983). Laterality of function in the infant: historical and contemporary trends in theory and research. In: G. Young, S.J. Segalowitz, C.M. Corter, & S.E. Trehub (Eds.), *Manual specialization and the developing brain.* New York: Academic Press, pp. 177–247.

Harris, L.J., & Carlson, D.F. (1988). Pathological left-handedness: an analysis of theories and evidence. In: D.L. Molfese & S.J. Segalowitz (Eds.), *Brain lateralization in children: developmental implications.* New York: Guilford Press, pp. 289–372.

Harris, L.J., & Carlson, D.F. (1993). Hand preference for visually-directed guiding in human infants and adults. In: J.P. Ward & W.D. Hopkins (Eds.), *Primate laterality: current behavioral evidence of primate asymmetries.* New York: Springer, pp. 285–305.

Hauser, M., Perry, S., Manson, J.H., Ball, H., Williams, M., Pearson, E., & Berard, J. (1991). It's all in the hands of the beholder: new data on free-ranging rhesus monkeys. *Behavioral and Brain Sciences, 14*, 342–344.

Hawn, P.R., & Harris, L.J. (1983). Hand differences in grasp duration and reaching in two- and five-month-old infants. In: G. Young, S.J. Segalowitz, C.M. Corter, & S.E. Trehub (Eds.) *Manual specialization and the developing brain.* New York: Academic Press, pp. 331–348.

Heffner, R.S., & Masterson, R.B. (1983). The role of the corticospinal tract in the evolution of human digital dexterity. *Brain, Behavior and Evolution, 12*, 161–200.

Hegstrom, R.A., & Konepudi, D.K. (1990). The handedness of the universe. *Scientific American*, Jan., 108–115.

Hepper, P.G., Shahidullah, S., & White, R. (1991). Handedness in the human fetus. *Neuropsychologia*, *29*, 1107–1111.

Hildreth, G. (1949). The development and training of hand dominance: I,II,III. *Journal of Genetic Psychology*, *75*, 197–275.

Holloway, R.L., & La Coste-LareyMondie, M.C. (1982). Brain endocasts in pongoids and hominids: some preliminary findings on the palaeontology of cerebral dominance. *American Journal of Physical Anthropology*, *58*, 101–110.

Hoogland, H.J., & de Haan, J. (1980). Ultrasonographic placental localization with respect to fetal position *in utero*. *European Journal of Obstetrics, Gynecology and Reproductive Biology*, *11*, 9–15.

Hopkins, B. (1994, October). *The developmental origins of handedness*. Proceedings of the European Science Foundation workshop: The development of sensory, motor and cognitive capabilities in early infancy. Acquafredda di Maratea, Italy.

Hopkins, B., Beek, P.J., & Kalverboer, A.F. (1993). Theoretical issues in the longitudinal study of motor development. In: A.F. Kalverboer, B. Hopkins, & R. Geuze (Eds.), *Motor development in early and later childhood: Longitudinal approaches*. Cambridge: Cambridge University Press, pp. 343–371.

Hopkins, B., & Butterworth, G. (1996). Dynamical systems approaches to the development of action. In: G. Bremner, A. Slater, & G. Butterworth (Eds.), *Infant development: recent advances*. Hove, UK: Psychology Press. pp.75–100.

Hopkins, B., Lems, W., Janssen, B., & Butterworth, G. (1987). Postural and motor asymmetries in newlyborns. *Human Neurobiology, 6*, 153–156.

Hopkins, B., Lems, Y.L., van Wulfften Palthe, T., Hoeksma, J., Kardaun, O., & Butterworth, G. (1990). Development of head position preference during early infancy: a longitudinal study in the daily life situation. *Developmental Psychobiology, 23*, 39–53.

Hopkins, W.D. (1994). Hand preferences for bimanual feeding in 140 captive chimpanzees (*Pan troglodytes*): rearing and ontogenetic determinants. *Developmental Psychobiology, 27*, 395–407.

Hopkins, W.D., & Bard, K.A. (1993). Hemispheric specialization in infant chimpanzees: evidence for a relation with gender and arousal. *Developmental Psychobiology, 26*, 219–235.

Hopkins, W. D., Bennett, A.J., Bales, S.L., Lee, J., & Ward, J.P. (1993). Behavioral laterality in captive bonobos (*Pan paniscus*). *Journal of Comparative Psychology, 107*, 403–410.

Hopkins, W.D., & de Waal, F.B.M. (1995). Behavioral laterality in captive bonobos (*Pan paniscus*): replication and extension. *International Journal of Primatology, 16*, 261–276.

Hopkins, W. D., & Washburn, D.A., & Rumbaugh, D.M. (1989). Note on hand use in the manipulation of joysticks by rhesus monkeys (*Macaca mulatta*) and chimpanzees (*Pan troglodytes*). *Journal of Comparative Psychology, 103*, 91–94.

Hughey, M.J. (1985). Fetal position during pregnancy. *American Journal of Obstetrics and Gynecology, 153*, 885–886.

Humphrey, D.E., & Humphrey, G.K. (1987). Sex differences in reaching. *Neuropsychologia, 25*, 971–975.

Humphrey, D.E., & Humphrey, G. K. (1988). Sex differences in lateralized preference for reaching and grasping in infants. In: M.A. Goodale (Ed.), *Vision and action: the control of grasping*. Norwood, NJ: Ablex.

Humphrey, T. (1964). Some correlations between the appearance of human fetal reflexes and the development of the nervous system. *Progress in Brain Research, 4*, 93–135.

Ittyeral, M. (1993). Hand preference and hand ability in congenitally blind children. *Quarterly Journal of Experimental Psychology, 46A*, 35–50.

Jacobson, M. (1978). *Developmental neurobiology*. New York: Plenum Press.

Johanson, D.C. (1985). The most primitive Australopithecus. In: P.V. Tobias (Ed.), *Hominid evolution, past, present and future*. New York: Liss, pp. 203–212.

Jones-Engel, L.E., & Bard, K. A. (1996). Precision grips in young chimpanzees. *American Journal of Primatology, 39*, 1–15.

Kelso, J.A.S. (1995). *Dynamic patterns: the self-organization of brain and behavior*. Cambridge, MA: MIT Press.

Kertesz, A., & Geschwind, N. (1971). Patterns of pyramidal decussation and its relationship to handedness. *Archives of Neurology, 24*, 326–332.

Kertesz, A., Polk, M., Black, S.F., & Howell, J. (1990). Sex, handedness, and the morphometry of cerebral asymmetries on magnetic resonance imaging. *Brain Research, 530*, 40–48.

Kim, S.G., Ashe, J., Georgopoulos, A.P., Merkle, H., Ellerman, J.M., Menon, R.S., Ogawa, S., & Ugurbil, K. (1993). Functional imaging of human motor cortex at high magnetic field. *Journal of Neurophysiology, 69*, 297–302.

Kinsbourne, M., & Hiscock, M. (1977). Does cerebral dominance develop? In: S.J. Segalowitz, & F.A. Gruber (Eds.), *Language development and neurological theory*. New York: Academic Press, pp. 171–191.

Kooistra, C.A., & Heilman, K.M. (1988) Motor dominance and lateral asymmetry of the globus pallidus. *Neurology, 38*, 388–390.

Kuhl, P.K. (1988). On handedness in primates and human infants. *Behavioral and Brain Sciences, 11*, 727–729.

Kurtzberg, D., Vaughan, H.G., Daum, C., Grellong, B.A., Albin, S., & Rotkin, L. (1979). Neurobehavioral performance of low-birthweight infants at 40 weeks conceptional age: comparison with normal full-term infants. *Developmental Medicine and Child Neurology, 21*, 590–607.

Kuypers, H.G.J.M. (1985). The anatomical and functional organization of the motor system. In: M. Swash & C. Kennard, (Eds.) Scientific basis of clinical neurology. Edinburgh: Churchill Livingstone, pp. 3–18.

Larson, C.F., Dodson, D.L., & Ward, J.P. (1989). Hand preferences and whole-body turning biases of lesser bushbabies (*Galago sengalensis*). *Brain, Behavior and Evolution, 33*, 261–267.

Leakey, L.S.B., Tobias, P.V., & Napier, J.R. (1964). A new species of the genus *Homo* from Olduvai gorge. *Nature, 202*, 7–9.

Lenneberg, E. (1967). *Biological foundations of language*. New York: Wiley.

LeMay, M. (1976). Morphological cerebral asymmetries of modern man, fossil man and nonhuman primate. *Annals of the New York Academy of Science, 280, 349*–366.

Levy, J., & Nagylaki, T. (1972). A model for the genetics of handedness. *Genetics, 72*, 117–128.

Liederman, J. (1983). Mechanisms underlying instability in the development of hand preference. In: G. Young, S.J. Segalowitz, C.M. Corter & S.E. Trehub (Eds.), *Manual specialization and the developing brain*. New York: Academic Press, pp. 71–92.

Liederman, J. (1988). Misconceptions and new conceptions about early brain damage, functional asymmetry, and behavioral outcome. In: D.L. Molfese & S.J. Segalowitz (Eds.), *Brain lateralization in children: developmental implications*. New York: Guilford Press, pp. 375–399.

Liederman, J., & Kinsbourne, M. (1980). Rightward motor bias in newborns depends upon parental right-handedness. *Neuropsychologia, 18*, 579–584.

MacNeilage, P.F. (1991). The "postural origins theory" of primate neurobiological asymmetries. In: N. Krasnegor, D.M. Rumbaugh, M.G. Studdert-Kennedy, & R. Schiefelbusch (Eds.), The biological foundations of language development. San Diego: Academic Press, pp. 165–188.

MacNeilage, P.F., Studdert-Kennedy, M.G., & Lindblom, B. (1987a). Primate handedness reconsidered. *Behavioral and Brain Sciences, 10*, 247–263.

MacNeilage, P.F., Studdert-Kennedy, M.G., & Lindblom, B. (1987b). Primate predatory, postural, and prehensile proclivities and professional peer pressures: postscripts. *Behavioral and Brain Sciences, 10*, 89–303.

MacNeilage, P.F., Studdert-Kennedy, M.G., & Lindblom, B. (1988). Primate handedness: a foot in the door. *Behavioral and Brain Sciences, 11*, 748–758.

Masataka, N. (1989). Population-level asymmetry of hand preference in lemurs. *Behaviour, 110*, 244–247.

Masataka, N. (1990). Handedness of capuchin monkeys. *Folia Primatologica, 55*, 189–192.

Matoba, M., Masataka, N., & Tanioka, Y. (1991). Cross-generational continuity of hand-use preferences in marmosets. *Behaviour, 117*, 281–286.

McCormick, C.M., & Maurer, D.M. (1988). Unimanual hand preferences in 6-month-olds: consistency and relation to familial-handedness. *Infant Behavior and Development, 11*, 21–29.

McDonnell, P.M. (1979). Patterns of eye–hand coordination in the first year of life. *Canadian Journal of Psychology, 33*, 253–267.

McDonnell, P.M., Anderson, V.S., & Abraham, W.C. (1983). Asymmetry of orientation of arm movements in three- to eight-week-old infants. *Infant Behavior and Development, 6*, 287–298.

McManus, I.C., & Bryden, M.P. (1991). Geschwind's theory of cerebral lateralization: developing a formal, causal model. *Psychological Bulletin, 110*, 237–253.

Michel, G.F. (1981). Right-handedness: a consequence of infant supine head-orientation? *Science, 212*, 685–687.

Michel, G.F. (1987). Self-generated experience and the development of lateralized neurobehavioral organization in infants. *Advances in the Study of Behavior, 17*, 61–83.

Michel, G.M., & Goodwin, R. (1979). Intrauterine birth position predicts newborn head position preferences. *Infant Behavior and Development, 2*, 29–38.

Michel, G.F., & Harkins, D.A. (1986) Postural and lateral asymmetries in the ontogeny of handedness during infancy. *Developmental Psychobiology, 19*, 247–258.

Michel, G.F., Ovrut, M.R., & Harkins, D.A. (1986). Hand-use preference for reaching and object manipulation in 6- through 13-month-old infants. *Genetic, Social, and General Psychology Monographs, 111*, 407–428.

Milliken, G.W., Forsythe, C., & Ward, J.P. (1989). Multiple measures of hand-use lateralization in the ring-tailed lemur (*Lemur catta*). *Journal of Comparative Psychology, 103*, 262–268.

Mittwoch, U. (1978). Changes in the direction of the lateral growth gradient in human development: left to right and right to left. *Behavioral and Brain Sciences, 2*, 306–307.

Morgan, M.J., & Corballis, M.C. (1978). On the biological basis of human laterality; II: The mechanisms of inheritance. *Behavioral and Brain Sciences, 2*, 270–277.

Moss, F.A. (1929). *Applications of psychology*. Boston: Houghton Mifflin.

Nathan, P., Smith, M.C., & Deacon, P. (1990). The corticospinal tracts in man: course and location of fibers at different segmental levels. *Brain, 113*, 303–324.

O'Callaghan, M.J., Tudehope, D.I., Dugdale, A.E., Mohay, H., Burns, Y., & Cook, F. (1987). Handedness in children with birthweights below 1000g. *Lancet, 1*, 1155.

Ogle, W. (1871). On dextral pre-eminence. *Transactions of the Royal Medical and Chirurgical Society of London, 54*, 279–301.

Oke, A., Keller, R., Mefford, I., & Adams, R.N. (1978). Lateralization of norepinephrine in human thalamus. *Science, 200*, 1411–1413.

Olson, D.A., Ellis, J.E., & Nadler, R.D. (1990). Hand preference in captive gorillas, orangutans and gibbons. *American Journal of Primatology, 20*, 83–94.

Ottaviano, S., Guidetti, V., Allemand, F., Spinetoli, B., & Seri, S. (1989). Laterality of arm movement in full-term newborn. *Early Human Development, 19*, 3–7.

Oxnard, C. (1982). *The order of man: a biomathematical anatomy of the primates.* Hong Kong: Hong Kong University Press.

Palmer, D. (1964). Development of a differential handedness. *Psychological Bulletin, 62,* 257–273.

Passingham, R.E. (1979). Brain size and intelligence in man. *Brain, Behavior and Evolution, 16,* 253–270.

Petrie, B.F., & Peters, M. (1981). Handedness: left/right differences in intensity of response and duration of rattle holding in infants. *Infant Behavior and Development, 3,* 215–221.

Porac, C., & Coren, S. (1981). *Lateral preferences and human behavior.* New York: Springer.

Previc, F.H. (1991). A general theory concerning the prenatal origins of cerebral lateralization in humans. *Psychological Review, 98,* 299–334.

Previc, F.H. (1994). Assessing the legacy of the GBG model. *Brain and Cognition, 26,* 174–180.

Ramsay, D.S. (1980). Beginnings of bimanual handedness and speech infants. *Infant behavior and Development, 3,* 67–77.

Ramsay, D.S, Campos, J.J., & Fenson, L. (1979). Onset of bimanual handedness in infants. *Infant Behavior and Development, 2,* 69–76.

Ramsay, D.S., & Weber, S.L. (1986). Infants' hand preference in a task involving complementary roles for the two hands. *Child Development, 57,* 300–307.

Ramsay, D.S., & Willis, M.P. (1984). Organization and lateralization of reaching in infants: an extension of Bresson et al.. *Neuropsycholgica, 22,* 639–641.

Roberts, A. M., & Smart, J.L. (1981). An investigation of handedness and headedness in newborn babies. *Behaviour and Brain Research, 2,* 275–276.

Rogers, L.J., & Kaplan, G. (1996). Hand preferences and other lateral biases in rehabilitated orang-utans (*Pongo pygmaeus pygmaeus*). *Animal Behaviour, 51,* 13–25.

Roney, L.S., & King, J.E. (1993). Postural effects on manual reaching laterality in squirrel monkeys (*Saimiri sciureus*) and cotton–top tamarins (*Saguinis oedipus*). *Journal of Comparative Psychology, 107,* 380–385.

Rönnqvist, L., & Hopkins, B. (1996, August). *Head position preference in the human newborn.* Proceedings of the XXVIth International Congress of Psychology, Montreal, Canada.

Rönnqvist, L., & von Hofsten, C. (1994). Neonatal finger and arm movements as determined by a social and an object context. *Early Development and Parenting, 3,* 81–94.

Satz, P. (1972). Pathological handedness: an explanatory model. *Cortex, 8, 121–135.*

Satz, P., Achenbach, K., & Fennel, E. (1967). Correlations between assessed manual laterality and predicted speech laterality in a normal population. *Neuropsychologica, 5,* 295–310.

Schwartze, H., & Schwartze, P. (1977). *Physiologie des foetal– neugeborenen– und kindesalters.* Berlin: Akademie Verlag.

Seltzer, C., Forsythe, C., & Ward, J.P. (1990). Multiple measures of motor lateralization in human primates (*Homo sapiens*). *Journal of Comparative Psychology, 104,* 159–166.

Seth, G. (1973). Eye–hand co-ordination and "handedness": a developmental study of visuomotor behaviour in infancy. *British Journal of Educational Psychology, 43,* 35–49.

Shaw, J. (1902). Right-handedness and left-braineness. *Lancet, 2,* 1486.

Smith, A. (1966). Certain hypothesized hemispheric differences in language and visual functions in human adults. *Cortex, 2,* 109–126.

Springer, S.P., & Deutsch, G. (1985). *Left brain, right brain.* New York: Freeman.

Stafford, D.K., Milliken, G.W., & Ward, J.P. (1990). Lateral bias in feeding and brachiation in *Hylobates*. *Primates, 31*, 407–414.

Steingrueber, H.J. (1975). Handedness as a function of test complexity. *Perceptual and Motor Skills, 40*, 263–266.

Steinmetz, H., Volkmann, J., Jäncke, L., & Fruend, H.J. (1991). Anatomical left–right asymmetry of language-related temporal cortex is different in left- and right-handers. *Annals of Neurology, 29*, 315–319.

Sugiyama, Y., Fushimi, T., Sakura, O., & Matsuzawa, T. (1993). Hand preference and tool use in wild chimpanzees. *Primates, 34*, 151–159.

Tanner, N.M. (1981). *On becoming human*. Cambridge: Cambridge University Press.

Taylor, D.C. (1976). *Beck's obstetrical practice and fetal medicine* (10th ed.). Baltimore, MD: Williams & Wilkins.

Thelen, E., Corbetta, D., Kamm, K., Spencer, J., Schneider, K., & Zernicke, R.F. (1993). The transition to reaching: mapping intention and intrinsic dynamics. *Child Development, 64*, 1058–1098.

Thelen, E., & Smith, L.B. (1995). *A dynamic systems approach to the development of cognition and action*. Cambridge, MA: MIT Press.

Tobias, P.V. (1981) The emergence of man in Africa and beyond. *Philosophical Transactions of the Royal Society of London, B*, 292, 43–56.

Tobias, P.V. (1987). The brain of *Homo habilis*: a new level of organization in cerebral evolution. *Journal of Human Evolution, 16*, 741–761.

Todor, J.I., & Doane, T. (1977). Handedness classification: preference versus proficiency. *Perceptual and Motor Skills, 45*, 1041–1042.

Tonooka, R., & Matsuzawa, T. (1995). Hand preferences of captive chimpanzees (*Pan troglodytes*) in simple reaching for food. *International Journal of Primatology, 16*, 17–35.

Toth, N. (1985). Archaeological evidence for preferential right-handedness in the lower and middle Pleistocene and its possible implications. *Journal of Human Evolution, 14*, 607–614.

Touwen, B.C.L. (1978). Variability and stereotypy in normal and deviant development. In: J. Apley (Ed.), *Care of the handicapped child*. London: Heinemann, pp. 99–110.

Turkewitz, G. (1977). The development of lateral differences in the human infant. In: S. Harnard, R.W. Doty, L. Goldstein, J. Jaynes & G. Krauthamer (Eds.), *Lateralization in the nervous system*. San Diego, CA: Academic Press, pp. 251–259.

Turkewitz, G., & Creighton, S. (1974). Changes in lateral differentiation of head posture in the human neonate. *Developmental Psychobiology, 8*, 85–89.

van Gelder, R.S., Dijkman, M.M.T.T., Hopkins, B., van Geijn, H.P., & Ho-Meau-Long, D.C. (1990). Prenatal development of head orientation preference. *International Journal of Prenatal and Perinatal Studies, 4*, 201–206.

van der Maas, H., & Molenaar, P.C.M. (1992). Stagewise cognitive development: an application of catastrophe theory. *Psychological Review, 99*, 395–417.

van der Staak, C. (1975). Intra- and interhemispheric visual-motor control of human arm movements. *Neuropsychologica, 13*, 439–448.

Ververs, I.A.P., de Vries, J.I.P., van Geijn, H.P., & Hopkins, B. (1994a). Prenatal head position from 12–38 weeks: I. Developmental aspects. *Early Human Development, 39*, 83–91.

Ververs, I.A.P., de Vries, J.I.P., van Geijn, H.P., & Hopkins, B. (1994b). Prenatal head position from 12–38 weeks: II. The effects of fetal orientation and placental localization. *Early Human Development, 39*, 93–100.

Visser, G.H.A., Zeelenberg, H.J., de Vries, J.I.P., & Dawes, G.S. (1983). External physical stimulation of the human fetus during episodes of low heart rate variation. *American Journal of Obstetrics and Gynecology, 145*, 579–584.

von Bonin, G. (1962). Anatomical asymmetries of the cerebral hemispheres. In: V.B. Mountcastle (Ed.), *Interhemispheric relations and cerebral dominance*. Baltimore, MD: Johns Hopkins University Press, pp. 1–6.

von Hofsten, C. (1982). Eye–hand coordination in the newborn. *Developmental Psychology, 18*, 450–461.

von Hofsten, C., & Rönnqvist, L. (1988). Preparation for grasping an object: a developmental study. *Journal of Experimental Psychology: Human Perception and Performance, 14*, 610–621.

Wada, J.A., Clarke, R., & Hamm, A. (1975). Cerebral hemispheric asymmetry in humans. *Archives in Neurology, 32*, 239–246.

Ward, J.P., Milliken, G.W., Dodson, D.L., Stafford, D.K., & Wallace, M. (1990). Handedness as a function of sex and age in a large population of *Lemur*. *Journal of Comparative Psychology, 104*, 167–173.

Warren, J.M. (1977). Handedness and cerebral dominance in monkeys. In: S. Harnad, R.W. Doty, L. Goldstein, J. Jaynes & G. Krauthamer (Eds.), *Lateralization in the nervous system*. New York: Academic Press, pp. 151–172.

Warren, J.M. (1980). Handedness and laterality in humans and other animals. *Physiological Psychology, 8*, 351–359.

Washburn, S.L. (1978). The evolution of man. *Scientific American, 239*, 194–204.

Westergaard, G.C. (1991). Hand preference in the use and manufacture of tools by tufted capuchin (*Cebus apella*) and lion-tailed macaque (*Macaca silenius*). *Journal of Comparative Psychology, 105*, 172–176.

Westergaard, G.C., & Suomi, S. J. (1993). Hand preference in the use of nut-cracking tools by tufted capuchin monkeys (*Cebus apella*). *Folia Primatologica, 61*, 38–42.

Wimmers, R.H., Savelsbergh, G., Beek, P.J., & Hopkins, B. (in press). Developmental changes in action: theoretical and methodological issues. *British Journal of Developmental Psychology*.

Yakovlev, P.I., & Rakic, P. (1966). Patterns of decussation of bulbar pyramids and distribution of pyramidal tracts on two sides of the spinal cord. *Transactions of the American Neurological Association, 91*, 366–367.

Yeni-Komshian, G.H., & Benson, D.A. (1976). Anatomical study of cerebral asymmetries in the temporal lobes of humans, chimpanzees and rhesus monkeys. *Science, 8*, 395.

Young, G. (1977). Manual specialization in infancy: implications for lateralization of brain functions. In S.J.Segalowitz & F.A. Gruber (Eds.), *Language development and neurological theory*. New York: Academic Press, pp. 289–331

Yu-Yan, M., Cun-Ren, F., & Over, R. (1983). Lateral symmetry in duration of grasp by infants. *Australian Journal of Psychology, 35*, 81–84.

PART IV

Perception and
Cognition

CHAPTER TWELVE

From Perception to Action: The Early Development of Knowledge

J. Gavin Bremner
Lancaster University, UK

Over the past 20 years or so a growing body of data on early perceptual competence has forced a change in the prevalent image of the young infant. In competition with the traditional Piagetian view of the infant as initially bereft of awareness of the world, the image of the competent infant has emerged, with even newborns credited with objective awareness of their surroundings. There has been a tendency to identify this as a simple matter of progress in science: as new techniques have emerged for studying young infants, data have accumulated apparently showing that Piaget was quite simply wrong and that infants are sophisticated perceivers from birth. Although current evidence indicates that there are some important limitations to newborn perception, the indication is that these limitations are largely overcome within a few months, and on some measures it appears that by around four months infants are well on the way to the sort of understanding of the world that Piaget saw emerging only gradually through the infant's systematic actions in the environment.

However, this revolution in our image of infancy has its own problems. Firstly, the evidence for early competence is largely based on variants of the habituation–dishabituation technique and, productive though the technique has been, it is not at all clear what status to accord to the capacity that leads the infant to look longer at a novel or discrepant stimulus. Does this constitute knowledge of the world (maybe as some have put it, reasoning about reality) or is it a more basic level detection of difference or discrepancy without understanding? Secondly, when we use measures of infant awareness based on the infant's directed action on the world, much more conservative estimates of ability emerge, more or less confirming the Piagetian image of the infant as gradual constructor of an objective world. I shall indicate that we cannot explain this *decalage* as a matter of a lag between perceptual and motor development, since a number of important phenomena cannot be explained as purely motor problems.

In this chapter I shall argue that we are indeed faced with a revolution in our image of infancy, but that the new image should be a good deal more complex than might appear at first sight. The basis of my argument will be that, while young infants do indeed possess impressive capacities for perceiving the world, a good deal must happen before these capacities are transformed into knowledge of the world. We need some minimal definition of what constitutes knowledge, and whereas successful action indicates knowledge of *how* to do something, it is not clear that perceptual capacities revealed in habituation–dishabituation studies qualify in this respect. My suggestion is that the lag between early perceptual capacity and ability revealed in directed action occurs because important developmental processes are at work through which perception is progressively brought into the service of action. And impressive as these early perceptual capacities are, we can only infer knowledge on the part of the infant once perceptual information is used systematically to guide action.

THE EVIDENCE FOR EARLY ABILITY

There are two primary sources of evidence that contribute to the view of the young infant as perceptually and conceptually competent. Recent research on visual perception in early infancy contributes to the view that from birth infants perceive objective properties of objects and space. And research on knowledge of objects and physical events suggests that as early as three months, infants have quite advanced awareness of the physical properties of the world.

Newborns as objective perceivers

The development of a range of techniques based on habituation of looking has undoubtedly revolutionised our knowledge of the visual perceptual capabilities of young infants. Development of infant-controlled procedures has made it possible to use these techniques successfully with newborns. Additionally, the version generally referred to as the *familiarisation–novelty* technique has brought enormous power to this sort of investigation, by making it possible during habituation trials to vary lower order stimulus variables while holding constant the variable of interest.

The use of this technique with newborns has provided important evidence regarding two important principles involved in perception of objective reality — shape and size constancy. Some time ago, using an operant conditioning technique, Bower (1966) obtained evidence suggesting that both shape and size constancy were present in early infancy. However, later work using habituation techniques did not reveal evidence for shape constancy before around six months (McKenzie,

Tootell & Day, 1980). Use of the familiarisation–novelty technique modified the story, however. Slater and Morison (1985) habituated newborns to one shape presented at different tilts and then presented the same shape in a new tilt (so presenting a novel retinal image) paired with a novel shape (that presented a retinal image that had been encountered during habituation). Newborns looked more at the novel shape, good evidence for shape constancy. Similarly, Slater, Mattock and Brown (1990) habituated infants to a particular object presented at different distances and then tested for novelty preference between the same object at a new distance and a differently sized object. Again, newborns showed size constancy by looking more at the novel size object. It appears that earlier studies failed to obtain size constancy in young infants because they did not vary object distance during habituation, a procedure that led infants to work at the level of object distance or retinal image size rather than true size.

These findings constitute probably the strongest evidence that even newborns perceive an objective world. One should not, however, jump to the conclusion that newborns perceive the world much as adults do. Apart from basic limitations such as low visual acuity (Norcia & Tyler, 1985), there appear to be other limitations that are theoretically more important. Probably the best example comes from work on perceptual completion. Kellman and Spelke (1983) habituated four-month-olds to the display shown at the top of Fig. 12.1, a moving rod behind a box. Following habituation, they tested for dishabituation on the two displays (presented singly)

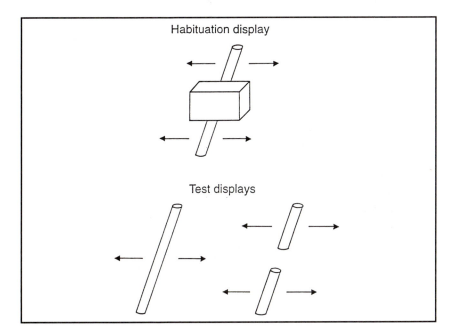

FIG. 12.1:   Stimuli used by Kellman and Spelke (1983).

shown at the bottom of the figure, a continuous rod and a broken rod constituted of the parts visible during habituation. The rationale was that, if infants employed perceptual completion and perceived a continuous rod during habituation, they would show a novelty preference for the broken rod, whereas if they had simply perceived what was visible, two rod parts, they would show a preference for the continuous rod. Kellman and Spelke obtained the first pattern, support for the notion that infants perform perceptual completion, filling in the invisible parts of an object in uniform motion. A number of studies have been done since that identify more closely the conditions under which perceptual completion occurs (Johnson & Aslin, 1996; Johnson & Nanez, 1995), but a crucial finding is that newborns do not show this phenomenon. Slater, Morison, Somers, Mattock, Brown and Taylor (1990) replicated Kellman and Spelke's effect with four-month-olds, but obtained the opposite result with newborns, that is, a looking preference for the continuous rod. It appears that newborns habituated to what was literally visible: the ability to perform perceptual completion appears to be absent at birth.

Object knowledge in early infancy

There is a sense in which Kellman and Spelke's task goes beyond the bounds of conventional perception, since it is about perception or awareness of invisible parts of an object. In that sense, it relates to issues about object permanence. Here again, the conventional view that object permanence emerges relatively late has been challenged by recent research. In one of the earlier studies of this sort (Baillargeon, Spelke & Wasserman, 1985) five-month-olds were presented with repeated familiarisation trials in which a flap, initially flat on the table, rotated 180 degrees about an axis perpendicular to infants' line of sight, and then back again to its original position. After these trials, a cube was placed in its path and two types of trial followed. In the possible event, the flap rotated but stopped at the point when it would have come in contact with the now hidden cube. In the impossible event, however, the flap rotated the full distance as before and so apparently moved through the position occupied by the cube, which disappeared in the process. Infants looked significantly longer at the impossible event, and Baillargeon et al. (1985) concluded that five-month-olds both understood the continued existence of the cube and realised that the flap could not move through the position it occupied.

In a later study, Baillargeon (1987a) replicated this result with younger infants, finding that 4.5-month-olds and some 3.5-month-olds responded in the same way as infants in the first study. It should be noted, however, that there is some ambiguity over the interpretation of these results. Two things happen in the impossible event: the flap moves through the position occupied by the cube and the cube disappears. One cannot say whether it is one or both of these violations that draws infants' attention, and it is possible that this is prompted solely by the unexpected disappearance of the cube. Such an interpretation requires no knowledge of the constraint the cube puts on the movement of the flap.

Another study, however, suggests that this more simple interpretation cannot explain the performance of older infants. Baillargeon (1987b) found that seven-month-olds have quite precise expectations about when the flap should stop rotating, expecting it to stop sooner in the case of a taller cube, but later in the case of a compressible object. These findings suggest really quite precise awareness of relations between objects, even when one object is occluded. And this is the general pattern that Baillargeon obtains in a range of studies: basic level awareness of object permanence and relationships between objects at around three or four months, replaced by more precise awareness some months later.

A further impressive example from Baillargeon's work relates again to understanding of when one object blocks the path of another. This time, infants are familiarised with a repeated event in which a truck rolls down a ramp and travels behind a screen, disappearing and then re-emerging at the other side. After familiarisation, two types of test events are given. In the impossible event, the screen is lifted to reveal a block resting on the track used by the truck, and is lowered again prior to the truck travelling down the ramp, behind the screen and re-emerging as usual. In the possible event, the same procedure is followed but for the fact that the block is placed just behind the path of the truck so that it does not block its progress.

Under these conditions, Baillargeon (1986) found that six- to eight-month-olds looked longer at the impossible event, and more recently, Baillargeon and DeVos (1991) obtained similar results with four-month-old infants. Also, there is some evidence of this awareness in even younger infants. Spelke, Breinlinger, Macomber and Jacobson (1992) familiarised 2.5-month-olds with an event in which a ball rolled behind a screen, whereupon the screen was lifted to show the ball at rest against an end wall. Then two types of test trial were given. In both, a block was lowered behind the screen into the path of the ball, leaving part of the box in view to indicate its continued presence. In the possible event the ball rolled behind the screen and when the screen was lifted was revealed at rest against the block, but in the impossible event it was revealed at rest in its position on familiarisation trials, against the end wall. Infants looked more at the impossible event, again suggesting that they are aware of the rules constraining the movement of objects.

Perceiving versus knowing

The evidence for newborn detection of shape and size constancy and young infants' awareness of the physical world is particularly impressive, and might lead us to the view that by around six months infants have developed a more or less adult knowledge of the world. However, we must question this conclusion both on theoretical and empirical grounds. At the theoretical level, it is not at all clear what we should call the abilities that are measured by habituation–novelty techniques and the variants used by Baillargeon and Spelke. Longer visual inspection of an event that is novel or that violates a physical principle certainly indicates awareness of some departure from what has gone before, but it is not at all clear what level we are dealing with. Certainly, one must ask whether it is appropriate to conclude as Baillargeon does that infants in their first half year are *reasoning* about physical reality. Here it is worth noting Piaget's (1954) distinction between acting in accordance with a particular principle and knowing this principle as such. Although visual activity is involved, it is not directly adapted to physical principles: infants simply look longer at a particular event, and there is no evidence that they are guiding their actions in accordance with the principles under test (as, for instance, infants might shape their reaching according to the size and distance of an object).

Another theoretical issue concerns the apparent fact that the phenomena detected by Baillargeon and Spelke emerge only after repeated familiarisation to a non-violation event. If infants possess an understanding of physical principles would we not expect them to reveal this in longer looking at a violation event straightaway? This suggests either that the knowledge revealed in these studies is particularly fragile, such that repeated exposure to a specific normal event is required to support it, or that the knowledge is derived purely from the familiarisation events presented within the study itself.

The major empirical issue concerns the fact that, despite these impressive early capacities, in their manual activities infants do not reveal knowledge of object permanence and rules governing physical reality. For instance, infants do not begin to search for hidden objects until around eight months, and even then they make persistent errors: firstly if the object is hidden in a new place (the A not-B error), and after 12 months, when the object is moved while invisible to a new place. These findings, first noted by Piaget (1954), have been replicated in many laboratories, and present a developmental picture that is much more in accord with his theory of sensori-motor development in which knowledge of object permanence and the objective world is gradually constructed through action.

One might attempt to reconcile these phenomena with the more recent work using habituation–novelty techniques by suggesting that what the infant lacks is not knowledge of objects but the requisite motor skill to retrieve hidden objects. However, it is clear that search failure cannot be due to simple motor limitations. Bower and Wishart (1972) showed that infants who did not search for an object under an opaque cup did search when the cup was transparent. So the appropriate action is available and it is something to do with object invisibility that provides the problem. And the later phenomena are not about the failure to produce an appropriate action but about failure to direct it appropriately on the basis of the events that have been presented.

One line of research puts this sort of failure neatly in opposition to the habituation-based work of Baillargeon and Spelke. Hood (1995) and later Hood, Uller and Carey (1996) presented 2-year-olds with variants of a retrieval task in which an object fell down a tube, coming to rest where it could be retrieved through an aperture. On test trials, a shelf was placed above the normal end point of the object's trajectory so that it obstructed the object's path. Despite this, 2-year-olds searched for the object below the shelf. This task has a similar structure to

Baillargeon's and Spelke's studies with young infants; in fact, Spelke et al. (1992) demonstrated that 4-month-olds would look longer at an event in which an object apparently fell through a shelf to land underneath.

As a whole, these studies present a real problem about how we can square the object-search phenomena with work reviewed earlier indicating that infants are apparently aware not just of the continued existence of a hidden object but of the implications of this existence for the movements of another object. In general, infants' performance in object-search tasks is several months behind their performance in habituation based tasks. And taking a specific comparison, the work by Hood et al. (1996) suggests that apparent awareness at 4 months of how a barrier affects a falling object is not reflected in appropriate action even by 2 years. One possibility put forward by cognitive scientists is that the hidden object representations detected in the early months are insufficiently strong to be used to guide action (Munakata, McClelland, Johnson & Siegler, 1994). This approach has the advantage of providing a possible explanation of the fact that in early infancy, awareness of sequences that violate principles such as object permanence emerge only after repeated exposure to a lawful event sequence. If the representation is fragile, detection of violation of the principle in which it is based may emerge only after the infant is repeatedly exposed to a sequence embodying the principle.

It is important to note that these workers' use of the concept of *representation* is rather different from the conventional notion of some internal copy of reality: the concept is applied here in the language of connectionist modelling, in terms of the connection between input and output units. In that way, the major criticisms of the concept of representation are avoided. In effect, this approach appears to be a systematic way of modelling the development of connections between perception and action. The data on perceptual competence in early infancy are not purely about perception, but about a very basic level connection between what is perceived and what the infant directs visual attention to, whereas the data from object-search tasks call for an explanation in terms of precise coordination between perception and action in which the perception of events is coordinated with complex motor activity.

Connectionist modelling may ultimately answer many of the questions here, and it is possible that the most promising approach will involve application of connectionist modelling to aspects of Gibsonian theory of direct perception and dynamic systems theory, as a means of investigating how perception and action become coordinated or *coupled* during development.

DIRECT PERCEPTION, DYNAMIC SYSTEMS THEORY, AND PERCEPTION–ACTION COUPLING

The notion that I shall be advancing in the remainder of this chapter is that young infants show quite sophisticated awareness of the physical world, an awareness that may best be conceptualised as a high level perceptual property, but that this awareness is not initially available to guide action. Seen in this light, a large part of development is about forming coordinations between developing perception and action.

The theory of direct perception

Although not presented initially as a developmental theory, Gibson's (1979) theory of *direct perception* is seen by many as the antithesis of the principles upon which Piaget's account is based. A basic principle of the theory is that the structure of the world is available in perceptual information picked up by the individual, particularly in the flow of perceptual information that results as the individual actively explores the environment. Perception is fundamentally a dynamic process which is continuous over time. Information about the objective nature of the world, its three-dimensionality etc., is contained in the dynamic perceptual flow, and there is no need to construct three-dimensionality through interpretation of depth cues. From the Gibsonian perspective, perceiving *is* knowing. And this knowing extends beyond perception of the structure of the world to perception of *affordances*; that is, the possibilities particular environmental features offer the individual in terms of action.

Many investigators are, however, uneasy about the *direct perception* approach, since although it says much about the availability of environmental structures and their "pick up" through dynamic perceptual processes, it says little about the structures of the mind that are necessary to support direct perception. So although the approach is enormously useful in reining us back from invoking representational processes as necessary prerequisites for all infant abilities, it leaves us in the dark about the minimum but undoubtedly necessary structures of the mind that are needed to support objective perception.

Dynamic systems theory and direct perception

If we are to fill the gaps in direct perception accounts, what is needed is a theoretical framework which gets the balance between environmental and organismic factors right. *Dynamic systems* theory stresses the need to analyse behaviour as the outcome of the functioning of a complex system. And what makes it a promising candidate is that this system need not be located within the individual, but can extend to the wider system of the organism and environment in interaction. Additionally, the approach is extremely flexible, being essentially "content free" and applicable to any problem or "content area" in which a complex system is involved.

A basic premise of the approach is that complex systems are self-organising: they arrive at new states simply through their own functioning. Also, it is claimed that the behaviour of a system can only be understood in terms of a complex interaction between different factors that contribute to its functioning. For instance, Thelen and Ulrich (1991) point out that those studying motor activity are mistaken in seeking to explain it purely in terms of some neural substrate, since the complexity of the activity is contributed to as much by the biomechanical properties of the limbs and muscles as by the functional characteristics of the motor cortex. For instance, much of the complexity involved in walking effectively "falls out of" bipedal dynamics, and there is no need to look for a neural control system that holds the key to it all. This is an important point when we compare this approach to more conventional cognitive approaches, since the implication is that the behaviour of the system cannot be explained by recourse to some single element (such as a representational structure). Instead, behaviour is an emergent property of a complete system composed of psychological, biological and physical components. Systems "prefer" particular states of equilibrium, but (and here is where development comes in) they tend to progress towards states of lower stability and eventually to new states of equilibrium, under the influence of particular forces acting from within or outside the individual. And part of the explanatory power of this approach lies in the claim that complex new states and their behavioural manifestations can be triggered by changes in quite simple parameters.

This approach, however, has its own problems. Application of the detailed analysis that it demands leads to a preoccupation with minute aspects of action, and there is a danger of being unable to see the larger psychological picture. But we should also apply critical analysis to more conventional approaches to ask whether they are too ready to invoke traditional adult psychological concepts, such as representation, reasoning and inference, when studying early infancy. There are certainly grounds to question whether data gathered from habituation procedures can be taken as evidence for mental representation, or reasoning, and yet these terms are often used in interpreting data from infants under six months. The issue is really about the appropriate level of analysis and hence the appropriate terminology to apply to the phenomena observed in early infancy. And I shall suggest that although there is a need for more or less conventional psychological explanation, this need may be limited to specific phenomena and to phenomena emerging later in infancy.

Although the major application of dynamic systems has been in the study of motor development in infancy, there is scope for applying the same analysis in a broader way so that it incorporates perceptual activities. Indeed, this is already happening in the analysis of visually guided action. And there is general potential for a link-up between this approach and Gibsonian theory. Both are essentially ecological systems theories, and the advantage of the dynamic systems approach is that, through putting together action systems and perceptual systems as components of an overall system, it may be possible to identify the minimum structures of the system that are required to permit objective perception. Where I think there is clear utility to a marriage between direct perception and dynamic systems is when it comes to the Gibsonian concept of *affordance*. The notion involved in this concept is that in addition to perceiving the world objectively, individuals directly perceive the connections between features of the world and their own actions. A good example here is affordances of surfaces for locomotion.

The notion is that organisms directly perceive whether or not particular surfaces support locomotion, and the point is that the affordance is determined not just by the properties of the surface but by the characteristics of the organism, its weight, style of locomotion and so on. Taking a developmental perspective, for the newly walking infant, only quite flat and stable surfaces support this new and rather precarious activity. And the interesting thing is that these young walkers are capable of perceiving the surfaces that afford locomotion, avoiding those that do not (Gibson, Riccio, Schmuckler, Stoffregen, Rosenberg & Taormina, 1987).

At first sight, direct perception of affordances seems implausible. They are not, after all, features of the world available to be picked up, but rather relationships between perceived features and the habits of the individual. This might lead us to the view that development of affordances must be a constructional process, in which representations of the relationship between perceived features and actions are built up. And as I shall indicate later, I think cognitive processes of this sort mediate the development of many affordances that relate to complex activities such as problem solving. However, dynamic systems may provide a simpler solution in the case of affordances relating to the more "automatic" aspects of behaviour. Savelsbergh and van der Kamp (1993) have provided a developmental model for the progressive detection of affordances by marrying direct perception with dynamic systems analysis of behavioural development. Basically, the notion is that the dynamic systems analysis must encompass the factors involved in the action system, the perceptual system, and those environmental features providing perceptual structure. As new action systems emerge, these mesh or do not mesh with certain features in the perceptual world. The mesh is reached through action, not as mental construction, but as an emergent property of the perceptuo-motor system.

A good example here would be the case of early object manipulation. Prior to the development of a controlled reach and grasp sequence, infants certainly should be able to perceive differences in object size, a crucial variable determining whether or not an object can be grasped. However the "graspability" of an object is determined by the relationship between object size and the maximum finger–thumb separation that will achieve a successful grasp. It is possible that detection of this affordance arises through the natural meshing of perceived object features and the characteristics of action.

It has already been widely recognised that Gibson's ecological approach and the dynamic systems approach might profitably be combined (Reed, 1982; Turvey, 1990). And recent ecological accounts of the development of affordances use terminology that has much in common with dynamic systems. For instance, Adolph, Eppler and Gibson (1993, p. 56) write, "An adequate description of an affordance entails specification of how action is constrained by the fit between environmental properties and action capabilities..." However, there appears to be a tendency for the link to stop at the level of common terminology, since the Gibsonian school tend to use generalities instead of specifying developmental processes with the mathematical precision available to dynamic systems. Thus we find it stated (p. 90) that development of perception of affordances occurs "... where observers notice and detect information for the animal-environment fit themselves through active exploration". This provides little evidence about what sort of processes are involved in exploration, and what is involved in noticing and detecting. Is the information detected simply through the fact of mobility, or is there active spatial problem solving involved that might call upon cognitive processes? So what is left unsaid here is just what sort of psychological processes are involved in detection of affordances. The strength of the dynamic systems approach is that it tries to specify these processes quite precisely, and in doing so suggests that at least in many cases the processes involved can be quite low level.

THE IMPLICIT–EXPLICIT DISTINCTION

In this section, my aim is to return to the linked issues of what we should call the capacities of young infants as revealed through current experimental techniques, how this awareness changes during infancy, and what processes produce this change. And it is here that I want to bring in the *implicit–explicit* distinction as a basic descriptive principle. Although this distinction has recently generated considerable interest, it appears to have almost as many interpretations as it has adherents. Some investigators apply the distinction in terms of knowledge revealed through action versus knowledge revealed through language. For instance, Gibson (1979, p. 260) defines explicit knowledge as information that can be linguistically expressed. Some define the distinction in a more general way. For instance, Karmiloff-Smith (1992) defines implicit knowledge or information as a form of representation not available to guide the mental activities of the individual, and proposes that this is transformed into explicit knowledge through a process of representational redescription. There is also a tendency to relate the distinction to conscious versus unconscious processes, with implicit learning conceptualised as the result of unconscious processing (Cleeremans, 1993) and *tacit knowledge* the outcome of such learning (Reber, 1993).

My suggestion is that there is another sense in which the distinction may be usefully applied, particularly in early infancy, a way that is in keeping both with ecological psychology, with its reluctance to invoke cognitive processes, and with cognitive approaches. We are faced with evidence that young infants perceive an objective and permanent world, but that they are far from being able to use this perception to guide action. In that sense, we may consider these perceptual abilities *implicit knowledge*, since although they involve detection of information vital for action guidance, they do not constitute *explicit knowledge* at the most basic level of "knowing how". And a major developmental process in early infancy involves the transformation of knowledge implicit in perception into explicit knowledge that can be used to guide action.

This definition need not conflict with other uses of the distinction, provided we are careful to define in each instance the level of psychological activity to which we are applying it. Thus, it becomes quite acceptable for a form of knowledge treated as explicit with respect to manual activity, to be redefined as implicit (procedural) knowledge with respect to linguistic activity. And it is even possible to subdivide knowledge used to guide manual activity by distinguishing between automatic guidance of action and purposive guidance of action (as in problem solving). The important point is that there are a set of levels at which knowledge becomes available to guide the activities of the individual, and this progression may be repeated during development on successively higher levels of psychological activity, or may jump levels through the operation of different processes. So defined, any form of knowledge is always implicit with respect to the higher level activity but explicit with respect to the lower level.

Linguistic activities are not a major focus during early infancy, and as already noted in this chapter, there is controversy over the degree to which it is appropriate to invoke mental processes in explaining early behaviour. However, there appears to be utility in a general distinction between knowledge implicit in perception and explicit perceptuo-motor knowledge that can be used to guide action. I shall suggest that we need to subdivide this distinction further to recognise the difference between use of information for automatic guidance of action and for guidance of purposive behaviour, as seen in problem solving. The distinction between automatic activities and purposive problem-solving activities appears fundamental, particularly in identifying the beginnings of what makes human psychology distinct, and it appears to me that it was the latter that Piaget was primarily concerned with. Furthermore, it makes sense to assume that knowledge judged explicit at the level of automatic action has to be transformed or supplemented before becoming explicit at the level of purposive flexible action typical of problem solving. It is here that Karmiloff-Smith (1992) identifies the need for representational redescription. But my account is very much about the processes occurring before that point, through which perception and action are first coordinated.

One clear advantage of interpreting infant development in terms of this implicit–explicit conceptualisation is that, rather than portraying infants as progressing from a state of no or little knowledge to a state of mature knowledge, they are conceptualised as in a sense knowing the world from the start, and development is treated as a set of changes in the way in which this knowledge or information is utilised as perception and action are progressively coupled.

DEVELOPMENTAL PROCESSES

The implicit–explicit distinction is developmentally descriptive because, in itself, it does not illuminate the processes underlying development. However, earlier sections have laid the ground for us to consider the sorts of process that might explain developmental changes during infancy. Gibsonian theory generates some straightforward predictions and dynamic systems analysis may in time provide a detailed account of some of the processes involved. The processes that emerge most clearly all relate in one way or another to the development of action, in particular to the development of locomotion. For instance, although direct perception is a matter of information pickup with no need for internal representation, perception is described as an active process. So one would assume that the effectiveness of perception would be closely related to motor development, in particular, that the onset of locomotion would lead to more effective and extensive detection of information. This might simply involve the pickup of further perceptual information, or in current terms, further implicit knowledge.

Important predictions emerge in relation to the concept of affordances. In the words of Adolph, Eppler and Gibson (1993, p. 52), "An affordance is the fit between an animal's capabilities and the environmental supports that enable a given action to be performed." And a given feature of the environment will hold one type of affordance for one species and a different one for another. This has an important developmental parallel, namely, that the affordances detected will depend on the infant's ability to act. To say that a particular surface affords crawling makes sense only in relation to infants who can crawl. So as new motor achievements come on the scene, new affordances emerge. Because these affordances are essentially relationships between environmental structure and the structure of action, it is here that dynamic systems theory may help us to understand the process by which new affordances are developed, through the meshing of the organismic and environmental sides of the system. And the thrust of this approach is to describe the emergence of new affordances as taking place in an automatic manner through the actions of the infant in his or her environment.

The development of affordances can be analysed in terms of the implicit–explicit distinction. Prior to emergence of a new affordance, the relevant environmental feature was available to perception. Thus, the environmental information specifying the affordance was implicit in perception. But it is not until this information is meshed in as part of a system including both perception and the appropriate action that we can say that the affordance has been detected. And since an affordance is a relationship between perception and action which in itself may be sufficient to guide action, in terms of my earlier definition, it constitutes explicit knowledge.

So what of the developmental processes involved in the emergence of new affordances? At one level, it would appear that development just happens through the natural functioning of the perceptuo-motor system. Perceptual capacity is either present at birth or develops early, and is transformed into explicit knowledge at the level of action as it becomes meshed with new actions. Of course, there is a lot buried in the statement that perception develops early. For instance, at a basic level, improvement in visual acuity is liable to enhance feature extraction. Also the emergency of stereopsis at 3 to 4 months (Granrud, 1986) provides more precise information about distance, and it may be no coincidence that accurate reaching for objects emerges around this time. But in this case, stereopsis probably does not so much provide new information about the world as provide perceptual support needed for accurate action. This is rather different from the subsequent meshing between this new action and perceptual information determining whether or how an object can be grasped, through which object knowledge becomes explicit in relation to reach-and-grasp actions. At a higher level, the evidence of Baillargeon, Spelke and their colleagues indicates the emergence of some level of awareness of object permanence and the rules governing physical reality as early as the third month, with development of the precision of this awareness continuing during the first year. However, this awareness is not revealed in the infant's manual actions until some months later. So although a great deal is happening on the perceptual level, the main point is that none of these developments in itself leads to the development of explicit knowledge, because that only emerges through couplings between current perception and new actions.

A major principal of the dynamic systems approach is that there is no need to go beyond consideration of the environmental, mechanical and biological constraints in the system in order to reach an adequate developmental explanation. Through its denial of the need to rely on mentalistic concepts, this approach has some clear advantages: reliance on mentalistic terminology (such as knowledge, understanding and reasoning) in explanations of infants' ability often seems inherently inappropriate. But one cannot help asking if there is no more to infant development than the natural emergence of functions that link behaviour to the environment. Although the dynamic systems approach may help to explain many of the basic activities of infants, activities which both emerge and are exercised at a relatively automatic unconscious level, this approach will have greater difficulties in dealing with the infant as an active problem solver engaged in means–ends analysis (Willatts, 1997). Although, in principle, the cognitive concepts that seem to be required in these cases can be incorporated within systems analysis, it is hard to see how the resulting system can be analysed with the same rigour as in the case of simpler behaviours. At these higher levels, the dynamic systems approach is applied as a metaphor, and it is not quite so clear that it has advantages beyond pointing out that multiple factors have to be taken into account in explaining development.

I believe that this distinction between automatic behaviours and the purposive ones seen in problem solving is crucial. Both forms are self-guided, but the latter are purposive in the sense that they involve deliberate manipulation and variation by the individual. It seems likely that this is not a rigid subdivision, since development may be partly a matter of behaviours becoming automatic after a period of achievement as a result of active problem solving. Thus, for instance, locomotion may become automatic, although its initial achievement may have been partly based on the infant trying out motor and postural variations. However, at a given point in development, there are some behaviours that appear automatic, while there are others that appear to involve problem solving under the control of a component of the system which we may want to call the mind, brain, or executive control system, depending on our theoretical stance.

It thus appears likely that affordances are acquired in some cases as a result of purposive problem solving rather than just through automatic functioning. Any new motor achievement such as locomotion permits further environmental exploration, but at the same time new problems are encountered, the solutions to which constitute new knowledge. In this respect, the global concept of learning through action that is encountered in the Gibsonian work needs to be unpacked, to investigate the different processes involved in learning through action.

It is possible to describe the product of development through these processes in terms of different forms of implicit-to-explicit shift. As already mentioned, detection of perceptual variables specifying an affordance make that affordance implicit in perception, but this cannot be called explicit knowledge until the infant can use it to guide action. What I am adding here is that there are two distinct processes through which perception comes to be used to guide action: firstly at a relatively automatic level, such as when perceptual flow information is used to guide locomotion or update position, and secondly, at a level that seems fundamentally cognitive, in which the infant is acting as a purposive problem solver, and discovers in the process certain ways in which perception and action fit together. Finally, this shift from implicit to explicit is not simply a matter of "plugging in" implicit knowledge to the action system. There is always something new in the sense that the connection involves the formation of an appropriate and often quite complex linkup between perception and action. The task of future research is to identify both the form of these connections and the processes leading to their formation. It is here that both dynamic systems analysis and connectionist modelling are liable to have important roles in providing precise specifications of the conditions for development.

REFERENCES

Adolph, K.E., Eppler, M.A., & Gibson, E.J. (1993). Development of perception of affordances. In C. Rovee-Collier & L.P. Lipsitt (Eds.) *Advances in Infancy Research*, Vol. 8. Norwood, NJ: Ablex, pp. 51–98.

Baillargeon, R. (1986). Representing the existence and location of hidden objects: objects permanence in six- and eight-month-old infants. *Cognition, 23*, 21–41.

Baillargeon, R. (1987a). Object permanence in 3.5- and 4.5-month-old infants. *Developmental Psychology, 23*, 655–664.

Baillargeon, R. (1987b). Young infants' reasoning about the physical and spatial properties of a hidden object. *Cognitive Development, 2*, 179–200.

Baillargeon, R., & DeVos, J. (1991). Object permanence in young infants: further evidence. *Child Development, 62*, 1227–1246.

Baillargeon, R., Spelke, E.S., & Wasserman, S. (1985). Object permanence in five-month-old infants. *Cognition, 20*, 191–208.

Bower, T.G.R. (1966). The visual world of infants. *Scientific American, 215*, 80–92.

Bower, T.G.R., & Wishart, J.G. (1972). The effects of motor skill on object permanence. *Cognition, 1*, 165–172.

Cleeremans, A. (1993). *Mechanisms of implicit learning: connectionist models of sequence processing*. Cambridge, MA: MIT Press.

Geert, P. van (1993). A dynamic systems model of cognitive growth: competition and support under limited resource conditions. In L.B. Smith & E. Thelen (Eds.) *A dynamic systems approach to development: applications*. Cambridge, MA: MIT Press, pp 265–332.

Gibson, J.J. (1979). *The ecological approach to visual perception*. Boston: Houghton Mifflin.

Gibson, E.J., Riccio, G., Schmuckler, M.A., Stoffregen, T.A., Rosenberg, D., & Taormina, J. (1987). Detection of the traversability of surfaces by crawling and walking infants. *Journal of Experimental Psychology: Human Perception & Performance, 13*, 533–544.

Granrud, C.E. (1986). Binocular vision and spatial perception in four- and five-month-old infants. *Journal of Experimental Psychology: Human Perception & Performance, 12*, 36–49.

Hood, B.M. (1995). *Gravity errors in preschool children*. Poster presented to the Biennial Meeting of the Society for Research in Child Development, Indianapolis.

Hood, B.M., Uller, C., & Carey, S. (1996). *Naive physical reasoning in two-year-olds: discrepancies with the infant data*. Poster presented to the 10th International Conference on Infant Studies, Providence. (Abstract: *Infant Behavior & Development, 19*, 512).

Johnson, S.P., & Aslin, R.N. (1996). Perception of object unity in infants: the roles of motion, depth, and orientation. *Cognitive Development, 11*, 161–180.

Johnson, S.P., & Nanez, J.E. (1995). Young infants' perception of object unity in two-dimensional displays. *Infant Behavior & Development, 18*, 133–143.

Karmiloff-Smith, A. (1992). *Beyond modularity: a developmental perspective on cognitive science*. Cambridge, MA: MIT Press.

Kellman, P.J., & Spelke, E.R. (1983). Perception of partly occluded objects in infancy. *Cognitive Psychology, 15*, 483–524.

McKenzie, B.E., Tootell, H.E., & Day, R.H. (1980). Development of visual size constancy during the first year of human infancy. *Developmental Psychology, 16*, 163–174.

Munakata, Y., McClelland, J., Johnson, M., & Siegler, R. (1994) Rethinking object permanence: do the ends justify means–ends? Paper presented to the Ninth International Conference on Infant Studies, Paris. (Abstract: *Infant Behaviour & Development, 17*, 842).

Norcia, A.M., & Tyler, C.W. (1985). Spatial frequency sweep VEP: visual acuity during the first year of life. *Visual Research, 18*, 1399–1408.

Piaget, J. (1954). *The construction of reality in the child* (trans. M. Cook). New York: Basic Books. (originally published in French, 1936).

Reber, A.S. (1993). *Implicit learning and tacit knowledge: an essay on the cognitive unconscious*. Oxford: Oxford University Press.

Reed, E.S. (1982). An outline of a theory of action systems. *Journal of Motor Behaviour, 14*, 98–134.

Savelsbergh, G.J.P., & van der Kamp, J. (1993). *A natural physical perspective on the development of infant eye–hand coordination: a search for the laws of control*. Annual report No. 16. Research & Clinical Center for Child Development, Hokkaido University, Sapporo.

Slater, A., Mattock, A., & Brown, E. (1990). Size constancy at birth: newborn infants' responses to retinal and real sizes. *Journal of Experimental Child Psychology, 49*, 314–322.

Slater, A., Mattock, A., Brown, E., & Bremner, J.G. (1991). Form perception at birth: Cohen and Younger (1984) revisited. *Journal of Experimental Child Psychology, 51*, 395–406.

Slater, A., & Morison, V. (1985). Shape constancy and slant perception at birth. *Perception*, *14*, 337–344.

Slater, A., Morison, V., Somers, M., Mattock, A., Brown, E., & Taylor, D. (1990). Newborn and older infants' perception of partly occluded objects. *Infant Behavior and Development*, *13*, 33–49.

Spelke, E.S., Breinlinger, K., Macomber, J., & Jacobson, K. (1992). Origins of knowledge. *Psychological Review*, *99*, 605–632.

Thelen, E., & Ulrich, B.D. (1991) Hidden skills: a dynamic systems analysis of treadmill stepping during the first year. *Monographs of the Society for Research in Child Development*, *56* [Special Issue].

Turvey, M.T. (1990). Coordination. *American Psychologist, 45*, 938–953.

Willatts, P. (1997). Beyond the "couch potato" infant: how infants use their knowledge to regulate action, solve problems, and achieve goals. In J.G. Bremner, A. Slater & G. Butterworth (Eds.) *Infant development: recent advances*. Hove: Erlbaum (UK) Taylor & Francis.

CHAPTER THIRTEEN

Sensory–Motor Coordinations: Their Relation to Cognition

Henriette Bloch
*Laboratoire de Psycho-Biologie du Développement,
EPHE-CNRS, Paris, France*

Among the most fruitful criteria for assessing phylogenetic evolution are the repertoires of action typical of a species, especially those modes that allow mastery over the milieu, whether it consists in using what the environment provides or in transforming it. In this respect techniques constructed by humans are not only rooted in acquired knowledge and culture, but they are also based on an individual psycho-biological exchange with the environment. From a psychological point of view, and because it is a universal need of organisms to interact with their environment, it is important to know how individuals acquire the status of an agent, i.e. how they generate observable effects consequent upon their own activity.

Agency develops over time with the formation of skills of varying levels, from gripping a small object which requires the pincer grip, to reading and writing, to the mastery of a musical instrument or driving a vehicle, and to the ever growing number of vigilance tasks due to the increasing technology of our societies. In the simplest, as in the most complex tasks, the skill is based on a precise agreement between perception and action; i.e. on an effective sensory–motor coordination. For instance, to thread a needle, it is necessary to direct the gaze accurately to the eye of the needle, while aiming and directing the thread toward the hole. Such a precise, complex act is in some way prepared for by a broad repertoire of actions that associate the eye with the hand. At first glance, the baby seems particularly poorly equipped with such skills. An apparent paradox is that the more a species is organised, the more it acts on its milieu, the more its initial ability to interact appears poor and slow to develop. Thus the question of when and how skills begin in man is raised. Yet, as Bruner remarked in 1970 p. 63: "There is simply no adequate literature on skill development in infancy, and such as there is tends to be concerned with the achievement of a norm, rather than with the close description of behaviour, whether a norm is achieved or not". Bruner recommended that the "pathetically simple" behaviours of the infant be studied. This wish was also expressed by Marr (1979) a few years later.

Since the 1970s the called for description has progressed a lot, yet studies concerning sensory–motor relations at the start of life are still fairly rare. In this domain speculation seems to be ahead of the facts. Sensory–motor relations are taken into account in all theories of development. They have appeared in models dating from two diverging intellectual traditions of the end of the 19th century: *cognitivism*, based on Helmholtz's ideas on the one hand, and *reductionism*, such as Hering's, on the other.

Empirical research today does not always refer explicitly to these theoretical constructs although they do influence the choice of experimental setting and the criteria for judgement, as well as giving the framework of interpretation that is often used. We will therefore present them first, before moving on to study the facts. Finally, we will examine whether the knowledge accumulated to date can validate or refute the models proposed.

THE MODELS

Three authors have presented a coherent body of proposals to explain the relations between perception and action and how these contribute to the child's knowledge of the outside world. Their constructs are summarized in the three figures which follow.

Piaget's model

The first model, chronologically speaking, is that of Piaget. The broad outlines were sketched as early as 1936, it was reformulated in 1947, and received a few minor adjustments in 1974. It aims to show a continuity between the processes that direct sensory–motor coordination and those that direct thought. Its starting point is a description of physical reality divided into two essential aspects: states and transformations. The physical environment is characterized both by a certain stability, due in particular to the fact that it is made of solids, and certain changes, due to changing view points which result from our own movements and the motion of objects.

Piaget's thesis is encapsulated in the following statements: (1) The tools that allow the individual to apprehend states are *descriptive*, whereas those that allow him to master transformations are *operators*; and (2) The former are necessarily subordinate to the latter for only they can retrace the link between an initial and a final state through both reproduction and manipulation.

The operators are built, first through action then through reasoning and they structure mental life. In perception–action relations, Piaget therefore has a tendency

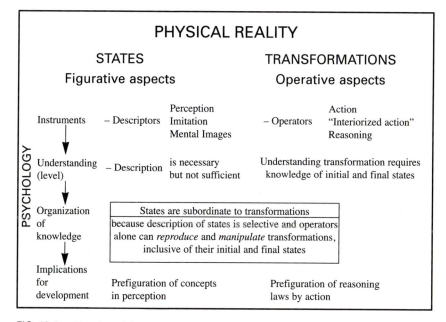

FIG. 13.1:   Piaget's model.

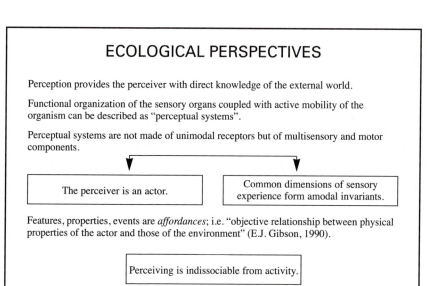

FIG. 13.2:   Gibson's model.

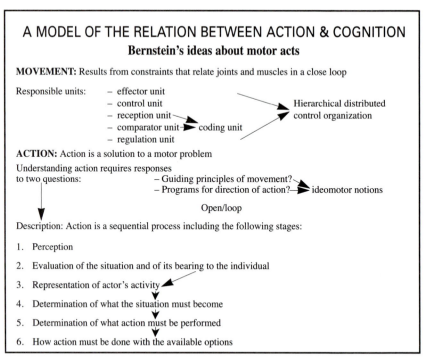

FIG. 13.3:   Bernstein's model.

to favour action (cf. Bloch, 1994). This does not, however, mean that action is organised without the help of perception—Piaget, let us remember, was the first to talk of "sensory-motricity"—but that it surpasses perception in that action is critical for building the operators. In the first instance, the operator of "reversibility" is constructed which, as we know, plays a central part in Piagetian theory.

According to Piaget, the newborn infant, in order to act, has at its disposal only reflex reactions. Reflexes are the source of the "circular reactions" that lead to voluntary movement. Their coordination to perception is elaborated during the first year of life, by gradually calling on the sensory spaces, first buccal, then visual, then visuo-manual. That the coordination of prehension and vision was very important to Piaget is well known. The coordination is established between the ages of 4 and 5 months, and according to Piaget, it marks not only the first stage of the organisation of action towards objects but also the first stage transition from spatial heterogeneity to spatial homogeneity.

Gibson's model

There is no doubt that the seductive power of Gibson's model is in large part due to its parsimony. Three theorems sum it up:

1. Perception is direct. It does not result from transformations of the input, because the excitation of the sensory-receptors, which Gibson referred to as "the proximal stimulus", is already organised to provide reliable information. Thus, thanks to the varying intensity of the light rays reaching the eye, there appear on the retina points of greater or lesser intensity, an "optic array of texture" that corresponds in every way to the physical texture of the source object (Gibson, 1961). The retinal distribution of texture indicate both the shape and the size of external objects. Objects of the same size, placed at different distances to the perceiver stand in the same relation to the same quantity of optic texture. They are perceived in their actual size without any need for unconscious inference to relate their apparent size to their spatial position. On the contrary, the "density of optical texture" (i.e. the grouping of stimulated retinal points) depends on the visual angle and varies with distance. The ordered variations of optic density make up a gradient that gives information about distance. Sensory organs are therefore to be considered as perceptual systems.
2. Perceptual systems all link movement to perception. The precision of the perceptual changes brought about by actual movements creates a sort of "functional equivalence" between perception and movement. According to Gibson, visual perception involves not only the eye but also all parts of the body that can accompany the movement of the eye, with movement of their own. Any perception is therefore multimodal.
3. The individual lives in an "ecological" universe; that is to say, in a world which is meaningful for him and where he can be effective. In the flux of stimulation he perceives that which is consistent with his potential actions. These are "affordances", which should be considered as objective relations between the physical properties of the environment and the perceiver's capacities for acting.

Unlike Piaget's theory, Gibson's model is not developmental but it can be applied to development since it suggests that sensory–motor associations exist whenever perception occurs. Furthermore, it is also useful since it harmonizes the growing capacity for action with an extension and refinement of affordances which occurs with increasing age.

Bernstein's model

Bernstein is well known for his explanation of the organisation of movement in terms of a reduction in degrees of freedom in motor components but his ideas on action, which comprise the other half of his theory, are less familiar. While, simple movement is thought to be organised as a closed loop, in the case of action, perception is involved at two different levels.

First, action requires the perception of the situation in which the actor finds himself. The "absolute" placing of the target-object (its position related to actor's position), its identification and the perception of a context are all part of building the action. Action also requires anticipation of the perceived change that will be brought about. This depends on the meaning of the situation for the actor, and on the representation that the actor has of his own capabilities and on the means from which he can choose to act. At this level, action is dependent on ideomotor thought. The higher the control of movement, the highest level being voluntary movement, the more the programming of the action is in open loop form: "The standard determinant both for programming the motor activity and its effecting and correction by feedback connections can only be the representation of a motor act by the brain in one way or another" (1967, p. 445).

Placed in a developmental perspective, action on this model would require cognitive capabilities (such as symbolic processes) which appear only relatively late in infancy.

Conclusion

Of the three theories outlined above, only Piaget's deals directly with the development of the relations between perception and action in infancy; it places sensory–motor coordinations at their heart and explains their links to cognitive development. The other two theories are simply general models of these relations. The resulting hypotheses concerning development differ fundamentally: According to Gibson, these relations do not depend on construction and they are cognitive from the start. According to Bernstein, movement organisation, which owes little to perception, predates the onset of true "motor acts" that owe a lot to it . The latter require, among other things, representational capacities that use higher structures of the CNS which are not functionally developed at birth. From Bernstein's point of view as from Piaget's, despite their different starting point, perception–action relations are complex and they are building blocks precisely because they refer to cognitive processes.

FACTS RECORDED IN EARLY INFANCY

The experimental study of perception–action relations in babies and of sensory–motor coordinations, to illustrate such relations, has expanded recently with the discovery of early perceptual capacities and differentiated early motor behaviours. At the same time, constraints and limitations of the sensory and motor systems at the very beginning of life have required attention to be focused on specific features of infant's perceptual and motor responses.

Though all sensory systems are functional at birth, in man, none is mature and motor immaturity is even more obvious. The newborn's spontaneous movements appear anarchic, clumsy and goalless. Anti-gravitational reactions are weak and fleeting. Postural maturation, both in its static and dynamic aspects, has a species-typical rate of postnatal development that is particularly slow. The first question is therefore whether and how a sensory–motor collaboration can occur between two systems that are not at the same level of development. With regard to this, advances in neuroanatomy and neurophysiology have provided important information revealing, for example, that cortical structures are clearly differentiated, that some cortico–subcortical connexions exist, and that several neural networks can be activated simultaneously in different parts of the CNS. To sum up briefly, these studies have shown that behavioural responses from birth bring into play different levels of the brain and a number of regions are responsible for sensory messages and for motor commands. Such is the case in the superior colliculus and in the parietal cortex that controls movements in relation to body position. The parietal cortex contains not only motor cells but also sensory neurones that are activated by visual or auditory, as well as somesthesic, stimulation. The former respond more quickly than the latter. Active groups of sensory neurones in motor areas encourage the view that there is a permeable frontier between perceptual sensitivity and movement and that any information picked out by the senses in the external world can contribute to elicit and control movement (Schwartz, 1994; König, Engel, Roefsema & Singer 1995; Jeannerod, Arbib, Rizzolatti & Sakata, 1995). Such relations can be considered as functional or even cognitive when perceptual information affects the parameters for movement.

Cognitive functioning in man is, however, widely spread in the CNS and involves the associative cortices that develop after the primary cortices. Relations between primary and associative cortices, as for all intracortical relations, are established over the long term. Thus a question is raised about the cognitive aspect of early sensory–motor associations and about the control that information extracted from the external world can exert on movement. This question is at the root of the distinctions which have been made about the role of vision as triggering or guiding a hand movement toward a visual target. It is therefore not enough to assess a sensory–motor coordination in order to bestow upon it cognitive status.

Perception-action relations in neonates:

Visuo-motor behaviour is what has been studied by researchers. Other sensory–motor associations, such as hand–mouth coordination, are known to be present at least as early as birth (Butterworth & Hopkins, 1988) and should be analysed by the same methods that have been developed for visuo-motor studies. Visual perception, like all perception, requires the mobility of the receptor organ. The mobility of the eyes has been established before birth with ultra-sonography. At birth, ocular tracking or visual pursuit can be observed as one of the items of the postnatal neurological examination. The vertical and horizontal movements of an object held in front of the newborn's eyes causes a movement of the eyes in the same direction as the stimulus. Horizontal pursuit is, however, better than vertical. It is also possible to test visual tracking of eccentric targets appearing at different distances from the centre position. A peripheral stimulus requires an orientation reaction towards the stimulus for fixation to occur in order to perceive the stimulus in central vision. This fixation capability is also demonstrated in habituation experiments. In newborns, it consists of discontinuous pauses of the gaze which show that the neonate's optomotor system is able to generate a similar response to that of the adult system, even if these responses are neither programmed nor combined as in the adult.

The oculomotor capacities are not taken as signs of perception–action relations because they concern only the visual system. The study of perception–action relations requires that at least two systems, recognised as independent—one sensory and the other motor—be brought together in the production of a response. Pursuit can be just through the ocular system, or it can associate head movement to eye movement. Only in the latter case can the perception–action relation be studied, when criteria for coupling and convergence of systems are assessed. Such studies are thus based on behaviour that does not necessarily need to bring into play different systems for a common goal (Bloch, 1989). In general, coordinated behaviours are considered to be of a higher level than non coordinated ones and eye–head pursuit is considered to be more elaborated than ocular pursuit. Two types of facts support this conception: *chronological order* and the *modes of functioning* of each system respectively.

Chronology: For example, ocular pursuit predates eye–head pursuit. This can be tested in situations where babies are free to move their heads. Before the head can be maintained upright (around the third month), it is possible to arrange for a comfortable sitting position, favouring a quiet alert state, with support for the body and head without reducing head turning movements. In a series of studies conducted with I. Carchon (Carchon & Bloch, 1993, 1994) we were able to show that newborns (3-days-old) displayed some portions of eye–head pursuit. However, it was significantly more frequent in the 45-day-olds (Fig. 13.4).

Not only did the frequency of head movements increase, but also the directional coupling between head and eyes grew. Fewer head movements in the opposite direction to the eyes and the target were recorded and, furthermore a stable temporal relation between the two movements began to be observed. This does not amount to complete synchronisation, since the different weights of the head and eyes makes this difficult. In fact, complete synchrony is not achieved even by adults (where the head movement generally lags a few milliseconds behind the eye). But the temporal ratio between eye movement and head movement tends to remain the same. It is therefore the beginning of a coordination, marked by a spatio-temporal coupling that we witnessed. It is paralleled by an increase in the extension and duration of pursuit. Such a sensory–motor association has proved impossible to demonstrate in newborn pre-term babies, though they can produce head movements during a visual pursuit. With F. Bassot, we tested healthy prematures at 35–37 weeks of gestational age, in a similar pursuit experiment as the full-term babies, in two conditions: With the head supported but free to move, and with the head fixed. As the results in Fig. 13.5 show, embedding head movement does not affect the performance. In both conditions, pursuit is performed only with the eyes. It seems that the lack of maturity of the cephalic motor system—the axial hypotonicity is

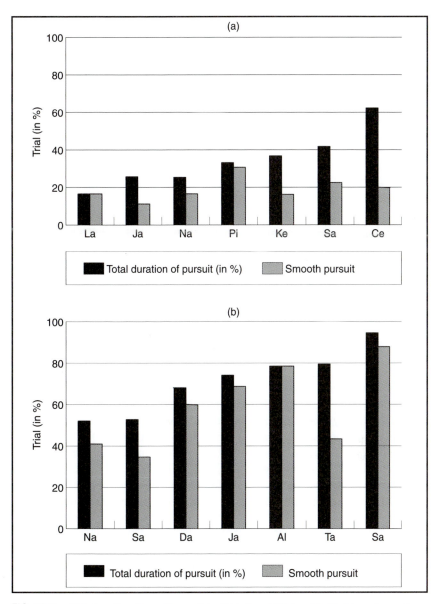

FIG. 13.4: Global portion of smooth pursuit (in %) in 3- and 45-day-olds (N=7 in each group).

even greater in prematures than in fullterm neonates—acts as a brake on establishing eye–head relations. We did however notice that certain fast, saccadic, movements of the eye sometimes primed a rapid deviation of the head. We will return to this point.

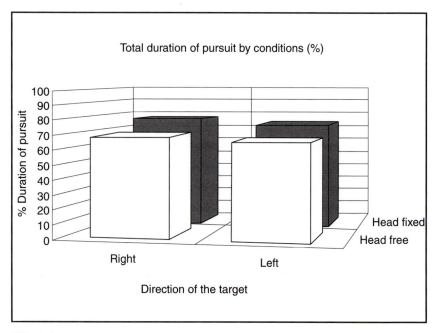

FIG. 13.5:   Duration of pursuit in prematures, comparing free head and fixed head conditions.

Modes of functioning: The modes of perceptual and motor functioning change with age. They make up more or less favourable conditions for sensory–motor coordination. For example, oculo-motor functioning in the young infant has been decribed as totally saccadic, rapid jumps from one point to another in space, of small and rigid amplitude, described by Aslin and Salapatek (1975) as "hypometric saccades". This saccadic functioning may reveal foveal immaturity and a programmed saccadic reflex. Roucoux, Culee and Roucoux (1983) compared this functioning (Bassot, Mellier & Bloch, 1994) to that of organisms with no fovea, which are unable to perform continuous pursuit with the eye, and hence use the head to ensure vision. In this case, the eye–head association is an automatic combination and the eye's saccades lead the head. We observed this type of relation in prematurely born babies of 35 weeks gestational age (Bloch, Bassot, Carchon & Lentié, 1992). In 71% of the analysed attempts (51 out of 72), when the subject was free to move his head, the start of a saccade provoked a head movement. This is infrequent in babies born full term. Full-term newborns are able to perform composite eye movement, with portions of smooth, slow movement and portions of saccades. The portions of smooth movement increase considerably between the first week and the second month. In 45-day-old infants, head movement accompanies the slow movement more systematically. We noticed in this case a coupling of the eye and the head that was precise enough for the eyes to remain centred on the target for durations relative to the position of the target in space and to its speed. In other words, the position of the eyes and the head were adjusted to the target clearly and together but, unlike in adults, this adjustment was not continuous.

Such data allow one to think that a more flexible and controlled visual function than a saccade provides favourable conditions for coordinating eye and head. It also seems to indicate that the task is differently defined for the infant. It might mean that the goal is no longer *don't lose the target* but *see what it is*. It has been shown that in both animals and adult humans visual attention, when engaged at specific locations or stimuli, exerts an inhibitory control on the generation of short saccades (Remington, 1980; Braun & Breitmeyer, 1988; Fisher & Weber, 1993). We may suppose that visual attention in the neonate and infant needs specific conditions adapted to the organism's capacity. We do not mean only the capacities of the receptor system but, more globally, the information-processing capacities. The results reported as follows are here to clarify this.

With I. Carchon (Carchon & Bloch, 1996) we presented mobile targets with only the direction of movement changed, either from the centre of the spatial field to the periphery or from the periphery to the centre. Subjects were 3-day-olds and 45-day-olds. They sat just in front of the central point of arrival or departure of the target. Every subject was fitted with electrodes on the outer oculo-motor muscles; movement of the eyes and of the head were filmed by two synchronised cameras. Using an attention "grabber" we made sure the baby fixated the central point before the target started moving. The latency of the first saccade was measured from the moment the subject had his eyes on the target. We also considered the frequency of the saccades in the central (0° to 24°) and the peripheral (24° to 48°) zones. We observed that the latency of the first saccade is much longer when the target starts from the middle. As shown in Fig. 13.6, the portion of smooth pursuit (in %) is larger and the frequency of saccades lower when the target is moving through the central zone, whatever the direction of travel. Furthermore it is in the central zone that the eye–head coupling is achieved (see Fig. 13.7): visual attention, shown by keeping the target in central vision thanks to the assistance of the head, is favoured by the target's central position. Such a position corresponding with the midline axis of the subject would allow him to frame the target in a system of spatial coordinates relative to his own ego-centred position. Overall the data aforementioned show that eye–head coordination occurs in coincidence with a mode of perceptual functioning that has become more powerful for extracting information from the stimulus.

The first stages of motor development have often been described as a change from reflex reaction to voluntary movement, through continuous improvement (Twitchell, 1970). Although we still have certain difficulties in defining one from the other type of movement, some criteria can be used for a distinction. According to Manning (1972), reflexes are characterized by short latency and large velocity, by only one muscular group intervening, by low and stable thresholds, and by stereotyped persistence if the stimulation that causes it recurs. By contrast, a

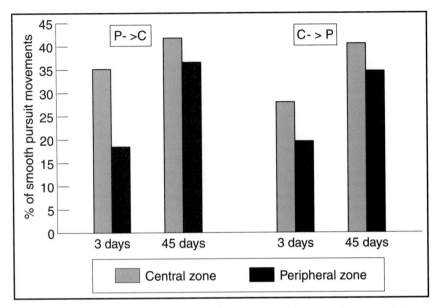

FIG. 13.6:   Smooth eye-movements (in %) in relation to the spatial position of the target, in 3-(N=13) and 45-day-olds (N=18).

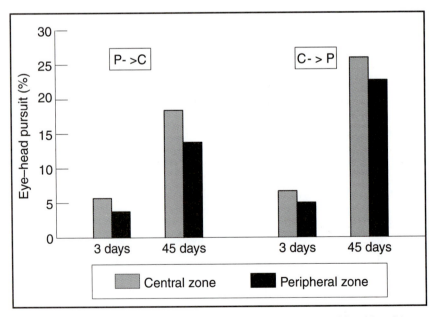

FIG. 13.7:   Head coupling with smooth eye-movement, in relation to the spatial position of the target (3- and 45-day-olds).

voluntary movement has a longer latency, a variable speed and it is aimed towards a goal. The problems of the nature of the movement and of its goal have considerably hindered researchers in the field of perception–action relations. The former, thanks to analyses of the parameters of movement can receive some answers but the latter is difficult to study at ages where neither instructions nor performance criteria are relevant (Bloch, 1989; Willatts, 1990).

The hypothesis of a filiation from reflex to voluntary movement has often been offered to account for the development of manual prehension from roots in the grasping reflex. This hypothesis has been rejected following observations of infants making contact or brushing, and even taking objects without grasping them, at a very early age (i.e. without a strong and global closure of the hand, Amiel-Tison & Grenier, 1985). The manual movements the baby performs when he perceives an object close to him, even when he does not reach the object, have also been considered as a stage in this development. The study of eye–hand coordination therefore appreared necessary to resolve the issue expressed in well-known debates brought about by first Bower (1974) and then von Hofsten's (1982) data. In well-controlled conditions, von Hofsten observed that the newborns produce slow manual approach movements that do not end in a contact but are closer if the baby is looking at the object. By placing newborns in conditions similar to those of von Hofsten, we were able, with K. Ennouri (Ennouri & Bloch, 1996) to confirm and give greater precision to these results. The analysis of manual movement showed that it has no precise direction at the onset, whether an object is present or not, and that it is made up of successive segments. There is no clear movement vector, but the intermittent visual fixation of the object brings about corrections that allow the hand to get close to the object. Fig. 13.8 shows the temporal relation between visual fixation and change in the hand direction. The comparison with what occurs during empty intervals permits one to see that, in this case, fixing a point in space does not lead to directing the hand toward that point. Since, as it appears, the direction of the hand movement is not determined by the position of the eyes, or the direction in which the head is facing, it cannot be considered as a reflexive projection of the arm and hand into a specific area of external space. Rather, it is indeed a movement relative to the presence of the fixed object. We will have to return to the possible interpretations of this result.

The fact that the hand movement has a longer latency than the eye movement seems to show that the triggering of this movement is not reflexive but that vision is involved. In a longitudinal study, von Hofsten (1984) noted that visual fixation of the object inhibited the hand's approach to the object between the first and the second month. It might be that a search for information on the object, made possible by foveal development, is responsible for this inhibition.

Correction of hand movements due to the perception of the target object does not tell us what type of information is responsible. It could be the position of the object—where is it?—or it could be its intrinsic qualities—what is it? The two types of information are not processed by the same part of the visual system (Atkinson

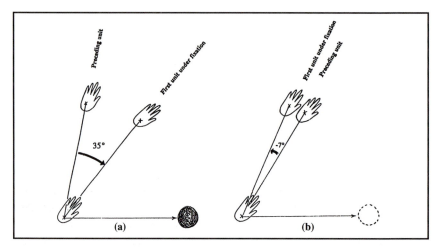

FIG. 13.8: Correction in hand-approach movement in relation to visual fixation in neonates when object is present and when there is no object (N=10).

(a) The first unit under each new eye fixation was more directed towards the object than the preceding unit, which was not under fixation. Correction as gain in direction due to the gaze is 35°

(b) No correction was observed in control trials when the gaze was fixing the virtual place of the object.

(from *Ennouri, K. & Bloch, H., 1995*)

& Braddick, 1989) nor are the motor commands that direct the movement of limbs towards a point in relation to the body position the same as those that govern acts in relation to object characteristics There seems to be a similar parallel between the system of visual localisation and the form analyser on the one hand and the system responsible for axial movement and that for pyramidal movement on the other. The slow myelination of the pyramidal tract stops the hand from taking part in shape analysis, hence the lateness of prehension. In order to check whether visual processing of form influences the manual approach movement, we compared visual fixations and hand movements toward three different objects. The experiment was on 3-day-olds. The length of testing time, which included at least four presentations of an object for 40 seconds each (two presentations on the right side and two on the left) with 20 seconds empty intervals, prevented us from showing all the objects to the same subject. The results are for independent groups (with 10 subjects randomly assigned to each). The empty intervals served as control trials, identical for all, and allowed us to verify that the groups were equivalent. This allowed us to link the different shapes with differences in reaching observed during the experimental trials. The objects chosen were a single colour sphere, a cube also of one colour and a sphere decorated with geometric muticoloured patterns. All three had identical volumes and subtended the same visual angle.

Hand movement and gaze were first considered separately, then their possible relations were examined. As expected, no significant differences were found between the three groups for the control trials. In the experimental trials, when an object was present, some differences appeared in relation to shape: babies looked more quickly and longer at the cube and the decorated sphere than at the simple sphere. The gain of hand movement toward the object was related to visual fixation and was more important for the cube and the decorated sphere than for the simple sphere. These results show that intrinsic qualities of the target object—what it is —are taken into account and therefore that central vision is involved and contributes to correct the hand movement. This supports the hypothesis that the relation between eye and hand is in some way cognitive from birth. The fact that perceptual knowledge however does not allow the hand to make adjusted contact with the object shows that its guidance is first directional and not precisely positional. The direction of reach could be specified more or less accurately from the qualities of object. We observed that the cube was more efficient for this than the sphere, which is according to the Gestalt laws. The information seems nevertheless insufficiently precise to guide the hand to the object or for it to open in an anticipatory shaping.

The development of sensory–motor coordinations and the notion of goal

During the first few months of life, the sensory and motor systems appear to become more and more precisely coordinated and in a less and less rigid manner. Nevertheless, their efficiency, comparing with child or adult, improves slowly as has been shown for eye–head as well as eye–hand coordination. For example, the approach trajectory of the hand becomes more direct and rapid around the third month and it more often reaches the object. This movement is however ballistic, the hand does not decelerate enough and it pushes the object away. This appears as a transitory behaviour which shows that mastery of the movement takes time, even when aiming the hand has progressed. The rate of progress has led some authors to link it to building of goals. According to McDonnell (1979) the infant first acts with no goal and only subsequently with the expectation of an effect. Such an expectation is the fruit of experience, that is to say of the perceived effects produced by the initially goalless movements. The problem of evaluating this hypothesis, which is still not resolved today, depends on being able to detect the goal of early actions. Should manual movement toward a visual object which does not end in contacting the object be considered as a prehension failure or as a movement that is well adapted to the infant's capabilities but which serves another goal? If what distinguishes action from movement is the attainment of a particular objective, as Bernstein claims, what are the relevant criteria? Or again, how can the affordance be characterized that determines the approach movement? In the studies of early infancy, goals can be inferred only from a lot of convergent data and need to be thoroughly verified.

Turkewitz (1979, p. 411) thought attention should be paid "to the stimulus conditions eliciting approach movements rather than to the nature of the movements per se". It is not certain whether we can establish a catalogue of the necessary and sufficient conditions. The importance of conditions does, however, suggest that the development of perception–action relations does not solely concern the development of the motor and perceptual systems but also deals with the situations and tasks encountered. Newell (1991) defended this point of view. Taking into account the conditions leads to questions about the variability of possible determinants. The following example illustrates this. In experimental studies, approach movements are toward objects close to the baby and are never movements of fully extended arms. We accidently noticed, however, in a daycare centre a 3-month-old baby stretching the arms out toward the caregiver when she was at a much larger distance than usually required. Someone less familiar, at the same distance, did not provoke such a movement. By successively presenting a familiar toy and a non-familiar but more attractive one, at distances beyond the reachable space, we were able to repeat this observation. This suggests that the meaning of the stimulus comes into play in determining the act, and conditions an expectation linked to it. In this case, meaning and expectation appear to be due to experience and the approach movement can be interpreted as the anticipation of a well-defined goal. It is difficult to generalize this interpretation to the behaviour of a three-day-old and the "affordance" relation does not receive any validation, in this case: the movement is far from being adjusted to the reachability of the target. So the question remains as to how a goal is built.

If we consider that goal and intention are equivalent concepts, we are led to suppose that they must exist before the act and direct it. The analysis of manual approach movement in the newborn does not incline us to interpret it in such a way. If, on the contrary, we distinguish between goal and intention, we can have a "factual" approach to a goal and consider it in Lashley's words (1951, p.119) as "a generalized pattern imposed upon specific acts as they occur" (our emphasis). From this point of view, we suppose that experience derived from feedback is not the sole origin of the goal, but that feedforward interventions are also involved. We asserted earlier that the neonate's hand movement was corrected in its course by fixation on the stimulus. Nothing, however, indicates that the correction is due to a calculation between the position of the superior limb in space and that of the visual stimulus. Nothing indicates that the mechanism used in correcting is "cognitive" in nature. It is, however, easy to envisage that the organisation of movement, particularly its discrete aspect, subdivided into segments, favours a comparison between the "efferent copy" and the perceived position of the stimulus at the time of fixation. This would imply that hand movement and visual perception have a common frame of reference. In this perspective, correcting the hand movement could have "as a goal" to put the hand and the eye in the same direction relatively to the body rather than to allow directly a better approach to the object. The presence of the object would merely ensure the anchoring of the gaze as long as is needed. The observed dependance on properties of shape could be due to the greater or lesser accuracy of visual anchoring. The first stage in the development of eye–hand coordination would therefore be devoted, one could say, to the building of the means to act, before clearly defined goals prescribe how they are used. The early development of eye–head relations calls for a similar conclusion: its goal, as we have pointed out, can change when the smooth eye movement has been controlled, so the head's movement can be combined with it. That argues for a sort of dialectical process in building means–goal relations.

In line with such a view, while considering how the earliest hand approach movements are segmented, Berthier (1994) recently presented a predictive model of development. His initial hypothesis is that the infant learns to conform motor strategies to his current level of motor control. Learning occurs with experience. The model is one of learning in situations of uncertainty (the baby cannot predict the consequence of a particular movement) with a "variation-selection" procedure that leads to optimal movement. Such a perspective has to be confirmed empirically. It leads us to think that, in the development of sensory–motor coordinated behaviours, goals are defined first from available actions and not the other way round. Only later will experience specify the goals allowed by the available means of activity.

TO COME BACK TO THEORIES

The empirical data recorded at the very beginnings of life lead to the view that sensory–motor relations are progressive constructs. They do exist from birth, but they are not immediately effective. Development is marked both by changes in their status and in their organisation. In visuo-motor coordinations, vision seems to act as the pilot but, at the beginning, vision is unable to overcome a series of motor constraints.

The objects of the environment obviously constitute attractive poles that allow perceptual and motor systems to try out their capabilities. The first goal of early coordinations, as rudimentary as they are, seems to be to ensure the actions themselves as potential instruments and directional, then temporal couplings, are steps in this process.

In doing so, coordinations come to support the acquisition of knowledge not only through their effects but also because they endorse what comes to be known through their own rules of functioning. Gibson supposed that these rules are automatically contained in the affordances of the external world but empirical data do not confirm that. We are rather of the opinion that sensory-motor relations come to build operators, as Piaget suggested.

It may be that the term "operator" has too strong connotations, regarding the actions observed in young infant. However, logical algorithms can come even from early acts that seem incomplete, as for example directing the eyes and the hand to a distal object may bring the object nearer and clearer in vision. Later, when the contact of the hand with the object pushes the object away, that disconfirms this first rule and this could be why approach movements become significantly less frequent up to the fourth month. Such variations or apparent regressions have been observed in the development of other sensory–motor coordinations, such as in hand–mouth coordination (Butterworth, 1989).

Sensory-motor coordinations have been considered as powerful tools for knowing the external world and we do not disagree with this view. Studying how the perceptual and motor systems fit together leads us to think that they also take part in the origin of self-knowledge.

REFERENCES

Amiel-Tison, C., & Grenier, A. (1985). *La surveillance neurologique au cours de la première année de la vie*. Paris: Masson.

Aslin, R.N., & Salapatek, P. (1975). Saccadic localization of visual pattern targets by the very young human infant. *Perception and Psychophysics*, *17*(3), 293–319.

Atkinson, J., & Braddick, O.J. (1989). "Where" and "what" in visual search. *Perception*, *18*, 181–189.

Bassot, F., Mellier, D., & Bloch, H. (1994). Detection of a target in low-visual future neonates. Abstracts 13th Meeting of ISSBD, Amsterdam, p. 323.

Bernstein, N. (1967). *The coordination and regulation of movements*. Oxford: Pergamon Press.

Berthier, N. (1994). Infant reaching study in a theoretical consideration. *Infant Behavior and Development*, *17* (Special ICIS Issue), 521.

Bloch, H. (1989). On early coordination and their future. In A. D. Ribaupierre (Ed.), *Transition mechanisms in child development* (pp. 259–282). New York: Cambridge University Press.

Bloch, H. (1994). Intermodal participation in the formation of action in the infant. In D. Lewkovicz & R. Lickliter (Eds.), *Development of intersensory perception: comparative perspective* (pp. 309–333). Hillsdale, NJ: Lawrence Erlbaum Associates Inc.

Bloch, H., Bassot, F., Carchon, I., & Lentié, J. P. (1992). Oculo-cephalic pre-coordinated movements in pre- and full-term neonates. *Infant Behavior and Development*, *15* (Special ICIS) Issue, 302.

Bloch, H., & Carchon, I. (1992). On the onset of eye–head coordinations in infants. *Behavioral and Brain Research*, *49*, 85–90.

Bower, T.G.R. (Ed.). (1974). *Development in infancy*. San Francisco: Atkinson, Freeman & Thomson.

Braun, D., & Breitmeyer, B. (1988). Relationship between directed visual attention and saccadic reaction times. *Experimental Brain Research*, *73*, 546–552.

Bruner, J.S. (1970). The growth and structure of skill. In K. Connolly (Ed.), *Mechanisms of motor skill development* (pp. 63–94). New York: Academic Press.

Butterworth, G.E. (1989). On U-shaped and other transitions in sensorimotor development. In A.D. Ribaupierre (Ed.), *Transition mechanisms in child development* (pp. 283–296). Cambridge: Cambridge University Press.

Butterworth, G., & Hopkins, B. (1988). Hand–mouth coordination in the newborn baby. *British Journal of Developmental Psychology, 6*, 363–414.

Carchon, I., & Bloch, H. (1993). Fonctionnement oculaire et coordination oculo-céphalique: méthode de traitement du signal électro-oculographique chez le nouveau-né et le nourrisson de 6 semaines. *Psychologie Française, 38*(1), 19–32.

Carchon, I., & Bloch, H. (1996). Visuo-cephalic relations in neonates and young infants. In F. Vital-Durand, J. Atkinson, & O.J. Braddick (Eds.), *Infants' vision* (pp. 249–263). Oxford: Oxford University Press.

Ennouri, K., & Bloch, H. (1996). Visual control of hand-approach movement in newborn. *British Journal of Developmental Psychology.*

Fisher, B., & Weber, H. (1993). Modes of saccade generation and their attentional control. *Experimental Brain Research, 16*, 595–610.

Gibson, J.J. (1961). Ecological optics. *Vision Research, 1*, 253–262.

Gibson, J.J. (1966). *The senses considered as perceptual systems.* Boston: Houghton Mifflin.

Gibson, J.J. (1979). *The ecological approach to visual perception.* Boston: Houghton Mifflin.

Jeannerod, M., Arbib, M.A., Rizzolatti, G., & Sakata, H. (1995). Grasping objects: The cortical mechanisms of visuo-motor transformation. *Trends in Neuroscience, 18*, 316–320.

Hughes, B.G., & Stelmach, G.E. (1986). On Bernstein as a contributor to cognitive theories of motor behavior. *Human Movement Science, 5*, 35–45.

König, P., Engel, A.K., Roefsema, P.R., & Singer, W. (1995). How precise is neuronal synchronization? *Neural Computation, 7*, 469–487.

Lashley, K.S. (1951). The problem of serial order in behavior. In L. A. Jeffress (Ed.), *Cerebral mechanisms in behavior* (pp. 112–146). New York: Wiley.

Manning, E. (1972). *An introduction to animal behavior.* London: William Clowes.

Marr, D. (1979). Representing and comparing visual informations. In P.H. Winston & R.H. Brown (Eds.), *Artificial intelligence: (Vol. II. Understanding vision, manipulation, computer design, symbol manipulation*, (pp. 313–335). Cambridge, MA: MIT Press.

McDonnell, P.M. (1979). Patterns of eye–hand coordination in the first year of life. *Canadian Journal of Psychology, 33*, 253–267.

Newell, K.M. (1991). Motor skill acquisition. *Annual Review of Psychology, 42*, 213–237.

Piaget, J. (1936/1952). *The origins of intelligence in children* (M. Cook, Trans.). New York: Basic Books. (Original work published 1936).

Piaget, J. (1947). *La psychologie de l'intelligence.* Paris: A. Colin.

Piaget, J. (1974). *Réussir et comprendre* [Succeeding and understanding]. Paris: Presses Universitaires de France.

Remington, R. (1980). Attention and saccadic eye movements. *Journal of Experimental Psychology: Human Perception and Performance, 6*, 726–744.

Roucoux, A., Culee, C., & Roucoux, M. (1983). Development of fixation and pursuit eye movements in human infants. *Behavioral Brain Research, 10*, 133–139.

Schwartz, A.B. (1994). Distributed motor processing in cerebral cortex. *Current Opinion in Neurobiology, 4*, 840–846.

Turkewitz, G. (1979). The study of infancy. *Canadian Journal of Psychology, 33*, 408–412.

Twitchell, T.E. (1970). Reflex mechanisms and the development of prehension. In K. Connolly (Ed.), *Mechanisms of motor skill development* (pp. 25–37). New York: Academic Press.

von Hofsten, C. (1982). Eye–hand coordination in the newborn. *Developmental Psychology, 18*, 450–461.

von Hofsten, C. (1984). Developmental changes in the organization of prereaching movements. *Developmental Psychology, 20*(3), 378–388.

Willatts, P. (1990). The goal directed nature of early sensorimotor coordinations. In H. Bloch & B.I. Bertenthal (Ed.), *Sensorimotor organizations and development in infancy and early childhood* (pp. 179–186). Dordrecht: Kluwer.

CHAPTER FOURTEEN

An Information-Processing Approach to Infant Perception and Cognition

Leslie B. Cohen
University of Texas, USA

If one takes the sheer volume of published reports as the standard, over the past 25 years, research on infant development has made extraordinary progress. In the late 1960s, I was fortunate to be among a mere handful of investigators who met informally for the first time to share research ideas about infant development. By the mid-1970s, a more formal group of approximately 200 researchers met for the first time at the 1st International Conference on Infant Studies in Providence, Rhode Island. The latest conference, the 10th biennial meeting, convened once again in Providence, with well over 1000 scientists attending. Back in the 1960s and early 1970s, it was a rare treat to find an article in a psychological journal on infant development. In 1978, a specialized journal devoted entirely to infant research, *Infant Behavior and Development*, published its first volume. Today, less than 20 years later, I would estimate that at least a fifth of all articles published concerning developmental psychology relate to some aspect of infancy.

Research on infant perception and cognition has been a major reason for this dramatic increase. Over the past decade alone, hundreds, if not thousands, of articles have appeared on topics ranging from infant audition to infant vision, from infant form perception to infant event perception, and from infants' categorical perception of phonemes to their categorization of animate objects.

Judged solely by the volume of published articles, progress in infant perception and cognition has been truly remarkable. But what about progress judged by a different standard, by the qualitative standard of whether researchers have made meaningful progress toward a coherent explanation of what does and does not develop perceptually and cognitively during the first year or two of life?

Unfortunately, by this standard, the enterprise often appears to be approaching a state of chaos.

Attempting to synthesize the conclusions of these myriad studies can be a confusing, if not totally bewildering experience. In some reports one reads that very young infants can hardly see, and must be at least three months of age before they can respond in any special way to a picture of a face (Dannemiller & Stephens, 1988) yet, according to others, even newborns are sophisticated enough to tell a face from a non-face (Morton & Johnson, 1991). Initial evidence suggested that infants had to be at least two months of age before they showed true habituation (Wetherford & Cohen, 1973), yet now there is evidence of habituation in the womb (Madison et al., 1986; Madison, Madison & Adubato, 1986). According to some reports, infants can demonstrate object permanence by three to four months of age (Baillargeon, 1987). But according to others, infants cannot actually distinguish one object from another until 12 months of age (Xu & Carey, in press). Considerable evidence suggests that infants cannot tell the difference between small numerosities (e.g., two items from three items) until they are approximately 5 or 6 months old (Strauss & Curtis, 1984); yet according to one recent study, they can add and subtract by 3 months (Wynn, 1992). The earliest age at which infants can categorize is 7 months (Cohen & Younger, 1983), or is it 3 months (Bomba & Siqueland, 1983), or perhaps even at birth (Granrud, 1987; Slater, Mattock, Brown & Bremner, 1991)? According to some, categorization begins with the ability to process basic level categories and then advances to more abstract, superordinate categories (Mervis, 1986). According to others, the pattern appears to be just the reverse (Mandler, 1988). Infants cannot really think, or form true concepts until they are 12 months of age (Mandler, 1992); yet they seem to be able to make inferences about objects as early as 2½ months of age (Spelke, Breinlinger, Macomber & Jacobson, 1992). According to some, infant perception and cognition are two sides of the same coin (Cohen, 1991). According to others, they are totally different currencies (Mandler, 1993).

What is happening in our field? Are we making real progress or aren't we? It may be enlightening to report on a totally unscientific and unreliable test I recently gave to a number of my colleagues. I showed them an oversimplified continuum, much like the one in Figure 14.1, which leads from sensation at one end, to perception, then to cognition, and finally, at the far end, to language.

I simply asked my colleagues to mark off where they thought the major divisions were along this continuum; which areas tended to go together and which tended to be distinctly different. In a sense I was attempting to measure my colleagues' categorical perception of these overlapping areas. The results were illuminating, if not surprising. Those whose research emphasized either end of the continuum — either sensation or language — tended to draw a single major boundary between perception and cognition as shown in the upper portion of the figure. It was obvious to them that sensation and perception were one and the same domain, while cognition and language were, collectively, a distinctly different domain. On the

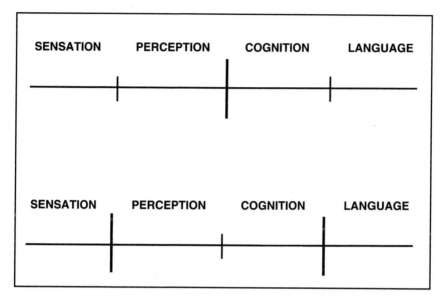

FIG. 14.1:   Possible categorical perception of traditional areas within experimental psychology.

other hand, those whose research emphasized perception or cognition had more difficulty finding a distinct difference between the two. Instead, they tended to draw two boundary lines, one between sensation and perception and the other between cognition and language as shown in the bottom portion of the figure. For them, perception and cognition represented different aspects of the same domain.

This poll of my colleagues provides just one of many indications that confusion about the fundamental relationship between perception and cognition may be at the heart of the apparent chaos that seems to characterize the field of infant perceptual and cognitive development. It suggests that the confusion in the experimental literature may be largely a result of the conflicting and divergent ways we, as researchers, frame our questions and organize the core concepts in our field. This conceptual disarray leads to disarray in the design and interpretation of seemingly straightforward experiments.

But our field need not settle for the sort of continuing confusion suggested by the aforementioned conflicting conclusions. In fact, out of this apparent chaos, one can find at least some semblance of order by interpreting the relevant studies in a unified manner. What is required is some organizing principle or framework for the facts we already have accumulated; something that can tie together topics as diverse as infant pattern perception and infant event perception, infant habituation and infant categorization. In this chapter, I shall argue that a viable candidate for such an organizing framework is the infant's developing information-processing ability. For some, what I shall propose may seem obvious; for others it may appear heretical, turning well-accepted beliefs upside down.

In some circles it apparently is in vogue to assume that processes such as attention, habituation, memory, and categorization—the methods by which infants deal with information in their environment—all improve with age; whereas the content of their information, the infant's perception, or knowledge, of patterns, objects, and events, the laws of physics, abstract concepts and categories, all are pre-wired, modular, and available very early in life. In this chapter I shall present the opposite thesis, that infant perception and cognition operate the other way around; that major developmental changes occur in the content of information, in what constitutes an integrated, meaningful unit of information for the infant. If we, as researchers, can determine what that unit is and how it becomes elaborated over age, we may discover that the processes for utilizing the information, i.e., the mechanisms of attention, habituation, memory, and categorization, all remain relatively constant throughout infancy.

Let me begin by clarifying what I mean by an information unit. When infants process almost any picture, object or event, they have the opportunity to do it at multiple levels. They can process it in terms of its independent parts or they can integrate those parts into a single higher level unit or whole. My proposal is that the primary developmental change over age is in the highest level of information infants can process as a single unit.

Let me provide an example. Several years ago Barbara Younger and I (Cohen & Younger, 1984) conducted a study in which we habituated 6- and 14-week-old infants to a simple angle (either 45 or 135 degrees) and then tested them on various transformations of that angle. These angles are shown in Fig. 14.2.

One of the test angles, A_fO_f, was identical to the one shown during habituation. A second angle, A_fO_n, was rotated so that although the angle remained the same, i.e., 45 or 135 degrees, the orientation of the individual line segments producing the angle had changed. A third angle, A_nO_f, was the reverse. The orientation of each line segment was unchanged, but the angle itself was novel; it changed from

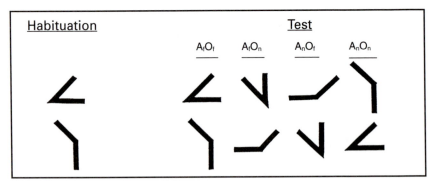

FIG. 14.2:   Design of Cohen and Younger (1984) angle experiment. Half of the subjects were presented the stimuli shown on the top line. The other half were presented the stimuli shown on the bottom line.

45 degrees to 135 degrees or the reverse. The fourth test angle, A_nO_n, was novel in both degrees of angle and line orientation.

Our assumption was that if the infants were processing the actual angle, i.e., the relationship between line segments, their looking times should dishabituate to those test stimuli in which the angle had changed, namely, A_nO_f and A_nO_n. On the other hand, if the infants were not processing the angle, but instead were simply attending to the orientation of individual line segments, the angle should be irrelevant, and they should dishabituate to stimuli in which the orientations had changed, namely, A_fO_n and A_nO_n.

Our results were somewhat unexpected, and may have provided us with an important clue as to how infant information-processing changes over age. Figure 14.3 shows the test data for both 6- and 14-week-old infants.

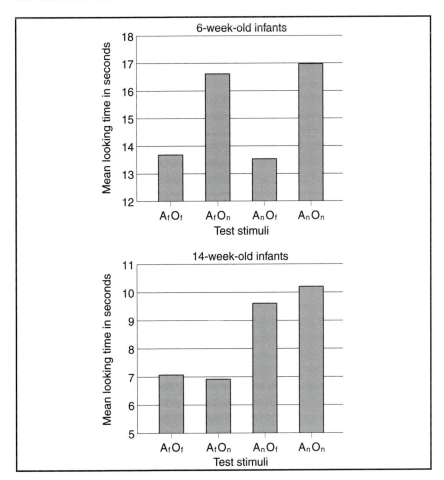

FIG. 14.3: Results of Cohen and Younger (1984) for both 6- and 14-week-old infants.

As can be seen from the upper portion of Fig. 14.3, the 6-week-olds dishabituated to A_fO_n and A_nO_n, but not to A_fO_f and A_nO_f. In other words, they noticed the change in orientation of the individual line segments but appeared oblivious to the change from a 45 degree angle to a 135 degree angle. In sharp contrast, as can be seen in the lower portion of Fig. 14.3, the 14-week-olds did just the opposite. They dishabituated to A_nO_f and to A_nO_n. They noticed the change in angle, but not the change in line segment orientation.

This pattern of results is provocative. It suggests what may be a general principle about the development of infant information-processing. At 6 weeks, the infants appear to process the stimuli as independent elements, as line segments in particular orientations, whereas at 14 weeks they appear to be able to integrate those elements into a larger whole, an angle, defined not by the orientation of individual line segments but by the relationship between those orientations.

As is often the case, one intriguing result can raise more questions than it answers. Is this part-to-whole progression unique to angle perception? Does the progression occur only from 1½ to 3 months of age, or is it a more general phenomenon that recurs repeatedly, albeit with different stimuli, at older ages? If it does tend to recur, what are the relevant parts and relevant wholes produced by those parts? Also, to what extent does this progression depend upon the type of procedure used? That is, would one find one pattern of results from a standard habituation task and yet a different pattern of results from, say, a discrimination learning or categorization task? At least partial answers to these questions are already available and we continue to explore these questions in our laboratory.

Answers to all of these questions appear to be linked. Considerable evidence, both direct and circumstantial, indicates that the transition from perceiving parts to perceiving wholes occurs at several different ages, but the particular age at which the transition occurs depends upon the nature of the stimuli involved.

A few examples may clarify this point. Three decades ago, in a study rarely cited these days, Bower (1966) reported operantly conditioning infants' head turns to a stimulus constructed from a circular disk upon which was placed a large X and two dots, similar to the object shown in Fig. 14.4.

Bower then tested for response generalization to the whole object and to the various parts of the object (i.e., the disk, the X, and the dots). He reported that through 4 months of age, the number of conditioned responses to the whole was equal to the sum of the responses to the parts. At 5 months, however, responses to the whole became greater than the sum of the parts. The obvious implication was that the disk, the X, and the dots were perceived as independent parts by infants under 5 months of age, whereas they were integrated into a unique whole or pattern at 5 months of age. So Bower both produced additional evidence for the part to whole progression, and did so using a different procedure, conditioned head turning.

Another implication, this time a developmental one, can be drawn from a comparison of Bower's (1966) results with those of Cohen and Younger (1984).

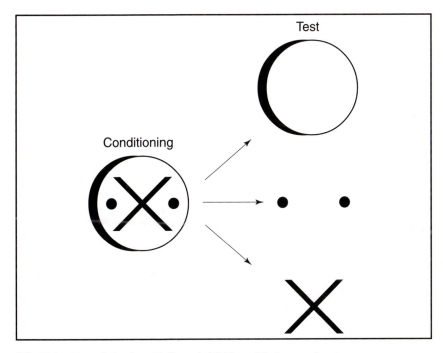

FIG. 14.4:   Type of stimuli used in Bower's (1966) conditioning experiment.

It will be recalled that Cohen and Younger, using simple angle stimuli, found the parts-to-whole transition occurring between 1½ and 3 months of age. Bower, using a more intricate pattern, found it between 4 and 5 months of age. Apparently, this transition does recur at older ages if the stimuli are complex enough. In fact, considerable additional evidence suggests that the period from 3 to 5 months of age may be particularly important in the transition from processing simple shapes or forms, such as circles or squares, as independent elements, to integrating those shapes or forms into relatively complex patterns. For example, Strauss and Curtis (1981) have reported that a more symmetrical, regular pattern of dots can be processed as a single unit at a somewhat younger age (at 3 months) than can a less symmetrical, irregular pattern (at 5 or 7 months). Columbo, Freeseman, Coldren & Frick, (1995) have also shown, with 4-month-old infants, that short-lookers (a characteristic of maturity) tend to process these same types of patterns initially as wholes, whereas long-lookers (a characteristic of immaturity) tend to process the patterns in terms of their elements.

For several years, Bertenthal (1993) has been investigating infants' perception of motion using point light displays. With adults, he finds that if the display is right side up, they perceive a coherent set of dots representing a person walking. However, if the display is upside down, they lose that coherence and perceive local groups of dots moving together. Five-month-old infants show the same disparity between right-side up and upside down dots. Apparently, they perceive the dots in a coherent, integrated way, as do adults. Three- or four-month-olds, on the other hand, respond in the same way whether the dot pattern is right side up or upside down. A reasonable interpretation, one that would be consistent with the present thesis, is that even in the right-side up display, the 3- to 4-month-old infants are perceiving local groups of dots, but not the overall integrated display of a person walking.

What about even more complex patterns, such as drawings of objects or animals? One might well expect the perceptual transition from parts to wholes to occur at or beyond 5 months of age. A few years ago, Barbara Younger and I (Younger & Cohen, 1986) examined how infants of different ages process line drawings of imaginary animals. The animals were constructed from identifiable parts—bodies, legs, tails, ears, etc.—combined in arbitrary ways. We also used a procedure designed specifically to test whether infants processed those parts independently or integrated them into an entire animal.

A general outline of this design, which we have subsequently used in many other experiments on a wide variety of topics, is shown in Fig. 14.5. For reasons which will become apparent in a moment, we have labeled it the "switch design", Cohen (1992).

The two essential characteristics of the switch design are first, that infants be habituated to at least two different stimuli, and second, that the critical test stimulus, also known as the "switched stimulus", be constructed from a novel combination of old parts or features previously presented in the habituation stimuli. As indicated in Fig. 14.5, infants would be habituated to two different stimuli, described as , 1 1 X and 2 2 X. The numbers refer to values of features a, b, and c respectively. The X for feature c simply means that the value of c is the same for both stimuli, and irrelevant in the present context. Also, as shown in Fig. 14.5, the subsequent

HABITUATION STIMULI

Features

a	b	c
1	1	X
2	2	X
•	•	•
•	•	•
•	•	•
•	•	•

TEST STIMULI

	a	b	c
same:	1	1	X
switched:	2	1	X
novel:	3	3	X

FIG.14.5:   Basic switch design: part-to-whole experiments

test items include a familiar stimulus seen during habituation, a totally novel stimulus, and most importantly, a switched stimulus. In the switched stimulus the critical feature values will all be familiar. For example, in Fig. 14.5 the critical feature values for the switched stimulus are 1 and 2. It is this combination or arrangement of those values that is novel. Infants have never before seen an A 1 paired with a B 2. If infants dishabituate to this switched stimulus, it cannot be because the individual parts are novel. They have all been seen before during habituation. It must be because the infants are sensitive to the new arrangement of those parts. In other words, this switch design can assess whether or not the infants are perceiving the stimulus as a whole or only as a set of independent parts.

To provide a concrete example of an effective use of the switch design, consider one study in a series of experiments reported some time ago on infant categorization by Younger and Cohen (1986). In this study, we habituated 4-, 7-, and 10-month-old infants to pictures of two different imaginary animals such as those shown in Fig. 14.6.

The experimental procedure (as shown in Fig. 14.7) precisely followed the switch design just described. The animals differed on three features, type of body, feet, and tail. Infants were habituated to two animals, each with different feature values; e.g., one had a bear-like body with webbed feet and a feathered tail, and the other had a giraffe-like body with club feet and a furry tail. (The type of ears

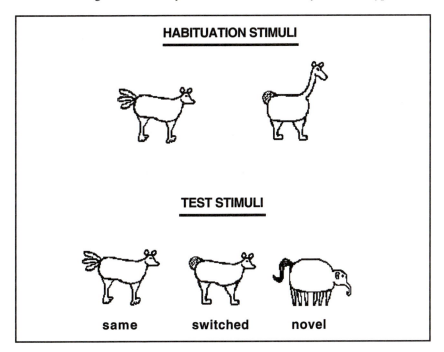

FIG. 14.6:   Examples of animal pictures used by Younger and Cohen (1986).

HABITUATION STIMULI					
	feet	**tail**	**body**	**ears**	**# of legs**
Animal 1	web	feather	bear	round	two
Animal 2	club	fluffy	giraffe	round	two

TEST STIMULI					
	feet	**tail**	**body**	**ears**	**# of legs**
Same	web	feather	bear	round	two
Switched	club	fluffy	bear	round	two
Novel	hoof	horse	elephant	human	six

FIG.14.7:   Application of simple version of switch design by Younger and Cohen (1986).

and number of feet did not vary across animals.) The critical test item, the switched stimulus, was a composite of parts taken from both habituation animals; two of the features came from the first habituation animal, whereas the other feature came from the second habituation animal. (A third animal, the elephant-like creature was also presented in the test as a novel control stimulus.) If infants responded to the switched animal as novel, it would indicate their ability to organize the parts and to respond to the animal as a whole. On the other hand, if they responded to the switched animal as old, it would indicate that for them the "animal" was merely a collection of independent parts.

Our results were quite clear. Both 7- and 10-month-olds did respond to this switched test animal as novel. They looked substantially longer at it than at a familiar animal they had seen during habituation. In contrast, the 4-month-olds looked no longer at the switched animal than at the familiar animal. Apparently for them, the switched animal was simply a collection of familiar and independent parts.

Thus, once again, we found evidence of a developmental transition from processing parts to processing wholes; this time, however, with more complex patterns than either the single angles used by Cohen and Younger (1984) or the simple disk used by Bower (1966). Also, this time the transition appears to occur at a somewhat older age, probably around 6 to 7 months of age.

We have now arrived at a developmental level at which infants apparently can process complex pictures or perhaps entire objects as single integrated wholes. What should be the next higher level in this sequence? One way of describing this developmental progression so far is that single lines became integrated into a simple form such as an angle; then simple forms, such as circles and Xs, were integrated into Bower-type and other simple patterns; and then simple patterns, such as line drawings of a foot, an ear, a tail, etc. were integrated into an entire animal. At each level of information processing, the wholes that infants processed can be described, at least in part, as the relationship among lower-order wholes, and those wholes, in turn, can be described as the relationship among yet lower-order wholes. Thus, each higher level involves processing relationships among wholes at the level just below it. Returning, then, to the question of what level an infant should attain after mastering relatively complex objects, the most plausible answer would be a level at which the whole is based upon the relationship between different complex objects.

Therefore, the next step in our research program was to investigate infants' reactions to a simple, classic type of relationship between objects: a direct launching event. A direct launching can be described as one object moving across a screen or surface until it comes into contact with a second object. Once contact is made the first object stops, and the second object then continues the motion of the first. To both Michotte (1963) and Leslie (1986) this direct launching of one object by another represents the prototypic causal event, and should be perceived directly and automatically as causal. Without getting into difficult theoretical issues relating to the possible meanings of direct or automatic perception, the most relevant questions for us would be how can one demonstrate that infants perceive the causal relationship between two objects, and at what age are they capable of doing so?

In answer to the first question consider the four types of events listed in the upper portion of Fig. 14.8.

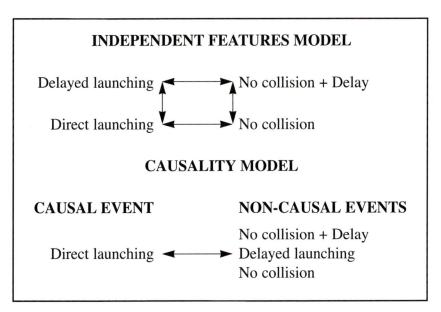

FIG. 14.8:   Schematic representation of two possible models for infants' processing of causal events.

The direct launching (lower left-hand corner of the square) has already been described. It is an event in which one moving object contacts a second object that then moves upon contact. This event is universally perceived as causal by adult observers. Now consider the same event but with a 1sec delay inserted between the first object's contact and the second object's movement. This delayed launching (upper left-hand corner of the square) is not perceived as causal by most adults. Neither is a no-collision event (lower right-hand corner), in which no delay occurs, but the second object moves prior to any contact by the first object. Of course, an event that includes both delay and no-collision (upper right-hand corner) is also not perceived by adults as causal.

How then do infants treat these events? One possibility is that they are not responding to the causal (or non-causal) relationship between objects. Instead, they are treating each dimension—the presence or absence of a delay, and the presence or absence of a collision—as an independent perceptual feature. If this is the case, then, assuming a simple additive model, the perceived difference between any two events would be indicated by the linear distance between those events in the square shown in Fig. 14.8. For example, one prediction would be that the perceptual difference between a no-collision event and a delayed launching event should be just as great as the difference between a direct launching event and an event involving no-collision and a delay. Either set of events involves a change in both temporal (delay) and spatial (collision) characteristics. Or, to take another example, the difference between a no-collision and a delayed launching, which differs temporally and spatially, should be greater than the difference between either a direct launching and no-collision, or a direct launching and a delayed launching, since each of these last two pairs differ along only one dimension.

On the other hand, if infants are responding in terms of the causal relationship between objects, then, as shown in the bottom portion of Fig. 14.8, the direct launching, which is the only causal event, should be perceived as quite different from the other three events. In contrast, the three non-causal events—the delayed launching, the no-collision, and the delay plus no collision—should all be perceived as being relatively equivalent.

Over the past several years we have conducted numerous experiments concerning infants' developing perception or understanding of causal events. In one of our earliest studies (Oakes & Cohen, 1990), we attempted to determine at what age infants organize simple launching-type events on the basis of causality, as depicted in the lower portion of Fig. 14.8. We showed 6- and 10-month-old infants videotaped recordings of moving, realistic toy objects. Infants were habituated either to a direct launching, a delayed launching, or a no-collision event, and then were tested on all three events. As a control, they were also tested on a very different event with totally different objects.

The results were quite interesting. The 6-month-olds showed no evidence of causal perception. They dishabituated when the objects or patterns of movement changed, but nothing about the relationship between the objects affected their looking time. In contrast, the 10-month-olds were sensitive to the causal relationship between the objects. They responded as one would predict from the lower portion of Fig. 14.8. When habituated to a direct launching—the only causal event—they dishabituated to both of the non-causal events: the delayed launching and no-collision. However, as shown in the lower portion of Fig. 14.9, when habituated to either non-causal event, they dishabituated only to the causal event, and not to the other non-causal event.

This early study, and later related studies from our laboratory and elsewhere, have yielded consistent results. When realistic objects are presented in the events, infants have to be approximately 10 to 12 months of age before they respond to the causal relationship between objects. When simpler, uniform shapes such as circles or squares are presented, some infants as young as 6 to 7 months may be able to respond in terms of causality. But with these very simple stimuli, the infants are not confronted with the initial task of integrating complex pattern and other information within the objects themselves. Also, even with these simple stimuli, 3- to 4-month-old infants seem to be unable to perceive the causal relationship (Cohen, 1994; Lecuyer, 1994).

Thus far, I have described a variety of studies conducted at different ages, which together support a recurring theme in infant perceptual development. The theme is constructivist. The infant at one age processes holistic units which become elements in the construction of higher-order units at a later age, and those units, in turn, become elements in the construction of yet higher orders at an even later age. I could have presented a great deal of additional evidence on infant pattern or object perception that would also be consistent with this theme. And although this repeating sequence does provide some overall organization for a rather diverse set of findings on infant perception during the first year of life, it certainly cannot be the whole story. The view also leads to a number of significant theoretical questions. For example, one could ask what might be the next perceptual unit or level of organization more complex than a simple event. Whatever the exact unit might be, it would be likely to involve the relationship between two or more simple events. Bauer (1996) has been examining just that sort of relationship in her investigation of infant memory during the second year of life. Her work indicates that, generally speaking, beginning in the second year, infants can remember and imitate sequences of events if they are in some meaningful temporal relationship to one another.

Another theoretical question would be: what happens to lower-order units once infants are capable of using them as elements in higher-order units? This is essentially a levels of processing question. Do infants lose the ability to process information at that lower level, or is that level still available to them, and if it is available, under what circumstances is it available? We know one thing from the studies I have already presented. Infants must, at least under the conditions of these studies, be top-down processors; that is, they initially attempt to process information at the highest level available to them. If they did not behave this way, then we would not consistently observe older infants tending to process information at higher levels

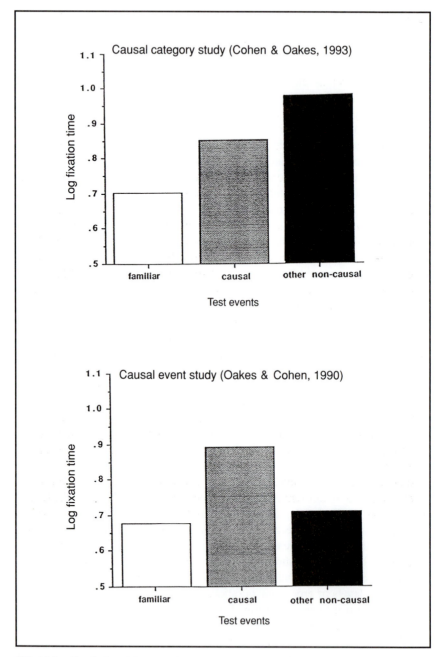

FIG. 14.9: Results from infant causal event studies. The upper figure is consistent with independent features model, whereas the bottom figure is consistent with the causal perception model.

than younger infants. There would be no reason, for example, for 3-month-olds to process whole angles rather than individual lines, or for 7-month-olds to process whole animals rather than individual body parts.

But if they do generally process information at the highest level available, does that imply they have lost the ability to process information at lower levels? I would argue that they certainly have not, and that this tendency to process at the highest level is an adaptive bias that easily can be overcome. Perhaps we can draw an analogy between an infant attempting to understand her perceptual world and a young child attempting to read. Initially, when learning to read, the child generally begins by processing the sounds of letters. She then moves on to words, then to phrases, and finally to the gist of entire sentences or paragraphs. This is plainly a constructive process similar to the one being proposed for infant perception more generally.

Once the child has become a competent reader, however, she has not lost the ability to process single words or letters under appropriate circumstances. While processing on such a lower level would not normally be useful or necessary, what if the child were to come to a passage that she did not understand? What if the construction of the sentence or the meaning of a word were unclear? More than likely, the child would drop down to a simpler word or letter level, and attempt to process the passage bottom-up from that lower level.

Perhaps something similar happens more globally in the realm of infant perception. Perhaps under conditions in which the object of perception is unclear or unknown, or if the information load is too great, infants will drop down to a lower level of processing. Some evidence has already been presented to suggest that information load may influence level of processing. Recall that some 6- to 7-month-olds can process a causal relation, but only if very simple objects are involved. If the objects are more realistic or complex, however, the infants apparently must be closer to 10 months of age to perceive the causal relationship.

Additional, more direct evidence on this issue has been reported by Cohen and Oakes (1993). As is apparent and as mentioned earlier, they replicated the Oakes and Cohen (1990) causality study with 10-month-old infants, but with one small modification: the objects varied from trial to trial. Recall that the critical conditions in these experiments were the ones in which infants were habituated to one non-causal event (either delayed launching or no-collision) and then tested on the familiar non-causal event, the causal event (direct launching) and the other non-causal event. The most important question was whether infants would respond to the other non-causal event as if it were familiar or novel. If they responded to it as familiar, it would indicate that perception was occurring at the level of causality, as depicted by the bottom portion of Fig. 14.8. If they responded to it as novel, it would indicate perception not in terms of causality, but at the lower level of the separate spatial and temporal parameters of the events, as depicted by the upper portion of Fig. 14.8.

The results, plotted in terms of response level to familiar non-causal, causal, and other non-causal test events, are shown in the upper portion of Fig. 14.9. The bottom portion of the figure simply displays the data from the earlier presented Oakes and Cohen (1990) study; i.e., the results when the same two objects are used in the event. As you can see, and as I mentioned earlier, 10-month-old infants clearly responded to the other non-causal event as familiar. In other words, they responded in terms of causality. But the results from the Cohen and Oakes (1993) study show that when different objects were used on each trial, 10-month-old infants now responded on the basis of the spatial and temporal perceptual characteristics, and not in terms of causality. According to some theoretical viewpoints (e.g., Leslie, 1986; Michotte, 1963), this variation from trial to trial in the objects used in the events should make no difference. The causal, non-causal distinction should be just as apparent. However, that clearly was not the case. Varying the objects from trial to trial — essentially presenting the infants with a category of events — made the task more difficult. It presumably forced the infants to process the events at a lower, perceptual level, rather than at the level of the causal relationship between objects.

Thus, the combined results from Oakes and Cohen (1990) and then from Cohen and Oakes (1993) indicate that, depending upon the circumstances, infants at the same age (i.e., 10-months) can process an event either in terms of the causal relationship or, if the perceptual demands are too great, at a lower, more immature level. A logical next question is whether this tendency, under certain circumstances, to drop to a lower level of processing, is merely an idiosyncratic feature of causal perception, or a more general feature of perceptual processing over a number of domains.

Earlier in this chapter, a study by Younger and Cohen (1986) was described in which infants were shown line drawings of imaginary animals. In that study (see Fig. 14.7), infants were habituated to two separate animals, each defined as particular values of three features. A total of 10 habituation trials were given, five with each animal. So, for example, an infant might have received five presentations of one animal that had webbed feet, a feathered tail, and a bear body along with five presentations of a second animal that had club feet, a fluffy tail, and a giraffe body. It will be recalled from the earlier description that 4-month-olds processed the animals in terms of their independent features, whereas 7-month-olds integrated those same features into a single, whole animal.

Actually, this study was only one of a series on infants' perception of correlated features. Two additional studies were almost identical to the first, but with one critical exception. Instead of three features being correlated (and the other two features remaining constant) as was the case in the first study, now three were correlated, but the other two varied randomly as is shown in Fig. 14.10. So now an infant would see four different animals rather than one with webbed feet, a feathered tail and a bear body and also four other animals with club feet, a fluffy tail, and a giraffe body. Of course the animals were presented in random order. In essence, the task was transformed from a simple object-recognition problem in

HABITUATION STIMULI

	feet	tail	body	ears	# of legs
Category 1	web	feather	bear	round	two
Category 1	web	feather	bear	round	four
Category 1	web	feather	bear	antlers	two
Category 1	web	feather	bear	antlers	four
Category 2	club	fluffy	giraffe	round	two
Category 2	club	fluffy	giraffe	round	four
Category 2	club	fluffy	giraffe	antlers	two
Category 2	club	fluffy	giraffe	antlers	four

TEST STIMULI

	feet	tail	body	ears	# of legs
Same	web	feather	bear	round	two
Switched	club	fluffy	bear	round	two
Novel	hoof	horse	elephant	human	six

FIG. 14.10:   Application of switch design by Younger and Cohen (1986) to a more complex category study.

which the infant had to remember two different objects, to a categorization problem with two categories, each having four exemplars.

In one such "category" study, 4- and 7-month-olds received a total of 12 habituation trials. The 4-month-olds performed precisely as they had done previously. They habituated rapidly and indicated by their test performance that they were processing the attributes independently . The 7-month-olds, in contrast, had great difficulty with the task. They didn't show any evidence of decreased looking during the 12 habituation trials. This difficulty in habituating is understandable if one assumes that the 7-month-olds were trying to process the animals as wholes. Unlike the previous study in which they had to remember only two different animals each with a different set of attribute values, the present study required the infant to remember either two distinct categories, or eight distinct animals with considerable overlap among attribute values.

In an effort to maximize the possibility that 7-month-olds would process the stimuli at some level, an additional study was conducted in which infants were not given a fixed number of habituation trials. Instead, they were continued in the habituation phase of the experiment until they reached a criterion of habituation. Under this more stringent condition, the question was whether the infants would now be able to process in terms of either categories or whole animals. The answer was that they could do neither. The 7-month-olds regressed to the level of

4-month-olds. They now processed the independent features rather than the animals as a whole.

So once again, we found evidence that when the information load was too great, infants reverted to a lower level of processing. In this instance, as opposed to the one involving 10-month-olds' perception of causality, we were dealing with 7-month-olds who dropped from processing a whole picture of an animal to processing particular features or attributes of that animal, but the processing strategy remained the same. If the information load was increased by making the task a category problem, infants reverted to a simpler level of processing.

The next question in this logical sequence is whether the same drop-down strategy would be at work with even simpler stimuli, but at younger ages. The answer may be that it is. Recall that early in this chapter an experiment by Cohen and Younger (1984) was described in which 3-month-olds processed a simple angle as the relationship between two lines (i.e., an angle); whereas 6-week-olds processed the same angle as separate line segments in particular orientations. Recently, Slater et al. (1991) has reported a series of studies on the angle perception of newborns. First, replicating the Cohen and Younger (1984) study with acute versus obtuse angles, he showed that newborns behaved like 6-week-olds: they processed the angles as separate line segments, and not as angles *per se*. Next, he converted the task into a category-like problem by presenting the same angle in different orientations on each habituation trial. Now it seemed, at least on first analysis, that newborns were responding in terms of angle rather than orientation. However, as even Slater has noted, a more conservative interpretation would be that, in this category context, the infants actually dropped down to some simpler level of processing, such as differences in low spatial frequency information at the apexes of acute versus obtuse angles, or differences in the degrees of visual angle subtended by the acute angles as a group versus the obtuse angles as a group. Without additional research, we cannot be certain what cues these newborns were using, but we can be certain that converting the task into a category problem changed the way the newborns responded to these angle stimuli, perhaps forcing a reduction in the level at which those stimuli were processed.

From the evidence presented so far, what conservative conclusions can be drawn regarding development of infant perception and cognition? At the very least, we are seeing a picture of development in which the level at which infants process information increases repeatedly with age. It appears to be the content or complexity of information units that is changing with development. An integration of information from multiple units at one level forms a single, more complex unit at the next higher level. Furthermore, once infants progress to that next level, they do not irretrievably lose the ability to process information at the lower level. On the contrary, infants merely have a tendency to be top-down processors. If they can process the information at their highest level, then they do so. But if the task is made too difficult for them, perhaps by introducing a category or presenting more complex, lifelike objects, the infants may well drop down to their next lower level, and attempt to process the information at that level.

If the content of information units changes with age, what about the processes that deal with these units? What about processes such as attention, habituation, memory, or categorization? As I have argued elsewhere (Cohen, 1991) it could be that these processes change very little developmentally. We know, for example, that when presented with a complex picture, older infants will tend to stop looking sooner than younger infants. Rather than interpreting this difference in terms of processing speed *per se*, it could simply be that as infants become older, while the duration of their attention to a single unit remains more or less constant, the units themselves have become larger, and more relational. Thus, for any given picture, the absolute number of units they need to process decreases.

We know that younger infants usually take longer to habituate than older infants. This difference in habituation speed is often taken as an indication that younger infants have poorer memories than older infants. But perhaps the ability to remember a relatively small number of units remains constant over age. The younger infants' lower processing level dictates that, for any given stimulus, the younger infant will have more units to remember than an older one. So it may not be that the younger infant has a poorer memory, but rather that the memory demands are simply greater at a younger age because of the increased number of units to be processed.

Early categorization research in our laboratory (Cohen & Caputo, 1978; Cohen & Strauss, 1979), produced evidence suggesting that infants had to be at least 7 months of age before they could form categories of objects. But these categories tended to include rather complex pictures such as photographs of dogs or faces. More recent research has provided evidence that infants as young as 3 months of age can form categories, but interestingly, these categories tend to be of simple geometric patterns, such as triangles or squares. Still more recent research suggests that even newborns may form categories, but these categories tend to be even simpler. They seem to be based upon sizes of blobs, degrees of visual angle, or some gross indication of object size. So it may be that an infant's ability to categorize also remains relatively invariant with age, and what really changes, once again, is the complexity of the units being categorized.

At this point, one might well ask how this information-processing approach can be reconciled with the abundant evidence presented in recent years that infants are much more cognitively precocious than had previously been believed. The answer is that many of these claims have been exaggerated. When one gets beyond the nativist rhetoric and carefully examines the research that has been done, one finds a pattern of unsubstantiated assumptions about what infants are supposedly thinking or inferring. (See Haith & Benson (in press) for a recent evaluation of this literature.) In those few cases in which an attempt has been made to test these nativist claims rigorously, the results have actually been more supportive of the developmental, information-processing approach advanced in this chapter.

One example is the growing body of research on infants' perception of causality. In the original studies on this topic, Leslie (1986) claimed that infants were built with a causal module that operated from a very early age, and automatically produced the perception of causality whenever the spatial and temporal conditions were appropriate. More recent evidence, some of which has been reported earlier in this chapter, indicates that the story is much more complex and constructivist than Leslie proposed.

In fact, a more accurate account of the development of infant causal perception, and of the primary cues infants seem to use at each stage of processing, would be the one proposed by Cohen (1994) and shown in Fig. 14.11. At an early phase, around 4 months of age, infants are sensitive to certain elements of a causal event. They can distinguish between continuous and discontinuous movement and can distinguish between objects based upon differences in those objects' features. It is not until somewhat later, around 6 or 7 months of age, that they begin to notice certain relationships between these objects and their movement, such as whether a particular movement goes with a particular object. At an even later age, usually around 10 months, these perceptual relationships are organized on the basis of the meaning of the event. In other words, at this age the infants are able to perceive the event in terms of its causality. However, there is yet more to learn, and it is not until around 14 months of age that infants can distinguish between different types of causal relationships, or begin to associate verbal labels with different causal events.

Another example would be the research on infants' understanding of an object's solidity. Spelke et al. (1992) has proposed that infants as young as 2½ months of

---

Process the elements in the event
     Is there movement?
     Is the movement continuous or discontinuous?
     Is there one object or two?
     What do the objects look like?

Process the relationship between objects and movement
     Is there a temporal delay between the objects and their movements?
     Is there a spatial gap between the objects and their movements?

Process the meaning of that relationship
     Is the first object causing the second object to move?
     Are the two objects moving independently?

Process the type of causal relationship
     Is the first object pushing the second object?
     Is the first object pulling the second object?

FIG. 14.11:   Possible developmental progression in infants' processing of simple causal events.

age understand that one solid object cannot pass through a second solid object. Once again, the suggestion is that infants come equipped with an innate, well-organized cognitive system. An understanding of solidity implies, at the very least, an understanding of the relationship between two objects. If Spelke's proposal were correct, it would seriously undermine our contention that such an understanding does not develop until much later in the first year of life.

Our extensive research on this topic (Cohen, 1995; Cohen, Gilbert & Brown, 1996) which included some essential control groups not used previously, indicated that Spelke was incorrect. She reported that infants as young as 2½ or 4 months of age responded with surprise (or at least looked longer) when one solid object appeared to pass through a second solid object. In our studies, infants as old as 7 months of age also looked longer when one object passed through a second object, but we also found that they looked longer even when the first object had an opening in it, so it was no longer impossible for the second object to pass through it. In fact, the infants were looking longer at the "passing through" events either because the first object moved for a longer period of time than when the first object stopped at the second object, or because, when compared with the habituation event, this "passing through" event was just more perceptually novel than the one in which the first object stopped at the second object. In neither case did the data require one to accept that the infants understood "solidity", or that they were responding to the nature of the physical relationship between the objects. In our studies, it was not until 10 months of age that the infants clearly responded on the basis of this solidity relationship. Recall that, perhaps not accidentally, this is the same age at which they also clearly begin to respond to a causal relationship between objects. With solidity, as with causality, our evidence has been much more consistent with a developmental, information-processing approach than with a modular or nativist approach.

Finally, what about the supposed continuum from sensation to perception to cognition to language? When a theoretical approach extends developmentally from informational units like low spatial frequency blobs, to simple forms, to complex objects, to simple perceptual relationships among objects, and then to meaningful relationships among such simpler perceptual relationships, attempting to draw distinct lines in this continuum seems rather arbitrary.[1] The arbitrariness is even more apparent when one considers that the information-processing approach emphasizes the continuity of development more than the change. The units of information

---

1   The same arbitrariness could be claimed for the boundary between cognition and language. Certainly certain linguists, e.g., cognitive semanticists, would not want to draw a sharp distinction between the two. Our own research on infants' labeling of objects (Lloyd, Cohen, Werker, Foster & Swanson, 1994; Lloyd, Werker & Cohen, 1993) and of actions (Casasola & Cohen, 1996) has made use of the switch design to show the same part-to-whole progression in infants' early labeling. Such a progression suggests that at least certain aspects of linguistic development should not be treated as a distinct domain.

change with age, but there is constancy in both the constructive process of building new units from old units, and the top-down processing bias. The processes that select, store, and group these units remain relatively constant as well. Processes such as attention, habituation, learning, memory, or even categorization may change little, if at all, during the first year of life. Placing an artificial boundary either between sensation and perception or between perception and cognition does a disservice to our understanding of these underlying processes, and erroneously encourages fragmented research based on the premise that these topics are truly distinct. The information-processing approach encourages just the opposite. It suggests that much of infant sensation, perception, and cognition during the first year of life can most accurately be characterized as a single domain, a domain that in some ways is gradually being constructed as the infant develops, but in other ways is under the control of the same processes whether the infant is a newborn or a toddler.

Where then do we stand in our effort to understand infant perception and cognition? Superficially, the flood of research in this area seems to have produced a spate of conflicting, chaotic results and contradictions. However, the picture is not that bleak. As promised earlier in this chapter, I have attempted to provide a theoretical framework for organizing a substantial portion of the relevant research in a developmentally useful way. That framework can best be characterized as an information-processing approach to infant perception and cognition. The approach certainly does not answer all of the questions or resolve all of the ambiguities. Indeed, it raises many unanswered questions. But on balance, it is consistent with a large body of research in the area, and it provides a starting point for analysis when conflicting results or inconsistencies appear in the literature. My hope is that continuing to apply the approach and the experimental procedures generated by it, such as the switch design, to an ever wider list of topics within infant perception and cognition, will lead to further insights, and will continue to reduce the apparent chaos in the field.

ACKNOWLEDGEMENTS

This chapter was based upon a conference paper presented by the author at the European Research Conference on The Development of Sensory, Motor, and Cognitive Abilities in Early Infancy, held in Acquifredda di Maratea, Italy, October 1994. Preparation of the chapter and much of the research reported in it were supported by Grant HD-23397 to the author from the National Institute of Child Health and Human Development. A special thanks goes to Geoffrey Amsel for his careful reading and many editorial improvements on earlier versions of the chapter. Correspondence should be addressed to Leslie B. Cohen, Department of Psychology, University of Texas at Austin, Austin, TX, USA 78712.

REFERENCES

Baillargeon, R. (1987). Object permanence in 3½ and 4½-month-old infants. *Developmental Psychology, 23*, 655–664.

Bauer, P. (1996). What do infants recall of their lives?: Memory for specific events by one-to two-year-olds. *American Psychologist, 51*, 29–41.

Bertenthal, B.I. (1993). Infants' perception of biomechanical motions: Intrinsic image and knowledge-based constraints. In C. Granrud (Ed.), *Visual perception and cognition in infancy*, (pp. 175–214). Hillsdale, NJ: Erlbaum.

Bomba, P.C., & Siqueland, E.R. (1983). The nature and structure of infant form categories. *Journal of Experimental Child Psychology, 35*, 294–328.

Bower, T.G.R. (1966). Heterogeneous summation in human infants. *Animal Behavior, 14*, 395–398.

Casasola, M., & Cohen, L.B. (1996, April). *The influence of language labels on infants' ability to discriminate between pushing and pulling.* Poster presented at the meeting of the International Conference on Infant Studies, Providence.

Cohen, L.B. (1991). Infant attention: An information processing approach. In M.J.W.P.R. Zelazo (Ed.), *Newborn attention: Biological constraints and the influence of experience* (pp. 1–21). Norwood, NJ: Ablex.

Cohen, L.B. (1992, May). *The myth of differentiation.* Invited symposium paper presented at the International Conference on Infant Studies, Miami.

Cohen, L.B. (1994, June). *How infants perceive the causality of physical events.* Paper presented at the Invited symposium; Mechanical and Intentional Causality at the International Conference on Infant Studies, Paris.

Cohen, L.B. (1995, March). *How solid is infants' understanding of solidity?* Symposium paper presented at the Society for Research in Child Development Meeting, Indianapolis.

Cohen, L.B., & Caputo, N. (1978, May). *Instructing infants to respond to perceptual categories.* Paper presented at the meeting of the Midwestern Psychological Association, Chicago.

Cohen, L.B., Gilbert, K., & Brown, P.S. (1996, April). *Infants' understanding of solidity: Replicating a failure to replicate.* Poster presented at the meeting of the International Conference on Infant Studies, Providence.

Cohen, L.B., & Oakes, L.M. (1993). How infants perceive simple causality. *Developmental Psychology, 29*, 421–433.

Cohen, L.B., & Strauss, M.S. (1979). Concept acquisition in the human infant. *Child Development, 50*, 419–424.

Cohen, L.B., & Younger, B.A. (1983). Perceptual categorization in the infant. In E. Scholnick (Ed.), *New trends in conceptual representation* (pp. 197–220). Hillsdale, NJ: Erlbaum.

Cohen, L.B., & Younger, B.A. (1984). Infant perception of angular relations. *Infant Behavior and Development, 7*, 37–47.

Columbo, J., Freeseman, L.J., Coldren, J.T., & Frick, J.E. (1995). Individual differences in infant fixation duration: Dominance of global versus local stimulus properties. *Cognitive Development, 10*, 271–285.

Dannemiller, J.L., & Stephens, B.R. (1988). A critical test of infant pattern preference models. *Child Development, 59*, 210–216.

Granrud, C.E. (1987, May). *Size constancy in newborn human infants.* Paper presented at the meeting of the Association for Research in Vision and Ophthalmology, Sarasota.

Haith, M.M., & Benson, J.B. (in press). Infant cognition. In D. Kuhn & R. Siegler (Eds.), *Handbook of child psychology: Vol. 2. Cognition, perception, and language development.* (5th ed.) New York: Wiley.

Lecuyer, R. (1994, June). *Causal and noncausal relations between collision events and their detection by 3-month-old infants.* Paper presented at the Invited symposium; Mechanical and Intentional Causality at the International Conference on Infant Studies, Paris.

Leslie, A.M. (1986). Getting development off the ground: Modularity and the infant's perception of causality. In P. v. Geert (Ed.), *Theory building in developmental psychology* (pp. 406–437). Amsterdam: North Holland.

Lloyd, V.L., Werker, J.F., & Cohen, L.B. (1993, March). *Age changes in infants' ability to associate words with objects.* Poster presented at the Society for Research in Child Development Meeting, New Orleans.

Lloyd, V.L., Cohen, L.B., Werker, J.F., Foster, R., & Swanson, C.S. (1994, June). *Gender and motion: Important factors in infants' ability to learn word-object associations.* Poster presented at International Conference on Infant Studies, Paris.

Madison, L.S., Adubato, S.A., Madison, J.K., Nelson, R.W., Anderson, J.C., Erickson, J., Kuss, L., & Gooslin, R.C. (1986). Fetal response decrement: True habituation? *Developmental and Behavioral Pediatrics, 7,* 14–20.

Madison, L.S., Madison, J.K., & Adubato, S.A. (1986). Infant behavior and development in relation to fetal movement and habituation. *Child Development, 57,* 1475–1482.

Mandler, J.M. (1988). The cradle of categorization: Is the basic level basic? *Cognitive Development, 3,* 247–264.

Mandler, J.M. (1992). How to build a baby: II. Conceptual primitives. *Psychological Review, 99,* 587–604.

Mandler, J.M. (1993, April). *On how to tell a concept from a percept.* Paper presented at the University of Texas Conference on Early Cognition and the Transition to Language, Austin.

Mervis, C.B. (1986). *Early lexical development: The role of operating principles.* Portions of this paper were presented at New England Child Language Association, Cambridge, MA.

Michotte, A. (1963). *The perception of causality.* New York: Basic Books.

Morton, J., & Johnson, M.H. (1991). CONSPEC and CONLEARN: A two-process theory of infant face recognition. *Psychological Review, 98,* 164–181.

Oakes, L.M., & Cohen, L.B. (1990). Infant perception of a causal event. *Cognitive Development, 5,* 193–207.

Slater, A.M., Mattock, A., Brown, E., & Bremner, J.G. (1991). Form perception at birth: Cohen and Younger (1984) revisited. *Journal of Experimental Child Psychology, 51,* 395–406.

Spelke, E.S., Breinlinger, K., Macomber, J., & Jacobson, K. (1992). Origins of knowledge. *Psychological Review, 99,* 605–632.

Strauss, M.S., & Curtis, L. (1981, April). *Infant perception of patterns differing in goodness of form.* Paper presented at the meeting of the Society for Research in Child Development, Boston.

Strauss, M.S., & Curtis, L.E. (1984). Development of numerical concepts in infancy. In C. Sophian (Ed.), *Origins of Cognitive Skills.* Hillsdale, NJ: Erlbaum.

Wetherford, M.J., & Cohen, L.B. (1973). Developmental changes in infant visual preferences for novelty and familiarity. *Child Development, 44,* 416–424.

Wynn, K. (1992). Addition and subtraction in infants. *Nature, 358,* 749–750.

Xu, F., & Carey, S. (in press). Infants' metaphysics: The case of numerical identity. *Cognitive Psychology.*

Younger, B.A., & Cohen, L.B. (1986). Developmental change in infants' perception of correlations among attributes. Child *Development, 57,* 803–815.

CHAPTER FIFTEEN

Stability in Mental Development from Early Life: Methods, Measures, Models, Meanings and Myths

Marc H. Bornstein
*National Institute of Child Health and Human Development,
Bethesda, Maryland, USA*

INTRODUCTION

The human infant's abilities to assimilate information in the environment and accommodate the mind to that information are requisite to beginning cognitive and social development. Mental growth in the human child consists of the increasing coordination of mind and reality. This chapter provides an overview of infancy studies that bear on the growth of rudimentary processes associated with assimilation and accommodation—sensing, perceiving, and cognizing—especially matters involved in stability of mental development from infancy. It does so in the context of a developmental perspective on information processing.

The chapter is organized as follows. First, I review briefly some *methods* and *measures* of studying elementary cognitions in young infants. Focus falls on one mode of infant information processing, habituation, the decline in infant attention to stimulation which is increasingly familiar. Measurement studies of procedural and psychometric characteristics of habituation show individual variation and adequate short-term stability of this phenomenon. Arguments for the interpretation of habituation as information processing and as an indicator of infant cognitive functioning are assessed on sundry bases, including notably the predictive validity of habituation for childhood cognitive performance. Second, I turn to some *models* of stability and continuity, and of the roles of experience in understanding cognitive development from infancy, especially with reference to habituation. Antecedents of habituation are also discussed in this framework. Third, I present data on some possible *meanings* of habituation in terms of sources of stability in mental growth. The chapter concludes with a homily on *myths* in the too-ready application of models of information processing in infancy. Habituation in cocaine-exposed infants is explored, and its implications are evaluated.

METHODS AND MEASURES

Habituation

One of the central challenges to infancy studies is the communication barrier. How can we probe the mind of infants? More specifically, how can we ask questions of normally mute and mentally undeveloped, motorically inept and attention-limited, state dependent and unmotivated—however attractive—little babies? Several procedures to study and communicate with infants have now been developed. One is *habituation*.

Habituation is the decrement in attending that infants show to a continuously available or repeated stimulus. Sit a baby in an infant seat, show the baby a stimulus, and record the pattern of the baby's looking (Fig. 15.1). When the stimulus first appears, the baby will normally orient and attend to it. If, however, the stimulus is made available continuously or is presented repeatedly, the baby's attention to it usually wanes. This decrement in attention indicates habituation.

Formally, researchers have almost universally adopted an infant-control procedure to implement habituation (Bornstein, 1985a; Horowitz, Paden, Bhana, & Self, 1972). Here a single infant "look" is the unit of analysis, and a stimulus is

FIG. 15.1: A laboratory arrangement to study habituation in infancy.

presented to the infant for the duration that the infant looks at it. The mean of the infant's first 2 (or so) looks is calculated to compute a baseline, and succeeding looks are tracked until a criterion of (say) 2 successive looks less than or equal to one-half of the baseline is reached. In practice, habituation is typically indexed quantitatively by temporal measures of duration and rate of looking—including the longest or peak look, the cumulative time the infant looks before the habituation criterion is reached, the decrement in looking, the slope, and the number of looks to habituation criterion. Of course, it could be that the decrement in infant attention reflects general changes in state, in receptor adaptation, or in effector fatigue. In some cases, it may. In others, however, it clearly does not, and experimental controls are normally put into place to rule out these alternative interpretations (see Bertenthal, Haith, & Campos, 1983; Bornstein, 1985a).

Psychometrics of habituation

Habituation has proved to be an important "individual differences" variable among infants. In this respect, it has been found to satisfy two prerequisite psychometric criteria reasonably well. Habituation is characterized by adequate individual variation, and it has been shown to be a moderately stable infant behavior, at least over the short term. Fig. 15.2 shows *individual variation* in habituation eventuating from the application of an infant-control procedure (Bornstein & Benasich, 1986). Plotted for each function is looking time (as a percentage of the baseline) against habituation trials (exposures). From a qualitative view, the infant at the top shows a linear or exponential decrease in habituation to criterion; the infant in the middle first increases then decreases looking; and the infant in the bottom shows a fluctuating looking pattern. This qualitative perspective on habituation is supported by quantitative measures of duration and magnitude. For example, infants who habituate in a linear or exponential fashion require about one-half the accumulated looking time to reach a constant criterion as increase–decrease and fluctuating infants, who require approximately equivalent amounts of time. As can be seen in Table 15.1, the range of individual variation for common habituation variables is substantial.

A number of studies of the second psychometric criterion of habituation, *short-term stability*, have also been conducted. In the study just referenced, the stability

TABLE 15.1

Individual Variation in Habituation: Age and Stimulus Held Constant

Variable	Range
Longest (peak) look	8.3 to 60.9 sec.
Accumulated looking time to criterion	23.3 to 157.2 sec.
Decrement	56 to 90%
Slope	−42.3 to −9.2
Trials to criterion	4.0 to 8.5

From Bornstein & Benasich, 1986.

of habituation was investigated qualitatively as well as quantitatively: mothers and their infants actually participated in two laboratory sessions spaced 10 days apart (Bornstein & Benasich, 1986). Fig. 15.2 shows the results of the second visit for infants who gave the individual-variation data in their first visit. The three same infants again appear in the top, middle, and bottom panels, respectively. Qualitatively, a nominal scale metric showed significant 10-day test–retest repeatability of habituation pattern. More typical are reports of the stability of

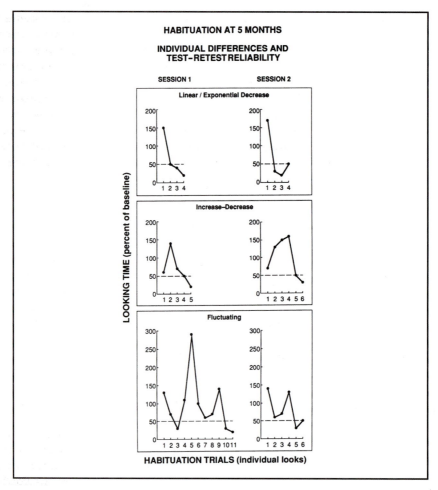

FIG. 15.2:   Results of two infant-control habituation sessions for three infants. These babies illustrate three main patterns of habituation and the short-term stability of habituation. The infant at the top shows a linear or exponential decrease to a 50% habituation criterion in two sessions; the infant in the middle first looks more, then rapidly habituates to criterion both times; and, the infant at the bottom shows a fluctuating looking-time function in each session before reaching the habituation criterion (Bornstein & Benasich, 1986).

quantitative habituation data. Fig. 15.3 summarizes the results of several studies of the short- to long-term stability of habituation. Plotted is test–retest stability (*r*) against test–retest interval (same day to 3 years). Each data point represents the result of a separate study. Tests administered closer in time yield higher stability estimates: day-to-day stability reaches .60. Of course, estimates of the stability of habituation can be expected to vary with state and age of the child, stimulus used, and so forth.

The imperfect stability of extant measures of infant habituation can be explained in several ways. Besides normal variation due to state, time, and the like, consider that young infants may process different aspects of a fixed stimulus than do older infants (Cohen, 1988). Habituation at different ages may therefore actually assess processing of different elements of the same physical stimulus leading to attenuation of stability. Furthermore, only one habituation task is normally given to an infant at any one time, and small samples are notoriously unreliable. Colombo, Mitchell, and Horowitz (1988) showed that the stability of infant performance could be raised by combining or aggregating tasks.

Habituation *qua* information processing

Successful habituation minimally implies neurologic integrity and sensory competence in the infant. Beyond that, habituation certainly represents an elementary kind of learning (e.g., Thompson & Spencer, 1966). Indeed, habituation has been interpreted in terms of classical (e.g., Rescorla & Wagner, 1972) as well as operant conditioning (e.g., Malcuit, Pomerleau, & Lamarre, 1988). Habituation

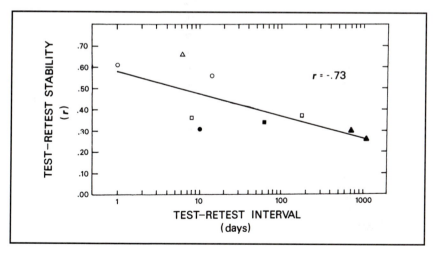

FIG. 15.3:   Test–retest stability (*r*) of measures of habituation duration and magnitude for infants first tested in the first six months of life as a function of test–retest interval (log days). (○ = Pêcheux & Lècuyer, 1983; ● = Bornstein & Benasich, 1986; □ = Colombo et al., 1987; ■ = Bornstein et al., 1988; △ = Rose et al., 1986; ▲ = Miller et al., 1979.)

is also primitive and widespread: fetuses habituate (e.g., Hepper & Shahidullah, 1992; Leader, 1994; Madison, Madison, & Adubato, 1985).

However, the decrement in attention in infants that is habituation is also thought to comprise processes that reflect the infant's passive or active development of some "mental representation" of the stimulus as well as the infant's ongoing comparison of new stimulation with that representation. As a consequence, infant habituation is construed today as (at least) the partial analog in adults of encoding, construction, and comparison with some kind of internal representation; that is, as *information processing*.

In 1780, the French philosopher Condillac described a sensationalist epistemology that in a way lets adults intuitively share in the habituation experience of the infant. Condillac invited his reader to imagine arriving at a chateau at night. In the morning, the shutters of the bedchamber are opened for just an instant, permitting the visitor a glimpse at a magnificent landscape. A second glimpse, or a third, each time would yield exactly the same sense impressions as the first, the impression that the landscape would yield if the shutters were left open. Just one glimpse is insufficient, Condillac argued, for the visitor to become familiar with the countryside; he could hardly recount what he had seen. But successive inspections allow the visitor to sort out the major features of the view, then to distinguish and relate more and more minor features to these, and finally to embrace the landscape.

Our understanding of habituation processes has not changed much since Condillac, unfortunately. In arriving at an information-processing interpretation, experimental and developmental investigators make intuitions about infant mind, and we require of them considerable evidence. The information-processing interpretation of habituation makes several predictions, and there is evidence to support each. It is therefore possible to wire a "nomological net" among age, population, stimulus, mental representation, and validity arguments in support of an information-processing interpretation of habituation.

First, on an information-processing interpretation older and more mature babies ought to habituate more efficiently than younger and less mature babies (see Fantz, 1964). Bornstein, Pêcheux, and Lècuyer (1988) recorded total accumulated looking times over weekly habituation sessions in the same infants between 2 and 7 months of age. As they aged across the first year, infants required less and less cumulative exposure to reach a constant habituation criterion. The second prediction of an information-processing interpretation of habituation is related to the foregoing one: normally developing babies ought to habituate more efficiently than babies born at-risk for cognitive developmental delay. Indeed, children with Down's syndrome or brain damage (e.g., micro- or anencephalia) fail to habituate or habituate relatively inefficiently (see Cohen, 1981; Friedman, 1975; Hepper & Shahidullah, 1992; Lester, 1975). The third information-processing prediction of habituation is that "simpler" stimuli ought to engender more efficient habituation in infants than more "complex" stimuli. Data from Caron and Caron (1969) indicate that infants of the same age (in their case, 3.5 months) required more time to encode information in a 24 x 24 checkerboard than in a 2 x 2 checkerboard. Fourth, if habituation involves processing information, infants habituated to one stimulus should later be able to distinguish a novel stimulus in comparison with their internal representation of the newly familiar stimulus. This argument has been adopted widely, if implicitly, in the discrimination and memory literature in infancy (e.g., Bornstein & Lamb, 1992; Salapatek & Cohen, 1987a,b). One experiment makes the case for the mental representation argument for habituation explicitly. Slater, Morison, and Rose (1983) habituated newborns to a stimulus, allowing them to use only one eye. Later, the babies recovered looking to a new stimulus, compared to the habituation stimulus, when they viewed the familiar and novel stimuli through the other eye. This "interocular transfer" indicates that information about the familiar stimulus acquired via habituation must be processed centrally in the brain.

Evidence supporting each of the first four predictions helps to validate an information-processing interpretation of habituation of attention infants. Further tests of the process as "cognitive" are provided by its validity in predicting other measures of cognition both contemporaneously and predictively. Fifth, then, normally developing infants and young children who habituate efficiently at the same time prefer complex over simple patterns, show advanced sensorimotor development, explore their environment rapidly, play in relatively more sophisticated ways, solve problems quickly and attain concepts readily, and excel at oddity identification, picture matching, and block configuration (for a summary, see Bornstein, 1985a).

Last but not least, habituation possesses moderate predictive validity. Table 15.2 summarizes research now documenting that infants who habituate efficiently in the first 6 months of life later, between 2 and at least 12 years of age, perform better on assessments of cognitive competence, including standardized psychometric tests of intelligence as well as measures of representational ability, including language and symbolic play. The averaged weighted normalized predictive correlation coefficient (Hedges & Oklin, 1985) across studies of populations of normal babies is about .57; for at-risk samples, it is .22; and for all samples combined, .33.

Although infant habituation is far from a perfect predictor, it has proven to satisfy key criteria that justify our confidence in the information-processing interpretation of its nature. Most notably, predictive validity has been found in populations of both normal and at-risk infants of different ages, exposed to different stimuli in different laboratories with different procedures for different measures in infancy and different measures in childhood. To be fair, of course, we do not know whether (or how many) studies have failed to obtain predictive validity on these measures.

It is not unimportant to note that habituation is not an epiphenomenon of laboratory investigation, but typifies infants' everyday interactions with people and objects in the world. A study of habituation in naturally occurring, home-based interactions of American and Japanese infants confirms this conclusion (Bornstein

TABLE 15.2

Habituation of Attention in the First Half-Year of Life in Relation to Measures of
Cognitive Competence in the Second Year of Childhood and Later:
Longitudinal Studies

| Authors[a] (Year) | N | Infancy | | Childhood | | Correlation[b] |
		Habituation measure	Age (months)	Cognitive measure	Age (years)	
Bornstein (1984, 1985a)	20	Amount	4	WPPSI (N=14)	4	.54
Bornstein (1985b)	18	Index[c]	5	RDLS-R	2	.55
Laucht, Esser, & Schmidt (1994)	221[d]	Amount	3	Total IQ	4.5	.20
Lewis & Brooks-Gunn (1981)	22	Amount	3	Bayley	2	.61
Miller et al. (1979)	29	Amount	2-4	Language Comprehension	3.3	.39
Rose, Slater, & Perry (1986)	21	Index[e]	1.5-6.5	WPPSI (N=16)	4.5	.63
				BAS (N=16)	4.5	.77
Sigman et al. (1991)[d]	67[d]	Amount[e]	Newborn	WISC-R (N=59)	12	.33

a Authors are listed in alphabetical order.
b All correlations are absolute values and significant at $p \le .05$; direction and nature of the
   correlation depend on the measures.
c Latent variable of baseline, slope, and amount.
d Sample consists of or includes preterm and/or at-risk infants; testing carried out at corrected age.
e Mean of total fixation time, duration of first fixation, average fixation duration, and average trial
   duration.

& Ludemann, 1989). Babies in both cultures habituated, and they were equivalent
on measures of habituation. Moreover, quantitative characteristics of habituation
at home matched those typically obtained in the laboratory. Habituation is thus
characteristic of, and similar in, infants growing up in different parts of the world.
Furthermore, a case can be made that habituation is broadly adaptive. Not only do
infants assimilate environmental information in habituating, but when infants
inhibit attending to familiar (or irrelevant) stimulation, they also liberate attentional
and cognitive resources which can then be deployed in new encounters with new
stimulation in the environment. Finally, the practical implications of representation
making on the part of infants should not be underestimated. Bowlby (1982) argued
that children construct mental representations—he called them "internal working
models"—of their parents over the earliest months (and years) of their lives and
that these representations exert far-reaching effects in child development.

Settled and unsettled issues about habituation

Like many simple phenomena, habituation is deceptively powerful, and it has been
used to study a variety of mental processes in infants (see Bornstein, 1985a).
Habituation has been used to investigate *detection* and *discrimination* abilities: when
habituation to one stimulus is followed by a test with a second stimulus, recovery
of looking or "dishabituation" to the test stimulus indicates detection and discrimination by the infant. People frequently treat discriminable properties, objects, or
events in the environment as effectively similar; that is, they *categorize*. The gener-

alization of habituation from one stimulus to other physically different, perceptually discriminable stimuli, for example, is taken to index such perceptual organization in the infant. Habituation also lends itself to the study of *memory*. By habituating infants and testing them immediately afterwards with the same stimulus, it is possible to study infant short-term recognition, as it is possible to institute a delay between habituation and test to study infant long-term recognition. Additionally, the effects of age, stimulus, and interference on memory all can be investigated in this way. In studies of *concept formation*, infants are habituated to a variety of stimuli from a given class, and subsequently tested for generalization of habituation to a novel member of that class versus dishabituation to a novel stimulus from a different class.

For all the progress which has been made in this domain of infant assessment in recent years, the nature and meaning of habituation *per se* are far from settled, however. For example, theoretical understanding of the processes of habituation dates back at least to the physiological speculation of Sokolov (1958/1963), which in itself is not altogether satisfying. Theory as to how habituation occurs is simple or complex, but still theory (see Cohen, 1973; Miller, Galanter, & Pribram, 1960). Perhaps habituation is *noumenal* in Kant's terminology—an unknown, possibly unknowable, yet logically necessary mental operation.

Further, habituation in infants appears to relate to indicators of intelligence in childhood, but prominent theories contrast about the structure and nature of intelligence (e.g., Carroll, 1982, 1993; Gardner, 1983; Neisser et al., 1996; Sternberg, 1985) and its development (see later), never mind its value or validity (e.g., Barrett & Depinet, 1991; Deese, 1993; Howe, 1988; Hunter, 1986; McClelland, 1973; Rabbitt, 1988). How habituation fits with these is far from clear. For example, Spearman (1904, 1923, 1927) asserted a general *g* factor theory of IQ, positing that *g* is inherited and universal and enters into all abilities. Fagan (1984) argued the *g* position for infancy work based on stability of intelligence data. Thurstone (1938; Thurstone & Thurstone, 1962) theorized that no general factor could account for all mental abilities, but rather he defined several independent, primary mental abilities (see, too, Gardner, 1983). Perhaps habituation is one of these. Some evidence supports a synthesis of these positions. Burt (1940) and Vernon (1961, 1969) proposed that *g* is a higher-order, more important factor than are secondary ability factors. Plomin (1986) suggested that differentiation of intellectual abilities occurs after the period of infancy, supporting an hypothesis which Garrett (1938, 1946) originally advanced that, across childhood, the organization of abilities changes *from* general and unified *to* specific and differentiated. Of course, domain general and specific domain abilities may coexist. What habituation in the infant is and where it stands in the stability debate are still at issue.

Habituation is also not the sole infant predictor of later mental functioning either. Research has correlated infant visual recognition memory expectations, and reaction time with later measures of cognitive functioning (e.g., DiLalla et al., 1990; Dougherty & Haith, 1997; Fagen & Ohr, 1990; Fagan & McGrath, 1981; Rose & Feldman, 1995; Rose, Feldman, Wallace, & Cohen, 1991). Furthermore, Bornstein,

Slater, Brown, Roberts, and Barrett (1996) have reported that at least two additional classes of infancy paradigms, beyond habituation and visual recognition memory, possess predictive value. These include means–ends problem solving and enabling relations, both forms of causal reasoning.

MODELS

The habituation example can serve as a model for exploring transitions in cognition during early development, as well as transactions between the infant and the environment that affect later development. Habituation studies also raise key issues which pervade thinking about the development of infant sensing, perceiving, and cognizing: two are *stability* in individuals and *continuity* in general development across time (see Bornstein & Lamb, 1992; Bornstein, Brown, & Slater, 1996; McCall, 1981). The two are now discussed with an emphasis on stability; afterward, a third, the role of *experience* in this domain of development, is introduced. These theoretical considerations lead to an exploration of the possible origins of infant cognitive skills.

Stability and continuity

Stability describes consistency in the relative ranks of individuals in a group with respect to the expression of an ability over time. For example, a stable ability would be one that some infants perform relatively well when they are very young and again perform well when they are older. *Continuity* describes consistency in the absolute level of an ability in a group over time. For example, a continuous ability would be one performed by a group of infants at approximately the same level when they are young and again when they are older. Of course, stability in individuals and continuity in a group are independent (Bornstein et al., 1996; McCall, 1981). So, for example, in a stability–continuity model, individuals in a group are consistent in their relative ranks over time, and the absolute level of group performance remains consistent over time (Fig. 15.4A). In a stability–discontinuity model, individuals in a group are consistent in their relative ranks over time, but the absolute level of group performance changes over time (Fig. 15.4B). And so forth, for instability–continuity (Fig. 15.4C) and for instability–discontinuity (Fig. 15.4D) models. Based on work described above, habituation in the first year is probably best described by the stability–discontinuity model.

In infancy studies of sensation, perception, and cognition, developmentalists are interested not only in performance, but also in cross-age expressions of stability and continuity, as well as their antecedents. Several possible types of individual stability can be identified. One is *stability of individual behavior*. Some ability X at Time 1 correlates with the same ability X at Time 2: identical abilities are assessed, and the rank order of individuals within the group is maintained. Another model is *stability of underlying construct*. Ability X at Time 1 correlates with a

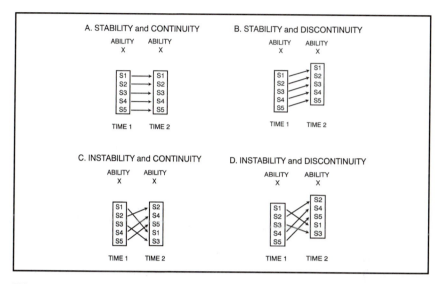

FIG. 15.4:   Patterns of stability and continuity in development. (A) *Stability and continuity*: individuals in a group are consistent in their relative ranks over time, and the absolute level of group performance remains consistent over time; (B) *Stability and discontinuity*: individuals in a group are consistent in their relative ranks over time, but the absolute level of group performance changes over time; (C) *Instability and continuity*: individuals in a group are inconsistent in their relative ranks over time, but the absolute level of group performance remains consistent over time; and (D) *Instability and discontinuity:* individuals in a group are inconsistent in their relative ranks over time, and the absolute level of group performance changes over time.

different but related ability X' at Time 2: X and X' are different abilities but reflect one underlying or latent construct which maintains the rank order of individuals on the two indicator abilities. A third model is *stability of developmental status*. Ability X at Time 1 correlates with a different ability Y at Time 2: X and Y are different abilities but maintain the rank order of individuals over time because the two follow the same developmental function.

The predictive validity of habituation could be characterized by stability of underlying construct, *if* habituation in infancy and intelligence in childhood share common characteristics of information-processing. Habituation to visual or auditory stimulation is thought to involve information processing capacities, like attention and memory, which are also implicated in intelligence testing (e.g., Bornstein, 1985a; McCall, 1994). Alternatively, the two could be related through stability of developmental status, *if* the two do not share such common function(s).

Experience

Findings of stability so early in life can entice infancy researchers into believing that endogenous processes may be at work. It would be premature to characterize stability of any infant measure as reflecting processes *in* the infant, however, without considering the potential roles of *experience* (see Aslin & Pisoni, 1980). Experience manifestly influences sensation, perception, and cognition as well as their development at every level of ontogenesis from cells to culture (Bornstein, 1992). In order to know how and why development proceeds in the individual, it is necessary to understand endogenous processes as well as potential contributions of experience. In early infancy, we can proximally and reasonably embody experience as the local environment and as "mother" (e.g., Barnard & Martell, 1995; Bradley, 1995). The child is never alone in development.

Just as several possible models of individual stability have been identified, so have several possible models of experience as well as their timing, including, for example, early, contemporary, or cumulative (early *and* contemporary) experience. Figure 15.5 illustrates three possible models of experience effects. In *early experience*, child performance at Time 2 reflects the effects of experience at Time 1 over and above stability in the child from Time 1 to Time 2 and the effects of contemporary experience at Time 2 (Fig. 15.5A). Data derived from ethology, behaviorism, and neuropsychology, like sensitive periods (see Bornstein, 1989) support this model. For example, Bornstein and Tamis-LeMonda (1990) conducted a naturalistic observational study of mother and infant activities and interactions in the home at 2 and 5 months. With respect to this early experience model, mothers' didactically encouraging their 2-month-olds to attend to properties, objects, and events in the environment predicted unique variance in infant tactile exploration of objects at 5 months, that is over and above (2- to 5-month) stability in infant tactile exploration and contemporary (5-month) maternal didactic stimulation.

In *contemporary experience,* child performance at Time 2 reflects the effects of experience at Time 2 over and above stability in the child from Time 1 to Time 2 and the effects of experience at Time 1 (Fig. 15.5B). In this model, later experiences are unique or override earlier ones. The data base for this model typically consists of recovery of functioning from early severe deprivation, failure of early intervention studies to show long-term effects, and the like (see Clarke & Clarke, 1976; Clarke-Stewart, 1991; Kagan, 1981). In Bornstein and Tamis-LeMonda (1990), mothers' didactic stimulation at 5 months shared unique variance with infant visual exploration of the environment at 5 months.

In *cumulative experience,* child performance at Time 2 reflects the combined effects of experiences at Time 1 and Time 2 over and above stability in the child from Time 1 to Time 2 (Fig. 15.5C). Cumulative effects presumably result from consistent environmental influences. In Bornstein and Tamis-LeMonda (1990), maternal didactic stimulation at 2 and at 5 months together predicted unique variance in infant nondistress vocalizing at 5 months.

Origins

The facts that by the middle of their first postnatal year infants differ in their ability to process information and that those individual differences in information processing are reasonably stable and moderately predictive of later childhood cognitive performance, beg the question of what the earlier origins of infant cognitive skills might be. Here, stability and the role of experience in early development are telling.

To determine the antecedents of habituation in 5-month-olds, Bornstein and Tamis-LeMonda (1994) obtained several sets of data in the context of a multivariate, short-term prospective, longitudinal design. Naturalistically occurring maternal

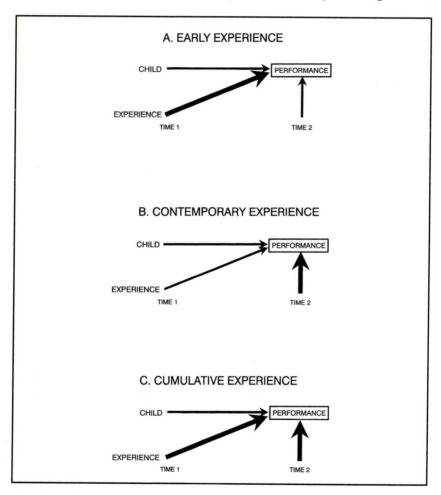

FIG. 15.5:   Three patterns of experience effects in development. (A) *Early experience*: child performance at Time 2 reflects the effects of experience at Time 1 over and above stability in the child from Time 1 to Time 2 and the effects of contemporary experience at Time 2. (B) *Contemporary experience*: child performance at Time 2 reflects the effects of experience at Time 2 over and above stability in the child from Time 1 to Time 2 and the effects of experience at Time 1. (C) *Cumulative experience*: child performance at Time 2 reflects the combined effect of experiences at Times 1 and 2 over and above stability in the child from Time 1 to Time 2.

behaviors were studied at home identically at 2 and at 5 months. At 2 months in the laboratory, infant visual discrimination ability was measured; at 5 months, infant habituation was evaluated. Laboratory and home sessions were conducted by different observers to eliminate observer knowledge about infant and mother performance at other times. In addition, maternal IQ was assessed. Models of stability and experience on habituation were then evaluated. Habituation at 5 months was uniquely predicted by infant visual discriminative capacity at 2 months, and habituation also shared unique variance with maternal responsiveness in the home at 5 months. So, there is some stability in very early infant functioning, and infant information-processing performance is also sensitive to concurrent maternal behavior. It will be a concern of future research to explore genetic components of habituation and novelty responsiveness and their predictive validity (see Benjamin, Li, Patterson, Greenberg, Murphy, & Hamer, 1996); this work is underway in my laboratory.

To attribute stability to the infant and to differentiate among different models of experience, it is clearly necessary to measure infant as well as pertinent early and late experiences. In the next section, potential sources of stability in infant performance are explored.

MEANINGS

The predictive association between infant habituation performance and childhood cognitive outcome stands as a strong endorsement of moderate stability in information processing in early life. However, the nature of the longitudinal association is at base correlational (Table 15.2), and other exogenous or endogenous variables may mediate the predictive association. How do stability and experience models apply to questions of the development of infant cognition?

Exogenous sources of stability

Models of experience indicate, as just seen, that the association between habituation in infancy and intellectual performance in childhood could be supported by an effective or consistent feature of the child's cognitive environment. Studies exist, however, that address (and, to a degree, undermine) major alternative environmental, interactional, and maternal factors that may carry that predictive relation. For example, key as it is sociodemographically in infancy, maternal education appears not to relate systematically to any common habituation variable in infants (Mayes & Bornstein, 1995).

Contributions of maternal behavior and IQ to stability assessments have also been investigated. In one long-term prospective study extending from 4 months to 4 years, mother–child dyads were seen at three points in development (Bornstein, 1985b). At 4 months, infant habituation was assessed in the laboratory; at 1 year, infant productive vocabulary was ascertained; and at 4 years, child intelligence was evaluated using the Wechsler series. At 4 months and at 1 year, didactics in mothers' interactions with children were also recorded during home observations (didactics included mothers' pointing, labeling, showing, demonstrating, and the like). Path analysis determined direct and unique longitudinal effects of independent variables on dependent variables (Fig. 15.6). Maternal didactic efforts at encouraging attention in infancy contributed to both the 1-year and 4-year child cognitive outcomes. However, infant habituation showed predictive links both to toddler productive vocabulary size at 1 year and to childhood intelligence test performance at 4 years *independent* of maternal early and late didactic contributions.

These findings were replicated and expanded upon in two short-term longitudinal follow-up studies. In the first, infant habituation at 5 months was evaluated in relation to two cognitive outcomes, language comprehension and pretense play sophistication, in the same children at 13 months (Tamis-LeMonda & Bornstein, 1989). Mothers' didactic activities (measured during naturalistic observations in the home) were also assessed at the two ages. Structural equation modeling was used to examine the unique contributions of infant habituation and maternal interactions to toddler cognitive abilities. Maternal behaviors influenced child development. However, habituation at 5 months predicted 13-month language comprehension, play sophistication, and representational competence (a latent variable constructed of the two indicator variables); moreover, habituation predicted the three outcomes *after* the influences of both 5- and 13-month maternal didactics were partialled out. In the second longitudinal follow-up study, infant habituation at 5 months, infant vocal and exploratory activities and mothers' didactic stimulation of infants at 5 months, as well as mothers' IQ were examined, all in relation to 13-month-olds' pretense play and attention span (Tamis-LeMonda &

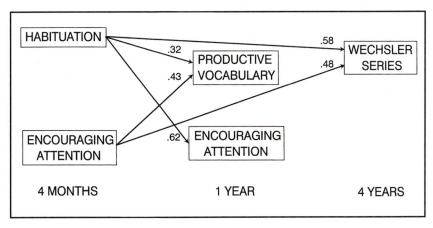

FIG. 15.6: Unrestricted path model (and ß-weights) among variables assessed to predict cognitive development between infancy and childhood (Bornstein, 1985b).

Bornstein, 1993). Maternal IQ was predictive, but infant habituation predicted toddler attention span and pretense play sophistication as well as exploratory competence (a latent variable constructed of the two indicator variables). Again, habituation predicted the three outcomes independent of the other infant activities, as well as maternal didactics and maternal IQ. Similarly, Laucht, Esser, and Schmidt (1994) found that 3-month habituation accounted for a small but significant proportion of variance in 4.5-year IQ *after* the significant contributions of 3-month Bayley MDI, indexes of biological and psychological risk, and parent education had all been partialled out.

External experiences and family influences, both genetic and experiential, undoubtedly play a role in child mental development, but they do not exclusively mediate stability (e.g., Bornstein, 1989; Broman, Nichols, & Kennedy, 1975; Gottfried, 1984; Plomin & DeFries, 1985; Sameroff, Seifer, Baldwin, & Baldwin, 1993; Scarr, Weinberg, & Waldman, 1993). A margin of stability in mental development appears to exist *in the child* independent of environmental contributions. Taken together, these findings specifically confirm direct and unique stability between infant habituation and childhood cognitive performance, controlling for diverse environmental experiences, including maternal education and didactic stimulation, as well as other influences (at least partially) external to the infant, like maternal IQ. Habituation in infancy appears to predict cognitive status in childhood in at least moderate degree, and the source of stability in some mental performance appears to reside in children.

Endogenous sources of stability

What endogenous mechanisms or processes might underlie stability in infant-to-child cognitive performance? Several possibilities—noncognitive and cognitive—have been proposed.

Noncognitive factors. Some mediators of stability might arise within the child, rather than from the child's experience, but represent noncognitive characteristics. Succeeding in infancy at habituation and in childhood on mental assessments presumably requires possessing perceptual acumen and (perhaps) motor skill as well as a persistent or vigilant temperament style. For example, sensing and perceiving acutely may enhance information pick-up as well as cognitive performance (e.g., Fisher, Bornstein, & Gross, 1985). Gottfried and Gilman (1985) found that visual skills of stereopsis and form perception (among other purely visual performance abilities) at 12 months correlated with measures of intellectual development at 42 months. Alternatively, some children might intentionally or continuously seek more optimal amounts, kinds, or patterns of environmental stimulation and experience, and through such consistent exposure improve their performance. Berg and Sternberg (1985) proposed that infants who seek and experience a greater variety of stimulating experiences may be in a better position to incorporate novel information into their thinking than infants with a more restricted history of experiences and, therefore, that experience with novelty leads to more varied learning and improves the child's capacity at problem solving. However, spontaneous exploratory activity in infants does not necessarily mediate stability (see earlier). A comprehensive index of infant activity—derived by tallying infants' looking at objects, touching objects, looking at mother, and nondistress vocalizing—predicted toddler exploratory competence; however, infant habituation did so over and above these novelty-seeking activities (Tamis-LeMonda & Bornstein, 1993).

Consider motivation or persistence or vigilance to be yet another potential noncognitive mediator of stability in the child. It could be that children who possess an attentive and resolute temperament do well at habituation in infancy and later in childhood at test taking that involves intelligence evaluations, independent of pure cognitive ability. Pasilin (1986) found that mothers' ratings of their preschoolers' persistence and attention to tasks related positively to children's performance on achievement tests. Habituation and motivation could share variance in infancy, just as intelligence test performance and motivation share variance in childhood (e.g., Guerin, Gottfried, Oliver, & Thomas, 1994; Sigman, Cohen, Beckwith, & Topinka, 1987; Zigler, Abelson, & Seitz, 1973). Motivation is often included in constructs of intelligence (e.g., Scarr, 1981). Indeed, in discussing both the philosophy and administration of his intelligence scales, Wechsler (1958, 1974, p. 6) was careful to define intelligence as a global multidetermined and multifaceted construct that embraces nonintellectual factors like motivation: "Intelligent behavior ... may also call for one or more of a host of aptitudes (factors) which ... involve not so much skills and know-how as drives and attitudes .... They include such traits as persistence, zest, impulse control, and goal awareness".

Relatedly, self-regulation of state of arousal could mediate longitudinal consistency in the child. As Rothbart (1986) has argued, in order to attend to the environment, adults and infants alike must be able to modulate their state of arousal. Indeed, Moss, Colombo, Mitchell, and Horowitz (1988) found that newborn performance on the Range of State cluster of the *Neonatal Behavioral Assessment Scale* (NBAS; Brazelton, 1973) was a factor in infant habituation-test performance: infants with better state control (those who were aroused from sleep to an intentive state without becoming distressed) discriminated novel from familiar stimuli better.

On these accounts, motivation or self-regulation could be a stable noncognitive construct from infancy to childhood and contribute, at least in part, to the predictive association between habituation in infancy and intelligence test performance in childhood. This general argument in favor of noncognitive explanation loses force, however, in the light of the fact that infant performance on other traditional developmental tests (such as the *Bayley Scales of Infant Development* among many) have proved historically and on many occasions to possess little or no predictive validity (Bayley, 1949; Kopp & McCall, 1980). That is, there is no reason that performance on other infant tests should not share variance with motivation or self-regulation the way habituation would, and therefore, if these generalized individual differences factors were carrying the predictive association, they should do so for traditional infant test performance and for habituation equivalently. Moreover, the abilities represented on standard infant tests reflect sensory, motor, action-consequence, and imitation skills rather than *information-processing* capacities, like the speed, accuracy, and completeness of encoding a stimulus into memory, that are indexed by habituation and that appear to relate to mental capacities which are measured by standard tests of intelligence in childhood (McCall, Eichorn, & Hogarty, 1977).

Information processing.   Perhaps habituation in infancy and performance on intelligence tests in childhood both reflect efficiency of information processing (Bornstein, 1985a, 1989; Colombo, 1995; Fagan, 1988; Fagan & Singer, 1983). Information processing embraces multiple mental abilities and functions: to detect and discriminate, encode and store, retrieve and recognize, and compare stimulus information. Thus, infants who habituate efficiently (who require briefer attention deployment to repeated or unchanging stimulation) are infants who scan and pick up information efficiently, assimilate information quickly, and/or construct memory engrams easily and faithfully. Children who solve the perceptual, language, abstract reasoning, and memory tasks that are assessed on childhood intelligence tests do likewise (Bjorklund & Schneider, 1996; Deary, 1995; Detterman, 1987a, b; McCall, 1994; Nettelbeck, 1987; Vernon, 1987).

The primary interpretation of habituation is in terms of *information-processing* efficiency: the speed, accuracy, and completeness of assimilating and accommodating environmental stimulation. Many infant procedures as well as child (and adult) IQ tests turn on just such performance processes. That is, IQ presumably reflects efficiency of information processing (Campione, Brown, & Ferrara, 1982; Cooper & Regan, 1986; Deary, 1995) and mental representation skills (Hunt, 1983), among other characteristics.

In turn, several different possible mechanisms could contribute to individual variation in information-processing efficiency (see Colombo, 1995). First, processing information could depend on some combination of attention and temperament. If, for example, some infants are poorly self-regulated or easily arousable, and information processing is inhibited by poor self-regulation or high arousal level, those factors would consistently interfere with performance. Gardner and Karmel (1983) observed that infants look at more intense visual stimuli when they are less aroused and at less intense visual stimuli when they are highly aroused. Thus, infants exhibit a tendency to approach or avoid environmental information as a reflection of both level of arousal and characteristics of the stimulation.

Second, the child's knowledge base, grounded in experience with varied kinds of stimulation and information, could contribute to information-processing performance (see, e.g., Bjorklund & Schneider, 1996; Ceci, 1990). Infants and children who know more possess more sophisticated cognitive schemas to which they can assimilate, learn, and remember new information more readily.

Last, it could be that individual differences in information processing reflect individual differences in some aspect of central nervous system functioning, such as speed of neurotransmission, which in infancy might in turn depend on myelinization, extent of dendritic branching, and neurochemical or biophysical parameters (see Colombo, 1995). In general, more mature nervous systems habituate more quickly than do immature nervous systems (Bergström, 1969; Graham, Anthony, & Zeigler, 1983). Pure information-processing capacity correlates with adult IQ in the range of -.30 to - .50 (Eysenck, 1987; Jensen, 1992; Vernon, 1987; see, too, Lehrl & Fischer, 1990). Speed of processing is a pervasive individual differences factor and underlies various aspects of childhood cognition (see also Hale, 1990; Kail, 1986, 1988, 1991). Nettelbeck (1987) and Anderson (1992), among others (Jensen, 1992), have speculated on the association between measures of information processing and IQ test performance. For example, Nettelbeck and Young (1989, 1990) confirmed a correlation in 6- and 7-year-olds between IQ and inspection time (accuracy in a two-choice visual discrimination task using a tachistoscopic threshold masking procedure). Of course, individual variation in processing speed may help to account for variation in childhood IQ (Nettelbeck, 1987), but differences in speed may still not sufficiently explain differences in intelligence. That is, processing speed may be "necessary for the appropriate development of intellectual aptitudes but not sufficient to determine them" (Nettelbeck & Wilson, 1994, p. 279). However, in a developmental study of 7- to 19-year-olds, Fry and Hale (1996) showed that individual differences in speed of information processing exerted a direct effect on working memory capacity which in turn was a direct determinant of individual differences in analytical or fluid intelligence. Cognitive development appears to represent a "cascade" wherein age-related changes in processing speed effect changes in working memory that enhance analytical intelligence (Kail, 1991, 1992; Kail & Park, 1992; Kail & Salthouse, 1994).

Thus, some infants process information in the habituation paradigm more quickly, needing to look less and reaching an habituation criterion more efficiently, and those same children tend to process information in tests of cognition and intelligence and perform well in them (Anderson, 1992; Bornstein 1985b; Colombo & Mitchell, 1988, 1991; Slater, 1995). Sigman et al. (1991) found that newborns' fixation length predicted children's span of apprehension at 12 years, a speed-of-processing task in which pre-adolescents had to say whether or not a target was present in a tachistoscopically presented array. Rose and Feldman (1995) examined relations between infant visual recognition memory and child performance at 11 years in a *Specific Cognitive Abilities* test (SCA: Cyphers, Fulker, Plomin, & DeFries, 1989; Thompson, Detterman, & Plomin, 1991). They found that nearly all their infancy measures related to the assessment perceptual speed. Finally, "short-looking" infants engage in more extensive stimulus scanning, whereas "long-looking" infants tend to focus for prolonged periods on parts of stimuli (Bronson, 1991). Freeseman, Colombo, and Coldren (1993) first identified

4-month-olds as short-lookers or long-lookers on the basis of their habituation performance and then tested the same children in visual discrimination tasks. They found that long-looking infants differed in the speed and nature of their information processing from short-looking infants: Short-looking infants required less familiarization with a stimulus to demonstrate a preference for a new stimulus, whereas long-looking infants needed more time to process the original stimulus information. Short-looking infants began by attending to global features and then moved to examine local features as exposure duration increased, a pattern of attention allocation that is commonly employed by adults. By contrast, long-looking infants focused on local elements during familiarization beyond the time required for discrimination of global features (Colombo, Freeseman, Coldren, & Frick, 1995). Short-looking infants also recognized perceptually degraded forms quickly, which long-looking infants required more time to do (Frick & Colombo, 1996).

Related processes.   It has been argued that the infant's ability to *inhibit attention* to uninformative stimulation underlies cognitive stability (McCall, 1994; McCall & Mash, 1995). Thus, infants who attend only briefly to already familiar stimulation, and children who perform well on intelligence tests, both more quickly detect repetitive or irrelevant information and turn their attention away from it and towards new and more informative stimulation. This view posits that superior mental performance and stability reflect the ability of infants, children, and adults to inhibit attention and action. Case (1985) showed that a strategy that directs the person to attend to only goal-relevant, and reciprocally to disregard redundant, information may increase dramatically the probability of success on working memory tasks. Children's performance in a variety of cognitive domains (including verbal self-regulation, lexical and discourse processing, and memory) can be accounted for, at least in part, by their improving ability to so inhibit attention (Dempster & Brainerd, 1995). In their longitudinal project, Sigman et al. (1991) included two verbal analogy tasks in which a pre-cue was presented that consisted of novel information either relevant or irrelevant to solving a problem. The strongest longitudinal predictions to emerge obtained between attention in infancy on the one hand and, on the other, 12-year IQ and the child's ability to inhibit attention to irrelevant novelty.

Perhaps, however, inhibition is a linked process to habituation; habituation reflects becoming familiar with a piece of stimulation, and inhibition is turning away from that same increasingly familiar stimulation. Indeed, Dempster (1991) argued that mature intelligence is typically characterized in terms of speed of information processing, the quality or quantity of information represented, executive processes, and processing capacity, but that it cannot be understood without reference to reciprocal inhibitory processes as well.

Relatedly, *memory* abilities could underlie both the infant and child/adult measures, and consistency in memory mediate developmental stability between them (Colombo, 1993; Larson & Alderton, 1990). Measures of memory in the first year predict IQ at 2–3 years of age (e.g., Fagen & Ohr, 1990). Habituation and memory appear to be integrally linked, as are memory and child and adult intelligence and cognitive performance. Jacobson et al. (1992) factor analyzed a battery of infant measures including reaction time, anticipation, fixation duration, novelty preference, elicited play, and *Bayley Scales* performance. One factor for processing speed emerged, and another for memory/attention. Later, Colombo (1993) hypothesized that these two factors are the principal ones underlying stability of cognition from infancy to childhood. However, Fry and Hale (1996), in the study cited earlier, disentangled causal influences and placed processing speed at the start of the mental cascade.

In summary, several possible related threads to the fabric of individual stability in child mental development have been woven, and many factors are found to contribute to mental development in the child. These include efficiency of information processing, attention inhibition, memory skills, motivation and persistence, as well as supportive experience. Although it is parsimonious to believe that a single mechanism underlies stable performance, that clearly need not be the case. There is nothing to say that this list of processes is exhaustive, or that these processes themselves are mutually exclusive. Nonetheless, significant, if moderate, stability lies in the child, above the contribution of the environment, and that stability is not simply or solely dependent on exploratory activity or noncognitive factors in the child. Each mechanism has some face validity and supporting empirical evidence, but each also begs penetrating questions and raises unresolved issues. If they are mediating processes, what underlies their commonality? Is each equally applicable to explaining the connection between the several infant predictors and the several child outcomes? These findings articulate with other arguments that support an information-processing interpretation of habituation—even if habituation is *not* information processing all the time. At base, prevailing empirical results substantiate a view of mental development across childhood that incorporates the notion of individual consistency. However, findings about habituation simultaneously point to potential myths in the meanings (in this case, *over-interpretation*) of prediction.

MYTHS

When children who were exposed to cocaine *in utero* first reached school age in the US, social response was uniformly grave. The problem is large and compelling. In many inner-city populations nearly 50% of women giving birth report or test positive for cocaine use at the time of delivery (Amaro, Fried, Cabral, & Zuckerman, 1990; Osterloh & Lee, 1989), and national estimates suggest that 10 to 20% of all infants born in the US are exposed to cocaine prenatally (Chasnoff, Landress, & Barrett, 1990).

Theory and research suggest relations between disturbances in orientation, attention, information processing, learning, and memory and prenatal cocaine exposure (see, e.g., Alessandri, Sullivan, Imaizumi, & Lewis, 1993; Bornstein, Mayes, & Tamis-LeMonda, 1996; Struthers & Hansen, 1992). For example adult rodent offspring exposed to cocaine prenatally exhibit a number of different apparently cocaine-related neurobehavioral sequelae, including notably impaired habituation (Heyser et al., 1994). Cocaine affects those areas of the brain that are involved in the regulation of states of attention (Mayes, 1994) by blocking the reuptake of monoaminergic neurotransmitters at the presynaptic neural junction (Gawin & Ellinwood, 1988; Kosten, 1990; Swann, 1990). Blocking reuptake leaves more dopamine, norepinephrine, and serotonin available within the synaptic space and results in both enhanced activity of these agents in the CNS and physiological reactions and behaviors. (The exaggerated alertness seen with cocaine use is believed to relate to specific effects of cocaine on the norepinephrine system; Richie & Greene, 1985.) Human infants exposed to cocaine prenatally exhibit increased norepinephrine levels in cerebrospinal fluid (Mirochnick et al., 1991). The norepinephrine system plays a role in the regulation of states of arousal, and in turn the maintenance of attention (Karmel, Gardner, & Magnano, 1991; Posner & Petersen, 1990; Rothbart & Posner, 1985). In this connection, Lidow (1995) has reported that, in rhesus monkeys, intermittent prenatal cocaine exposure resulted in cerebral cortices with highly abnormal structural characteristics, including disrupted cortical laminar architecture with an increased number of cells in the underlying white matter suggesting impaired neuronal migration. These findings may reflect disrupted monoaminergic system regulated processes that control cell differentiation and migration. Prenatal cocaine exposure also results in vasoconstriction of blood vessels in placenta and fetus (Moore, Sorg, Miller, Key, & Resnik, 1986). Repeated prenatal cocaine exposure eventuates in chronic fetal hypoxemia and decreased nutrient transfer (Woods, Plessinger, & Clark, 1987), and diminished blood flow would have deleterious consequences for fetal growth (Zuckerman, Frank, Hingson, & Amaro, 1989).

To be sure, infants exposed prenatally to cocaine are also typically exposed to other prenatal and postnatal risk factors that can impair development. Pregnant women who abuse cocaine also typically expose their fetuses to other substances of abuse (alcohol, tobacco, opiates, marijuana, and amphetamines), and they have pregnancies complicated by preterm delivery and intrauterine growth retardation. Postnatally, infants priorly exposed to cocaine often continue to be exposed to parental substance abuse, they are more frequently neglected and abused, and they have parents with more depressive symptomatology and higher overall stress and anxiety (Mayes, 1995). Any one or all of these factors may adversely influence the development of infant information processing.

For these reasons, we prospectively studied habituation in babies exposed to cocaine *in utero* and in a group of sociodemographically matched, drug-free controls. We tested *all* babies blind to drug exposure status, and or analyses controlled for maternal sociodemographic and systemic infant perinatal differences. In our first study of newborn performance on the Brazelton (1973) NBAS, relative to matched controls, cocaine-exposed babies showed depressed performance on all clusters, but they performed significantly worse on the habituation cluster (Mayes, Granger, Frank, Schottenfeld, & Bornstein, 1993). These findings supported our initial hypotheses about the detrimental effects of cocaine on very early information processing.

In a second study, we tested babies at 3 months of age to determine the effects of prenatal cocaine exposure directly on infant-control habituation (Mayes, Bornstein, Chawarska, & Granger, 1995). Surprisingly, the majority of infants in cocaine-exposed and -free groups reached an habituation criterion, and among infants who did, no significant group differences emerged in habituation (or in recovery to a subsequent novel stimulus). However, compared to the control group, infants exposed prenatally to cocaine were significantly more likely to fail to start the habituation procedure, and, those who did were significantly more likely to react with irritability at the start of the procedure. Perhaps the effects of cocaine on infant performance are not solely or exclusively "cognitive" in nature. Common to both the neurotransmitter reuptake and vasoconstriction effects of cocaine on infants is the dysregulation of state of arousal. Novel stimulation increases arousal and the regulation of arousal gates orientation and attention and thus, information processing, learning, and memory (Posner & Petersen, 1990; Rothbart & Posner, 1985).

In order to examine arousal regulation and its effects in cocaine-exposed infants, we standardized a "novel-repeat" laboratory procedure to evaluate infants coping with consistent novelty (Mayes, Bornstein, Chawarska, & Granger, 1995). We studied affective expressions and behavioral states in 3-month-olds who were cocaine-exposed or -free. Infants exposed prenatally to cocaine were more likely to display negative affect and less likely to exhibit positive affect; they were also more likely than drug-free infants to exhibit a crying state in reaction to a novel stimulus. Notably, Azuma and Chasnov (1993) reported poor task persistence and increased irritability and distractability among cocaine-exposed 3-year-olds who participated in standardized testing.

You never know with young infants when you start what you are going to find. We were moved by these data away from an information-processing prediction of cocaine effects to one concerned with arousal regulation. All drug-exposed babies may *not* be disadvantaged in terms of information processing *per se*: drug-exposed babies who completed habituation did not differ in their information-processing characteristics from drug-free babies growing up in relatively similar socioeconomic conditions. However, our testing revealed an arousal regulation problem in cocaine-exposed babies. In turn, impairments in self-regulation of arousal need to be considered in terms of their own predictive implications for children's social and cognitive development.

Obviously, too, these unexpected findings reinforce concerns about specifying sources of influence—beyond experience—when making deductions about perceptuocognitive performance from the newborn period and early infancy.

CONCLUSIONS

Concerning the development of cognition, I have reviewed some methods, measures, models, meanings, and myths. A central issue in developmental study is evaluation of forces bound up in ontogenetic advance. Central to understanding developmental advance is recognizing the contributions of infant *and* of experience, as well as their transaction. In this chapter, I have indicated some ways in which these two principal forces jointly contribute to developmental outcome. Notably, infants appear to bring substantial individuality of ability to their own development. Indeed, research indicates moderate predictive validity in individual cognitive development, whether in habituation, responsiveness to novelty, or understanding causal relations.

At the same time, experiences in the environment, often embodied for infants in parents, also contribute to children's earliest cognitive growth. How transactions between the child and parent begin and evolve, the nature of their distribution and sequential structure, what their psychophysiological underpinnings may be, what their consequences are, and how their positive effects may be facilitated in the dyad as a boon to the child, represent critical and perennial research questions in human development. A multivariate and transactional approach, such as described in this program of research, promises a more comprehensive characterization of the antecedents in infancy of childhood cognitive competencies.

Infancy is a starting point of life. Infancy may also represent a critical setting point in the life of the child. At minimum, this research lends some scientific credence to Milton's observation in *Paradise Regained* (IV, 220), that: "the childhood shows the man."

ACKNOWLEDGEMENTS

This chapter summarizes selected aspects of my research, and portions of the text appear in previous scientific publications. I thank H. Bornstein, O. M. Haynes, A. Herron, L. Mayes, C. S. Tamis-LeMonda, and B. Wright.

REFERENCES

Alessandri, S.M., Sullivan, M.W., Imaizumi, S., & Lewis, M. (1993). Learning and emotional responsivity in cocaine-exposed infants. *Developmental Psychology, 29*, 989–997.

Amaro, H., Fried, L.E., Cabral, H., & Zuckerman, B. (1990). Violence during pregnancy and substance use. *American Journal of Public Health, 80*, 575–579.

Anderson, M. (1992). *Intelligence and development: A cognitive theory.* Oxford: Blackwell.

Aslin, R.N., & Pisoni, D.B. (1980). Some developmental processes in speech perception. In G. Yeni-Komshian, J. Kavanagh, & C. Ferguson (Eds.), *Child phonology: Perception and production* (pp. 67–96). New York: Academic Press.

Azuma, S.D., & Chasnov, I.J. (1993). Outcome of children prenatally exposed to cocaine and other drugs: A path analysis of three-year data. *Pediatrics, 92,* 396–402.

Barnard, K.E., & Martell, L.K. (1995). Mothering. In M.H. Bornstein (Ed.), *Handbook of parenting* (Vol. 3, pp. 3–26). Mahwah, NJ: Lawrence Erlbaum Associates.

Barrett, G.V., & Depinet, R.L. (1991). A reconsideration of testing for competence rather than for intelligence. *American Psychologist, 46,* 1012–1024.

Bayley, N. (1949). Consistency and variability in the growth of intelligence from birth to eighteen years. *Journal of Genetic Psychology, 75,* 165–196.

Benjamin, J., Li, L., Patterson, C., Greenberg, B.D., Murphy, D.L., & Hamer, D.H. (1996). Population and familiar association between the D4 dopamine receptor gene and measures of novelty seeking. *Nature Genetics, 12,* 81–84.

Berg, C.A., & Sternberg, R.J. (1985). Response to novelty: Continuity versus discontinuity in the development course of intelligence. In H.W. Reese (Ed.), *Advances in child development and behavior* (Vol. 15, pp. 1–47). New York: Academic Press.

Bergström, R.M. (1969). Electrical parameters of the brain during ontogeny. In R. J. Robinson (Ed.), *Brain and early behavior: Development in the fetus and infant* (pp. 15–37). New York: Academic Press.

Bertenthal, B.I., Haith, M.M., & Campos, J.J. (1983). The partial–lag design: A method for controlling spontaneous regression in the infant–control habituation paradigm. *Infant Behavior and Development, 6,* 331–338.

Bjorklund, D.F., & Schneider, W. (1996). The interaction of knowledge, aptitude, and strategies in children's memory performance. *Advances in Child Development and Behavior, 26,* 59–89.

Bornstein, M.H. (1984). *Infant attention and caregiver stimulation: Two contributions to early cognitive development.* Paper presented at the International Conference on Infant Studies, New York City.

Bornstein, M.H. (1985a). Habituation of attention as measure of visual information processing in human infants: Summary, systematization, and synthesis. In G. Gottlieb & N.A. Krasnegor (Eds.), *Measurement of audition and vision in the first year of postnatal life: A methodological overview* (pp. 253–300). Norwood, NJ: Ablex.

Bornstein, M.H. (1985b). How infant and mother jointly contribute to developing cognitive competence in the child. *Proceedings of the National Academy of Sciences (USA), 82,* 7470–7473.

Bornstein, M.H. (1989). Sensitive periods in development: Structural characteristics and causal interpretations. *Psychological Bulletin, 105,* 179–197.

Bornstein, M.H. (1992). Perception across the life span. In M.H. Bornstein & M.E. Lamb (Eds.), *Developmental psychology: An advanced textbook* (pp. 155–209). Hillsdale, NJ: Lawrence Erlbaum Associates.

Bornstein, M.H., & Benasich, A.A. (1986). Infant habituation: Assessments of short-term reliability and individual differences at five months. *Child Development, 57,* 87–99.

Bornstein, M.H., Brown, E.M., & Slater, A.M. (1996). Patterns of stability and continuity in attention across early infancy. *Journal of Reproductive and Infant Psychology, 14,* 195–206.

Bornstein, M.H., & Lamb, M.E. (1992). *Development in infancy: An introduction* (3rd ed.). New York: McGraw Hill.

Bornstein, M.H., & Ludemann, P.L. (1989). Habituation at home. *Infant Behavior and Development, 12,* 525–529.

Bornstein, M.H., Mayes, L.C., & Tamis-LeMonda, C.S. (in press). Habituation, information processing, mental development, and the threat of cocaine exposure in infancy. In P.G. Hepper & M. Kendal-Reed (Eds.), *Perinatal sensory development: Psychology and psychobiology*. Cambridge: Cambridge University Press.

Bornstein, M.H., Pêcheux, M.G., & Lècuyer, R. (1988). Visual habituation in human infants: Development and rearing circumstances. *Psychological Research, 50*, 130–133.

Bornstein, M.H., Slater, A., Brown, E., Roberts, E., & Barrett, J. (1996). Stability of mental development from infancy to later childhood: Three "waves" of research. In G. Bremner, A. Slater, & G. Butterworth (Eds.), *Infant development: Recent advances* (pp. 191–215). Hove, UK: Erlbaum (UK) Taylor & Francis.

Bornstein, M.H., & Tamis-LeMonda, C.S. (1990). Activities and interactions of mothers and their firstborn infants in the first six months of life: Covariation, stability, continuity, correspondence, and prediction. *Child Development, 61*, 1206–1217.

Bornstein, M.H., & Tamis-LeMonda, C. (1994). Antecedents of information-processing skills in infants: Habituation, novelty responsiveness, and cross-modal transfer. *Infant Behavior and Development, 17*, 371–380.

Bowlby, J. (1982). *Attachment and loss:* Vol. 3. *Loss*. New York: Basic Books.

Bradley, R.H. (1995). Environment and parenting. In M.H. Bornstein (Ed.), *Handbook of parenting* (Vol. 2, pp. 235–261). Mahwah, NJ: Lawrence Erlbaum Associates.

Brazelton, T.B. (1973). *Neonatal behavior assessment scale*. Philadelphia: Lippincott.

Broman, S.H., Nichols, P.L., & Kennedy, W.A. (1975). *Preschool IQ: Prenatal and early developmental correlates*. Hillsdale, NJ: Lawrence Erlbaum Associates.

Bronson, G. (1991). Infant differences in rate of visual encoding. *Child Development, 62*, 44–54.

Burt, C. (1940). *The factors of the mind: An introduction to factor analysis in psychology*. London: University of London Press.

Campione, J.C., Brown, A.L., & Ferrara, R.A. (1982). Mental retardation and intelligence. In R.J. Sternberg (Ed.), *Handbook of human intelligence* (pp. 392–491). Cambridge: Cambridge University Press.

Caron, A.J., & Caron, R.F. (1969). Degree of stimulus complexity and habituation of visual fixation in infants. *Psychonomic Science, 14*, 78–79.

Carroll, J.B. (1982). The measurement of intelligence. In R.J. Sternberg (Ed.), *Handbook of human intelligence* (pp. 29–119). Cambridge: Cambridge University Press.

Carroll, J.B. (1993). *Human cognitive abilities: A survey of factor-analytic studies*. Cambridge: Cambridge University Press.

Case, R. (1985). *Intellectual development: Birth to adulthood*. New York: Academic Press.

Chasnoff, I.J., Landress, H.J., & Barrett, M.E. (1990). The prevalence of illicit drug or alcohol abuse during pregnancy and discrepancies in mandatory reporting in Pinellas County, Florida. *New England Journal of Medicine, 322*, 102–106.

Clarke, A.M., & Clarke, A.D.B. (Eds.) (1976). *Early experience: Myth and evidence*. New York: Free Press.

Clarke-Stewart, K.A. (1991). Developmental psychology in the real world: A paradigm of parent education. In F.S. Kessel, M.H. Bornstein, & A.J. Sameroff (Eds.), *Contemporary constructions of the child* (pp. 179–193). Hillsdale, NJ: Lawrence Erlbaum Associates.

Cohen, L.B. (1973). A two-process model of infant visual attention. *Merrill-Palmer Quarterly, 19*, 157–180.

Cohen, L.B. (1981). Examination of habituation as a measure of aberrant infant development. In S. L. Friedman & M. Sigman (Eds.), *Preterm birth and psychological development* (pp. 241–253). New York: Academic Press.

Cohen, L.B. (1988). An information-processing approach to infant cognitive development. In L. Weiskrantz (Ed.), *Thought without language* (pp. 211–228). Oxford: Oxford University Press.

Colombo, J. (1993). *Infant cognition: Predicting later intellectual functioning.* Newbury Park, CA: Sage.

Colombo, J. (1995). On the neural mechanisms underlying developmental and individual differences in visual fixation in infancy: Two hypotheses. *Developmental Review, 15,* 97–135.

Colombo, J., Freeseman, L.J., Coldren, J.T., & Frick, J.E. (1995). Individual differences in infant fixation duration: Dominance of global versus local stimulus properties. *Cognitive Development, 10,* 271–285.

Colombo, J., & Mitchell, D.W. (1988). Infant visual habituation: In defense of an information-processing analysis. *Cahiers de Psychologie, 8,* 455–461.

Colombo, J., & Mitchell, D.W. (1991). Individual differences in early visual attention: Fixation time and information processing. In J. Colombo & J. Fagen (Eds.), *Individual differences in infancy: Reliability, stability, prediction* (pp. 193–228). Hillsdale, NJ: Lawrence Erlbaum Associates.

Colombo, J., Mitchell, D.W., & Horowitz, F.D. (1988). Infant visual attention in the paired-comparison paradigm: Test–retest and attention–performance relations. *Child Development, 59,* 1198–1210.

Colombo, J., Mitchell, D.W., O'Brien, M., & Horowitz, F.D. (1987). The stability of visual habituation during the first year of life. *Child Development, 57,* 474–488.

Condillac, E.B. (1780/1948). (Bonnot Abbè de). *La logique.* In G. Le Roy (Ed.), *Oeuvres philosophiques de Condillac* (Vol. 2, pp. 374–375). Paris: Presses Universitaires de France.

Cooper, L.A., & Regan, D.T. (1986). Attention, perception, and intelligence. In R. J. Sternberg (Ed.), *Handbook of human intelligence* (pp. 123–169). Cambridge: Cambridge University Press.

Cyphers, L.H., Fulker, D.W., Plomin, R., & DeFries, J.C. (1989). Cognitive abilities in the early school years: No effects of shared environment between parents and offspring. *Intelligence, 13,* 369–386.

Deary, I.J. (1995). Auditory inspection time and intelligence: What is the causal direction? *Developmental Psychology, 31,* 237–250.

Deese, J. (1993). Human abilities versus intelligence. *Intelligence, 17,* 107–116.

Dempster, F.N. (1991). Inhibitory processes: A neglected dimension of intelligence. *Intelligence, 15,* 157–173.

Dempster, F.N., & Brainerd, C.J. (Eds.). (1995). *New perspectives on interference and inhibition in cognition.* Orlando, FL: Academic Press.

Detterman, D.K. (1987a). Theoretical notions of intelligence and mental retardation. *American Journal of Mental Deficiency, 92,* 2–11.

Detterman, D.K. (1987b). What does reaction time tell us about intelligence? In P. A. Vernon (Ed.), *Speed of information processing and intelligence* (pp. 177–199). Norwood, NJ: Ablex.

DiLalla, L.F., Thompson, L.A., Plomin, R., Phillips, K., Fagan, J.F., Haith, M.M., Cyphers, L.H., & Fulker, D.W. (1990). Infant predictors of preschool and adult IQ: A study of infant twins and their parents. *Developmental Psychology, 26,* 759–769.

Dougherty, T.M. & Haith, M.M. (1997). Infant expectations and reaction time as predictors of childhood speed of processing and IQ. *Developmental Psychology, 33,* 146–155.

Eysenck, H.J. (1987). Speed of information processing, reaction time, and the theory of intelligence. In P.A. Vernon (Ed.), *Speed of information processing and intelligence* (pp. 21–67). Norwood, NJ: Ablex.

Fagan, J.F. (1984). The relationship of novelty preferences during infancy to later intelligence and later recognition memory. *Intelligence, 8,* 339–346.

Fagan, J.F. (1988). Evidence for the relationship between responsiveness to visual novelty during infancy and later intelligence: A summary. *European Bulletin of Cognitive Psychology, 8*, 469–475.

Fagan, J.F., & McGrath, S.K. (1981). Infant recognition memory and later intelligence. *Intelligence, 5*, 121–130.

Fagan, J.F., & Singer, L.T. (1983). Infant recognition memory as a measure of intelligence. In L.P. Lipsitt (Ed.), *Advances in infancy research* (Vol. 2, pp. 31–79). Norwood, NJ: Ablex.

Fagen, J.W., & Ohr, P.S. (1990). Individual differences in infant conditioning and memory. In J. Colombo & J. Fagen (Eds.), *Individual differences in infancy: Reliability, stability, prediction* (pp. 155–192). Hillsdale, NJ: Lawrence Erlbaum Associates.

Fantz, R.L. (1964). Visual experience in infants: Decreased attention to familiar patterns relative to novel ones. *Science, 146*, 668–670.

Fisher, C.B., Bornstein, M.H., & Gross, C.G. (1985). Left–right coding skills related to beginning reading. *Journal of Developmental and Behavioral Pediatrics, 6*, 279–283.

Freeseman, L.J., Colombo, J., & Coldren, J.T. (1993). Individual differences in infant visual attention: Four-month-olds' discrimination and generalization of global and local stimulus properties. *Child Development, 64*, 1191–1203.

Frick, J.E., & Colombo, J. (1996). Individual differences in infant visual attention: Recognition of degraded visual forms by four-month-olds. *Child Development, 67*, 188–204.

Friedman, S. (1975). Infant habituation: Process, problems, and possibilities. In N. Ellis (Ed.), *Aberrant development in infancy: Human and animal studies* (pp. 217–239). New York: Halstead Press.

Fry, A.F., & Hale, S. (1996). Processing speed, working memory, and fluid intelligence: Evidence for a developmental cascade. *Psychological Science, 7*, 237–241.

Gardner, H. (1983). *Frames of mind: The theory of multiple intelligences.* New York: Basic Books.

Gardner, J.M., & Karmel, B.Z. (1983). Attention and arousal in preterm and full-term neonates. In T. Field & A. Sostek (Eds.), *Infants born at risk* (pp. 69–98). New York: Grune & Stratton.

Garrett, H.E. (1938). Differentiable mental traits. *Psychological Record, 2*, 259–298.

Garrett, H.E. (1946). A developmental theory of intelligence. *American Psychologist, 1*, 372–378.

Gawin, F.H., & Ellinwood, E.H. (1988). Cocaine and other stimulants. *New England Journal of Medicine, 318*, 1173–1182.

Gottfried, A.W. (1984). Issues concerning the relationship between home environment and early cognitive development. In A.W. Gottfried (Ed.), *Home environment and early cognitive development* (pp. 1–4). New York: Academic Press.

Gottfried, A.W., & Gilman, G. (1985). Visual skills and intellectual development: A relationship in young children. *Journal of the American Optometric Association, 56*, 550–555.

Graham, F.K., Anthony, B.J., & Zeigler, B.L. (1983). The orienting response and developmental processes. In D. Siddle (Ed.), *Perspectives in human research* (pp. 371–430). New York: Wiley.

Guerin, D.W., Gottfried, A.W., Oliver, P.H., & Thomas, C.W. (1994). Temperament and school functioning during early adolescence. *Journal of Early Adolescence, 14*, 200–225.

Hale, S. (1990). A global developmental trend in cognitive processing speed. *Child Development, 61*, 653–663.

Hedges, L.L., & Oklin, I. (1985). *Statistical methods for meta-analysis.* Orlando, FL: Academic Press.

Hepper, P.G., & Shahidullah, S. (1992). Habituation in normal and Down's Syndrome fetuses. *The Quarterly Journal of Experimental Psychology, 44,* 305–317.

Heyser, C.J., McKinzie, D.L., Athalie, F., Spear, N.E., & Spear, L.P. (1994). Effects of prenatal exposure to cocaine on heart rate and nonassociative learning and retention in infant rats. *Teratology, 49,* 470–478.

Horowitz, F.D., Paden, L., Bhana, K., & Self, P. (1972). An infant-controlled procedure for studying infant visual fixations. *Developmental Psychology, 7,* 90.

Howe, M.J.A. (1988). Intelligence as an explanation. *British Journal of Psychology, 79,* 349–360.

Hunt, E.B. (1983). On the nature of intelligence. *Science, 219,* 141–146.

Hunter, J.E. (1986). Cognitive ability, cognitive aptitudes, job knowledge, and job performance. *Journal of Vocational Behavior, 29,* 340–362.

Jacobson, S.W., Jacobson, J.J., O'Neill, J.M., Padgett, R.J., Frankowski, J.J., & Bihun, J.T. (1992). Visual expectation and dimensions of infant information processing. *Child Development, 63,* 711–724.

Jensen, A.R. (1992). The importance of intraindividual variation in reaction time. *Personality and Individual Differences, 13,* 869–881.

Kagan, J. (1981). *The second year: The emergence of self-awareness.* Cambridge, MA: Harvard University Press.

Kail, R. (1986). Sources of age differences in speed of processing. *Child Development, 57,* 969–987.

Kail, R. (1988). Developmental functions for speeds of cognitive processes. *Journal of Experimental Child Psychology, 45,* 339–364.

Kail, R. (1991). Developmental change in speed of processing during childhood and adolescence. *Psychological Bulletin, 109,* 490–501.

Kail, R. (1992). Processing speed, speech rate, and memory. *Developmental Psychology, 28,* 899–904.

Kail, R., & Park, YS. (1992). Global developmental change in processing time. *Merrill-Palmer Quarterly, 38,* 525–541.

Kail, R., & Salthouse, T.A. (1994). Processing speed as a mental capacity. *Acta Psychologica, 86,* 199–225.

Karmel, B.Z., Gardner, J.M., & Magnano, C.L. (1991). Attention and arousal in infancy. In M.J. Weiss & P.R. Zelazo (Eds.), *Newborn attention: Biological constraints and the influence of experience* (pp. 339–376). Norwood, NJ: Ablex.

Kopp, C.B., & McCall, R.B. (1980). Stability and instability in mental test performance among normal, at-risk, and handicapped infants and children. In P.B. Baltes & O.G. Brim, Jr. (Eds.), *Life-span development and behavior* (Vol. 4, pp. 33–61). New York: Academic.

Kosten, T.R. (1990). Neurobiology of abused drugs: Opioids and stimulants. *Journal of Nervous and Mental Disease, 178,* 217–227.

Larson, G.E., & Alderton, D.L. (1990). Reaction time variability and intelligence: A "worst performance" analysis of individual differences. *Intelligence, 14,* 309–325.

Laucht, M., Esser, G., & Schmidt, M. (1994). Contrasting infant predictors of later cognitive functioning. *Journal of Child Psychology and Psychiatry, 35,* 649–662.

Leader, L.R. (1994). Fetal habituation in growth retardation and hypoxia. In H.C. Lou, G. Greisen, & J.F. Larsen (Eds.), *Brain lesions in the newborn* (pp. 326–329). Munksgaard, Copenhagen: Alfred Benzon Symposium 31.

Lehrl, S., & Fischer, B. (1990). A basic information psychological parameter (BIP) for the reconstruction of concepts of intelligence. *European Journal of Personality, 4,* 259–286.

Lester, B.M. (1975). Cardiac habituation of the orienting response to an auditory signal in infants of varying nutritional status. *Developmental Psychology, 11,* 432–442.

Lewis, M., & Brooks-Gunn, J. (1981). Visual attention at three months as a predictor of cognitive functioning at two years of age. *Intelligence, 5*, 131–140.

Lidow, M. (1995). Prenatal cocaine exposure adversely affects the development of the primate cerebral cortex. *Synapse, 21*, 332–341.

Madison, L.S., Madison, J.K., & Adubato, S.A. (1986). Infant behavior and development in relation to fetal movement and habituation. *Child Development, 57*, 1475–1482.

Malcuit, G., Pomerleau, A., & Lamarre, G. (1988). Habituation, visual fixation and cognitive activity in infants: A critical analysis and an attempt at a new formulation. *Cahiers de Psychologie Cognitive, 8*, 415–440.

Mayes, L.C. (1994). Neurobiology of prenatal cocaine exposure: Effect on developing monoamine systems. *Infant Mental Health, 15*, 134–135.

Mayes, L.C. (1995). Substance abuse and parenting. In M.H. Bornstein (Ed.), *The handbook of parenting* (Vol. 4, pp. 101–125). Mahwah, NJ: Lawrence Erlbaum Associates.

Mayes, L.C., & Bornstein, M.H. (1995). Infant information-processing performance and maternal education. *Early Development and Parenting, 4*, 91–96.

Mayes, L.C., Bornstein, M.H., Chawarska, K., & Granger, R.H. (1995). Information processing and developmental assessments in three-month-old infants exposed prenatally to cocaine. *Pediatrics, 95*, 539–545.

Mayes, L.C., Granger, R.H., Frank, M.A., Schottenfeld, R., & Bornstein, M. (1993). Neurobehavioral profiles of infants exposed to cocaine prenatally. *Pediatrics, 91*, 778–783.

McCall, R.B. (1981). Nature–nurture and the two realms of development: A proposed integration with respect to mental development. *Child Development, 52*, 1–12.

McCall, R.B. (1994). What process mediates prediction of childhood IQ from infant habituation and recognition memory? Speculations on the roles of inhibition and rate of information processing. *Intelligence, 18*, 107–125.

McCall, R.B., Eichorn, D.H., & Hogarty, P.S. (1977). Transitions in early mental development. *Monographs of the Society for Research in Child Development, 42*(3, Serial No. 171).

McCall, R.G., & Mash, C.W. (1995). Infant cognition and its relation to mature intelligence. *Annals of Child Development, 10*, 27–56.

McClelland, D. C. (1973). Testing for competence rather than for "intelligence". *American Psychologist, 28*, 1–14.

Miller, D.J., Ryan, E.B., Arbeger, E., McGuire, M.D., Short, E.J., & Kenny, D.A. (1979). Relationships between assessments of habituation and cognitive performance in the early years of life. *International Journal of Behavioral Development, 2*, 159–170.

Miller, G.A., Galanter, E., & Pribram, K H. (1960). *Plans and the structure of behavior.* New York: Holt, Rinehart & Winston.

Mirochnick, M., Meyer, J., Cole, J., Herren, T., & Zuckerman, B. (1991). Circulating catecholamine concentrations in cocaine-exposed neonates: A pilot study. *Pediatrics, 88*, 481–485.

Moore, T.R., Sorg, J., Miller, L., Key, T., & Resnik, R. (1986). Hemodynamic effects of intravenous cocaine in the pregnant ewe and fetus. *American Journal of Obstetrics and Gynecology, 155*, 883–888.

Moss, M., Colombo, J., Mitchell, J.W., & Horowitz, F.D. (1988). Neonatal behavioral organization and visual processing at three months. *Child Development, 59*, 1211–1220.

Neisser, W. Boodoo, G., Bourchard, T.J., Boykin, A.W., Brady, N., Ceci, S.J., Halpern, D. F., Loehlin, J.C., Perloff, R., Sternberg, R.J., & Urbina, S. (1996). Intelligence: Knowns and unknowns. *American Psychologist, 51*, 77–101.

Nettelbeck, T. (1987). Inspection time and intelligence. In P.A. Vernon (Ed.), *Speed of information processing and intelligence* (pp. 295–346). Norwood, NJ: Ablex.

Nettelbeck, T., & Wilson, C. (1994). Childhood changes in speed of information processing and mental age: A brief report. *British Journal of Developmental Psychology, 12*, 277–280.

Nettelbeck, T., & Young, R. (1989). Inspection time and intelligence in 6-year-old children. *Personality and Individual Differences, 10,* 605–614.

Nettelbeck, T., & Young, R. (1990). Inspection time and intelligence in 7-year-old children. *Personality and Individual Differences, 11,* 1283–1289.

Osterloh, J.D., & Lee, B.L. (1989). Urine drug screening in mothers and newborns. *American Journal of Diseases in Children, 143,* 791–793.

Pasilin, H. (1986). Preschool temperament and performance on achievement tests. *Developmental Psychology, 22,* 766–770.

Pêcheux, M.G., & Lécuyer, R. (1983). Habituation rate and free exploration tempo in 4-month-old infants. *International Journal of Behavioral Development, 6,* 37–50.

Plomin, R. (1986). *Development, genetics, and psychology.* Hillsdale, NJ: Lawrence Erlbaum Associates.

Plomin, R., & DeFries, J.C. (1985). *Origins of individual differences in infancy: The Colorado Adoption Project.* New York: Academic Press.

Posner, M I., & Petersen, S.E. (1990). The attention system of the human brain. *Annual Review of Neuroscience, 13,* 25–42.

Rabbitt, P. (1988). Human intelligence (critical review of R.J. Sternberg's work). *Quarterly Journal of Experimental Psychology, 40A,* 167–185.

Rescorla, R. A., & Wagner, A.R. (1972). A theory of Pavlovian conditioning: Variations in the effectiveness of reinforcement and nonreinforcement. In A.H. Black & W.F. Prokasy (Eds.), *Classical conditioning: II Current research and theory* (pp. 64–99). New York: Appleton-Century-Crofts.

Richie, J.M., & Greene, N.M. (1985). Local anesthetics. In A.G. Gilman, L.S. Goodman, T.N. Rall, & F. Murad (Eds.), *The pharmacologic basis of therapeutics* (7th ed., pp. 309–310). New York: Macmillan.

Rose, S.A., & Feldman, J.F. (1995). Prediction of IQ and specific cognitive abilities at 11 years from infancy measures. *Developmental Psychology, 31,* 685–696.

Rose, S.A., Feldman, J.F., Wallace, I.F., & Cohen, P. (1991). Language: A partial link between infant attention and later intelligence. *Developmental Psychology, 27,* 798–805.

Rose, D.H., Slater, A., & Perry, H. (1986). Prediction of childhood intelligence from habituation in early infancy. *Intelligence, 10,* 251–263.

Rothbart, M.K. (1986). Longitudinal observation of infant temperament. *Developmental Psychology, 22,* 356–366.

Rothbart, M.K., & Posner, M.I. (1985). Temperament and the development of self-regulation. In H. Hartlage & C.E. Telzrow (Eds.), *Neuropsychology of individual differences: A developmental perspective* (pp. 93–123). New York: Plenum.

Salapatek, P., & Cohen, L. (Eds.). (1987a). *Handbook of infant perception: From sensation to perception* (Vol. 1). New York: Academic Press.

Salapatek, P., & Cohen, L. (Eds.). (1987b). *Handbook of infant perception: From perception to cognition* (Vol. 2). New York: Academic Press.

Sameroff, A.J., Seifer, R., Baldwin, A., & Baldwin, C. (1993). Stability of intelligence from preschool to adolescence: The influence of social and family risk factors. *Child Development, 64,* 80–97.

Scarr, S. (1981). Testing *for* children: Assessment and the many determinants of intellectual competence. *American Psychologist, 36,* 1159–1166.

Scarr, S., Weinberg, R.A., & Waldman, I.D. (1993). IQ correlations in transracial adoptive families. *Intelligence, 17,* 541–555.

Sigman, M., Cohen, S.E., Beckwith, L., Asarnow, R., & Parmelee, A.H. (1991). Continuity in cognitive abilities from infancy to 12 years of age. *Cognitive Development, 6*, 47–57.

Sigman, M., Cohen, S.E., Beckwith, L., & Topinka, C. (1987). Task persistence in 2-year-old preterm infants in relation to subsequent attentiveness and intelligence. *Infant Behavior and Development, 10,* 295–305.

Slater, A. (1995). Individual differences in infancy and later IQ. *Journal of Child Psychology and Psychiatry, 36,* 69–112.

Slater, A.M., Morison, V., & Rose, D. (1983). Locus of habituation in the human newborn. *Perception, 12,* 593–598.

Sokolov, Y.N. (1958/1963). *Perception and the conditioned reflex* (S. W. Waydenfeld, Trans.). New York: Macmillan.

Spearman, C. (1904). "General intelligence" objectively determined and measured. *American Journal of Psychology, 15,* 201–293.

Spearman, C. (1923). *The nature of "intelligence" and the principles of cognition.* London: Macmillan.

Spearman, C. (1927). *The abilities of man.* London: Macmillan.

Sternberg, R.J. (1985). *Beyond IQ: A triarchic theory of intelligence.* Cambridge: Cambridge University Press.

Struthers, J.M., & Hansen, R.L. (1992). Visual recognition memory in drug-exposed infants. *Journal of Developmental and Behavioral Pediatrics, 13,* 108–111.

Swann, A.C. (1990). Cocaine: Synaptic effects and adaptations. In N.D. Volkow & A.C. Swann (Eds.), *Cocaine in the brain* (pp. 58–94). New Brunswick, NJ: Rutgers University Press.

Tamis-LeMonda, C.S., & Bornstein, M.H. (1989). Habituation and maternal encouragement of attention in infancy as predictors of toddler language, play, and representational competence. *Child Development, 60,* 738–751.

Tamis-LeMonda, C.S., & Bornstein, M.H. (1993). Antecedents of exploratory competence at one year. *Infant Behavior and Development, 16,* 423–439.

Thompson, L.A., Detterman, D.K., & Plomin, R. (1991). Associations between cognitive abilities and scholastic achievement: Genetic overlap but environmental differences. *Psychological Science, 2,* 158–165.

Thompson, R.F., & Spencer, W.A. (1966). Habituation: A model phenomenon for the study of neuronal substrates of behavior. *Psychological Review, 73,* 16–43.

Thurstone, L.L. (1938). *Primary mental abilities.* Chicago: University of Chicago Press.

Thurstone, L.L., & Thurstone, J. (1962). *Test of primary mental abilities* (Rev. ed.). Chicago: Chicago Science Research Association.

Vernon, P.E. (1961). *The structure of human abilities.* London: Methuen.

Vernon, P.E. (1969). *Intelligence and cultural environment.* London: Methuen.

Vernon, P.E. (Ed.). (1987). *Speed of information processing and intelligence.* Norwood, NJ: Ablex.

Wechsler, D. (1958). *The measurement and appraisal of adult intelligence.* Baltimore, MD: Williams & Wilkins.

Wechsler, D. (1974). *Wechsler intelligence scale for children: Revised.* New York: The Psychological Corporation.

Woods, J.R., Plessinger, M.A., & Clark, K.E. (1987). Effect of cocaine on uterine blood flow and fetal oxygenation. *Journal of the American Medical Association, 257,* 957–961.

Zigler, E., Abelson, W.D., & Seitz, V. (1973). Motivational factors in the performance of economically disadvantaged children on the Peabody Picture Vocabulary Test. *Child Development, 44,* 294–303.

Zuckerman, B., Frank, D.A., Hingson, R., & Amaro, H. (1989). Effect of maternal marijuana and cocaine use on fetal growth. *New England Journal of Medicine, 320,* 762–768.

Author Index

Author Index

Subject Index

Subject Index